LISTENING TO SILENCES

LISTENING TO SILENCES

New Essays in Feminist Criticism

Edited By

Elaine Hedges

Shelley Fisher Fishkin

New York   Oxford
OXFORD UNIVERSITY PRESS
1994

Contents

PART III

LISTENING TO SILENCES

Introduction

ELAINE HEDGES AND
SHELLEY FISHER FISHKIN

It is by now thirty years since Tillie Olsen, in a talk at the Radcliffe Institute in 1963, first formally introduced many of the ideas that in 1978 would comprise her groundbreaking book, *Silences*. In the years since then the subject she introduced has become central to feminist literary inquiry. Today her insights and her arguments—expanded, modified, redefined, and even contested—continue to provide crucial critical and contextual frameworks for a wide range of scholars and writers.

The book *Silences* took for its subject, in the words of one of its earliest reviewers, the disruption of the creative process in the person who wishes to write but cannot, or who publishes one book only, or who is ultimately stifled (*Book Review Digest*, 987). It dealt not with the "natural" silences—those periods in the creative life when the soil lies fallow in expectation of being tilled later—but with what Olsen called the unnatural silences—those that result from "circumstances" of being born into the wrong class, race, or sex, being denied education, becoming numbed by economic struggle, muffled by censorship, or distracted or impeded by the demands of nurturing. Its subject—and its implied audience—included men and women, the privileged and the poor, the educated and those deprived of an education. As Olsen put it in her dedication, the book was written

> [F]or our silenced people, century after century their beings consumed in the hard, everyday essential work of maintaining human life. Their art, which still they made—as their other contributions—anonymous; refused respect, recognition, lost.

And it was written, as well,

> [F]or those of us (few yet in number, for the way is punishing), their kin and descendants, who begin to emerge into more flowered and rewarded use of our selves in ways denied to them—and by our very achievement bearing witness to what was (and still is) being lost, silenced.

A collage of autobiography, argument, and extensive quotation from other writers and their works, the book included one essay that carried special meaning for women. In "One Out of Twelve: Writers Who Are Women in Our Century," first delivered at a session of the Modern Language Association in 1971, Olsen began to provide explanations, even a theory, for women's absence from, or disproportionately small presence in, literature and the literary canon. Her arguments ranged from explaining women's lesser productivity in terms of the consuming demands on them of marriage and motherhood, to charting women's fairly systematic exclusion from, or only minimal representation in, literature courses and anthologies. At a time when feminists in the academy were just beginning to recognize the pervasive absence of women writers from literary histories, textbooks, and courses—indeed, the absence of women or the study of women from all academic disciplines—Olsen's essay immediately struck a responsive chord. It put the subject of silence at the center of the feminist literary critical map. With it, Olsen pioneered a whole new critical territory.

Throughout the 1970s "silence" became an increasing focus of feminist attention. Marge Piercy's poem, "Unlearning to Not Speak," published in 1973, two years after Olsen's MLA talk, became an important feminist text, often reprinted. Adrienne Rich was by then also exploring the subject, in both her poetry and her prose. The MLA session at which Olsen delivered "One Out of Twelve" was also the occasion when Rich delivered "When We Dead Awaken," an essay that would become another early feminist landmark, where Rich broke silence to address the reality in her own life of many of those disabling circumstances that Olsen was identifying. In 1981 critic Susan Gubar cited Olsen's *Silences,* and Rich's *On Lies, Secrets, and Silence* (1979), in which "When We Dead Awaken" was reprinted, as crucial texts that drew attention to "the centrality of silence in women's culture, specifically the ways in which women's voices have gone unheard" ("The 'Blank Page,' " 259).

Gubar's and Sandra Gilbert's own groundbreaking study of nineteenth-century British and American women authors, *The Madwoman in the Attic,* which appeared in 1979, was clearly indebted to Olsen's work, as it was to that of her predecessor, Virginia Woolf, whose *A Room of One's Own,* with its poignant parable of Shakespeare's silenced sister, had been one of Olsen's own sources of inspiration. In the same year as *Madwoman,* Gilbert and Gubar's *Shakespeare's Sisters,* a collection of essays on women poets, also paid tribute to *Silences* as one of the "pioneering achievements" that helped them create their own book (xxiii).

Recognition of the importance of Olsen's work continued to develop throughout the 1980s, and a genealogy could be seen in the making. Thus, for example, Joanna Russ's *How To Suppress Women's Writing,* 1983, drew on *Silences* in chapters that explored the social, cultural, and psychological obstacles to women's creative expression. And in "The Transformation of Silence into Language and Action" in 1984, Audre Lorde's injunctions that women share "a war against the tyrannies of silence" and that "there are [still] so many silences to be broken" clearly paralleled, while further developing, Olsen's concerns (41, 44). In 1986 Elizabeth Meese could refer to *Silences* as "one of the most frequently cited texts of twentieth-century feminism" (91); and two years later Patricia Yeager could assert that Olsen's discoveries, her "eloquent typology of literary silences," had become "indispensable . . . to feminist criticism as a collective enterprise" (153–54).

By the mid-1980s, though, it was also being argued that feminist literary criticism had moved beyond and even away from Olsen's discoveries and emphases. Her focus in *Silences* was primarily on external impediments to the writing process; particularly, in the case of women, on their more limited access to education, cultural pressures that dissuaded them from taking themselves seriously as artists, the fragmentation of their time amidst the duties and distractions of motherhood, or the workings of a male literary establishment that excluded them. The new critical perspective, deriving from poststructuralism—which saw texts, in Frederic Jameson's words, not as "seamless webs and triumphant narrative progressions" but as works with gaps and breaks, discontinuities and absences—focused on silences that were intrinsic rather than external to the text (167–68). Such silences, in turn, might reveal reticences culturally imposed upon women, the workings of a repressed ideology, or, alternatively, women's deployment of silence as a form of resistance to the dominant discourse. By 1985, therefore, Ann Rosalind Jones, for example, was urging that critics attend to internal silences, "to what is repressed or only obliquely suggested in woman-authored texts" (96); and by 1990 Janis Stout could state that the study of textual silences had become one of "the most provocative and liveliest developments in criticism in the past twenty years" (2).

Yet such new critical perspectives had not, in fact, been wholly unanticipated by Olsen. Patricia Yeager saw Olsen's work as "an essential tool to help us think about textual lacunae" (154). In *Silences* Olsen had pointed, for example, to the taboos under which women have historically labored in representing the body and sexuality, and to their textual resort to male masks (Rebecca Harding Davis) or to riddle and "slant truth" (Emily Dickinson). In addition, as scholars had begun demonstrating by 1986, Olsen had also frequently used textual silences in her own creative work, as a way, for instance, of resisting conventional narrative closure. Both Elizabeth Meese and Shelley Fisher Fishkin had explored the ways in which Olsen's use of the white space on the page, both in *Silences* and in her daybook and reader, *Mother to Daughter, Daughter to Mother* (1984), offered invitations to the reader to participate in the writing of the text, to add their own words and meanings—in Meese's words, "to break the silences by inscribing themselves" (Meese, 112; Fishkin, "Borderlands," 160).

Tillie Olsen's *Silences,* then, over thirty years after her first public presentation of some of its ideas, is a text that clearly continues to matter. We are still in the process of asessing its influence and its importance. This collection of essays, therefore, is intended both to trace a genealogy and to offer a spectrum of the ways in which contemporary feminist criticism continues to respond to Olsen's discoveries. The collection is not, however, hagiography. Some contributors reveal their deep indebtedness to Olsen's ideas and critical procedures, while others qualify and quarrel with them. Simultaneously paradigmatic and problematic, her work, as well as feminist critical treatment of the idea of "silence" itself, will be examined from a range of points of view that suggest the rich and diverse possibilities and applications still being derived from the concept she introduced.

The book is divided into three parts. Part I consists of a set of essays focused on Olsen's own work: on the genesis of *Silences,* on the book's impact by now on three generations of scholars and writers, and on the operations of silence in her own fiction. Part II extends the book's scope to an examination of the subject of silence as it is being investigated by contemporary feminist critics studying literary texts by nineteenth- and twentieth-century women writers. This part demonstrates the range of critical approaches that are presently being employed to examine silence—silence as presence and as absence, as inscribed in the text and as external to it, as both oppressive and empowering. Part III explores a different, but closely related, set of silences: those within the academy, as the site of the production of the literary criticism in Parts I and II. In *Silences* Olsen had expressed the hope that higher education would be a particularly emancipatory space for women, and in many ways it has been. Yet her insistence that we remain vigilant about the dynamics of silence and silencing requires that we not ignore the ways, both overt and covert, in which this new space may nonetheless continue to mute women's voices or prevent women from coming to voice.

Part I begins with Diane Middlebrook's essay, "Circle of Women Artists: Tillie Olsen and Anne Sexton at the Radcliffe Institute," which provides a rare and moving glimpse of Olsen's first formal presentation, at the Radcliffe Institute in 1963, of some of the ideas that would become the basis for *Silences.* In recreating the conditions that first encouraged Olsen to shape for a public audience those "accumulations," as she called them—the reading and note-taking of decades that were the rich repository of her thinking—the essay also offers us an early instance of the powerful impact of Olsen's ideas. For the poet Anne Sexton, Olsen's talk, as Middlebrook reports, was not something merely heard, but something that "entered my life and is changing it."

Such impact, as it has been felt by three generations of writers, scholars, and literary critics, is the subject of Shelley Fisher Fishkin's extensive survey, "Reading, Writing, and Arithmetic: The Lessons *Silences* Has Taught Us." Through interviews and conversations conducted with over sixty writers, critics, editors, and publishers, as well as through an examination of the letters Olsen received from readers when her book was published, Fishkin charts the broad influence of Olsen's ideas, as well as of the reading lists of lost or forgotten women writers that she produced and circulated in the 1960s and early 1970s. Both those lists and the book *Silences,* as Fishkin demonstrates, have profoundly changed what we read and the ways in which we read and write. Fishkin's essay offers an overview of some of the many ways in which Olsen's ideas helped to encourage and generate new research and new critical paradigms, to open up the literary canon, and to empower women both to find their own creative and critical voices and to explore new or formerly taboo subjects.

Constance Coiner and Deborah Rosenfelt, with whose studies of Olsen's *Tell Me A Riddle* Part I concludes, are two critics whose scholarly research has been significantly shaped by their attention to and admiration for Olsen's work. Yet such admiration does not preclude revisionary judgment. As

Rosenfelt explains in "Rereading *Tell Me a Riddle* in the Age of Deconstruction," she first read Olsen's stories as a young radical in the late 1960s, when she saw them as continuous with the radical literature of the thirties. Rereading the works in the light of postmodernist critical practice, and specifically examining their textual silences, she now finds in them not only opposition but accommodation to the conservative discourse of the decade of the 1950s in which they were written. Seeing them as moving "between silence as trope and silence as absence, between the utopian yearning for a world free of [the circumstances that hinder creativity] and necessary textual accommodations to more limiting and emergent ideologies," Rosenfelt concludes that Olsen wrote "both against and with the age." Thus, while the stories offer powerful critiques of certain social and political silences or silencings of the fifties, they also inscribe silences of their own.

In dialogue with Rosenfelt, Constance Coiner in " 'No One's Private Ground': A Bakhtinian Reading of Tillie Olsen's *Tell Me a Riddle*," also attends to silences—gaps and absences—in the texts. Coiner, however, reads the silences she examines in the context of the multivocality that also characterizes the works. Both the silences and the multivocality, she concludes, are invitations to the reader to actively participate in the creation of meaning—an interpretation that recalls those by Meese and Fishkin. Applying Bakhtin's concept of heteroglossia, Coiner argues that Olsen's honoring and recording of multiple voices, especially those of the socially marginalized, democratizes the writing process, and that in encouraging readers to make connections among the voices and to fill in their silences, Olsen is, in a further democratic gesture, refusing traditional authorial control.

The essays in Part II include further examples, like Rosenfelt's and Coiner's, of postmodernist critical approaches to silences, as well as others that demonstrate the continuing applicability and relevance of many of the approaches Olsen pioneered. The critics in this section explore a rich variety of interrelated silences. Their essays include studies of circumstances that silenced women writers in the past; silences in mainstream literary history and in feminist criticism itself; strategies for breaking silence and for creating spaces in which new voices and messages may be heard; and the creative dimensions of silence, its potential as a site of feminist resistance.

In beginning Part II with Carla Peterson's " 'Further Liftings of the Veil': Gender, Class, and Labor in Frances E. W. Harper's *Iola Leroy*," we have chosen an essay that reflects Olsen's commitment to the recovery of lost works by women but that approaches the work it studies—and recent critical treatment of it—through the contemporary interest in textual silences. Frances Harper's *Iola Leroy* was one of the key "lost" texts by nineteenth-century black women writers recovered by feminist criticism in the 1980s. Yet by privileging this novel over other of Harper's prose works, such as those serialized in the *Christian Recorder* in the 1860s, 1870s, and 1880s, and by reading it solely through the prisms of gender and sentimental culture, critics have replicated silences in the text itself, silences that reveal Harper's own anxieties and ambivalences regarding issues of black labor in the urban north and of leadership within the black community in the post-Frederick Douglass era. Such textual and critical silences must be broken, Peterson argues, if we are to do justice to the complexity of Harper's work and thought and to that of the social and political environment in which they developed. Her essay, like Deborah Rosenfelt's in Part I, is thus an example of contemporary interest in the ways in which textual silences can mask ideology—the author's or the critic's—and also of the ways in which feminist criticism itself may inadvertently engage in "distortions around difference," inscribing new silences while in the very process of breaking old ones.

Where Peterson's focus is on silence as omission and distortion, other essays in Part II examine the potentially empowering aspects of silence, as well as the interplay of silence and speech within a text. King-Kok Cheung's study of Joy Kogawa's novel, *Obasan,* is a rich analysis of the complex and conflicting operations of silence within the culture of Japanese Canadians at the time of World War II. The oppressive silencing imposed by government censorship is contrasted to several kinds of positive silence, including the stoic and protective silences of the heroine's grandmother and the heroine's own silent, "attentive" listening, which enables her to read the grandmother's silences and balance the truths they contain against those embodied in the angry antiwar rhetoric of her more westernized aunt. Cheung's analyses in her essay of the expressive powers of silence is a useful corrective to our western tendency to valorize speech and language. In reminding us that in Chinese and Japanese the character for "silence" signifies positive qualities of alertness and sensitivity, she registers an implicit critique of our western ethnocentric tendency to dismiss or disparage as mere passivity culturally rooted behaviors different from our own. In so doing, her work contributes to the larger enterprise that Olsen's *Silences* nurtured: that of seeking out and listening to new voices, including those that challenge our own cultural assumptions.

A similar admonition to attentive listening is enjoined on white readers by Kate Adams, in an essay on the poetry of Cherríe Moraga, Gloria Anzaldúa, and Leslie Marmon Silko. Adams challenges us to suspend some of the assumptions we have derived from reading Anglo-American poetry in order to understand and appreciate the work of these women of color. Here again, however, it is the interplay of speech and silence within the texts that interests the critic. Adams argues that, as part of the "rescue work" these Chicana and Native American poets must do to retrieve from historical silence and obscurity the cultural information necessary to an understanding of their poetry, they must challenge and transform the white space—that blank space of silence—that conventionally surrounds and isolates a poem as an autonomous object. What Moraga, Anzaldúa, and Silko create, she demonstrates, are poems embedded in extrapoetic material—history, autobiography, oral tales, even photographs—"informative nets that surround and interact with the poem"—which perhaps more genuinely replicate the function and activity of poetry in their traditional cultures. Adams's essay, with its impassioned plea for silent, attentive listening by white critics and readers, is an eloquent example of the "advocacy scholarship"—careful research infused with emotion and commitment—for which *Silences* itself is the model, and an example, as well, of the critic who "bears witness"—the position Olsen also urges and adopts herself in her work.

Given Olsen's own emphasis in *Silences* on "the silence of the marginal"— on the "writer of a class, sex, color still marginal in literature, and whose coming to written voice at all against complex odds is exhausting achievement" (9)—it is fitting that so many of the essays in Part II of this collection deal with works by minority women. Joanne Braxton's and Sharon Zuber's essay, "Silences in Harriet 'Linda Brent' Jacobs's *Incidents in the Life of a Slave Girl*," in fact takes Olsen's statement about the silence of the marginal writer as its starting point. Their essay explores the complex ways in which, in her autobiographical work, Jacobs courageously broke the silence of that most marginalized group, slave women. The novel itself, as they point out, marks the discovery of a voice; and its treatment of the taboo subject of slave women's sexuality specifically broke what had been a profound cultural silence about white male sexual coercion of slave women. While also concerned with showing how Jacobs, both within her own experience of slavery and within the text of her novel, used silence as a weapon of resistance, their approach, with its emphasis on speech as the fundamental empowerment, underscores Olsen's own passionate belief in the need to retrieve the voices of the submerged. It is a critical approach that also represents an important theoretical position for many contemporary African-American critics who question the "death of the author" in postmodernist thought as a stratagem that threatens to silence the voices of marginalized writers at the very moment in history when those voices are being rediscovered (Wall, 8, 11).

Like Cheung, and Braxton and Zuber, Patricia Laurence in "Women's Silence as a Ritual of Truth: A Study of Literary Expressions in Austen, Brontë and Woolf," is interested in the expressive, and ultimately the resistant, possibilities of women's silence. Laurence rereads the texts of the three canonical authors she examines in order to discover in them—specifically in the verbal silences of various of their female characters—active strategies of choice and resistance. Building on the explorations of women's speech and silence by feminist linguists and psychologists as well as on the work of poststructuralists like Foucault and Derrida, Laurence traces what she sees as a female tradition of writing in which silences—whether they take the form of observing, listening, thinking, meditating, dreaming, or deliberately refusing to respond to the speech of others—become "active presences." For such characters as Austen's Fanny Price and Anne Elliot, Brontë's Jane Eyre, and Woolf's Mrs. Ramsay and Rhoda in *The Waves,* such silences, Laurence claims, offer ways of questioning or rejecting conventionally assigned social roles and, as well, ways of conveying truths or insights unavailable through conventional discourse.

In *Making a Difference: Feminist Literary Criticism,* 1985, Gayle Greene and Coppelia Kahn observed that feminist criticism began by deconstructing dominant male patterns of thought and social practice and reconstructing female experience previously silenced, hidden, or overlooked (6). While, as most of the essays in Part II demonstrate, such reconstructions are still necessary and therefore still being undertaken, we are also by now getting feminist deconstructions of some of our earliest reconstructions. Where Peterson applies this procedure to Frances Harper's critics, Carla Kaplan, in the final essay in Part II, applies it to an entire aspect of Olsen's critical legacy: the model that her emphasis on recuperating silences established for our earliest feminist reading practice. In "Reading Feminist Readings: Recuperative Reading and the Silent Heroine of Feminist Criticism," Kaplan reexamines three of feminist criticism's earliest exemplary texts—Charlotte Perkins Gilman's "The Yellow Wallpaper," Susan Glaspell's "A Jury of Her Peers," and Isak Dinesen's "The Blank Page"—in order to question the model of reading that feminist interpretation of those texts, and specifically of their silenced heroines, established. That reading model, Kaplan argues, was based on identification of reader and heroine, and it tended to ignore class and race differences among women. Responding, like Peterson, to our conteomporary concern with difference, Kaplan offers suggestions for a new reading practice that would avoid the assumption of "sameness" that identification of character and reader presupposes. In recognizing the distance that feminist criticism has traveled from Olsen's preoccupation with the "tragedies of female silence," and in finding the earliest reading models based on that preoccupation no longer tenable, Kaplan offers a major challenge. Nonetheless, she concludes that feminist criticism must continue to derive much of its aim and methodology from the impulse, which Olsen's work fostered, to recover and recuperate silence.

That work of recovery and recuperation takes place primarily inside the academy, a site that can either encourage or inhibit it. In keeping with Olsen's own insistence in *Silences* on the importance of the material conditions of cultural production, the essays in Part III of this collection therefore explore the circumstances surrounding the production of literary criticism in the academy, the space inside which the authors of that criticism live their professional lives. The authors of the essays in this section examine various silences that affect us as teachers and scholars, asking and trying to answer the crucial question of what it will take to make the academy more responsive to the voices of women and minorities now that these groups are a large presence within it. These essays examine a wide range of concerns, from the institutional structures, traditional practices, and cultural expectations of the academy that can inhibit female faculty's productivity to the content of the curriculum that can inhibit students' understanding.

The section begins with an essay by Constance Coiner, "Silent Parenting in the Academy," which dramatically documents the extent to which higher education continues to ignore or be silent about this central reality—parenting—in academic women's lives, and in the lives of many academic men as well. Twenty years and more after Olsen's MLA talk raised the question of responsibility for children and drew attention to the drains on women who must juggle motherhood and a career, very few adequate parental-leave policies are yet in place. Coiner's essay calls for major changes in how we structure academic careers, with specific recommendations for that restructuring.

Parenting—specifically mothering—is also the subject of Diana Hume George's essay, " 'How Many of Us Can You Hold to Your Breast?': Mothering in the Academy." Herself a poet and a teacher, George reveals in this essay the ways in which for some women, especially those who teach writing, teaching can become an extended and often exhausting form of mothering, given the gender expectations that both students and women faculty are likely to bring to the relationship. Her largely autobiographical essay poignantly and forcefully confirms Olsen's observations in *Silences* about motherhood as the one human relationship that means being constantly interruptible, responsive, and responsible, and that can thus lead to the silencing or curtailment of the mother's own creative work.

Several essays in Part III explore various kinds of speech which, if no longer wholly silenced in the academy, still encounter serious impediments there. Rebecca Mark's "Teaching from the Open Closet" confronts the situation of the lesbian or gay teacher. Mark, however, moves beyond the ways in which lesbian and gay faculty have been silenced in the past to explore both the possibilities and the continuing challenges of speaking out in the classroom. Her essay speculates on what a more open discussion of sexuality might mean in liberating both the content and the pedagogy of the academy. Breaking a culturally, socially, and politically mandated silence in the classroom has its costs, as Mark recognizes, but it also has the potential to open the classroom to perspectives that can enrich and enliven students' education.

In a related vein, Norma Alarcón's essay, "Cognitive Desires: An Allegory of/for Chicana Critics," examines the still marginal position in the academy of minority ethnic women, in this case the Chicana scholar. Such a scholar, Alarcón argues, is positioned not only between nation states, but also—given the academy's institutional structure—between often conflicting departments, disciplines, and schools of critical discourse. She and her text, therefore, are often continually displaced: do they belong in Ethnic Studies, in Women's Studies, in Spanish or English departments? And do the critical discourses of each or any of these disciplines allow the text to be satisfactorily heard? In challenging "privileged linguistic practices" that don't always hear, or can't translate, what the Chicana text says, Alarcón is reminding us, as Peterson and Adams did in Part II, that our contemporary critical discourses may still, however inadvertently, distort or silence some of the very texts they are concerned to retrieve.

Where Alarcón is concerned with the Chicana critic's "borderland" or conflicted identity, her uneasy position in the interstices between departments, disciplines, and critical schools of thought, so too are Judith L. Sensibar and Judith Bryant Wittenberg concerned with a similarly uneasy "in-between" status that can befall certain other kinds of feminist critics. In their essay, "Silences in the In-Between: Feminist Women Critics and the Canon," they explore some of the problems encountered by women writing feminist criticism on a male canonical author such as Faulkner. Exclusion from or only token inclusion in the most prestigious professional activities, such as conferences or the preparation of scholarly editions; limited access to collections of primary source materials; and marginalization (ironically, as more male critics adopt feminist critical approaches) are some of the experiences they cite to make us aware of gender inequities that are still operative. In addition, as feminist critics working on male authors, they may feel marginalized by or excluded from networks of feminist critics working on women authors, and also silenced by their own self-doubt, as they are sometimes forced—often by their own students—to question the legitimacy of their critical enterprise. They conclude, however, that despite the "in-betweenness" of the space they inhabit—neither at the center nor quite at the margin of academic discourse— it is an important space that they will continue to occupy, and one which, now that they have articulated its ambiguities, may in time become less troubled and more habitable.

If for critics like Alarcón, Sensibar, and Wittenberg, spaces within the academy are still blurred, or inhospitable, for Lillian Robinson spaces for the speech and writings of the working class are even less availabe and are still in need of definition, clarification, and expansion. Robinson contributed the text for the section of *Silences* that dealt with political censorship, and in the present essay, " 'The Great Unexamined': Silence, Speech, and Class," she explores what, quoting Olsen, she sees as the remaining "great unexamined": the issue of class, around which criticism, as Carla Peterson's essay in this volume also recognizes, still remains largely silent. In attempting to lift that silence, Robinson argues for the need to "honor the widest possible range of expression," including political action, as part of the "speech" of the poor and the oppressed. In explaining her belief in the need for a cultural theory that sees actions as "symbolic speech," Robinson is at one with others who are currently arguing for an expanded definition of expressive acts and for greater understanding of the ways in which class helps shape or construct expression. Her essay here is a valuable extension of her earlier work on class and litera- ture, *Sex, Class, and Culture* (1978.)

Robinson concludes her essay with an analysis of two recent anthologies of working-class writings, in which she raises the important question of the relation between such literature and the activism on which it is often based—whether such literature becomes a substitute for political action. She concludes, however, that despite the problematic relationship between "lit- erature" and working-class life, such writings do represent empowerment through language for that first generation of working-class men and women to come to writing—that generation with which Olsen herself has always been so deeply concerned and to whom *Silences* is dedicated.

Empowerment in this sense is also very much the central concern of the essay with which this collection concludes: Robin Dizard's "Filling in the Silences: Tillie Olsen's Reading Lists." This essay also returns us, as it were, to the beginning of the book—Fishkin's discussion of the importance of Olsen's reading lists to three generations of scholars and writers in and outside the academy. Dizard's eloquent discussion of those reading lists, which, as she recognizes, "led the way into the current debate over the canon," conveys a rich sense of their pluralism, their breadth, depth, and imaginative variety, as well as their sensitivity to the marginalized and the dispossessed. In describing Olsen's lists and their purpose—"to extend range and comprehension, provide balance"—Dizard contrasts them to the more prescriptive lists proposed by Allan Bloom in *The Closing of the American Mind* and E. D. Hirsch in *Cultural Literacy*. In so doing, she raises questions that, in this time of continued controversy over multiculturalism and the nature of American education, remain crucial to how we define our purpose in the academy, and crucial, therefore, to the enterprise of feminist criticism as well.

While it concludes this book, Dizard's essay does not represent closure. The issues her essay raises about the curriculum and American education are presently the subject of intense discussion and debate; similarly, the examination of silence, whether in women's lives or in their texts, is far from foreclosed. While feminist critical interest in the nature and operations of silence has expanded beyond Olsen's initial emphasis on it as repressive, and while the voices and texts of more and more women continue to be recovered and heard, it is still the case, as Anne Balsamo and Paula A. Treichler point out in "Feminist Critical Studies: Questions for the 1990s," that "[b]y no means has the last decade ended the forms of women's silence." There are still, as they go on to say, silences because women are not speaking, silences because women are not heard, silences because their voices are not understood, and silences because their voices are not preserved (6). From the cultural silences imposed on adolescent girls that Carol Gilligan is investigating, to the latest revelations of the extent to which women have kept and still keep silent about sexual harassment or rape, the need to continue to struggle against the silencing effects of dominant constructions of gender, race, class, and sexuality is apparent. This struggle must continue to inform feminist literary criticism. That criticism, meanwhile, must also continue to engage in the work of excavation, of the discovery and recovery of the many texts that are still lost or undervalued, especially those of minority women, as well as in the work of encouraging new voices to come to speech through writing. If, as this collection has shown, some contemporary feminist criticism disputes Olsen's emphases and goes beyond them, such disputes nonetheless significantly build on her work. Whatever directions future explorations of the paradigms of "silence" and "silencing" may take, feminist criticism will remain indebted—to use the phrase Olsen used about Rebecca Harding Davis's work—to Olsen's "pioneering firsts" (116).

WORKS CITED

Balsamo, Anne, and Paula A. Treichler. "Feminist Critical Studies: Questions for the 1990s." *Women and Language* xiii, 1 (Fall 1990): 6.
Fishkin, Shelley Fisher. "The Borderlands of Culture: Writing by W. E. B. Du Bois, James Agee, Tillie Olsen and Gloria Anzaldúa." *Literary Journalism in the Twentieth Century*. Ed. Norman Sims. New York: Oxford UP, 1990. 133–82.
Gilbert, Sandra M., and Susan Gubar. *The Madwoman in the Attic. The Woman Writer and the Nineteenth-Century Literary Imagination*. New Haven: Yale UP, 1979.

————. *Shakespeare's Sisters. Feminist Essays on Women Poets.* Bloomington: Indiana UP, 1979.

Gilligan, Carol, Nona P. Lyons, and Trudy J. Hammer, eds. *Making Connections. The Relational Worlds of Adolescent Girls at Emma Willard School.* Cambridge: Harvard UP, 1990.

Greene, Gayle, and Coppelia Kahn, eds. "Introduction" to *Making a Difference. Feminist Literary Criticism.* London: Methuen, 1985.

Gubar, Susan. "The 'Blank Page' and the Issue of Female Creativity." *Critical Inquiry* (Winter 1981): 243–64.

Jameson, Frederic. *Postmodernism, or, the Cultural Logic of Late Capitalism.* Durham, NC: Duke UP, 1991.

Jones, Ann Rosalind. "Inscribing Femininity: French Theories of the Feminine." *Making a Difference. Feminist Literary Criticism.* Ed. Gayle Greene and Coppelia Kahn. London: Methuen, 1985. 80–112.

Lorde, Audre. "The Transformation of Silence into Language and Action." *Sister Outsider. Essays and Speeches.* New York: Crossing, 1984. 40–44.

Meese, Elizabeth A. *Crossing the Double-Cross. The Practice of Feminist Criticism.* Chapel Hill: U of North Carolina P, 1986.

Mitchell, Sally. Cited in *Book Review Digest.* New York: H. H. Wilson, 1979. 987.

Olsen, Tillie. *Mother to Daughter, Daughter to Mother.* New York: The Feminist Press, 1984.

Olsen, Tillie. *Silences.* New York: Delta, 1979.

Piercy, Marge. *To Be of Use.* Garden City, NY: Doubleday, 1973.

Rich, Adrienne. *On Lies, Secrets, and Silence. Selected Prose 1966–1978.* New York: Norton, 1979.

Robinson, Lillian S. *Sex, Class, and Culture.* Bloomington: Indiana UP, 1978.

Russ, Joanna. *How to Suppress Women's Writing.* Austin: U of Texas P, 1983.

Stout, Janis P. *Strategies of Reticence. Silence and Meaning in the Works of Jane Austen, Willa Cather. Katherine Anne Porter, and Joan Didion.* Charlottesville: UP of Virginia, 1990.

Wall, Cheryl A., ed. *Changing Our Own Words. Essays on Criticism, Theory, and Writing by Black Women.* New Brunswick, NJ: Rutgers UP, 1989.

Yaeger, Patricia. *Honey-Mad Women: Emancipatory Strategies in Women's Writing.* New York: Columbia UP, 1988.

PART I

Circle of Women Artists:
Tillie Olsen and Anne Sexton
at the Radcliffe Institute

Diane Middlebrook

One Sunday in November 1960, *The New York Times* carried a front-page story announcing an experimental new program designed to "harness the talents of 'intellectually displaced women' " whose careers had been interrupted.[1] The program was to be called The Radcliffe Institute; its founder was Mary Ingraham Bunting, the recently inaugurated president of Radcliffe, the women's college at Harvard University. The program would make twenty fellowships available to women who wished to return to fulltime intellectual or artistic work. President Bunting devised the program to address what she described as the "climate of unexpectation" in which mature women struggled for professional visibility, once they had stepped off a career path in order to raise a family.[2] The Radcliffe Institute was to be a place where women could make up for lost time, using the facilities of the Harvard libraries and laboratories.

The announcement of this new fellowship program stirred ripples nationwide. Seventeen hundred women applied for the twenty available places, a few of which were set aside for working artists.[3] The poets Anne Sexton and Maxine Kumin were appointed Radcliffe Scholars that first year, as were visual artists Barbara Swan and Lois Swirnoff. Tillie Olsen learned of the Radcliffe Institute from Sexton, who had met Olsen only in the pages of *New World Writing* in 1960, when the same issue that published Sexton's "Dancing the Jig" also carried Olsen's novella, "Tell Me a Riddle." This story became one of Sexton's sacred texts, a work she reread and hoped to emulate. Impulsively, she had written Olsen a fan letter,[4] out of which grew a correspondence that inspired Sexton to press for Olsen's appointment to the Radcliffe Institute.

Anne Sexton, Maxine Kumin, and Barbara Swan received reappointments to continue at the Radcliffe Institute during the academic year 1962–63; Tillie Olsen joined them in September. After Olsen got settled in Cambridge she and Sexton made a date for lunch in Harvard Square. They were not really strangers: Olsen had encountered Sexton's work in literary magazines, and after reading *To Bedlam and Part Way Back* had cut Sexton's picture from the back jacket to mount on the wall over her desk along with the faces of Tolstoy,

A briefer version of this material appears in Diane Middlebrook, *Anne Sexton: A Biography*. New York: Houghton Mifflin, 1991.

Whitman, and "others who sustain and judge me."[5] But Sexton's diffidence surprised Olsen. "I recognized from reading *Bedlam* what a reader Anne was, what a hunger for ideas she had. Yet she would say to me, over and over, 'It's Maxine who's the real intellectual! I'm a poet, but I don't have real brains.' "[6] From that first meeting, Sexton and Olsen felt drawn together by the sense of being artists plunged into the unfamiliar mores of academia. Olsen, like Sexton, held no college degree, although six years before she had been a creative writing fellow at Stanford University, commuting there from San Francisco for the required seminars. But she had been a reader all her life, a frequenter of libraries, raised in a family that prized books and knowledge.

As a Radcliffe Scholar, Olsen, fifty, was older than most of the others. She had also lived in a different social world. Most of the scholars had led privileged lives and felt economically secure. To her amazement, Olsen found that, "like characters in a John Cheever novel," almost every one of the Radcliffe Scholars that year had spent some time in psychoanalysis; she observed that their view of what it meant to be a woman came straight out of Freud and other male-oriented models of human motivation. According to Sexton, Maxine Kumin, in particular, was attracted to Freudian ideas that year; she was discussing Freud in a course and wanted the other Radcliffe Scholars to share her excitement over *Civilization and Its Discontents* and *The Ego and the Id*.[7]

Olsen, the wife of a printer and a working mother with four daughters, looked elsewhere for her insights into family dynamics. "I had a different understanding of the situation of women," she recalled, "beginning with my Socialist upbringing, reinforced throughout my life. It had to do with looking for societal roots, causes, circumstances for so much attributed to the personal, the psychological only." Later, Olsen was to comment in *Silences* on the disadvantages she perceived in the psychotherapeutic assumptions prevalent in that era, which, she observed, could be especially formidable "for the analyzed writer-woman; deflecting, blinding, robbing of sources of one's own authority (that is: basic woman-experience comprehensions, and 'motherhood-truths' not yet incorporated into literature and other disciplines, let alone into psychiatric theory and practice)."[8]

At Radcliffe that year her feminist views came strongly to the fore when she was told about the psychological profiles that were being gathered at the Institute. The Scholars were expected to take a battery of psychological tests as well as be interviewed by the Radcliffe-appointed social scientist Martha White. It was one of Dr. White's working hypotheses that the high-achieving Radcliffe Scholars reflected the influence of strong fathers. "This method, this 'study' of us seemed to me to be both an unproductive and, indeed, insulting way of trying to understand why we were 'exceptional,' seemingly different in motivation and achievement from other women," said Olsen. "As I said to Connie Smith (the Institute's director), 'We have intellects, powers of observation, life experiences. The best thing the Institute could do would be to get us together to discuss that *why?* I was asking for a shared, conscious process of coming to comprehension, which came into being seven years later. It is called 'consciousness-raising.' " Olsen's influence was directly responsible for much of the bracing criticism of women's situation that circulated at the Institute that year.

Tillie Olsen loved Sexton and Kumin instantly. A passion for literature was a common bond that set them apart from other Radcliffe Scholars, making their differences seem more fascinating than divisive. And with Sexton, Olsen shared another bond: a taste for unfashionable poets. Sexton confided to Olsen how horrified she'd been when her fondness for "lady poets" had been ridiculed by other poets when she'd first joined John Holmes's class at the Boston Center for Adult Education. Olsen remembered,

> We were walking along the Charles River, under the sycamores changing to their fall colors; it was my first fall in New England. I quoted Sara Teasdale and Anne said "Oh, so you love her too! But you must never, never admit it to anyone." I said, "What do you mean?" She told me that once she had let slip in a writing class her feeling for Teasdale, and discovered that S. T. was considered the lowest of the low. Our love of Sara Teasdale or Edna St. Vincent Millay didn't shame us with each other. We never needed to be guarded or to dissemble. Besides the deepest caring for each other's work, it was the love for and the talking about the writers—accepted or not—who were life to us that created the special bond between us then. We shared old loves and new discoveries.
>
> "Having been with you today, I feel like a writer again," Anne wrote me once. I might have written those identical words to her. That was what we did for each other.

Tillie Olsen, and then the sculptor Mariana Pineda, joined Barbara Swan, Maxine Kumin, and Anne Sexton as a tightly knit cohort of artists at the Radcliffe Institute in 1963. They joked about being "The Equivalents": President Bunting's formula for mixing artists with scholars holding advanced degrees. (Maxine Kumin held a Master's Degree; but she was being resocialized by Anne.) Olsen and Sexton formed a close friendship with Barbara Swan, one of the visual artists among what Swan dubbed "the Premier Cru," the first group of Radcliffe Scholars.[9] Like Tillie Olsen, Swan had been assigned an office in the wood-frame house on Mt. Auburn Street that sheltered the Scholars' program. Swan dismissed the Institute's "rabbit warren of tiny rooms" as a hopeless place for a painter to work, so she did her painting at home. But she got acquainted with the other scholars by sketching them. Throughout the 1960s Swan drew or painted portraits of Sexton and her friends that convey their sense of being artists *for* each other, being artists where art mattered. Unfortunately, she did not sketch a portrait of Tillie Olsen, but Olsen did bring back to her home in California one of Swan's favorite etchings, a portrait of Emily Dickinson.

Olsen's year at the Institute was a time of intellectual exploration as well. One of the books she read for the first time was Virginia Woolf's *A Room of One's Own,* and Sexton read it too: sandwiched between books on psychiatry and on witchcraft, in contrast to which "*A Room of One's Own* was health," she said[10]—possibly under the influence of Tillie's skepticism about psychiatry.

Since girlhood, Olsen had copied out treasured passages from library books, which she would annotate with her own thoughts. She brought with her to Radcliffe an enormous collection of them, bundles of loose pages accumulated over the years, all shapes and sizes. With Anne she shared translations from Rilke and pages of copy-outs from the letters of Emily Dickinson, and from James's and Kafka's notebooks. When the time came for her to present work in the regularly scheduled Tuesday seminar, Olsen selected passages focused on the theme that years later evolved into her book, *Silences*. "It was called 'The Death of the Creative Process,' " Olsen remembered.

> I'd intended to read, not give a talk. But suddenly they told me they *had* to have a title to send out with the spring schedule, and it having been that kind of climbing-walls writing morning, I said fliply, "Oh, call it 'Death of the Creative Process.' " So it was that I had to pull together, think about, organize out of the years' and years' accumulation of source material, what became the "Silences" piece. I brought with me, in a large file envelope which after the seminar Anne borrowed, much of the makings of it. Not only passages from other writers, my own thoughts, but also deeply personal at-the-time records of how it had been with me—I hadn't remembered they were there, except what I had to read from, along with other material, as part of the talk. At our graduation one of our sister Scholars did a marvelous satire on the way I gave this talk: little notes and cards and papers falling to the floor.

Tillie Olsen's wide-ranging speculations in her seminar touched many chords in Anne Sexton. She had never really experienced a writer's block. Yet Olsen brought home in compelling phrases the hidden damages writers suffer from self-inflicted causes, too: drinking, laziness, snobbishness, selling out— the vices listed by Hemingway in "The Snows of Kilimanjaro."[11] Olsen's reading of this passage in particular roused Sexton's never-dormant worries about her own dependencies. "I was thinking, what's blunted the axe of my creativity? These devices of mine, the pills. Of course they blunt my pain; but the pain can write."[12]

When Sexton looked back that summer over her two years at the Radcliffe Institute, she singled out Tillie Olsen's presentation as the high point. She told Martha White:

> Tillie's seminar probably changed my writing as much as anything. That amazed you, as I recall. You don't know how exceptional she is. There aren't very many writers around like that. That had real impact, changed me more than six courses. It's something I'll never forget. I didn't just hear it: it's entered my life and is changing it.
>
> MW: Was it the topics she discussed?
>
> AS: It was the way she did it, with a total commitment to perfection. And what she said about failure: that you have to wait, let it come. Everything has been 'you must *succeed*'—even at the Institute you must succeed. And she put in a theory of failure, how you can waste yourself. At that moment I was so worried about failure. Artists always are. You're looking for this

wonderful thing that you may never get. Tillie rededicates you. That's what she did for me; I couldn't speak afterward, I was in a state of shock. Tillie's seminar went way overtime, but if anyone had stopped her, I would have chopped their head off.[13]

After the seminar Sexton borrowed Olsen's notes; she and her secretary spent many hours typing the "copy-outs" to keep in her own files: sixty-three pages of them.[14]

In Tillie Olsen Sexton found a unique mentor. Olsen was a tutor of the long view, an excruciatingly deliberate writer who hoarded words and knew how to be patient. Just as important to Sexton, Olsen mistrusted the currently fashionable languages of psychology—so influential in Sexton's work—and existential philosophy, with their emphases on selfhood and solitude. Sexton too was wrestling for a different vision of the human being, one she felt was embodied in religious people though not in churches. Tillie's stash of copy-outs was at once comic and magical, an eccentric and authentic kind of spirituality. She sought Olsen's good opinion very carefully ("Tillie is so harassed," she told another member of the Institute; "I try not to bother her"[15]), but Olsen saw what hungers Sexton was bringing to the table. Olsen felt Sexton needed to be more deeply rooted in dailiness. "She was hungry not only for all that fed her true writer self," Olsen observed, "but also for validation of that self, not the least the being valued for her own vision and achievement."[16]

After Olsen's two-year appointment at the Institute was over, she returned to San Francisco. But she and Sexton remained in close touch for several years. Olsen took to sending Sexton a special kind of birthday greeting. A devotee of second-hand stores, Olsen had a collection of old calendars, out of date but handsomely printed. She would select one for Sexton on which the days of the month were current, with a request that Anne send it back the next year it was current. By this device she acknowledged both her hopes and her fears about Sexton's continuing survival.

Sexton's suicide in 1974 ended their friendship, but not their relationship. As Olsen put it, looking back, "What vanishes when time goes on is what a human being meant to others in their time. The living impact of her poetry, her struggle to write it, her fight for life, and her death: these continue on and on, with ever-deepening significance." And the work that Olsen consolidated at Radcliffe that year goes on speaking to and for the creative process.

NOTES

1. Fred M. Hechinger, "Radcliffe Pioneers in Plan for Gifted Women's Study," *New York Times* 20 Nov. 1960, p.1.

2. Dr. Mary Ingraham Bunting, interview with Middlebrook, Cambridge, Mass., 2 Dec. 1982.

3. Arline Grimes, "Scholars Praise Radcliffe Institute," *Boston Herald* 8 Oct. 1961.

4. A. S. to Tillie Olsen, 5 April 1960, *Anne Sexton: A Self-Portrait in Letters,* ed. Linda Gray Sexton and Lois Ames (Boston: Houghton Mifflin Company, 1977), pp. 102–103.

5. Tillie Olsen to A. S., post card 7 Nov. 1960, n.d., Harry Ransom Humanities Research Center, University of Texas at Austin (HRHRC).

6. Tillie Olsen, interview with Middlebrook, San Francisco, 12 June 1987.

7. A. S. to Dr. Martin Orne, therapy tape, 10 Jan. 1963, private collection.

8. Tillie Olsen, *Silences* (New York: Delacourt Press/Seymour Lawrence, 1978), p. 253. Olsen's criticism is supported by the prevalence of a clinical attribution of "penis-envy" to active professional women who sought treatment for depression; for example, see Elizabeth Zetzel, M.D., "On the Incapacity to Bear Depression" (dated 1965), in *The Capacity for Emotional Growth,* (London: Hogarth Press, 1970), pp. 103–112; Zetzel was a respected analyst practicing in Boston during those years.

9. Barbara Swan, "Premier Cru," *Radcliffe Quarterly,* June 1986, pp. 17–18.

10. A. S. to Dr. Martin Orne, therapy tape, 21 March 1963, private collection.

11. Olsen quoted Hemingway: " 'He had destroyed his talent himself—by not using it, by betrayals of himself and what he believed in, by drinking so much that he blunted the edge of his perceptions, by laziness, by sloth, by snobbery, by hook and by crook; selling vitality, trading it for security, for comfort.' " *Silences,* p. 10.

12. A. S. to Dr. Martin Orne, therapy tape, 21 March 1963, private collection.

13. A. S., interview with Martha White, July 1963, Radcliffe College Archives.

14. Sexton Miscellaneous Files, HRHRC.

15. A. S., interview with Martha White, July 1963.

16. Quoted in *Silences,* p. 218.

Reading, Writing, and Arithmetic: The Lessons *Silences* Has Taught Us

SHELLEY FISHER FISHKIN

A reader picking up *Harper's Magazine* in October 1965 would have learned from the cover that a number of famous writers "and others" contributed to the issue. "And others" included Tillie Olsen—whose exclusion from the cover list of contributors gave ironic resonance to the themes of omission, erasure, and invisibility that her article so eloquently explored.

In ways that the editors of *Harper's* never suspected, "and others" was a marvelously rich and prescient by-line for Tillie Olsen—one which she mischievously contemplates reclaiming some time in the future.[1] For Olsen's project in that *Harper's* article on "Silences in Literature," the first published version of material that thirteen years later would be incorporated into her book *Silences,* involved coming to terms with—and throwing her lot in with—the "others" whose voices had been drowned out and forgotten in the course of literary history, and with the "others" whom circumstances had prevented from coming to voice at all.

The notion, now accepted as a truism, that a woman's personal experiences could be directly relevant to her insights as a critic was as foreign to the world of literary criticism in the United States in 1965 as the concept of analyzing "silences" was. The "New Criticism," of course, was by then solidly enthroned. The text itself—and the text most definitely *by* itself—was championed as the proper object of criticism. In that critical climate, Olsen's concern not only with the lack of texts, but also with the details of the lives of those who failed to produce texts, stood out as particularly bold and original. Olsen wrote for all those silenced, and for all those not silenced. In her view, the achievement of those who were not silenced (including herself) bore witness by its very existence to what might have been, in the shadows of what never was.

In an effort to understand the impact of *Silences* on our time, I interviewed or corresponded with more than sixty scholars, critics, creative writers, publishers, and editors. They ranged in age from their twenties to their seventies. They lived on the East and West coasts, in the Southwest, the Northwest, the Midwest, and Puerto Rico. They worked both inside and outside the academy and the world of academic publishing. They were male and female (although predominantly female) and were white, black, Chicana, Puerto Rican, and Asian-American. I examined scores of articles and books that included references to or discussions of *Silences.* I consulted Olsen's own heavily annotated copy of *Silences,* as well as the file of letters she had received about the book, which she generously made available to me. I also conducted several extended interviews with Olsen herself.[2] This research documents a story that has not yet been told: it is the story of Tillie Olsen "and others"—some of those others whose lives she changed with the lessons she taught.

A clear consensus emerged from these investigations: *Silences* changed what we read in the academy, what we write, and what we count; it also gave us some important tools to understand and address many of the literary, social, economic and political silencings of the present and the potential silencings of the future. The critical habits it encouraged and helped instill are still with us in the classroom and in the bookstore, informing what literature is read and taught and the ways in which it is interpreted and evaluated. The problems and dangers Olsen underlined show no signs of disappearing, and her analysis remains as contemporary today as it was when it was first written.

Before examining the influence of this volume and its impact on our time, this essay will outline how *Silences* came to be, and what, in brief, it set out to do.

The Genesis of *Silences*

The book *Silences* was long in accumulation, as Olsen has said. But she didn't hoard her insights until the book was completed. Her earliest public discussion of the subject of silences was a talk titled "Death of the Creative Process," which she delivered from notes at the Radcliffe Institute as part of a weekly colloquium series during the academic year 1962–1963, when she was an Institute Scholar.[3] The article Olsen published in *Harper's* in 1965 was edited from the taped transcript of this talk. Photocopies of the article seemed to turn up everywhere. Olsen had clearly touched a nerve. Other early talks—on real-life "Shakespeare's Sisters" silenced by circumstance—included a presentation on a panel titled "The Woman Writer in the Twentieth Century," moderated by Elaine Hedges at the Modern Language Association Convention in 1971, sponsored by the Women's Commission of the MLA.[4] At M.I.T. in 1973 and 1974, Olsen gave "seeding talks" on the subject of "Denied Genius" that focused on "the blood kin of great men," such as Sophie Thoreau, Alice James, and Dorothy Wordsworth (Olsen 1988). In the early 1970s Olsen began publishing, in the *Women's Studies Newsletter,* lists of books to read, reread, and teach, by unjustly forgotten women writers.[5] These lists originally grew out of a course Olsen had taught at Amherst in the fall of 1969 on "The Literature of Poverty, Work, and the Human Struggle for Freedom" (Olsen 1988).[6] Like the *Harper's* article, these lists were widely mimeographed, photocopied, and circulated across the country.

"The women's movement and the freedom movement," Olsen has said, "created an atmosphere that made [her writing on the subject of silences] possible" (Olsen 1988). Olsen's work, in turn, helped give another dimension to those movements, as it encouraged a generation of activists and scholars to make the ideals that animated their lives shape the ideals that inspired their scholarship. The women's movement was making the case for taking women's experiences seriously, and here was Olsen handing out road maps on how to do just that in the study of literature. While many pondered the significance in their lives of the slogan "the personal is the political," Olsen gave them clues as to how to let that insight inform their work, how to understand the linkage between the personal circumstances of writers' lives and the art they produced, between their position in the larger society and the culture's tendency to valorize or dismiss their creative work. The same impulse that led civil rights activists to integrate lunch counters soon began to prompt young academics (often veteran demonstrators themselves) to try to integrate syllabi, to overcome exclusionary practices based solely on gender or race or class. Those who struggled to develop the earliest women's studies courses were particularly indebted to Olsen's reading lists, which gave them a sense that there *was* a literary heritage to be mined, that women's experiences could be made visible, could be studied and taught. Through her early article and reading lists, and through the hundreds of copies of them that circulated around the country, the ideas Olsen would weave together in book form in 1978 reached larger and larger numbers of writers, critics, and teachers in the 1960s and 1970s.

Silences, the book version of this material, is dedicated to "our silenced people, century after century their beings consumed in the hard, everyday essential work of maintaining human life. Their art, which still they made—as their other contributions—anonymous; refused respect, recognition, lost;" and also to "those of us (few yet in number, for the way is punishing), their kin and descendants, who begin to emerge into more flowered and rewarded use of our selves in ways denied to them . . ." (ix). In a handscrawled note on the dedication page in her own copy of the book, Olsen wrote, "we who are most of humanity" (Olsen, Annotations ix). Clearly her book is addressed to the largest audience possible.

The first essay, "Silences in Literature—1962," based on the Radcliffe talk (and revised from the version of the talk published in 1965 in *Harper's*) is Olsen's statement about the connection between circumstances (social, economic, psychological, etc.) and the production of art. Olsen's meditation on the preconditions needed for creativity to flourish draws heavily on writers' journals and letters and includes reflective comments by Rimbaud, Melville, Balzac, Joseph Conrad, Thomas Mann, Katherine Anne Porter, Franz Kafka, Rainer Maria Rilke, Katherine Mansfield, and Olsen herself.

In the second essay, "One Out of Twelve: Writers Who Are Women in Our Century—1971," based on the MLA talk, Olsen examines "twentieth-century literature course offerings, and writers decreed worthy of critical attention in books and articles," (24) and interrogates the striking absence of women. "Why?", she asks insistently, "What, not true for men but *only for women,* makes this enormous difference? . . . Why are so many more women silenced than men? Why, when women do write (one out of four or five works published) is so little of their writing known, taught, accorded recognition?" (24–25).

The third essay, "Rebecca Harding Davis—1971, 1972," which was written as an afterword for the Feminist Press 1972 reprint of Davis's 1861 story "Life in the Iron Mills," is an extended biographical and critical reconsideration of a writer Olsen felt had been unjustly neglected.

Olsen's wild and quirky "Part Two" dances fugue-like around themes she lays out in clear expository prose in "Part One." In this experimental section, Olsen dramatizes the theme of "silence" with peculiar immediacy and intensity by confronting the reader, throughout the section, with the "visual silence" of blankness on the page.[7] Her bold use of white space focuses the reader's attention on the books that are not there, the words that are absent—the emptiness that gapes from the pages of literary history (Fishkin 1990, 151–60). It also reminds us of the endless interruptions that still contribute to silences and silencings of those "consumed in the hard, everyday essential work of maintaining human life." "Part Two," a montage of fragments, may be read as it was written, with interruptions, in bits and pieces, in time stolen between chores. In the blank spaces between the fragments the reader is given permission to pause, to think, to insert her own response, to recall her own experience, to listen to her own voice in addition to the voices of others.

In both the conventionally structured and the experimental parts of her book, Olsen draws our attention to a range of silences, including "work aborted, deferred, denied," "censorship silences," "political silences," and "silences where the lives never came to writing." She explores silences imposed by domestic responsibilities, by economic hardship, by corroded self-confidence, by "the cost of 'discontinuity' (that pattern still imposed on women)" (39).

Olsen requires that we come to terms with the blankness we confront in literary history when we look for writing by women, working people, and people of color. Are the pages blank because these groups were silenced by circumstances? Because they never came to the point at which there was literacy, leisure, space, and energy to write in the first place? Or are the pages blank because society erased their words through rejection, dismissal, or devaluation? Olsen demands that we ponder all of these questions, that we ask whether the silence we encounter is there because potential writers have been mute—or because we have been deaf.

The Lessons

Reading

Silences has helped change what we read. It has given scholars and publishers the confidence to approach buried and forgotten texts with fresh eyes and new understanding, to appreciate journals and other private writings, and to read in women's artifacts (such as quilts) stories and plots invisible to previous generations.

The reading lists that grew out of Olsen's Amherst course and out of the talks she gave on women writers whom she urged us to read, reread, and teach, contained so many names that were obscure and unfamiliar then— Rebecca Harding Davis, Fanny Fern, Elizabeth Stuart Phelps, Zora Neale Hurston, Agnes Smedley, Sarah Wright—so many books impossible to find, out of print.[8] The appetite those lists whetted would not have to stay hungry for long. In 1970, Olsen translated the spirit of her "reading lists" into action by convincing Florence Howe to make reprinting forgotten works a central mission of the Feminist Press. As Howe recounts the story, in 1970, when Tillie Olsen "gave *Life in the Iron Mills* to the Feminist Press and said she had written a biographical and literary afterword that we could have as well, that changed the whole course of publishing for the Press." Up to that point the Feminist Press had planned to bring out "short biographical pamphlets about writers and women of distinction in all kinds of work, and . . . feminist children's books," observes Howe, "but we had not thought of doing works from the past until [Tillie] handed [us] *Life in the Iron Mills,* and followed that up the following year with *Daughter of Earth*" (Howe). Since those beginnings in the early 1970s, the Feminist Press has reprinted works by Charlotte Perkins Gilman, Margaret Fuller, Mary Wilkins Freeman, Meridel LeSueur, Josephine Herbst, Edith Summers Kelley, Fielding Burke, Tess Slesinger, June Arnold, Mary Austin, Katharine Burdekin, Mona Caird, Helen Hull, Elizabeth Janeway, Josephine Johnson, Edith Konecky, Paule Marshall, Moa Martinson, Myra Page, Elizabeth Stuart Phelps, Elizabeth Robins, Jo Sinclair, Helen Smith, Susan Warner, Dorothy West, Sarah Wright, Zora Neale Hurston, and many others.

At first the Feminist Press had the reprint field to itself. Then other publishers, recognizing the validity of the idea as well as its commercial potential, began series of their own. Virago, the Seal Press, and the Women's Press launched reprint series in the mid-70s, and Kitchen Table/Women of Color Press, Oxford, Beacon, Rutgers, Pandora, Illinois, Cornell's Industrial and Labor Relations Press, Northeastern, and scores of others began them in the '80s. These series, usually in paperback, have transformed the scope of what can be read and taught in the literature classroom.

Rutgers's "American Women Writers Series," for example, under the editorial direction of Joanne Dobson, Judith Fetterley, and Elaine Showalter, has resurrected neglected work from the 1820s to the 1920s by such writers as Fanny Fern, Lydia Maria Child, Rose Terry Cooke, Harriet Prescott Spofford, Harriet Beecher Stowe, E.D.E.N. Southworth, Louisa May Alcott, Alice Cary, Catharine Maria Sedgwick, Elizabeth Stuart Phelps, Maria Cummins, Mary Austin, Caroline Kirkland, Constance Fenimore Woolson, and Nella Larsen. The "Northeastern Library of Black Literature," guided by Series Editor Richard Yarborough, has reprinted work by writers such as George Schuyler, William Demby, Julian Mayfield, Claude McKay, Richard Wright, W.E.B. Du Bois, J. Saunders Redding, Jessie Redmon Fauset, Albert Murray, and Gayle

Jones. The "Literature of American Labor" series launched by Cornell's Industrial and Labor Relations Press, edited by Cletus E. Daniel and Ileen A. DeVault, has reissued novels by Theresa Malkiel and K. B. Gilden. And Oxford University Press's "Schomburg Library of Nineteenth-Century Black Women Writers," shaped by series editor Henry Louis Gates, Jr., has made the work of writers such as Pauline Hopkins, Anna Julia Cooper, Frances E. W. Harper, Nancy Prince, Angelina Weld Grimke, Mary Seacole, Harriet Jacobs, Mrs. N. F. Mossell, Phillis Wheatley, Effie Waller Smith, Katherine Davis Chapman Tillman, Charlotte Forten Grimke, Elizabeth Keckley, Maria W. Stewart, Mrs. A. E. Johnson, Alice Dunbar-Nelson, Ann Plato, Emma Dunham Kelley, Ida B. Wells-Barnett, and Sojourner Truth available to scholars and teachers.

The same impulse that led publishers to begin reprint series led them to publish new anthologies of forgotten writers as well, books designed to make their way easily into college classrooms. The scholars who proposed and edited these anthologies often found their inspiration in *Silences*. As Mary Anne Ferguson put it (paraphrasing Whitman on Emerson), "I was simmering, simmering, simmering. Tillie brought me to a boil" (Ferguson 1988). *Images of Women in Literature,* a widely taught anthology now in its fifth edition, was the result. Ferguson was not the only scholar on whom *Silences* had this effect. Others include Michele Murray (*A House of Good Proportion: Images of Women in Literature*); Mary Helen Washington (*Black-Eyed Susans: Classic Stories By and About Black Women, Invented Lives: Narratives of Black Women 1860–1960,* and *Midnight Birds: Stories by Contemporary Black Women*); Helen Barolini (*The Dream Book: An Anthology of Writings by Italian American Women*); Arlyn Diamond and Lee Edwards (*American Voices, American Women*); and Susan Koppelman (*Between Mothers & Daughters, Images of Women in Fiction, Old Maids: Short Stories by Nineteenth Century U.S. Women Writers,* and *The Other Woman*) (Olsen 1988; Washington 1988; Koppelman 1988). The most recent anthology that is an outgrowth of Olsen's work on the subject of silences is *The Heath Anthology of American Literature,* which endeavors to integrate previously forgotten writers fully into American literary study, and which promises to transform the way American literature is taught in college classrooms for years to come (Lauter 1991; Heath 1990; Gordon 1990; McMillen 1991).[9]

Silences has stimulated the rediscovery of "lost" women writers outside the English-speaking world as well. The Swedish edition of *Silences,* for example, included an extended afterword by Swedish critics that cited Olsen's text as having inspired their recovery of Scandinavian women writers whom literary history had forgotten.[10]

The attention Olson paid to diaries, letters, and other neglected genres prompted scholars to take these forms more seriously than they had previously been taken. Once again, some striking anthologies, such as *Revelations,* Mary Jane Moffat's and Charlotte Painter's collection of women's diaries, were the result. Moffat wrote Olsen,

My Diaries course, which would never have happened but for you, was wonderful. . . . Charlotte Painter & I are preparing a collection of extracts from women's diaries & letters for Random House. . . . Our focus is on the inner life, the steps toward individuality women have recorded in the life-in-process diary form. We include examples of lives you introduced me to, or suggested: Ruth Benedict; Kathe Kollwitz; Dorothy Wordsworth; Alice James. We were interested in the diary or journal as a valid literary form for women. . . . I think of you as "Tillie Appleseed." Generations will thank you as I do now, far too sparingly (Moffat to Olsen, 15 October 1973).

Olsen's efforts to seek out and value women's words about women's lives, no matter how seemingly trivial or unimportant, helped inspire a scholar like Elizabeth Hampsten, in *Read This Only To Yourself,* to read critically the private letters of ordinary women (Hampsten 1988, 1982), and prompted Annette Kolodny to recover lost words of American pioneer women (Kolodny 1988, 1984). Teaching us to value, record, and collect that which, in Virginia's Woolf's phrase, "explains much and tells much," (45) *Silences* also stimulated the gathering of oral histories. It inspired Jean Reith Schoedel, for example, to collect in her book *Alone in a Crowd: Women in the Trades Tell Their Stories* the oral histories of women who work as steelhaulers, pipefitters, bindery workers, plumbers, longhaul truckers, bus drivers, sailors, carpenters, and firefighters.[11]

Olsen's determination to value women's experiences and their efforts to articulate that experience prompted many students and teachers to listen for muffled speech in places where they had previously assumed there was only silence. *Silences* originated in Olsen's awareness of the silencing of faculty wives at Stanford (where she held a writing fellowship in 1956–57) and Amherst (where she was a visiting professor and writer in residence in 1969–70) just as much as it derived from her consciousness of the silencing of working-class people in the Midwest and San Francisco (Olsen 1988). Teachers of middle-class students report that *Silences* allows their students to see the often hidden silences that enveloped their own mothers, sisters, grandmothers, and aunts, and to understand the myriad ways in which circumstances can constrict and stifle creativity (Kolodny 1988). Teachers of working-class and of first-generation college students report the key ways in which this book helps their students approach all of their college reading with new understanding— and with a sturdy respect for the dignity of their own voices and their own potential voices (Marcus 1988). *Silences* yoked eloquence and insight in a language that spoke to both the common reader and the academic critic (Stimpson 1988).

Writing

Silences has also helped change what we write as literary critics and feminist theorists. Catharine Stimpson put it succinctly: "it was simply one of the texts that helped to found a field" (Stimpson 1988). That field, of course, was feminist criticism and women's studies. For one thing, *Silences* helped put the idea of "silencing" itself on the table for discussion—an idea that Lillian Robinson, glancing back to Olsen, calls perhaps the most empowering of feminist critical tools (Robinson 1987, 23). Olsen's attention to the social forces that silence voices of the marginalized and powerless, to the material circumstances that inhibit creativity, to the politics of reputation and of censorship, and to the psychology of self-censorship, all helped scholars develop compelling critical frameworks.

Olsen's pioneering work in *Silences* on the nature of literary reputation (exemplified in her essay on Rebecca Harding Davis) helped stimulate widespread questioning about the construction of the literary canon by such critics as Lillian Robinson and Paul Lauter. It informed the kinds of questions Robinson raised in her widely-reprinted essay, "Treason Our Text: Feminist Challenges to the Literary Canon," and has influenced her approach to such issues as how one might evaluate working-class women's writing, private writing by women, and popular culture, as well as traditional canonical texts (Robinson 1983, 1978). Lauter, whose most recent book, *Canons and Contexts,* explores "alternative assumptions about literary value" (128) also acknowledges his indebtedness to Olsen (Lauter 1991).

Olsen's ideas about silencing were central to Jane Marcus's discussion of "the silenced women of history" in her essay "Still Practice: A/Wrested Alphabet: Toward a Feminist Aesthetic" (1984). Indeed, Marcus credits *Silences* with making it possible for her to break her own silence as a critic. She notes, "I was in silence and silenced when Tillie's book came out. *Silences* became my Bible in that it allowed me to identify with people who were more oppressed than I was. Hearing Tillie speak after having been silenced herself for so long made me feel I had to try because I was less oppressed than other people who were silenced" (Marcus 1988). The result was a host of influential articles and books from Marcus on the challenge of hearing and decoding women's voices in literature, and on the dynamics of the forces that would silence them.

Olsen's writing on silence and silencing was the "subtext" for Annette Kolodny's reinterpretation of the literary treatment of the American West in her book, *The Land Before Her* (Kolodny 1988, 1984), and for Norma Alarcón's revision in *This Bridge Called My Back* of the cultural significance of the figure of "La Malinche" (Alarcón 1988, 1983). It helped inspire Elaine Hedges's recovery and reinterpretation of Charlotte Perkins Gilman's *The Yellow Wallpaper* as a text intimately concerned with the silences inscribed by turn-of-the-century gender relations (Hedges 1988, 1973).

[Speaking personally for a moment, I might add that Olsen's charge that we recover and attend to voices that had been dismissed or ignored for reasons of race or class or gender helped prompt me to explore the role that several forgotten black speakers—a ten-year-old servant, a cook, and a teenaged slave—played in the development of Mark Twain's art in *Huckleberry Finn* (Fishkin 1993); it also encouraged me to reevaluate the role played by neglected or maligned women writers and women family members throughout Mark Twain's career (Fishkin 1994)].

Bonnie Zimmerman, Rosario Ferré, Linda Wagner Martin, Margaret Randall, Hortense Spillers, and many others also cite Olsen's ideas about silencing and silence as having been central to their ability to frame empowering critical paradigms, whether those paradigms focus on exclusion or erasure based on sexual preference, gender, race, class, political views, or all of the above (Zimmerman 1988; Ferré 1988; Wagner-Martin 1988; Olsen 1988; Spillers 1988).[12] As Linda Wagner-Martin commented, "it would be hard to find a feminist critic [of our generation] who was not influenced in key ways by *Silences*."

In addition, Olsen's exploration of the theme of silence has helped shape critical writing and research agendas in fields outside of literature. Legal theorist Robin West, for example, draws heavily on *Silences* in her examination of the voices that were left out of legal history and the law (West 1988); and the book was also the background for Susan Griffin's interpretation of pornography as "a desire to silence eros" in her book *Pornography and Silence* (Griffin 1981, vii, 1).

In addition to stimulating critical writing, *Silences* has helped inspire new creative writing—poetry, drama and fiction. It encouraged the Chicana writer Helena María Viramontes to draw, from her own culture, luminous, moving short stories (Viramontes 1985; 1988), and helped move Asian-American playwright Genny Lim to put on stage the drama that inhered in the culture *she* knew well (Lim 1988).[13] Gloria Naylor has said that "*Silences* helped me keep my sanity many a day" (Naylor to Olsen, 29 July 1988). Sandra Cisneros refers to *Silences* as " 'the Bible.' I constantly return to it" (Cisneros 1988). Margaret Atwood has observed that what Olsen has to say in *Silences* "is of primary importance to those who want to understand how art is generated or subverted and to those trying to create it themselves" (Atwood 1982). And Mary Stewart, referring to a collection of her poetry, wrote that ". . . it was *Silences* that gave me this poem, which in turn gave me all the poems that have followed . . ." (Stewart to Olsen, 28 September 1985). *Silences* was similarly inspiring for Alice Walker: ". . . As much as I learned from *Tell Me A Riddle,* I learned even more from Tillie's landmark classic and original essay "Silences: When Writers Don't Write," which I read while living in Cambridge in the early 70s, raising a small daughter alone and struggling to write myself" (Walker, n.d.). And Walker has also noted, "There are a few writers who manage in their work and in the sharing of their understanding to actually help us to live, to work, to create, day by day. Tillie Olsen is one of those writers for me" (Walker 1982). *Silences* has helped inspire other creative talents, including those of Maxine Hong Kingston, Ursula Le Guin, Alix Kates Shulman, Caryl Churchill, Margaret Randall, Margaret Laurence, Joyce Johnson, and Anne Sexton (Kingston 1982; Le Guin 1987; Schulman 1979; Churchill 1987, p. 77; Olsen 1988; Magnuson 1988; Middlebrook 1991).

Silences also played an empowering role for older writers. As Susan Gubar has observed, "no one else has recorded [as] faithfully [as Tillie Olsen has] the tribulations and triumphs of speech after long silence" (Gubar 1988). Teaching the importance of being aware of but not defeated by what Olsen called "foreground silences" (when many years of silence precede the first creative effort), Olsen's book also inspired *A Wider Giving: Women Writing after Long Silence* (1988), an "anthology of poetry, prose and autobiographical narrative by contemporary women writers who made their major commitment to creative writing after the age of forty-five,"[14] and other first books of fiction by older women such as *The Calling,* by Mary Gray Hughes (Marcus 1988).

Olsen's book prompted many writers to explore in both fiction and nonfiction themes that had been largely taboo before, but which *Silences* foregrounded; foremost among these was the complex tensions between art and motherhood. Ursula Le Guin, for example, in a 1987 meditation on this subject, confesses that she "stole (many of the) quotations [in a recent work of hers] from Tillie Olsen's *Silences,* a book to which" her own work, she writes, "stands in the relation of an undutiful and affectionate daughter: 'Hey, Ma, you aren't using this, can I wear it?' " Le Guin retains a special affection for Olsen's book because of the ways in which it empowered her as a writer: "Along in the seventies, when feminism tended to identify the Mother as the Enemy . . . I had three kids whom I liked and a mother whom I liked and a mother-in-law whom I liked, and I felt guilty. I felt I should not speak from my own experience, because my experience was faulty—not right" (Le Guin 1987). *Silences* encouraged Le Guin to value the truth of her own experience— without suppressing the complexities and tensions that experience entailed. For other women it cleared a space in which, secure in the knowledge that they were not alone, they could explore the anguished choices they had to make— often daily—between children and work. As Deborah Rosenfelt has put it, "*Silences* reassured women that they weren't crazy. It gave us permission to speak about things we had buried or kept to ourselves before" (Rosenfelt 1988).

Olsen forged bonds between the writers *about* whom she wrote, and the writers *for* whom she wrote. "Here we all are, then," wrote Alix Kates Shulman, "the writers invoked in *Silences* and those of us who read them, comprising a writers' workshop. We are sitting in a circle, sharing our experiences and ideas, . . . searching for a common truth, growing stronger and more confident and more determined through our mutual support and inspiration" (532–33). Readers sensed, quite rightly, that Tillie Olsen, too, was a warm and welcoming member of that circle. Indeed, Olsen herself once claimed with characteristic modesty, "I assure you I am not as good a writer as some of you may think I am. It is you and what you bring to it . . . the common work that we do together" (Olsen 1983, 64).

Arithmetic

Just as *Silences* has changed the way we read and the way we write, it has also changed the way we count. The book demonstrated the dramatic power of a "rhetoric of arithmetic"[15] to make explicit conditions of exclusion, imbalance, and neglect. Affirming and building on work by Elaine Showalter and Florence Howe, Olsen's essay, "One Out of Twelve: Writers Who Are Women in Our Century" (originally published in 1972, and republished in *Silences* in 1978) taught the simple lesson that adding up the number of women (and minorities) present in "literature courses, required reading lists, textbooks, quality anthologies, the year's best, the fifty years' best, consideration by critics or in current reviews," etc. was itself a valuable critical tool.[16] Over the next twenty years that tool would be picked up, for example, by Bonnie Zimmerman in her 1982 essay "One Out of Thirty: Lesbianism in Women's Studies Textbooks"; by Paul Lauter in his 1983 article on "Race and Gender in the Shaping of the American Literary Canon"; and by Charlotte Nekola, in her 1987 essay, "Worlds Unseen: Political Women Journalists and the 1930s." The practice of "counting" remains enormously useful to dramatize and document in concrete terms the inequalities and inequities women and minorities continue to confront. *Silences* taught us *how* to count, and it taught us *that* we count. Respect for ourselves, our voices, and those of our foremothers (however faint and forgotten) is one of the most important legacies it has left us.

Dissenting Voices

Not every reader, it should be said, has been enthralled with *Silences*. When the book appeared, several critics, in fact, faulted Olsen for having inscribed in it her own set of silences or distortions. Joyce Carol Oates, for example, observed that "there is little or no mention" in the book of successful women writers of our time, and suggested counter-examples to Olsen's relatively bare roster (Oates 1978, 33–34). (Oates went on to characterize "the thinking that underlies *Silences*" as "simply glib and superficial if set in contrast to the imagination that created *Tell Me a Riddle* and *Yonnondio*" (Oates 1978, 34)). Reviewer Phoebe-Lou Adams faulted Olsen's neglect of the psychological obstacles writers often put in their own paths. Olsen, Adams wrote, "blames everything except that standard known as writer's block, while quoting the lamentations of a number of writers (mostly men) who suffered no other impediment" (Adams 1978, 96). More recently, Mickey Pearlman and Abby Werlock have taken exception to Olsen's characterization of Rebecca Harding Davis's place in her society (129–30), and some readers have complained about the book's "whiny" tone, and the spirit of rhapsodic self-pity that they find pervades its prose.[17]

Nellie McKay, citing the large output of writing by black women in the nineteenth century who wrote and spoke (although for a relatively small audience) feels that the concept of "silence" may be less relevant than the theme of "silencing" for these African-American women writers who overcame often crushing "circumstances" to publish prolifically in African-American newspapers and magazines. These writers, largely absent from Olsen's lists, McKay notes, can be considered "silent" only from the standpoint of the mainstream culture that chose not to hear them (McKay 1988). While Mary Anne Ferguson credits *Silences* with having stimulated her own awareness of a number of black writers with whom she had been unfamiliar (Ferguson 1988), other critics share McKay's view that for all its efforts to be attentive to black writers, the book was ultimately "thinner" on bibliographies for black and third-world writers than it was for white ones. However, it is perhaps unfair to fault Olsen for not being aware of the numerous African-American writers whose works have been recovered during the quarter-century since she began her investigation of the subject of silences, especially since her work helped create a climate among scholars and publishers that made possible this recovery process. Any evalua- tion of the relationship between *Silences* and writing by people of color must ultimately take into account the views of the large number of minority writers and critics—including Alice Walker, Gloria Naylor, Sandra Cisneros, Hortense Spillers, Genny Lim, Norma Alarcón, Helena María Viramontes, and Maxine Hong Kingston—who cite *Silences* as a text that has been centrally important for them. As Maxine Hong Kingston put it, "Tillie Olsen helps those of us condemned to silence—the poor, racial minorities, women—find our voices" (Kingston 1982).

Attacks on the Lessons

Silences's legacy includes not only new habits of reading, writing, and count- ing, but also new habits of vigilance. For *Silences* has helped us understand the dynamics of "silencing" and has given us the tools to cry "foul" when we see in action the forces that silence. It is a book that addresses, in addition to the silences of the past, the silencings of the present and potential silencings of the future. What Olsen flagged as "censorship silences" (9; 142); silences stemming from "critical attitudes; exclusions" (238); "political silences" (9; 143); "silences where the lives never come to writing" (10; 151); and "virulent destroyers: premature silencers" (9–10; 148) are, unfortunately, still very much with us.

Reading

Take "censorship silences," for example. An offensive is currently being mounted on several fronts regarding what, and whom, we read. National studies reveal that the number of challenges to specific library books and school materials increased steadily from 1983 to 1990 (Reichman 8; Ervin 1991). A significant number of the censorship initiatives against schools and libraries have been sponsored by organized far-right groups such as Donald Wildmon's American Family Association (formerly the National Federation of Decency); Robert Simonds's Citizens for Excellence in Education, the activist wing of the National Association of Christian Educators; Phyllis Schlafly's Eagle Forum; and Beverly LaHaye's Concerned Women for Amer- ica ("People for" 1986–87, 9). Through efforts ranging from challenging specific texts in school districts and in the courts to taking over school boards, these groups have worked to remove from classrooms and libraries novels, textbooks, and other curricular material that challenges traditional sex roles, or that praises the contributions of minorities, women, or labor unions to American society (Reichman 27–45). They have helped to create what watchdog groups like People for the American Way call an alarming "climate of intolerance" in American secondary school classrooms ("People for" 1987–88; "People for" 1988). In this climate of intolerance students' own writing is not immune from attack: in Lolo, Montana a group of fundamentalist parents persuaded the school board to ban students' writing journals. They objected to the candor and openness that writing journals inspired ("People for" 1986–87, 14).

Silencing in college classrooms tends to take more subtle forms. Rather than "censorship silences," here we find what Olsen referred to as the silencing that stems from "critical attitudes; exclusions" and their potentially devastating effect on those who, due to "class, sex, or color" are "still marginal in literature, and whose coming to voice at all against complex odds is an exhausting achievement" (146). *Silences*'s legacy in publishing—reprint series and textbooks like the *Heath Anthology*—may make it easier than ever before to integrate previously neglected women and minority writers into college courses. Many individuals and institutions, however, have launched a campaign to exclude these voices from the curriculum. In the 1980s individuals like Allan Bloom and former Secretary of Education William Bennett publically challenged the validity of courses, reading lists, and programs of study that valued contributions of women and minorities to world culture. In the 1990s scholars who share Bloom's and Bennett's perspective unite under the banner of the National Association of Scholars (NAS) to achieve the same goals. This organization's journal, *Academic Questions,* frequently runs attacks on feminist criticism and African-American Studies (Weisberg 1991, 34–39; S. Diamond 1991, 45–48).

NAS members find the idea of expanding the canon to include those previously excluded from it repugnant. Their rhetoric often waxes hyperbolic: one member urged colleagues to fight the good fight against "a new dark ages, preserving what is worth preserving amid the barbaric ravages in the countryside and the towns of academe" (quoted in Weisberg 1991, 37). Those "barbaric ravages" refer to many of the texts recovered by scholars inspired by Olsen's *Silences* or written by imaginative writers whom Olsen's work helped empower. A budget of half a million dollars a year, mainly from conservative foundations, funds NAS members' fight to keep college courses and curricula as close as possible to what they were when *they* were in college. NAS arguments have captured the imagination of a number of mainstream publications—including *Time, The Atlantic Monthly,* and *The New Republic*—who have added their voices to a chorus of diversity bashing. Despite these efforts, however, it is unlikely that the NAS and its supporters will succeed in rolling back twenty years of innovative and responsible curricular transformation on American campuses.[18]

If Tillie Olsen's book *Silences* alerts us to the dangers of the silencings of the American Family Association, Citizens for Excellence in Education, and the National Association of Scholars, it also urges us to be more sensitive to the dynamics of our own silencings. We must make sure that efforts to expand the canon do not simply replace it with a counter-canon with its own new and different patterns of exclusion or ghettoization—patterns that may grow out of ethnocentrism or homophobia, diseases not confined, unfortunately, to diversity bashers.

The last decade, for example, has seen a dramatic increase in writing by Latinas. As Puerto Rican feminist writer Rosario Ferré has put it, "(Escribimos) porque le tenemos mas miedo al silencio que a la palabra."[19] Despite the heady proliferation of new Latina voices, Latina writers are rarely included in American literature courses or women's literature courses, and only recently have they made their way into literary anthologies. Scholars need to cultivate the critical and linguistic skills to respond to these voices with the intelligence and respect they deserve. Teachers of American literature, for example, need to make sure that they don't exclude from their syllabi and criticism works that draw on multiple linguistic and cultural traditions—such as Gloria Anzaldúa's book *Borderlands /La Frontera*—because they are afraid of grappling with a text that maps the borderlands of our culture.[20]

Writing

What we write, and who gets to write, is in jeopardy as well. We must continue to attend to what Olsen labeled "political silences (143)"—including "complete silencing by governments (143)." The *Writers in Prison Committee Reports,* prepared annually by International PEN, remind us of the writers around the world who have been imprisoned, and are still in prison, for the political content of their work, victims of brutal silencing by their governments.

Troubling as well are the "silences where the lives never come to writing" due to such factors as illiteracy and poverty. According to Henry Louis Gates, Jr., forty-four percent of African-Americans today cannot read the front page of a newspaper (Gates 1988). The functional literacy rate of the free black population in America in 1865 was probably higher than it is today.[21] We are also reminded that more than 75 percent of the women in the world today are women of color, and of these, ninety percent are illiterate.[22] Who will write their stories?

Olsen's book, with its groundbreaking discussions of the agonizing tensions between motherhood and creativity, between sustaining life and creating art, makes us particularly sensitive to those whose "lives never come to writing" because Federal restrictions on birth control and abortion information or denied access to abortion clinics effectively sentence them to early unwanted motherhood. Recent years have witnessed a disturbing increase in violent attacks on abortion clinics and on doctors and nurses who perform abortions, including, in 1993, the murder of one doctor. Patients have been the victims of public humiliation, psychological warfare, and entrapment by fake clinics.[23] The ultimate victim of these attacks and prohibitions is the woman (typically poor, young, and trapped) who will be locked out of the cultural conversation by the demands of the unwanted pregnancy she must carry to term.

Arithmetic

The way we "count" is under attack as well. For a number of students and professors, two black writers on an American literature syllabus is one too many. What the token woman was to the course syllabus of an earlier era, the token African-American or Asian-American or Native-American writer way be to the course syllabus of the 1990s. Those who attack multicultural initiatives in education complain about "bumping" a "good" white male writer and replacing him with a "bad" minority writer. If genius, as Olsen suggests frequently throughout *Silences,* is an equal opportunity employer, we must break down the spurious argument that "diversity" and "quality" are oppositional terms, and we must insist that the writers we teach "count" because their work matters.

There is another sense in which the way we count is being challenged. Olsen drew our attention to what she called "virulent destroyers: premature silencers." It is an accurate phrase to describe the devastating illness, AIDS. AIDS activists across the country have rallied to the slogan "Silence = Death," urging people to speak up for urgent research and treatment, as well as for compassion and civil rights for AIDS victims. The amount of potential creativity lost to AIDS is staggering, yet we are encouraged to "discount" that phenomenon as something that happens only to people who "don't count." Like the Danes who donned armbands identifying themselves as Jews to foil the Nazis' efforts to determine whom to count in their genocidal plans, we have to resist efforts to divide and conquer: we have to insist, as *Silences* taught us, that we all can and do count. *Silences*'s legacy today is the courage to assert that "we all count"—and that we have the right to read—and write—ourselves.

NOTES

This essay would not have been possible without the help of Tillie Olsen, who generously shared her time and her thoughts with me during the spring of 1988, and who continued to make her personal papers and correspondence available to me during the years that followed. I am also grateful to Elaine Hedges, Carla Peterson, Lillian Robinson, Jeffrey Rubin-Dorsky, and Sarah Weddington for their critical comments and suggestions. An earlier version of this paper was presented at the Modern Language Association Convention in 1988.

    1.   Olsen 1988. She is considering reclaiming the by-line as "Ann Dothers."
    2.   The individuals whose names I will be citing represent only a small fraction of the number of people—inside and outside academia—for whom *Silences* has been an extremely important book.

3. While Olsen herself refers to this talk as having taken place in 1962, the date on the transcript of the tape of the talk in the Humanities Research Center at the University of Texas at Austin is March 15, 1963. For more information on Olsen's experience at the Radcliffe Institute 1962–1963, see Diane Middlebrook's essay in this volume. Olsen also gave several other undocumented informal talks around this time, such as one at the Boston Public Library in 1963 (Ferguson 1988).

4. Other panelists were Adrienne Rich, Ellen Peck Killoh, and Elaine Reuben (see Hedges 1972).

5. See "Tillie Olsen's Reading List," in *Women's Studies Newsletter,* I: 2, p.7; I:3, p.3; I:4, p.2; II: 1, pp. 4–5.

6. Paul Lauter recalls the title of this course as "The Literature of Poverty, Oppression, Revolution, and the Struggle for Freedom" (Lauter 1991).

7. The page where Olsen notes a period of silence in Jane Austen's life, for example, is completely blank except for the following: "Jane Austen (1775–1817). The years 1800–1811. Woman reasons: she was powerless in all major decisions deciding her life, including the effecting of enabling circumstances for writing" (140).

8. The notes prefacing an early reading list suggest that "each entry should be read with the following in mind. (1) The hard and essential work of women, in and out of the home ('no work was too hard, no labor too strenuous to exclude us'). (2) Limitations, denials imposed; exclusions and restrictions in no way necessitated by biological or economic circumstances. (3) How human capacities born in women— intellect, organization, art, invention, vision, sense of justice, beauty, etc.—denied scope and development, nevertheless struggled to express themselves and function." Mimeographed sheet titled "From Women's Studies Newsletter, I, 3 (Spring 1973) TILLIE OLSEN'S READING LIST II/WOMEN: A LIST OUT OF WHICH TO READ." I am grateful to Julie Allen for providing me with copies of the original reading lists.

9. *Silences* helped prompt Paul Lauter to organize through the Feminist Press the "Reconstructing American Literature" project in 1979, which led to the publication in 1983 of a volume of syllabi, course materials, and commentary under that title (Lauter 1991). *The Heath Anthology* (1990) was an outgrowth of that project.

10. Olsen 1988. *Silences* has also been translated into Norwegian and Dutch.

11. Schoedel wrote, "Finally, I want to help overcome what my favorite writer, Tillie Olsen, calls 'women's silences of centuries.' Accounts of women's lives, in particular working class women's lives, have not been viewed as worth recording" (xiii).

12. Other critics not previously mentioned for whom *Silences* has been important include Elizabeth Meese, Dale Spender, Valerie Trueblood, Alix Kates Shulman, Helen MacNeil, Sandra Whipple Spanier, and Adrienne Rich, who commented on the significance of *Silences* for criticism: "Tillie Olsen's *Silences* will, like *A Room of One's Own,* be quoted wherever there is talk of the circumstances in which literature is possible" (Rich 1982).

13. *Silences* "offered a lot of solace and inspiration" to Lim, who found it "very exciting. It encouraged me to do the work I often doubted doing." Plays of Lim's such as "XX," which deals with the oppression of women from ancient China to the contemporary United States, have been produced in San Francisco. A collection of her plays (which she characterizes as "hard-edged feminist" drama) will be published in Hawaii (Lim 1988).

14. Citing Olsen's recognition of the importance of "foreground silences," Sondra Zeidenstein writes, " In breaking the silence imposed by their culture, [the writers in *A Wider Giving*] have had to give themselves time and permission, seek out training, face

rejection and self-doubt, fight the negativity sometimes ingested from their own mothers, begin to develop their craft and, hardest of all, summon the strength again and again to continue." (Zeidenstein xiii–xiv).

15. I am indebted to Carla Peterson for the concept of a "rhetoric of arithmetic" (Peterson 1988).

16. Olsen was not the first to use the concept of "counting." Indeed, she readily credits both Showalter and Howe with having sparked her awareness of the value of this technique. In the essay Olsen cites Elaine Showalter's article, "Women and the Literary Curriculum" (*College English,* May 1971) as a pioneering precursor. (Olsen 1982, 28) Olsen notes: "I have developed this almost compulsive what I call the Florence Howe Test, after the person I first saw do it. You take any anthology, any list—look at the contents of a magazine, or at who is being discussed in a book of criticism, a textbook. . . . You run your finger down and you count the number of men who are in it and you count the number of women, and you discover that in the second century in which women have come to writing at all, usually you will find one woman in about every nine to ten men. It is astonishing that you find this disparity even in the fields of poetry and story—which women have been more likely to write in the past because they presumably do not take as much time, or rather, they fit in more easily between other things, better than forms that require long, concentrated attention—it is astonishing that is, if you assume that human beings are born with similar capacities when it comes to thinking, to dreaming, to creating. I am of those who very strongly believe that this capacity to create is inherent in the human being and has not to do with the body, with the sex into which you are born. I believe that there is the strongest relationship between circumstances and actual creative production" (Olsen 1972). Olsen's distinctive contribution was introducing a larger audience to this valuable tool.

17. These complaints were raised by several graduate students, both women and men, in my American Studies graduate seminar at the University of Texas at Austin in the spring of 1990. Two years earlier I heard similar comments from a prominent feminist critic I had interviewed who did not wish to be cited by name.

18. In an article on campus trends, *Time Magazine,* for instance, noted with disapproval the fact that "a University of Texas professor of American Studies has constructed a course on 19th-century writers to alternate between famous white men one week and obscure women the next, in part to illuminate 'the prison house of gender.' " *Time*'s assumption, of course, was that the women writers were obscure because they deserved to be obscure—not because social or political factors might have helped deny their work the attention it deserved (Henry 66). See also D'Souza 51–79. For two cogent and eloquent challenges to the position embodied in the *Time* article, see Paul Lauter's *Canons and Contexts* and Henry Louis Gates, Jr.'s *Loose Canons: Notes on the Culture Wars.*

19. "[We write] because we have more fear of silence than of speech." (Direct translation: of words) Rosario Ferré, "Porque Escribe la Mujer." Variant on this quotation contained in "Entrevista breve con Rosario Ferré," conducted by Krista Ratkowski Carmona, supplied by Ferré. Stanford speech (which was in Spanish) replaced "I" of Carmona interview with "Women." Ferré spoke of the importance of *Silences* to her own work in an interview (Ferré 1988).

20. Two related areas of concern are the ghettoization within women's studies courses of material on women of color (see Zinn and also Alarcón, 1990) and the ghettoization and exclusion of gay and lesbian writers from a range of academic enterprises (see Beam et al., 1988; Poulson-Bryant; "As Quiet as It's Kept"; Mc-

Daniel). Unfortunately, homophobia in academia has led to a rise of self-censorship on the part of a number of gay and lesbian scholars (Zimmerman 1988).

21. Gates noted that he arrived at this statement through consultation with historian John Hope Franklin.

22. Statistics gathered by Norma Alarcón (personal communication).

23. I am indebted to *Roe v. Wade* attorney Sarah Weddington for sharing with me her clipping file of hundreds of articles on this subject, documenting instances of harassment, violence, and intimidation in every section of the country.

WORKS CITED

Adams, Phoebe-Lou. Review of *Silences*. *Atlantic Monthly*. Sept. 1978, 96.

Alarcón, Norma. "Chicana Feminist Literature: A Re-vision Through Malintzin/or Malintzin: Putting Flesh Back on the Object." *This Bridge Called My Back: Writings by Radical Women of Color*. Ed. Cherríe Moraga and Gloria Anzaldúa. Albany, N.Y.: Kitchen Table Press, 1983.

———. Telephone interview. Fall 1988.

———. "The Theoretical Subject(s) of *This Bridge Called My Back* and Anglo-American Feminism." *Making Face, Making Soul: Haciendo Caras*. Ed. Gloria Anzaldúa. San Francisco: Aunt Lute Foundation, 1990. 356–69.

Alcott, Louisa May. *Alternative Alcott*. Ed. Elaine Showalter. New Brunswick: Rutgers UP, 1987.

———. *Moods*. Ed. Sarah Elbert. New Brunswick: Rutgers UP, 1991.

Anzaldúa, Gloria. *Borderlands/La Frontera: The New Mestiza*. San Francisco: Spinsters/Aunt Lute, 1987.

Arnold, June. *Sister Gin*. Afterword by Jane Marcus. New York: The Feminist Press, 1989.

"As Quiet As It's Kept: The Literary Contributions of Black Lesbians and Gays." Press release. Ad Hoc Committee of Black Lesbian and Gay Writers. March 1988.

Atwood, Margaret. [Blurb]. Tillie Olsen. *Silences*. Sixth Printing, December 1982. Front cover.

———. "Obstacle Course." *New York Times Book Review*. 30 July 1978.

Austin, Mary. *A Woman of Genius*. Afterword by Nancy Porter. New York: The Feminist Press, 1985.

———. *Stories from the Country of Lost Borders*. Ed. Marjorie Pryse. New Brunswick: Rutgers UP, 1987.

Barolini, Helen, ed. *The Dream Book: An Anthology of Writings by Italian American Women*. New York: Schocken, 1985.

Beam, Joseph, Becky Birth, July Blackwomon, et al. "We are Black Lesbian and Gay Writers." Mimeograph. March 24, 1988.

Blow, Richard. "Mea Culpa." *The New Republic*. 204:7 (18 Feb. 1991): 32.

Burdekin, Katherine. *Swastika Night*. Afterword by Daphne Patal. New York: The Feminist Press, 1985.

Burke, Fielding, *Call Home the Heart*. Introduction by Alice Kessler-Harris and Paul Lauter and afterwords by Sylvia J. Cook and Anna W. Shannon. New York: The Feminist Press, 1983.

Caird, Mona. *The Daughters of Danaus*. Afterword by Margaret Morganroth Gullett. New York: The Feminist Press, 1989.

Cary, Alice. *Clovernook Sketches and Other Stories.* Ed. Judith Fetterley. New Brunswick: Rutgers UP, 1987.

Chevigny, Bell Gale, *The Woman and the Myth: Margaret Fuller's Life and Writings.* New York: The Feminist Press, 1976.

Child, Lydia Maria. *Hobomok and Other Writings on Indians.* Ed. Carolyn L. Karcher. New Brunswick: Rutgers UP, 1986.

Chopin, Kate. *The Storm and Other Stories* (with *The Awakening*). Edited with an introduction by Per Seyersted. New York: The Feminist Press, 1974.

Churchill, Caryl. Interview. *Interviews with Contemporary Playwrights.* Kathleen Bestko and Rachel Koenig. New York: Beech Tree Books/William Morrow, 1987.

Cisneros, Sandra. Telephone interview. Fall 1988.

Connor, Collins. "Book, Magazine, Banned from Middle School." *St. Petersburg Times.* Hernando Times Edition. 4 February 1987, p.1.

Cooke, Rose Terry. *"How Celia Changed Her Mind" and Selected Stories.* Ed. Daphne Patai. New Brunswick: Rutgers UP, 1988.

Cooper, Anna Julia. *A Voice from the South.* Introduction by Mary Helen Washington. New York: Oxford UP, 1988.

Cummins, Maria. *The Lamplighter.* Ed. Nina Baym. New Brunswick: Rutgers UP, 1989.

Davis, Rebecca Harding. *Life in the Iron Mills.* Biographical interpretation by Tillie Olsen. New York: The Feminist Press, 1972.

Demby, William. *The Catacombs.* Introduction by Nathan A. Scott, Jr. Boston: Northeastern UP, 1991.

"The Derisory Tower." *The New Republic.* 204:7 (18 February 1991): 5–6.

Diamond, Arlyn, and Lee Edwards, eds. *American Voices, American Women.* New York: Avon, 1973.

Diamond, Sara. "Readin', Writin' and Repressin'." *Z.* February 1991. 45–48.

D'Souza, Dinesh. "Illiberal Education." *Atlantic Monthly.* 267:3 (March 1991): 51–79.

DuBois, W. E. B. *The Quest of the Silver Fleece.* Introduction by Arnold Rampersad. Boston: Northeastern UP, 1989.

Dunbar-Nelson, Alice. *The Works of Alice Dunbar-Nelson.* Ed. Gloria T. Hull. Three volumes. New York: Oxford UP, 1988.

Ervin, Edie. Telephone interview. Spring 1991.

Fauset, Jessie Redmon. *There is Confusion.* Introduction by Thadious Davis. Boston: Northeastern UP, 1989.

Ferguson, Mary Anne. *Images of Women in Literature,* fifth edition. Boston: Houghton Mifflin, 1991.

———. Telephone interview. Fall 1988.

Fern, Fanny. *Ruth Hall and Other Writings.* Ed. Joyce Warren. New Brunswick: Rutgers UP, 1986.

Ferré, Rosario. Personal interview. Palo Alto. Spring 1988.

———. "Porque Escribe La Mujer." Keynote speech delivered at conference on "Mujer, Cultura y Feminismo." Stanford University. Spring 1988.

Fishkin, Shelley Fisher. "Mark Twain and Women." In *Cambridge Companion to Mark Twain,* edited by Forrest Robinson. New York and Cambridge: Cambridge, 1994 (forthcoming).

———. *Was Huck Black? Mark Twain and African-American Voices.* New York: Oxford, 1993.

———. "The Borderlands of Culture: Writing by W. E. B. Du Bois, James Agee, Tillie Olsen and Gloria Anzaldúa." *Literary Journalism in the Twentieth Century.* Ed. Norman Sims. New York: Oxford UP, 1990. 133–82.

Freeman, Mary E. Wilkins, *The Revolt of Mother and Other Stories.* Afterword by Michele Clark. New York: The Feminist Press, 1974.

Gates, Henry Louis, Jr. "Dealing with Diversity." Talk. American Studies Association Convention. Miami. 28 October 1988.

———. *Loose Canons: Notes on the Culture Wars.* New York: Oxford University Press, 1992.

Gilden, K. B. *Between the Hills and the Sea.* Ithaca: ILR Press, 1989.

Gilman, Charlotte Perkins, *The Yellow Wallpaper.* Afterword by Elaine Hedges. New York: The Feminist Press, 1973.

Gordon, Larry. "Anthology Rattles Tradition." *Los Angeles Times.* 27 August 1990, p. 1.

Griffin, Susan. *Pornography and Silence: Culture's Revenge Against Nature.* New York: Harper and Row, 1981.

Grimke, Angelina Weld. *Selected Works of Angelina Weld Grimke.* Ed. Carolivia Herron. New York: Oxford UP, 1991.

Grimke, Charlotte Forten. *The Journals of Charlotte Forten Grimke.* Ed. Brenda Stevenson. New York: Oxford UP, 1988.

Gubar, Susan. Letter to the author. Fall 1988.

Hampsten, Elizabeth. *Read This Only To Yourself: The Private Writings of Midwestern Women.* Bloomington: Indiana UP, 1982.

———. Telephone interview. Fall 1988.

Harper, Frances E. W. *Complete Poems of Francis E. W. Harper.* Ed. Maryemma Graham. New York: Oxford UP, 1988.

———. *Iola Leroy or Shadows Uplifted.* Introduction by Frances Smith Foster. New York: Oxford UP, 1988.

Heath Anthology of American Literature Newsletter. 1990, No. IV and Spring 1991, No. V.

Hedges, Elaine. "Afterword." Charlotte Perkins Gilman. *The Yellow Wallpaper.* Old Westbury: The Feminist Press, 1973.

———. Telephone interview. Fall 1988.

———. Ed., "Women Writing and Teaching." *College English.* 34:1 (October 1972).

Henry William A., III. "Upside Down in the Groves of Academe." *Time.* 1 April 1991. 137:13: 66–69.

Herbst, Josephine, *Rope of Gold.* Introduction by Alice Kessler-Harris and Paul Lauter. Afterword by Elinor Langer. New York: The Feminist Press, 1984.

Hopkins, Pauline. *Contending Forces: A Romance Illustrative of Negro Life North and South.* Introduction by Richard Yarborough. New York: Oxford UP, 1988.

———. *The Magazine Novels of Pauline Hopkins.* Introduction by Hazel Carby. New York: Oxford UP, 1988.

Howe, Florence. Telephone interview. Fall 1988.

Hull, Helen R. *Islanders.* Afterword by Patricia McClelland Miller. New York: The Feminist Press, 1988.

———. *Quest.* Afterword by Patricia McClelland Miller. New York: The Feminist Press, 1990.

Hurston, Zora Neale, *I Love Myself When I am Laughing . . . And Then Again When I Am Looking Mean and Impressive.* Ed. Alice Walker. Introduction by Mary Helen Washington. New York: The Feminist Press, 1979.

International P.E.N. Writers in Prison Report. July 1988.

Jacobs, Harriet. *Incidents in the Life of a Slave Girl.* Introduction by Valerie Smith. New York: Oxford UP, 1990.

Janeway, Elizabeth. *Leaving Home.* With a New Preface by the Author and an Afterword by Rachel M. Brownstein. New York: The Feminist Press, 1987.

Johnson, Mrs. A. E. *Clarence and Corinne; or God's Way.* Introduction by Hortense J. Spillers. New York: Oxford UP, 1988.

———. *The Hazeley Family.* Introduction by Barbara Christian. New York: Oxford UP, 1988.

Johnson, Josephine W. *Now in November.* Afterword by Nancy Hoffman. New York: The Feminist Press, 1991.

Jones, Gayle. *White Rat.* Introduction by Mae G. Henderson. Boston: Northeastern UP, 1991.

Keckley, Elizabeth. *Behind the Scenes, Or, Thirty Years A Slave, and Four Years in the White House.* Introduction by James Olney. New York: Oxford UP, 1988.

Kelley, Edith Summers. *Weeks.* Afterword by Charlotte Goodman. New York: The Feminist Press, 1982.

Kelley, Emma Dunham. *Megda.* Introduction by Molly Hite. New York: Oxford UP, 1988.

Kingston, Maxine Hong. [Blurb.] Tillie Olsen. *Silences.* Back Cover. New York: Delta/Seymour Lawrence, 1982.

Kirkland, Caroline M. *A New Home, Who'll Follow?* Ed. Sandra Zangarell. New Brunswick: Rutgers UP, 1990.

Kolodny, Annette. *The Land Before Her: Fantasy and Experience of the American Frontiers 1630–1860.* Chapel Hill: U of North Carolina P, 1984.

———. Telephone interview. Fall 1988.

Konecky, Edith. *Allegra Maud Goldman.* Introduction by Tillie Olsen. Afterword by Bella Brodzki. New York: The Feminist Press, 1976.

Koppelman, Susan, ed. *Between Mothers & Daughters.* Old Westbury: The Feminist Press, 1985.

———. Ed. *Images of Women in Fiction.* Bowling Green, Ohio: Bowling Green University Popular press, 1973.

———. Ed. *Old Maids: Short Stories by Nineteenth Century U.S. Women Writers.* London and New York: Pandora Press, 1984.

———. ed. *The Other Woman.* Old Westbury: The Feminist Press, 1984.

———. Telephone interview. Fall 1988.

Larsen, Nella. *'Quicksand' and 'Passing'.* Ed. Deborah E. McDowell. New Brunswick: Rutgers UP, 1986.

Lauter, Paul. *Canons and Contexts.* New York: Oxford UP, 1987.

———. Ed. *The Heath Anthology of American Literature.* Lexington, Mass.: D.C. Heath and Company, 1990.

———. Personal interview. Washington, D.C. Spring 1991.

———. Telephone interview. Spring 1988.

———. "Race and Gender in the Shaping of the American Literary Canon: A Case Study from the Twenties." *Feminist Studies 9.* 1983. Reprinted in Rosenfelt and Newton. *Feminist Criticism and Social Change.* 10–44.

———. *Reconstructing American Literature: Courses, Syllabi, Issues.* Old Westbury: The Feminist Press, 1983.

Le Guin, Ursula. "A Woman Writing, or the Fisherwoman's Daughter." Paper published by the graduate school of Tulane University, 1987.

LeSueur, Meridel, *Ripening: Selected Work, 1927–1980*. Edited with an introduction by Elaine Hedges. New York: The Feminist Press, 1982.

Lim, Genny, Telephone interview. Fall 1988.

McDaniel, Judith. "We Were Fired." *Sinister Wisdom*. 1982.

McKay, Claude. *Home to Harlem*. Edited with an introduction by Wayne F. Cooper. Boston: Northeastern UP, 1987.

McKay, Nellie. Telephone interview. Fall 1988.

McMillen, Liz. "Controversial Anthology of American Literature: Ground-Breaking Contribution or a 'Travesty'?" *Chronicle of Higher Education*. 16 January 1991, A 15.

McNeil, Helen. "Speaking for the Speechless." *Times Literary Supplement*. 4 November 1980.

Magnuson, James. Personal interview. Austin. Fall 1988.

Malkiel, Theresa S. *Diary of a Shirtwaist Striker*. Introduction by Francoise Basch. Ithaca: ILR Press, 1990.

Marcus, Jane. *Art and Anger: Reading Like a Woman*. Columbus: Ohio State UP, 1988.

———. "Still Practice, A/Wrested Alphabet: Toward a Feminist Aesthetic." In Shari Benstock, ed. *Feminist Issues in Literary Scholarship*. Bloomington: Indiana UP, 1987. 79–97.

———. Telephone interview. Fall 1988.

Marshall, Paule. *Brown Girl, Brownstones*. Afterword by Mary Helen Washington. New York: The Feminist Press, 1981.

Martinson, Moa. *My Mother Gets Married*. Translated and with an Afterword by Margaret S. Lacy. New York: The Feminist Press, 1988.

———. *Women and Appletrees*. Translated and with an Afterword by Margaret S. Lacy. New York: The Feminist Press, 1985.

Mayfield, Julian. *The Hit and the Long Night*. Introduction by Phillip M. Richards. Boston: Northeastern UP, 1989.

Meese, Elizabeth. "Deconstructing the Sexual Politic: Virginia Woolf and Tillie Olsen." In *Crossing the Double Cross; The Practice of Feminist Criticism*. Chapel Hill: U of North Carolina P, 1986. 89–113.

Middlebrook, Diane. "Tillie Olsen and Anne Sexton at the Radcliffe Institute." [1991] In Fishkin and Hedges, ed. *Listening to Silences*. 17–22.

Moffat, Mary Jane, and Charlotte Painter, eds. *Revelations: Diaries of Women*. New York: Random House, 1974.

———. Letter to Tillie Olsen. 15 October 1973.

Mossell, Mrs. N. F. *The Work of the Afro-American Woman*. Introduction by Joanne Braxton. New York: Oxford UP, 1988.

Murray, Albert. *Train Whistle Guitar*. Introduction by Robert G. O'Meally. Boston: Northeastern UP, 1989.

Murray, Michele, ed. *A House of Good Proportion: Images of Women in Literature*. New York: Simon and Schuster, 1973.

Naylor, Gloria. Letter to Tillie Olsen. 29 July 1988.

Nekola, Charlotte. "Worlds Unseen: Political Women Journalists and the 1930s." In Charlotte Nekola and Paula Rabinowitz, eds. *Writing Red: An Anthology of American Women Writers, 1930–1940*. New York: The Feminist Press, 1987. 189–98.

Oates, Joyce Carol. Review of *Silences*. *The New Republic*. 29 July 1978, 32–34.

Olsen, Tillie. Annotations and marginalia, 1987. *Silences*. (1978). New York: Delta/Seymour Lawrence, 1979.

————. "Death of the Creative Process." Transcription of seminar given at Radcliffe Institute for Independent Study. 15 March 1963.

————. *Mother to Daughter, Daughter to Mother: A Daybook and Reader.* New York: The Feminist Press, 1985.

————. "One Out of Twelve: Writers Who Are Women in Our Century—1971." Reprinted in Tillie Olsen. *Silences* (1978). New York: Delta/Seymour Lawrence, 1979, 22–46.

————. "Part One—Silences." In Tillie Olsen. *Silences* (1978). New York: Delta/ Seymour Lawrence, 1979, 1–118.

————. "Part Two: Acerbs, Asides, Amulets, Exhumations, Sources, Deepenings, Roundings, Expansions." In Tillie Olsen. *Silences* (1978). New York: Delta/ Seymour Lawrence, 1979, 119–283.

————. Personal interviews. Santa Cruz and San Francisco. Spring 1988.

————. "Rebecca Harding Davis—1971, 1972." Reprinted in Tillie Olsen. *Silences* (1978). New York: Delta/Seymour Lawrence, 1979, 47–118.

————. *Silences* (1978). N.Y.: Delta/Seymour Lawrence. 1982.

————. "Silences in Literature." *Harper's Magazine.* October 1965.

————. "Silences in Literature—1962." Reprinted in Tillie Olsen. *Silences* (1978). New York: Delta/Seymour Lawrence, 1979. 5–21.

————. *Tell Me a Riddle: A Collection.* Philadelphia: Lippincott, 1961.

————. "Tillie Olsen: From a Public Dialogue Between Olsen and Marilyn Yalom, Stanford Center for Research on Women." 5 November 1980. In Marilyn Yalom, ed. *Women Writers of the West Coast.* Santa Barbara: Capra Press, 1983.

————. "Tillie Olsen's Reading List II/Women: A List Out of Which to Read." Women's Studies Newsletter. I:3. Spring 1973. n.p.

————. "A Visit with Tillie Olsen." University of Vermont. 1972. n.d.

————. *Yonnondio: From the Thirties.* New York: Dell, 1975.

Page, Myra. *Daughter of the Hills: A Woman's Part in the Coal Miners' Struggle.* Introduction by Alice Kessler-Harris and Paul Lauter. Afterword by Deborah S. Rosenfelt. New York: The Feminist Press, 1986.

Pearlman, Mickey, and Abby H. P. Werlock. *Tillie Olsen.* Twayne's United States Authors Series. Boston: G.K. Hall, 1991.

Peterson, Carla. Personal interview. Miami. Fall 1988.

People for the American Way. *Attacks on the Freedom to Learn: 1985–1986 Report, 1986–1987 Report,* and *1989–1990 Report.*

————. *Press Clips: June/July/Aug./Sept.* 1988.

Phelps, Elizabeth Stuart. *Doctor Zay.* Afterword by Michael Sartisky. New York: The Feminist Press, 1987.

————. *Silent Partner.* Afterword by Mari Jo Buhle and Florence Howe. New York: The Feminist Press, 1983.

————. *The Story of Avis.* Ed. Carol Kessler. New Brunswick: Rutgers UP, 1987.

Plato, Ann. *Essays.* Introduction by Kenny J. Williams. New York: Oxford UP, 1988.

Poulson-Bryant, Scott. "Gay Power; Black Pride." *The Village Voice.* 12 April 1988.

Prince, Nancy. "A Narrative of the Life and Travels of Mrs. Nancy Prince." In *Collected Black Women's Narratives,* ed. Anthony G. Barthelmy. New York: Oxford, 1988.

Redding, J. Saunders. *Stranger and Alone.* Edited with an introduction by Pancho Savery. Boston: Northeastern UP, 1989.

Reichman, Henry. *Censorship and Selection: Issues and Answers for Schools.* Chicago: American Library Association and American Association of School Administrators. 1988.

Rich, Adrienne. [Blurb] Tillie Olsen. *Silences.* New York: Delta/Seymour Lawrence, 1982. Back Cover.

Robins, Elizabeth. *The Convert.* Introduction by Jane Marcus. New York: The Feminist Press, 1980.

Robinson, Lillian. "Canon Fathers and Myth Universe." *New Literary History.* Vol. 19. 1987: 23–35.

———. Personal interviews. San Francisco, Spring 1988. Austin, Spring 1991.

———. *Sex, Class and Culture.* Bloomington: Indiana University Press, 1978.

———. "Treason Our Text: Feminist Challenges to the Literary Canon." In Elaine Showalter, ed. *The New Feminist Criticism.* New York: Pantheon Books, 1985. 105–21. Originally published in Tulsa Studies in Women's Literature 2, 1983.

Rosenfelt, Deborah. Telephone interview. Fall, 1988.

Schlafly, Phyllis, ed. *Child Abuse in the Classroom.* Westchester, Illinois: Good News Publishers, 1985.

Schlesinger, Arthur M., Jr. *The Disuniting of America.* New York: W.W. Norton, 1992.

Schoedel, Jean Reith. *Alone in a Crowd: Women in the Trades Tell Their Stories.* Philadelphia: Temple UP, 1985.

Schuyler, George Samuel. *Black Empire.* Edited with an afterword by Robert A. Hill and Kent Rasmussen. Boston: Northeastern UP, 1991.

———. *Black No More.* Introduction by James A. Miller. Northeastern UP, 1989.

Seacole, Mary. *Wonderful Adventures of Mrs. Seacole in Many Lands.* Introduction by William L. Andrews. New York: Oxford UP, 1988.

Sedgwick, Catharine Maria. *Hope Leslie.* Ed. Mary Kelley. New Brunswick: Rutgers UP, 1987.

Showalter, Elaine. "Women and the Literary Curriculum." *College English.* May 1971.

Shulman, Alix Kates. "Overcoming Silences: Teaching Writing for Women." *Harvard Educational Review* 49:4 (Nov. 1979): 527–33.

Siegel, Fred. "The Cult of Multiculturalism." *The New Republic.* 204:7 (18 February 1991): 34–40.

Sinclair, Jo. *The Changelings.* Afterwords by Nellie McKay, Johnetta B. Cole and Elizabeth H. Oakes; biographical note by Ellsabeth Sandberg. New York: The Feminist Press, 1985.

Slesinger, Tess. *The Unpossessed.* Introduction by Alice Kessler-Harris and Paul Lauter. Afterword by Janet Sharistanian. New York: The Feminist Press, 1984.

Smedley, Agnes, *Daughter of Earth.* Afterword by Paul Lauter. New York: The Feminist Press, 1973.

Smith, Barbara. Telephone interview. Fall 1988.

Smith, Effie Waller. *The Collected Works of Effie Waller Smith.* Introduction by David Deskins. New York: Oxford UP, 1991.

Smith, Helen Zenna. *Not So Quiet . . .* Afterword by Jane Marcus. New York: The Feminist Press, 1989.

Southworth, E. D. E. N. *The Hidden Hand.* Ed. Joanne Dobson. New Brunswick: Rutgers UP, 1988.

Spanier, Sandra Whipple. "Kay Boyle: In a Woman's Voice." In Alice Kessler-Harris and William Brian, eds. *Faith of a (Woman) Writer.* Westport: Greenwood Press, 1988.

Spender, Dale. *Man-Made Language,* second edition. London: Routledge & Kegan Paul. 1985.

————. *Women of Ideas (And What Men Have Done to Them)*. London: Ark Paperbacks, 1983.

Spillers, Hortense. Telephone interview. Fall 1988.

Spofford, Harriet Prescott. *"The Amber Gods" and Other Stories*. Ed. Alfred Bendixen. New Brunswick: Rutgers UP, 1989.

Stewart, Maria W. *Spiritual Narratives: Maria W. Stewart, Jarena Lee, Julia A. J. Foote and Virginia W. Broughton*. Introduction by Sue E. Houchins. New York: Oxford UP, 1988.

Stewart, Mary. Letter to Tillie Olsen. 28 September 1985.

Smedley, Agnes. *Daughter of Earth*. Afterword by Paul Lauter. New York: The Feminist Press, 1973.

Stimpson, Catharine. "Tillie Olsen, Witness as Servant." In *Where the Meanings Are: Feminism and Cultural Spaces*. New York: Methuen, 1988. 67–76.

————. Telephone interview. Fall 1988.

Stowe, Harriet Beecher, *Oldtown Folks*. Ed. Dorothy Berkson. New Brunswick: Rutgers UP, 1987.

Tillman, Katherine Davis Chapman. *Works of Katherine Davis Chapman Tillman*. Ed. Claudia Tate. New York: Oxford UP, 1991.

Trueblood, Valerie. Review of *Silences*. *American Poetry Review*. May/June 1979.

Truth, Sojourner. *A Narrative of Sojourner Truth, A A Bondswoman of Olden Times, with a History of Her Labors and Correspondence Drawn from Her "Book of Life."* Introduction by Jeffrey Stewart. New York: Oxford UP, 1991.

Viramontes, Helena María. *The Moths and Other Stories*. Houston: Arte Público Press, 1985.

————. Telephone interview. Fall 1988.

Wagner-Martin, Linda. Telephone interview. Spring 1988.

Walker, Alice. [Blurb] Tillie Olsen. *Silences*. New York: Delta/Seymour Lawrence, 1982.

————. Text of remarks. Tillie Olsen Day. San Francisco. n.d.

Warner, Susan. *The Wide, Wide World*. Afterword by Jane Tompkins. New York: The Feminist Press, 1987.

Washington, Mary Helen, ed. *Black-Eyed Susans: Classic Stories By and About Black Women*. Garden City, N.Y.: Anchor Press, 1975.

————. Ed. *Invented Lives: Narratives of Black Women 1860–1960*. Garden City, N.Y.: Anchor Press, 1987.

————. Ed. *Midnight Birds: Stories by Contemporary Black Women*. Garden City, N.Y.: Anchor Press, 1980.

————. Telephone interview. Fall 1988.

Weisberg, Jacob. "N.A.S. Who Are These Guys Anyway?" *Lingua Franca: The Review of Academic Life*. April 1991. 31–39.

Wells-Barnett, Ida B. *The Selected Works of Ida B. Wells-Barnett*. Introduction by Trudier Harris. New York: Oxford UP, 1991.

West, Dorothy. *The Living is Easy*. Afterword by Adelaide M. Cromwell. New York: The Feminist Press, 1982.

West, Robin. "Postmodernism and Feminist Legal Theory." Paper presented at Legal Theory Workshop, Yale University Law School. Sept. 1988.

————. Telephone interview. Fall 1988.

Wheatley, Phillis. *The Collected Works of Phillis Wheatley*. Ed. John C. Shields. New York: Oxford UP, 1988.

Woolson, Constance Fenimore. *Woman Artists, Woman Exiles: "Miss Grief" and Other Stories*. Ed. Joan Weimer. New Brunswick: Rutgers UP, 1988.

Wright, Richard. *Lawd Today.* Edited with an introduction by Arnold Rampersad. Boston: Northeastern UP, 1986.

Wright, Sarah E. *The Child's Gonna Live.* Appreciation by John Oliver Killens. New York: The Feminist Press, 1986.

Zeidenstein, Sondra, ed. *A Wider Giving: Women Writing After a Long Silence.* Goshen, Conn.: Chicory Blue Press, 1988.

Zimmerman, Bonnie. "One Out of Thirty: Lesbianism in Women's Studies Textbooks." In Margaret Cruikshank, ed. *Lesbian Studies: Present and Future.* Old Westbury: The Feminist Press, 1982.

————. Telephone interview. Fall 1988.

Zinn, Maxine Baca, and Lynn Weber Cannon, Elizabeth Higgenbotham, and Bonnie Thornton Dill. "The Cost of Exclusionary Practices in Women's Studies." In Gloria Anzaldúa, ed. *Haciendo Caras: Making Face, Making Soul.* Spinsters/Aunt Lute: 1990. 29–41.

Rereading *Tell Me a Riddle* in the Age of Deconstruction

DEBORAH SILVERTON ROSENFELT

Rereading from a Different "Subject Position"

I first read *Tell Me a Riddle* as a young activist in the optimistic late sixties, and when I wrote about it several years later, I stressed its continuities with the radical literature of the thirties, including Olsen's own *Yonnondio,* and its importance in keeping that tradition alive (Rosenfelt 1980, 1981). This essay rereads those stories from a different "subject position," constituted during years of conservative Republicanism as well as years of deconstruction in academia. The *Riddle* I read now seems to me more ambiguous, more shadowed, less seamless internally than the text I "produced" then, though no less powerful. Perhaps because the Reagan-Bush era is not unlike the fifties, an era in which a movement that seemed to promise revolutionary change was succeeded instead by an era of reaction, *Tell Me a Riddle* now seems to me to reveal its embeddedness in the discourses and contradictions of the fifties as strongly as its affiliations, still clear but less univocally affirmed than I once assumed, with the 1930s genre Paula Rabinowitz has defined as women's revolutionary fiction (see especially Chapter 2). The stories of *Tell Me a Riddle* invite us to consider what happens textually when the revolutionary consciousness that has informed the literature of a radical social movement survives into a nonrevolutionary era.

Two different resonances of the concept of silences will structure my discussion of *Tell Me A Riddle.* "Silences in": silence as trope, as textual presence, as figure for all the material circumstances that, as Olsen documents in *Silences,* deny human creativity: lack of time, money, familial and social support, traditions of one's own, confidence in one's right to public language, an available discourse that will allow one to "tell the truth." "Silences of": silence as textual absence, as repression, as contradiction, as the site where ideology resides. The field between these two interpretive zones is the location where humanism, a set of assumptions affirming a unified and innately creative self, encounters postmodernism's anti-humanist assumptions of a textuality shaped by history and ideology, virtually divorced from the intentional creativity of an individual authorial subject. Framed differently, my discussion engages in what Frederic Jameson terms "the simultaneous recognition of the ideological and utopian functions of the artistic text" (299). It is informed both by Olsen's taxonomy of silencings in *Silences,* categories that cumulatively imply their counterforce, the utopian yearning for a world free of the negative "circumstances" of class and gender that deny and distort the human capacity for expression; and by Macherey's argument that "the work exists above all by its determinate absences, by what it does not say, in its relation to what it is not," and that "the concealed order of the work is thus less significant than its real determinate disorder" (155).

I do not mean to create a facile opposition between Olsen's work and that of Althusserian postmodernists like Macherey. Foregrounding in its very syntax the recalcitrance and the contingency of the medium of language itself, Olsen's writing inscribes one of the fundamental tensions of modernity: that between an older, humanistic faith in the capacity of language to represent something beyond itself, to correspond to as well as to simulate reality, and to issue coherently from the consciousness of a unified self or subject; and the postmodernist recognition of language as an arbitrary self-contained system of signs, organized into discourses that write us as much as we write them. Olsen's taxonomy of silences in *Silences* sometimes approximates the notion of gaps, ruptures in the text produced by a disparity between what is experienced and what it is possible to say, especially when she writes about the textual (mis)representation of women's bodies. Still, for Olsen as a critic and as a writer of fiction, silence as presence takes precedence over silence as absence. Her work enacts a covenant with readers to create a more just, less silencing material world. I have worried that, in reflecting on the ideological as a dimension of her work, in viewing her writing as shaped by as well as opposed to the discourses of its era, this essay might seem to betray that covenant. Nothing could be farther from my intent. Still, my current critical practices, though not strictly deconstructionist, are inevitably informed by some of the postmodernist assumptions that gave rise to deconstruction, especially those incorporating materialist accounts of ideology. My readings work themselves out on the slippery field between the two interpretive zones, the zone of "silences in" and that of "silences of." Moving between them, I explore two intersecting themes in the stories of *Tell Me a Riddle,* themes that exemplify its affiliation with and opposition to its times: the expression and repression of, respectively, political radicalism and women's embodiment and desire. I focus especially on "Tell Me a Riddle" and "Hey Sailor, What Ship?" for the first discussion, and on "I Stand Here Ironing" and "O Yes" for the second.[1]

Political Radicalism

In *First Drafts, Last Drafts: Forty Years of the Creative Writing Program at Stanford,* Olsen writes at some length of the complex roots of her work and of the "circumstanced time" in 1955–56 that made it possible for her to complete "Hey Sailor, What Ship?", to write all of "O Yes," and to write the first third of "Tell Me a Riddle."

1955–56. Profound earthquake years, presage years—for me; for my country, for our world. . . . Year of writing resurrection for me—yet year of arterial closeness to death and dyings of the four human beings ineradicably dearest to me: my mother, my father-in-law Avrum, Seevya, and Genya (whose last days of dying are inscribed in "Tell Me A Riddle"). All four of that great vanishing generation whose vision, legacy of belief—in one human race, in infinite human potentiality which never yet had had circumstances to blossom, in the ever-recurring movement of humanity against what degrades and maims—I tried to embed in that novella.

. . . World year of escalating nuclear threat—and seeming defeat for the petition movement of millions the earth over to totally disarm. . . .

. . . Year that began still in the McCarthyite shadow of fear; of pervasive cynical belief that actions with others against wrong were personally suspect, would end in more grievous wrong. . . .

. . . Year of the Supreme Court decision against segregation "which generates feelings of inferiority"; of Rosa Parks, Birmingham, Little Rock. Year of the first happenings of freedom movements, movements against wrong, which were to convulse and mark our nation and involve numberless individual lives.

So was burgeoned "O Yes" ("Baptism"). So was begun "Tell Me A Riddle" (63–64).

Olsen's insistence on "the ever-recurring movement of humanity against what degrades and maims" pervades the stories of the *Riddle* volume and unites them with all her work. Her working-class background, her political experience in the American left, and her immersion in the humanistic traditions of world literature ensure *Tell Me a Riddle*'s deeply critical stance toward the shallowness and repressiveness of fifties culture in the United States. At the same time, these stories inevitably inscribe certain culturally dominant "structures of feeling," Raymond Williams's term for emerging patterns of value and cultural expression.[2] To observe this contradiction is to note the encounter in the stories between silence as trope and silence as absence, between the utopian yearning for a world free from "what degrades and maims" and necessary textual accommodations to more limiting emergent ideologies.

Out of the many characterizations of the social and cultural world of the 1950s, I draw especially on Richard Ohmann's and Elaine Tyler May's. In the post-war years, Ohmann reminds us, the United States dominated the "free world . . . militarily, politically, and economically" (389). It was an era of unprecedented material prosperity, when working-class people as well as professionals and capitalists "participated in the steady growth of total product" (389). Class differences were masked and social struggle reduced in this atmosphere of prosperity. Advertising helped to create and sustain support for an increasingly privatized way of life built around home, family, and automobile. "Politics," writes Ohmann, "seemed nearly irrelevant to such a life," and "the boundaries of respectable political debate steadily closed in through the 1950s" (390). It was, of course, the era of McCarthyism and the Cold War, a time when the dominant political, social, economic, and cultural apparatuses of the country—Congress, the courts, most labor unions, the entertainment industry—collaborated in the vigorous repression of leftist politics and culture.

It was also an era shadowed by the memory of the terrible holocausts of World War II and by the pervasive threat of nuclear annihilation. Elaine Tyler May argues in *Homeward Bound* for a connection between Cold War anxieties and the rise of a "powerful ideology of domesticity" (20):

> A home filled with children would create a feeling of warmth and security against the cold forces of disruption and alienation. Children would also be a connection to the future and a means of replenishing a world depleted by war deaths (23).

Further, May argues, both women's sexual energies and the entrance of more middle-class white women into the labor market were regarded as threats to the familial order; women's "increasing sexual and economic emancipation" could become a "dangerous, destructive force" if their energies were not safely contained within the home (109).

> The modern family would, presumably, tame fears of atomic holocaust, and tame women as well. With their new jobs and recently acknowledged sexuality, emancipated women outside the home might unleash the very forces that would result in a collapse of the one institution that seemed to offer protection: the home (113).

May demonstrates the powerful effects of "the ideology of sexual containment," especially on the lives of women in white middle-class families.

The expression and repression of a radical political vision and history opposing the dominant cultural ideologies and practices described by Ohmann and May form a central dynamic of both "Tell Me a Riddle" and "Hey Sailor, What Ship?" Both critique powerfully the alienation and disengagement from public life that constitute the most preeminent social "silencing" of the era, while mourning the lost sense of community and betrayed vision of political progress and inscribing the confusion and loss of a generation of activists in a hostile decade. Simultaneously, both reveal the volume's filiations with other works of the decade in their inscription of betrayal, alienation, and despair. Both also incorporate a "structure of feeling" that Ohmann has described as characteristic of fifties literature, in which resistance is depoliticized, and unwillingly reinscribe, even in protesting against it, the ideology of female containment and domestication that May identifies as central to the period.

In both stories, the narrative form of the text itself is secretive, riddling; unfolding in the present, the narrative is continuously disrupted by intimations of the past, a past secreted in brief revelations and fragments of conversation and memory, rather than made manifest, as though the experience of the past is too complex, too different, for the present to contain, but too disruptive for it utterly to repress. Until Eva's dying delirium in "Riddle," the history of the embattled central couple's activist youth and the passion of Eva's social commitments remain unspoken, submerged except in fragments—glimpses of "a girl exile in Siberia," "an orator of the 1905 revolution," flarings up of Eva's internationalist rage at the rabbi, the candles; of her socialist rage at the ravages of capitalism on urban life—fragments that disrupt the order and ordinariness, chronological and social, of the present. As the past becomes ever more intrusive, embracing revolutionary vision and experience, bitter poverty, and the "monstrous shapes" of history that intervened between the thirties and the fifties—the Holocaust, the war, the atomic bombing of Hiroshima and Nagasaki—this narrative counterpoint reveals that Eva's withdrawal, though grounded in sheer exhaustion and though a logical extension of her long containment within the domestic sphere, has deeper causes still: a terrible disillusionment with modern history, an overpowering sense of the enormous disparity between the revolutionary idealism that inspired her youthful activism and the staggering complacency of contemporary life. David's longing for the Haven, then, is a longing also to escape from Eva, from her intransigent difference, from the repressed critique of their current existence implied by her very being.

Olsen's strategies of disclosure concerning Whitey's past are similar to those in "Tell Me a Riddle." Through his internal monologues, fragmented to represent his deterioration, through his exchanges with the family members, through their references to his past visits and their shared history, and through his declamation of "The Valedictory" of the condemned revolutionary José Rizal, the text gradually constructs the able seaman and social activist Whitey once was, contrasting his lost heritage, a time of brotherhood, to the diminished present, when even his union has no place for him, and when an anticommunist discourse precludes the public expression of sentiments like those in "The Valedictory," relegating them to nostalgic renditions in private living rooms. The narrative form of these stories produces a textual silencing that reinscribes in order to protest a historical and social silencing.

In "Riddle," the silencing cannot be maintained. Eva's deathbed explosion of words, fragments of songs, speeches, and poems from her radical, engaged youth, is quite literally the "return of the repressed," the emergence from underground of a political and social discourse contained temporarily beneath the glossy materialist surfaces of the era, an eruption of words bottled up in Eva's consciousness, much as women's bodies were contained within the home. To David, it seems that she has hidden an infinitely microscopic tape recorder within her, "trapping every song, every melody, every word read, heard, and spoken—and that maliciously she was playing back only what said nothing of him, of the children, of their intimate life together" (109). Her dying discourse thus reverses the anterior silencings in her life and in the text, articulating what has not been said and declining to speak the rest.

In Eva's final flood of words the utopian impulse infusing all the stories in *Tell Me a Riddle* receives its fullest articulation. Her words finally shatter David's numbness and restore his own vision: ". . . the bereavement and betrayal he had sheltered—compounded through the years—hidden even from himself—revealed itself,/uncoiled,/released,/*sprung*—and with it the monstrous shapes of what had actually happened in the century" (111). David's recognition of the significance of his and Eva's shared heritage and shared love and the final suggestion that Eva's legacy will be passed on to her granddaughter Jeannie suggest a mood of hope, of belief.

Yet these pages, like the novella as a whole, are fraught as well with a sense of the failure of the old revolutionary vision. "The world of their youth," thinks David, "dark, ignorant, terrible with hate and disease—how was it that living in it, they had not mistrusted man nor themselves, had believed so beautifully, so . . . falsely?" (113). Remembering the passion of belief in his youth, David yearns to pass it on to his children and grandchildren, *"that joyous certainty, that sense of mattering . . . of being one and indivisible with the great of the past, with all that freed, ennobled man"* (113). But an imagery of packaging and selling concludes the passage:

> Package it, stand on corners, in front of stadiums and on crowded beaches, knock on doors, give it as a fabled gift.
>   "And why not in cereal boxes, in soap packages?" he mocked himself (113).

This imagery is simultaneously compelled by and condemnatory of the commercialism and consumer fetishism that became hallmarks of the fifties. In this passage, David's consciousness both holds the contradiction and implies the incongruity between his old beliefs and the diminished, if comfortable, world of fifties America.

I have been struck in this rereading of "Tell Me a Riddle" by the frequent repetitions, in different contexts, of the word "betrayal." In the Los Angeles episode, the word is used twice, once as the older people talk incongruously across the Duncan Phyfe table of *"hunger; secret meetings; human rights; spies; betrayals; prison; escape"*—a conversation comically interrupted by a grandchild asking for Coke during a commercial break in a TV program (104). This is the context we expect for such a word. But elsewhere in the passage, the word is used differently, as David tries to mediate his anxiety about Eva's oddness and his own lack of financial success, and goes on, "detail after detail, the old habit betraying of parading the queerness of her for laughter" (104). In this passage, Olsen uses the word for its dual implications, to reveal and to abuse trust. It is Eva whom David betrays, both as her husband and as her onetime comrade. This passage illuminates and foreshadows the reference to "the bereavement and betrayal he had sheltered—compounded through the years—hidden even from himself" (120). Eva's dying delirium forces him to acknowledge the extent to which he has collaborated with the betrayal of history: that is, betrayed his own past history as idealist and activist, and accepted the "monstrous shapes of what had actually happened in the century"—the betrayals that history has perpetrated on those who believed in a vision of progress. He longs to "let her die, and with her their youth of belief out of which her bright, betrayed words foamed; stained words, that on her working lips came stainless"—here again the sense that history has mocked the revolutionary idealism of the century's early decades (121–22). And finally,

. . . as if he had been instructed he went to his bed, lay down, holding the
sketch (as if it could shield against the monstrous shapes of loss, of betrayal,
of death) and with his free hand took hers back into his (124).

For David, this personal reconcilation with his dying wife must now take place
within a historical context that she has forced him to acknowledge, to remember. "Riddle"'s central drama has enacted the confrontation between two
forms of consciousness, two postures that developed among once political
people in response to the political and spiritual losses of the fifties: the accommodation of David, the central male figure, and the alienation of Eva, an
alienation concealing a repressed rage. In dying, Eva shocks David (and the
community of readers who share his acceptance of things as they are) out of
an accommodationist stance and into a potentially oppositional one.

Interestingly, Al Richmond, the West Coast leftist whose mother Genya
Gorelick is one of the models for Eva, notes the tension between alienation
and opposition in 1962 in an exchange of letters with Olsen concerning his
review of *Tell Me a Riddle:*

> Your characters (Eva and Whitey) are rebels, they are at odds with society as
> it is, and yet they are outside the recognizable social frameworks of rebel-
> lion. This is a tragedy of the contemporary age, and this is what conveys the
> impression of alienation. . . .
>   I found your stories powerfully moving for several reasons, some in-
> tensely personal, and among them is this: you capture a prevalent mood of
> our generation and within that, in your own very original way, you reaffirm
> values that are certainly not unique to this generation, but which did ani-
> mate it when it was at its spiritual crest.

Richmond is correct, I think, in suggesting that these stories capture a prevailing mood of alienation; a mood compounded for leftists and former leftists by
the collapse of their political culture, even while the stories affirm the libera-
tory values of the preceding generation of progressives. "Riddle" should be
read in the context of other fictions of not just existential but political crisis of
the late forties, fifties, and early sixties, like Ellison's *Invisible Man* and
Clancy Sigal's *Going Away.* The concluding question of Sigal's book, a ram-
bling novel of the road that belongs to a distinctively masculinist tradition, is
nevertheless the fundamental question posed by "Tell Me a Riddle" as well:
"The historic agencies of change are collapsed; and with them I. Why? I must
find out" (504).

Yet if both Olsen's working-class background and her political consciousness produce a text suffused with grief and rage over the silencing of a once-
vital progressive culture, and critical of the ideologies of the era's emergent
middle class, at the same time her fiction, like Ellison's and Sigal's, inevitably
engages some of the period's dominant "structures of feeling." Ohmann,
drawing on Williams, argues that postwar fiction through the mid-seventies is
characterized by a particular "structure of feeling" in which "social contradictions were easily displaced into images of personal illness" (390). In fiction by
writers ranging from Sylvia Plath to Philip Roth, from John Updike to Mary

McCarthy, Ohmann notes a narrative pattern in which illness, especially mental disorientation or derangement, becomes an alternative to an acceptance of distorted social relations—"male supremacy, class domination . . . and the compensatory drive to best others in school, government, moral righteousness, public recognition" (392). "The movement into illness and toward recovery," Ohmann argues, "is the basic story" on which novels of the era play variations (395–96). Recovery in these works can only be "the achievement of personal equilibrium vis-a-vis the same untransformed external world" (395). Ohmann argues convincingly that this "structure of feeling" serves the needs and represents the interests of the professional-managerial class, its members also serving as the gatekeepers whose judgments and journals established the postwar literary canon. Ohmann thus brings a far more dialectical analysis to bear on the "mood" of accommodation noted by Marcus Klein in 1962 in his classic study *After Alienation,* a mood Klein celebrates as characteristic of "the best of our contemporary literature,"

> the mood that occurred when rebellion had exhausted itself, when suddenly the manner in which the individual . . . might meet society was no longer so certain, when there was no politics to speak of and when there were no orthodoxies to speak of to restrict one's freedom, and when all theories of society had been shattered (29).

Both "Tell Me a Riddle" and "Hey Sailor, What Ship?" contain elements of this "structure of feeling," though Olsen's deep working-class roots qualify and alter its fictive inscription. Whitey's alcoholism and Eva's cancer, the sources of their physical disintegration and the emblems of their inability or refusal to accommodate themselves to fifties America, link them to other postwar heroes whose illness becomes an individualized response to an apparently untransformable social order, while differentiating them from those whose accommodation to a world in which "there was no politics to speak of" is signaled by their recovery.

In Olsen's fiction, the protagonists do not recover from their illnesses and are never reconciled to loss and betrayal. In these narratives, accommodation is displaced onto more peripheral figures. Whitey's inevitable "going down" is juxtaposed to the poor but respectable family life represented by Lennie, his former comrade, and Helen and their daughters. Remembering and respecting their ties to Whitey, honoring their mutual activist past, Lennie and Helen nevertheless have themselves arrived at a necessary accommodation to their unheroic era, an accommodation Whitey refuses. Their familial health, though shadowed by Helen's sheer exhaustion, is contrasted to Whitey's illness. His illness has psychic roots in sexual maladjustment: he needs liquor to have sex, and he can have sex only with whores. In linking unhealthy, extrafamilial sexuality with Whitey's fall, and in juxtaposing his consequent isolation to the healthy if struggling domesticity of the family to which he returns, inevitably to leave again, "Hey Sailor" does seem to share in the "structure of feeling" Ohmann noted, as well as in the reconstitution of domesticity described by May. It is not so much that "there is no politics to speak of" here, for politics forms the primary content of Whitey's conversations and consciousness; rather, the narrative has no choice other than to expel Whitey, the carrier of sickness, from the domestic terrain, which is the text's only signifier of hope not relegated to a lost past. Adjustment on specifically familial terrain marks the terms of accommodation here: an accommodation consonant with the ideologies of domesticity and sexual containment documented by May and much like those Ohmann describes in the recoveries of the dominant novels of the period.

The representation of Jeannie's role at the conclusion of "Tell Me a Riddle" acts similarly. Like Whitey, Eva neither recovers nor reconciles herself to the diminished world in which she lives her adult life; she herself rejects the narrowly familial in her very dying, insisting on her participation in a larger historical discourse. Jeannie's attendance at her deathbed enables Eva to pass on her legacy to her grandchild; Jeannie reminds Eva of Lisa, the passionate young Tolstoyan who became her teacher in her youth. Olsen represents, through the connection between grandmother and granddaughter (and, reading intertextually, through the growth from the judgmental, conventional Jeannie of "Hey Sailor" to the generous, compassionate Jeannie of "Riddle"), a legacy in which the activism of one generation will illuminate the consciousness of the next.

Through the process that moves David toward his moment of recognition, the reader is invited to share Eva's critique of an ideology of individualism and accommodation. Even so, the pattern here of illness and recovery, a recovery in which the man and the woman are reconciled, though in death, through their grandchild's intervention, is consistent with both May's and Ohmann's analyses of the era's dominant ideologies. In Jeannie's very goodness and self-sacrificing nurturance of others, as in the highly personal nature of her quest for meaningful, expressive work, the raging intensities and political passions of her grandmother are domesticated and, as I read the text today, diminished. As Macherey suggests, Jeannie's presence provides for the "fictive resolution of ideological conflicts," a precarious resolution threatened by the powerful shapes of loss and betrayal that haunt the text as a whole.

In these stories, then, Olsen seems to me both to profoundly critique the mores and the ideologies of the era, and, more unwillingly than unwittingly, to cede them power. Eva and Whitey, the repositories of revolutionary consciousness, are anachronistic, actors in a textual order structured by the inexorable plot of their expulsion from it. Yet the narrative that finally expels them into exile and death, domesticating social history as family legacy and revolutionary rage as personal decency, is also the narrative that writes their lives and redeems them from the silence to which fifties culture consigned the radical past.

Women's Embodiment and Desire

The same fundamental tension between the ideological and the utopian, between the representation and the subversion of dominant ideas and practices, is inscribed in the other stories of *Tell Me a Riddle* as well. I will explore that tension in "I Stand Here Ironing" and "O Yes" by examining their representation of women's desire and women's embodiment.

The female body in Olsen's work speaks not a discourse of erotic desire, but another set of yearnings: for justice, for wholeness, for "circumference," in the Dickinsonian sense of the word. "Many a woman writer seeking circumference—of whom I am one . . . ," she writes in *Silences*, "has had to abide by, solace herself with trespass vision. . . . They do not suffice" (247). In *Tell me a Riddle*, Olsen rewrites women's desire as social, political, communal, esthetic rather than simply as erotic. Her comments in *Silences* on the difficulties of representing women's embodiment gloss her own practices and frustrations as a writer.

In "One Out of Twelve: Writers Who Are Women in Our Century" (1971), the essay that now forms a second chapter of *Silences*, Olsen takes issue with Hortense Calisher's approval, in a critical essay, of "the feminism that comes straight from the belly, from the bed, and from childbed. A sensibility trusting itself for what it is, as the other half of basic life." For Olsen, this passage represents a kind of silencing:

> Constriction to the stereotypic biological-woman (breeder, sex-partner) sphere. Not only leaving out (what men writers usually leave out), ongoing motherhood, the maintenance-of-life, and other angel in the house so determiningly the experience of most women once they get out of bed and up from childbed, but other common female realities as well.
> And it leaves out the rest of women's biological endowment as born human (including the creative capacity out of which women and men write) (42–43).

Later in *Silences*, Olsen offers a two-page gloss on her comments in "One Out of Twelve," under the heading "Constriction to One Dimension—III: Confinement to Biological (Sex-Partner) Woman." Again she alludes to Woolf: " 'Killing the angel in the house,' I think I solved . . . but the second (problem), telling the truth about my own experiences as a body, I do not think I solved. . . . Fifty years after," Olsen comments, "still to be solved." For "one's experiences as a body" are "the least understood, the most tormentingly complex . . . to wrest to truth" (253–54).

The passage moves from the silencing: "Telling the truth about one's experiences as a body, forbidden, not possible, for centuries" (253), to the possibility for a freer textuality that will correspond to a greater knowledge of, freer use of, women's bodies by women ourselves: "Telling the truth about one's body: a necessary, freeing subject for the woman writer" (254). Thus, as in Olsen's fiction, there is a utopian movement in these two pages from repression (forbidden, not possible) to resistance (necessary, freeing), and from physicality to textuality. The intervening paragraphs devote special attention to the problem initiated in the encounter with Calisher's essay:

> The problem of finding one's own truth through the primacy accorded sexuality by our times. The pornographic, the Freudian, times. Our freer—that

is, voluntary about reproduction—times. Our still restrictive, defining sexuality as heterosexual, times (254–55).

Evoking the connection between the physical ("free use" of the body, "rights
of one's own body denied") and the textual ("telling the truth about one's
experience as a body"), this passage recognizes the long unavailability of an
appropriate discourse about the female body as itself a silencing material
circumstance. Nor, as Olsen suggests, does the contemporary discourse of
sexuality provide an adequate mediation; sexuality is still coded as heterosexuality, and "the primacy accorded sexuality" in general obliterates other variants of women's bodily knowledge.

Olsen's interpretive slant here bears some resemblance to Macherey's, in
its articulation of an arena—the female body—that has lacked a discourse
adequate to its demystified textual representation. Her interpretation bears
some semblance as well to Foucault's, who sees the history of sexuality's
construction as one in which sexuality has been articulated with progressive
exhaustiveness, making various forms of the sexualized confession a central
genre of our times. Foucault of course is not interested in "the question of the
place, proportion, *actual* importance of sexuality in our (now) longer-lived,
more various, woman lives" (255). Olsen remains at odds with those who
would argue, like Foucault, that there can be no "actual," no reality, uncon-
structed through discourse—the emphasis on "actual" is her own. In *Silences,*
language mediates but does not engender "reality." Yet, like Macherey, Olsen
in this passage provides a basis for interpreting the deformations and absences
in the texts of the past, in this case women's texts; unlike Machery or Foucault, she articulates a utopian hope for the texts of the future, as they mediate the "unworked through, unassessed relationship between body difference
and the actual power relationship permeating associations between the sexes"
(254–55).

Silences suggests that Olsen's fiction rewrites women's desire to subvert
what Carolyn Heilbrun, quoted in a note in this section of *Silences,* calls "the
exploration of experience only through sexuality, which is exactly where men
have always told them that such an exploration should take place." Olsen's
narratives, critical and fictive, resist reducing the representation of women's
bodies to narratives of female erotic desire. She shares with the line of criticism influenced by Cixous and Irigaray a sense that, as Arleen B. Dallery puts
it in her discussion of *écriture feminine,* "through writing the body, woman's
body is liberated from the objectification and fragmentation of male desire"
(58). But she specifically opposes the discourse that privileges eroticism,
jouissance, as the only or primary expression of women's embodiment, and
that inscribes women's desire as exclusively erotic rather than social or political or religious or esthetic. Like the George Eliot described by Nancy Miller
in *Subject to Change,* Olsen would distinguish herself from "those women
writers whose language is structured exactly like the unconscious that Freud
has assigned to them, those writers (and their heroines) whose ambitious
wishes are contained *entirely* in their erotic longings" (35).

In "I Stand Here Ironing," for example, Emily's coming of age is represented not as a traditional budding into erotic womanhood, but as the acquisition of the physical powers of the mime, whose embodiment is expressed not in sexuality but in a redemptive art. "O Yes" thematizes the destructive effects of racism and the "hidden injuries of class" on the friendship of two girls, but structurally it is also a story of maternal desire, or rather, a desire shaped by but exceeding the maternal, a desire that, like the bodies of the two girls, is differentiated by race. The black mother dreams of freedom and spiritual transcendence; the white mother longs for the "place of strength" that seems to her represented by her black friend's community. Olsen's insistence on a larger compass for female desire is one of the dimensions of her work that remains powerful to contemporary women readers.

At the same time, the writing out of female sexual passion, of erotic desire, in her work partially conforms to the era's deep fears about female sexuality, leaving unchallenged the ideology of female sexual containment May identifies as a hallmark of the time (especially 114–34). In "O Yes," as well, the binary opposition between the black and white families, in which the black mother and child come to represent for the white mother both physicality and human community, suggests how even progressive white writers in the era construct racial differences in a way that inscribes white desire rather than black subjectivity, in this case displacing white female physicality onto a black other.

In "I Stand Here Ironing," written in the early fifties, the girl Emily's body inscribes the limits and possibilities for trespass vision, a dialectic between the experience of oppression and the impulse to creative power. The maternal narrator, responding in the sustained monologue that constitutes the story to the question of a teacher or counselor at Emily's school, broods on the circumstances that have circumscribed her daughter's life; she herself reads her daughter's body as both a figure and a product of the same "silencings" later rendered discursively in *Silences*. Emily's physicality at first seems to inscribe the undeveloped potential of her inner life. Unlike her golden-haired sister, "quick and articulate and assured," able since childhood to entertain company with jokes and riddles, Emily, "dark and foreign-looking," has spent much of her life sitting silent. Gradually, her different body, physically immature, often verbally inarticulate, becomes the medium for a different kind of expression, neither sexual nor verbal, the expressiveness of the mime. Her body, unmarked sexually, acquires onstage a compelling fluidity that evokes the release of laughter in her audience:

> Was this Emily? The control, the command, the convulsing and deadly clowning, the spell, then the roaring, stamping audience, unwilling to let this rare and precious laughter out of their lives? (19).

Emily's body in pantomime stands for the woman artist; like the woman who writes fiction with trespass vision, she must be, in Henry James's words, "one on whom nothing is lost" (*Silences*, 62, 247), drawing the sources of her art from her observations of those around her, and transforming them into her own embodied language.

Metaphors of embodiment and appetite pervade the narrative. A beautiful baby, Emily, says her mother, "would lie on the floor in her blue overalls patting the surface so hard in ecstasy her hands and feet would blur" (2). Left at eight months with a neighbor "to whom she was no miracle at all," she greets her anxious mother at the end of the working day with "a clogged weeping that could not be comforted" (3). Her gift, inadequately supported "has as often eddied inside, clogged and clotted, as been used and growing." "Clogged," "clotted"—metonyms for the constriction of the life's blood in human veins, metaphor for the congealing of talent.

Susan Bordo argues that hysteria, agoraphobia, and anorexia, "embodied rather than discursive demonstration," mark both women's protest against patriarchal expectations of femininity and tragic self-defeat, ironically countering "the stifling of the female voice through one's own voicelessness" (21). This is true of Emily, and signifies disturbance. At times "food sickens her" and she barely eats (5, 7); later she develops "the enormous appetite that is legendary in our family" (10). Yet she is able also to transform embodied demonstration from self-destructiveness into art, though she remains "as imprisoned in her difference as she had been in anonymity" (10). Recognizing with despair the limitations on Emily's potential for a sustained and gratifying art spoken through her body, the maternal narrator both relinquishes her daughter—"Let her be"—and issues one final utopian hope, for her, for all of us: "Only help her to know—help make it so there is cause for her to know—that she is more than this dress on the ironing board, helpless before the iron" (12). "I Stand Here Ironing," then, proffers a maternal narrative in which the mother reads her daughter's body as the site where the dialectics of silencing and speech, of circumstance and agency, are played out. Desire has been reinscribed in this maternal narrative as a hunger to cross the distance between what, given the circumstances of our lives, we can actually produce and "what is in (us)" as potential. It is a utopian hunger for a world that will nurture rather than extinguish human creative capacity.

The mother's tale reveals as well a deep, explicit ambivalence about the maturation of her daughter's body into its new loveliness. It is a relief to the mother that Emily's physical development has lagged years behind her contemporaries'; for "she was too vulnerable for that terrible world of youthful competition, of preening and parading, of constant measuring of yourself against every other, of envy. . . . She tormented herself enough about not looking like the others . . . without having it all magnified by the merciless physical drives" (9). Emily, nineteen at the moment of narration, like the maternal narrator at the time of her birth, is written out of a narrative of erotic development or romantic initiation. The coincidence in age between maternal narrator at the time of Emily's birth and the daughter whose story she now tells suggests that this mother may see in her daughter's sublimated expressiveness the counterpoint to her own experience, her own silencings as a young mother struggling to bring up a child in poverty after having been abandoned by the child's father.

Interestingly, Olsen's early journals and poems indicate that at Emily's age and earlier, she herself knew the "merciless drives" well; these private writings from her own young womanhood are suffused with a sensuous and sometimes explicitly sexual feeling that rarely finds its way into her published fiction. (Sexual desire in her published work is almost always ascribed to men, and almost always associated with some form of disturbance.) Women's erotic subjectivity is one "truth" not told in her fiction. In part this absence derives from her conscious choice to elaborate a different compass for women's desire. Yet the pages in *Silences* on this subject were written long afterwards, when the literature and theory of the women's movement had made available a discourse for representing, and thinking about representing, women's erotic subjectivity. It seems likely that the absence of such representation in the stories, even in those about the coming of age of young women, owes something both to Olsen's own experience in the rhetorically anti-erotic world of the political left and to fifties ideologies of female sexual containment, as well as to her own trajectory of maturation. In any case, if Emily's physical immaturity, her asexual androgyny, have protected her against the savagery of the mating and dating games of fifties America, the absence of "merciless drives" as a narrative force leaves unchallenged the ideology of sexual containment that May defines as central to the era, even as the narrative of the development of woman as artist challenges ideologies of female domesticity. In "I Stand Here Ironing," however, women's sexuality is feared not because it threatens the stability of the social order, but rather because its expression must be so fraught with danger for women in so patriarchal a world. Women's desire in this story, then, both partakes of and opposes prevailing attitudes about women's social and sexual relations.

A discourse of bodily constriction and expression figures also in "O Yes," Olsen's story about the gradual, inexorable "sorting" in junior high of two girls, one black, one white, who have been friends since early childhood. "O Yes" thematizes difference in part as different trajectories into silence. Carol is tracked on the upwardly mobile course that will sever her from the undifferentiated, innocently multicultural world of her childhood and excise from the grammar of her daily life the common language of that world. Parry's energy and physicality are molded increasingly by her maturation into a black working-class culture whose linguistic and bodily forms signal and produce her increasing estrangement from social approval and social power. Hence Olsen's name for her, Parialee.

"O Yes" remains a powerful and painfully relevant protest against the relations of race and class that track black and white children into different worlds. What is silent in the Machereyan sense of the term but visible after an intervening decade of work on difference and narrative is the extent to which "O Yes" shares certain racial attitudes of its time, specifically a propensity manifest in other progressive white-authored works of the era to read into black experience what is absent from, repressed in, white middle-class culture.³ Its binary structure, built around the representation of two pairs of mothers and daughters, black and white, allocates to the black pair those dimensions of experience longed for by and denied to white, middle-class women of the period—physicality, sexuality, and human community.

In the first section of the story, set in a black church where Carol and her mother are attending Parry's baptism, the words and music of the black church service, enacted textually, call forth a physicality of response from the parishioners. In a series of present participles, the text mimics the motion of the preacher: "running round the platform, stopping and shaking imaginary sleepers. . . . Looping, scalloping his voice—'grea-aa-aat Daaaay.' All the choirs thundering. . . ." The movement becomes contagious, and screams from the congregation evolve into "an awful thrumming sound . . . like feet and hands thrashing around, like a giant jumping of a rope" (44). Carol is moved at first by the preacher's voice to her own remembrances of motion, the physicality of unfettered girlhood that she has once shared with her friend:

> Tag. Thump of the volley ball. Ecstasy of the jump rope. Parry, do pepper. Carol, do pepper. Parry's bettern Carol, Carol's bettern Parry. . . (43).

But the screaming, the apparently uncontrolled movement of the parishioners, enacting a ritual of liberation from bondage that she cannot recognize as ritual, are too much for her. She longs for the second time to be able to compress the sound and motion "into a record small and round to listen to far and far as if into a seashell—the stamp and rills and spirals all tiny (but never any screaming)" (47). The final horror for her is the vision of one of her schoolmates, "the thrashing writhing body struggling against the ushers with the look of grave and loving support on their faces. . ." (48). Finally, inadequately protected by her fantasies of containment, she faints; nor can she hear Alva's repeated attempts to explain the service, the meaning of religion for those to whom "it's like a hope in their blood, their bones," to whom "church is home" and "the only place they can feel how they feel and maybe let it come out." Willing Alva to silence, she is excluded from Alva's internal monologue, a monologue that marks the closure of the story's first half by rendering Alva's private vision of despair and transcendence.⁴

The second part of "O Yes" offers one lyric passage in which Carol and Parry are united one last time in the sheer physical pleasure of a girlhood still precariously unmarked by gender or by race:

> In the wind and the shimmering sunset light, half the children of the block are playing down the street. Leaping, bouncing, halooing, tugging the kites of spring. In the old synchronized understanding, Carol and Parry kick, catch, kick, catch. And now Parry jumps on her pogo stick (the last time), Carol shadowing her, and Bubbie, arching his body in a semicircle of joy, bounding after them, high, higher, higher (56).

The joyousness of this passage, representing textually the sovereign bodies of two young girls moving in synchrony, is parodied sadly in a later one, in which Parry visits Carol, sick at home with the mumps, to bring her schoolwork. The scene is all fast jivetalk and frantic motion, speech that represents Parry's increasing social "difference," and movement that flippantly conceals her pain: we, unlike Carol, know that their teacher has assumed Parry to be the daughter of Carol's maid, and has given her instructions with a patronizing racism congruent with that assumption. So Parry whirls, talking nonstop, through Carol's room, a movement Olsen again evokes by the paratactic accumulation of participial phrases:

> Removing the books and binders, ranging them on the dresser . . . , marking lipstick faces—bemused or mocking or amazed—on each paper jacket. . . . Fluffing out smoothing the quilt with exaggerated energy. . . . Tossing up and catching their year-ago, arm-in-arm graduation picture, replacing it deftly, upside down, into its mirror crevice. . . . Adding a frown line to one bookface. Twanging the paper fishkite, the Japanese windbell overhead, setting the mobile they had once made of painted eggshells and decorated straws to twirling and rocking. And is gone (58–59).

Carol feverishly mocks this motion, finally sleeping after a disordered night. In the final pages of the story, the narrative turns from Carol's consciousness to that of her mother, Helen; the pivotal paragraphs reiterate Carol's location at the outer borders of childhood, surrounded by the "furnishings of that world of childhood she no sooner learned to live in comfortably, then had to leave." Her "just budding breast" is exposed as she reaches to hold her stuffed animal. These interpellations remind us that this too is a narrative of coming-to-age. But, as with Emily's adolescence, the young girl's budding breast is not the sign of the onset of erotic desire, but of a different order of longing, prefigured by Alva's monologue and coursing through Helen's life as well.

The nature of that desire can be better assessed by examining Alva's soliloquy more closely. In this monologue Olsen attributes to Alva a vision that combines the maternal and the Biblical. Pregnant at fifteen and alone, she hears a voice call her and follows a small boy down a path that leads through darkness to a vision of hell, before the child leads her upwards on a motorbike, first greasing her feet "with the hands of my momma when I was a knee baby."

> Eyes he placed all around my head, and as I journeyed upward after him, it seemed I heard a mourning: "Mama Mama you must help carry the world."
> The rise and fall of nations I saw. And the voice called again Alva Alva, and I flew into a world of light, multitudes singing, Free, Free I am so glad (52).

The monologue traces the movements of women's desire as redefined by Olsen and as framed in the rhetoric of the black sermon, which it glosses, as Coiner suggests in her essay in Part One of this volume. For Olsen, that movement is inevitably characterized by the development of a profound sense of social connectedness, social responsibility: "Mama Mama you must help carry the world," a sense of connectedness ultimately associated, as Elaine Orr argues, with spiritual transcendence and liberation.

Jessica Benjamin's work on women's desire can also assist in the interpretation of this passage. Benjamin notes the paradox that motherhood is the closest our culture has come to an image of feminine activity, though the mother herself "is not culturally articulated as a sexual subject, one who actively desires something for herself—quite the contrary" (83). Benjamin argues that "finding women's desire . . . requires finding an alternative to the phallic structures, to the symbolic mode. And that means an alternative mode of structuring the psyche, not just a symbol to replace the phallus" (92). The alternative mode she proposes uses the concept of intersubjectivity, "what happens between individuals, and within the individual-with-others, rather than within the individual psyche." This mode, she suggests, provides a "different arena for experiencing will, agency, and desire." Benjamin argues that receptivity, a possibility for agency and subjectivity, are aspects of the infant self that require recognition from another to develop fully. The confidence in one's inner resources is also founded in the experience of the other's integrity and separateness, "her ability to tolerate and create limits for our impulses, which permits us the freedom of spontaneous interaction." The self that develops through such experiences of mutual recognition, Benjamin argues, is a different modality from the symbolized ego of phallic structuring. For her, the "intersubjective mode of desire has its counterpart in spatial rather than symbolic representation, and . . . this mode does have something to do with female experience": "what is experientially female is the association of desire with a space, a place within the self," from which "a force imbued with the authenticity of *inner* desire" can emerge. Finally, desire is associated with the quest for freedom:

> Woman's desire, I believe, can be found not through the current emphasis on freedom from: as autonomy or separation from a powerful other, guaranteed by identification with an opposing power. Rather, we are seeking a relationship to desire in the freedom to: freedom to be both with and distinct from the other. . . . The discovery of our own desire will proceed, I believe, through the mode of thought that can suspend and reconcile such opposition (between subject and object), the dimension of recognition between self and other (97–98).

Alva's monologue, narrating her mythic and spiritual journey to religious revelation, with its reenactment of archetypal passages from death to rebirth in terms of African-American spiritual discourse, enacts a process curiously like Benjamin's psychoanalytically grounded interpretation of women's desire. The voice that calls her, "Alva. Fear not, I have loved you from the foundation of the universe," figures the recognition of integrity that Benjamin regards as essential to the full articulation of capacity. The small child who guides Alva seems to combine the characteristics of both man and woman; a baby boy who carries but discards a phallic stick, he greases Alva's feet with hands that recall her mother's holding. The child, then, is also Alva's mother and her infant self. The articulation and blurring between maternal and filial, masculine and feminine identities, intimates a desire like that Benjamin hypothesizes: for and enabled by freedom to be both with and distinct from the other, to achieve recognition from the other, to assume responsibility for the other, in acts of mutual recognition that constitute love but that transcend the purely maternal. To the extent that Benjamin encodes women's desire as sexual subjectivity and that Olsen writes a specifically sexual subjectivity for women out of her text, they do not share an identical analytic stance. Alva's monologue reenacts a process of black spiritual liberation, and it is this discourse that interests Olsen, this language to which she consciously gives voice.[5] But in reconfiguring the psychic landscape of desire to insist on the profundity of interconnectedness, the primacy of recognition for individual and social wellbeing, and simultaneously the existence of a women's desire that exceeds the maternal to demand a larger compass, Olsen anticipates aspects of Benjamin's discussion by thirty-five years.

"O Yes" concludes with an episode that marks Carol's maturation into identity with and compassion for a larger human community and that represents Helen's unarticulated longings, marking her at last as a mother who also "actively desires something for herself." Helen, downstairs, turns on the radio, and from it issues the same "storm of singing" that led to Carol's fainting in the church. Hearing it, she races down, "shrieking and shrieking," and demanding that her mother "turn it off." She collapses weeping in her mother's arms, finally wanting to know "why . . . they sing and scream like that," taking comfort from Helen's silent rocking, an enactment of the classic maternal stance of "soothing, holding, and containment" (Benjamin 86). Carol confesses finally her shame at the betrayals of her friendship with Parry, and for the first time names and recognizes her relatedness to Vicky, the "bad girl" of her school whose ecstasy at the church has triggered her fainting spell. "Oh why is it like it is," she cries, "and why do I have to care?"

> Her mother can only hold her silently, thinking: *caring asks doing. It is a long baptism into the seas of humankind, my daughter. Better immersion than to live untouched. . . . Yet how will you sustain?* (61).

And we learn that the white maternal body too is the site of longing, a longing textually repressed and silenced until the narrative can no longer contain it and it erupts to mark a tentative closure—countering the filial and cultural inscription of the mother as one without desire, without subjectivity:

> While in her, her own need leapt and plunged for the place of strength that was not—where one could scream or sorrow while all knew and accepted, and gloved and loving hands waited to support and understand (62).

This passage uses precisely the spatial metaphors that Benjamin suggests are definitive of women's desire. Within this mother-woman, need leaps and plunges like an animal corralled against its will. The nature of Helen's need is never specified, never spoken, but the solace for which she yearns is figured by a community of support that will nurture her as she nurtures Carol, as the ushers in the black church nurtured the congregants. As in Alva's monologue, Olsen in this paragraph rewrites maternality to inscribe the power of desire that exceeds the literally maternal, desire that is silenced here in the holding gestures of motherhood within the nuclear family. From this closing tableau of Helen, the mother who holds her daughter while longing silently for the solace of her own needs, it is a short step to the silent grandmother of "Tell Me a Riddle," who, her mothering done, rejects the maternal holding stance outright in her quest for "coherence, transport, meaning."

Again, the content of desire here is not erotic; women's erotic subjectivity is as silent in "O Yes" as in Olsen's other published work. "O Yes," then, explicitly opposes ideologies of domesticity, if not of sexual containment, by locating the silent longing of mothers for extrafamilial release and solace at the structural climaxes of the narrative. Opposing racism and exposing "the hidden injuries of class," the text nevertheless shares with other works of its day a structure of feeling that inevitably privileges white subjectivity, in this case by reinscribing a set of racial relationships that subsume black female experience within a context of white female desire. The desire of the white maternal body is invoked by imagery associated with the black church, black experience, and black maternality; the dynamic of physical containment and physical expression is played out by associating images of containment with Carol, the white daughter, freedom of movement with Parry and her community. The rhetoric of Helen's final monologue, read alongside that of Alva's monologue in the structurally similar location at the conclusion of the first section of "O Yes," inscribes Alva as the idealized "other" to the white woman's longing; somehow Alva, in her plenitude of vision, her participation in the black community represented by the church, her apparent access to religious revelation, has (or represents) what Helen wants.

Perhaps such a problematic is inevitable in a white-authored text that uses the different positionalities of white mothers, white daughters, black mothers, black daughters to explore the unfoldings of sameness and difference. As Jay Clayton points out, white writers can write with empathy and imaginative power about blacks, but "a work by a white writer cannot function in the same way as a work by a black. It cannot create the same kind of community for African Americans because it does not issue from the same pragmatic situation" (389). For Clayton, narrative can act to form communal bonds among members of specific ethnic and cultural communities; "minority writers are authorized as narrators in part by their prior status as listeners" within these communities (388).

Still, the women of "O Yes" mirror for one another what for Olsen is their common humanity, a commonality disrupted by the divisions of class and race, and differently inscribed by their different cultural practices. Indeed, Alva's silence in rendering her soliloquy is also a stance of resistance within the terms of the text to just such an appropriation as I have described. If neither Alva nor Helen chooses to speak fully out loud, to explain to Carol all that their experience has taught them, their silences may figure the unrepresentability of black experience and longing to whites, and of mothers' desires that exceed the maternal to daughters. "O Yes," then, like Olsen's other work, becomes the locus where powerful contradictions between the inscription and the subversion of dominant ideologies, in this case those governing the intersections of race and gender, play themselves out.

Conclusion

In this paper, I have tried to work through the relationship between my profound admiration for and debt to Tillie Olsen's work, which I turn to again and again for its beauty and wisdom, and the mode of reading preeminent in the past decade, which asks that we look at the operations of history and ideology in the language of the texts we love as well as those with which we quarrel. Understanding better the relations among the human silences Olsen thematizes in the stories of *Tell Me a Riddle* and the textual silences and contradictions that encode the ideologies of the era has increased my admiration for her work. Olsen writes both against and with the age, informed by historical memory of the past, attuned to the movements that will shape the future. If *Tell Me a Riddle,* like all cultural texts, is ideologically inscribed, it is also linguistically organized and socially engaged in ways that trace Olsen's specific authorial presence and will, a will that affirms the utopian against the odds. The fullness of *Tell Me a Riddle's* engagement, at the level of ideological inscription and as utopian aspiration, with the central social conflicts of its time is one of the marks of its significance as a work of art.

NOTES

1. Page citations to the stories in the *Tell Me a Riddle* volume refer to the Delta paperback printing cited in the bibliography. Olsen made minor but interesting revisions in subsequent editions, but since I am concerned here with the embeddedness of the stories in their era of origin, I have used the earlier version.

2. In Ch. 9 of *Marxism and Literature,* Williams defines this term extensively and distinguishes between "structures of feeling" and "more formal concepts of 'world-view' or 'ideology' " (132). I use "structures of feeling" and "ideology" more or less interchangeably in this paper, relying on the first term especially in drawing on Richard Ohmann's essay, which in turn makes extensive use of Williams's construct, more faithful than my own to Williams's original intent.

3. Norman Mailer's *The White Negro* is probably the most obvious and self-conscious example, but of course white admiration for (and sometimes appropriation of) black culture has a long history and has been variously inscribed in white American literature and culture in different eras.

4. Constance Coiner's essay in Part One of his book illuminates the relations among author, characters, and reader concerning what the characters speak, think but do not say, hear and fail to hear. My discussion of "O Yes" is in dialogue with hers.

5. According to William McPheron, who prepared the text for *First Drafts, Last Drafts,* Olsen's notes for "O Yes" include "years of jottings" on African-American

diction and syntax; the story deliberately gives voice to "strains of American English which for racial and class reasons are often excluded from the written medium" (65).

WORKS CITED

Benjamin, Jessica. "A Desire of One's Own: Psychoanalytic Feminism and Intersubjective Space." In Teresa De Lauretis, ed. *Feminist Studies/Critical Studies*. Bloomington: Indiana UP, 1986.

Bordo, Susan. "The Body and the Reproduction of Femininity: A Feminist Appropriation of Foucault." In Alison M. Jaggar and Susan R. Bordo, eds. *Gender/Body/ Knowledge: Feminist Reconstructions of Being and Knowing*. New Brunswick: Rutgers UP, 1986.

Clayton, Jay. "The Narrative Turn in Recent Minority Fiction." *American Literary History* 2:3 (Fall 1990):375–93.

Coiner, Constance. "Literature as 'No One's Private Ground': A Bakhtinian Reading of Tillie Olsen's *Tell Me a Riddle*." *Feminist Studies,* 18:2 (Summer 1992):257–81.

———. "Literature as Resistance: The Intersection of Feminism and the Communist Left in Meridel Le Sueur and Tillie Olsen." In Lennard J. Davis and M. Bella Mirabella, eds. *Left Politics and the Literary Profession*. New York: Columbia UP, 1990.

Dallery, Arleen B. "'The Politics of Writing (the) Body': *Écriture Feminine.*" In Alison M. Jaggar and Susan R. Bordo, eds. *Gender/Body/Knowledge: Feminist Reconstructions of Being and Knowing*. New Brunswick: Rutgers UP, 1986.

Ellison, Ralph. *Invisible Man*. New York: Random House, 1952.

Foucault, Michel. *The History of Sexuality. Vol. I: An Introduction*. Translated by Robert Hurley. New York: Vintage/Random House, 1980.

Jameson, Fredric. *The Politiical Unconscious: Narrative as a Socially Symbolic Act*. Ithaca: Cornell UP, 1981.

Klein, Marcus. *After Alienation: American Novels in Mid-Century*. Cleveland: World Publishing Company, 1962.

Macherey, Pierre. *A Theory of Literary Production*. Translated by Geoffrey Wall. London: Routledge, 1978, 1989.

Mailer, Norman. *The White Negro*. San Francisco: City Lights Books, 1957.

May, Elaine Tyler. *Homeward Bound: American Families in the Cold War Era*. New York: Basic Books, 1988.

McPheron, William. *First Drafts, Last Drafts: Forty Years of the Creative Writing Program at Stanford*. Stanford: Stanford University Libraries, 1989.

Meese, Elizabeth A. *Crossing the Double-Cross: The Practice of Feminist Criticism*. Chapel Hill: U of North Carolina P, 1986.

Miller, Nancy K. *Subject to Change: Reading Feminist Writing*. New York: Columbia UP, 1988.

Ohmann, Richard. "The Shaping of a Canon: U.S. Fiction, 1960–1975." In Robert von Hallberg, ed. *Canons*. Chicago: U of Chicago P, 1983.

Olsen, Tillie. Untitled Essay. In McPheron, 1989.

———. *Silences*. New York: Delacorte Press, 1978.

———. *Tell Me a Riddle*. New York: Dell Delta, 1956, 1957, 1960, 1961.

———. Unpublished journals and poems. Olsen's private papers.

Orr, Elaine Neil. *Tillie Olsen and a Feminist Spiritual Vision*. Jackson: UP of Mississippi, 1987.

Rabinowitz, Paula. *Labor and Desire: Women's Revolutionary Fiction in Depression America*. Chapel Hill: U of North Carolina P, 1991.

Richmond, Al. Unpublished letter to Tille Olsen. 1962.

Rosenfelt, Deborah. "Divided Against Herself: The Life Lived and the Life Suppressed in Agnes Smedley and Tillie Olsen." *Moving On* (April–May 1980):15–20, 23.

———. "From the Thirties: Tillie Olsen and the Radical Tradition." *Feminist Studies* 7: 3 (1981):371–406.

Sigal, Clancy. *Going Away*. New York: Dell, 1961.

Williams, Raymond. *Marxism and Literature*. Oxford: Oxford UP, 1977.

"No One's Private Ground": A Bakhtinian Reading of Tillie Olsen's *Tell Me a Riddle*

Constance Coiner

"Commitment" is more than just a matter of presenting correct political opinions in one's art; it reveals itself in how far the artist reconstructs the artistic forms at his [/her] disposal, turning authors, readers, and spectators into collaborators.

> Terry Eagleton, referring in his *Marxism and Literary Criticism* to Walter Benjamin's "The Author as Producer"

In the stories collected in *Tell Me a Riddle* Tillie Olsen examines the marginalization and potential empowering of various groups of oppressed people, particularly women, by experimenting with potentially democratizing modes of discourse. Deborah Rosenfelt has rightly placed Olsen in

> . . . a line of women writers, associated with the American Left, who unite a class consciousness and a feminist consciousness in their lives and creative work, who are concerned with the material circumstances of people's lives, who articulate the experiences and grievances of women and of other oppressed groups—workers, national minorities, the colonized and the exploited—who speak out of a defining commitment to social change ("Thirties" 374).

Although *Tell Me a Riddle* shows a range of marginalized lives, Olsen is far from content with merely portraying this multiplicity in American society. As Rosenfelt observes, Olsen writes out of a "commitment to social change," and I will discuss some of Olsen's narrative/political strategies that exemplify that commitment.

The modes of discourse with which Olsen experiments in developing her narrative strategies are those she has derived and recreated from long and careful listening to the voices of marginalized people. The cacophony of their voices, Olsen recognizes, comprises a potentially democratizing force. Noting some of Olsen's uses of empowering discursive forms in *Silences*, Elizabeth A.

A shorter version of this article appeared in *Feminist Studies*, volume 18, number 2 (Summer 1992): 257–81. Permission to reprint is granted by the publisher, *Feminist Studies*, Inc., c/o Women's Studies Program, University of Maryland, College Park, MD 20742.

Meese writes that "by means of a polyvocal chorus she [Olsen] questions silence and allows others to participate in the same process. . . . She then calls upon the reader to write the text—no longer her text, but occasioned by it and by the voices speaking through it" (110). The experiments noted by Meese as well as several other experiments pervade *Tell Me a Riddle.*

Some of Olsen's specific uses of discursive modes and the political/social changes they work to bring about are prefigured in Mikhail Bakhtin's general concept of "heteroglossia." For Bakhtin there are two competing forces in language use: "Every concrete utterance of a speaking subject serves as a point where centrifugal as well as centripetal forces are brought to bear" (*Dialogic* 272). The "centripetal" or "monologic" force presses toward unity, singularity of meaning; it attempts to assert its dominance by silencing uses of language that deviate from it. On the other hand, the "centrifugal" or "heteroglossic" force resists the dominance of monologism by fragmenting and disrupting it. The myriad heteroglossic voices of the marginalized comprise a social and political force against the tyranny of dominant discursive modes in any language community. Those such as Olsen who observe, record, and honor the multiple heteroglossic voices engage in the democratizing enterprise of amplifying dominated and marginalized voices.

Bakhtin's metaphor of "carnival" displays the nexus of heteroglossia and political/social power. Carnival, with its various simultaneous activities, is a site in which many of the usual societal impositions of class and order are suspended while the populace participates in multiple ways of parodying or mimicking the dominant culture's behavior. Terry Eagleton has described Bakhtin's notion of carnival in these terms: "The 'gay relativity' of popular carnival, 'opposed to all that [is] ready-made and completed, to all pretence at immutability,' is the political materialization of Bakhtin's poetics, as the blasphemous, 'familiarizing' language of plebeian laughter destroys monologic authoritarianism with its satirical estrangements" (*Against* 117). In *Tell Me a Riddle,* in several instances of carnival-like atmosphere, heteroglossia is unleashed to engage in a powerful, playful satirizing of the dominant culture.

The nurturing and recording of heteroglossia has democratizing potential, but heteroglossia itself and the recording of it also contain hazards both for the multiplicity of speakers and for those who listen to their voices. The collection of stories in *Tell Me a Riddle* presents a wide range of individual, marginalized voices competing for our attention. Unless readers/listeners make connections among a variety of voices, many of which are foreign to their own, the potential for genuine democracy latent within the cacophony of heteroglossia is lost. If they remain unconnected from each other, the competing voices lapse into a white-noise excess of sound that becomes unintelligible. Rejecting many traditional modes of authorial control, Olsen refuses opportunities to make connections for us and presses us to make connections among those voices ourselves. The social/political act of connecting otherwise isolated and marginalized voices realizes the democratizing potential of heteroglossia, and Olsen demands that we participate in such action.

To participate properly, we must be permeable to multiple voices, and in some characters in *Tell Me a Riddle,* Olsen shows us both the benefits and risks of receptivity to heteroglossia. Multiple voices often compete within a single character, displaying that character's complex web of ties to others and to the past. Heteroglossia on this level often operates in *Tell Me a Riddle* and other works by Olsen to undermine and offer alternatives to bourgeois individualism. But Olsen does not idealize the individual permeable to heteroglossia; she shows us hazards that exist in individual manifestations of heteroglossia (e.g., Whitey's isolation in "Hey Sailor, What Ship?" and the multiple voices that threaten to overwhelm the narrator of "I Stand Here Ironing"). *Tell Me a Riddle* asks us to be cognizant of the dangers we face as we assume the role Olsen insists we assume—that of active readers alert to the connections among a multiplicity of marginalized voices.

Throughout the stories in *Tell Me a Riddle* Olsen pits heteroglossic modes of discourse she associates with the oppressed against oppressors' monolingual/monological modes of discourse. In the title story, Jeannie's sketch of Eva "coiled, convoluted like an ear" suggests Olsen's narrative/political strategies. Olsen's writing, like an ear "intense in listening," is permeable to the heteroglossic differences constitutive of a complex social field. The stories collected in *Tell Me a Riddle* strain away from the prevailing narrative and social order by "hearing" and incorporating the suppressed voices of mothers, those of the working class, and the dialects of immigrants and African-Americans; by deconstructing the opposition between personal and political; and, in the title story, by honoring the communal polyphony of a dying visionary.

A second and related narrative/political strategy is a reworking of traditional relationships among writer, text, and reader. The stories collected in *Tell Me a Riddle* subvert the concept of textual ownership, affirming the reader not as an object but, reciprocally, as another subject. Many dominant discursive practices still take for granted that the act of reading will be a subjection to a fixed meaning, a passive receiving of what Bakhtin terms "monologue." In Bakhtin's view of monological discourse, the writer directly addresses the readers, attempting to anticipate their responses and deflect their objections; meanings are seen as delivered, unchanged, from source to recipient. In Bakhtin's terms, monologue is "deaf to the other's response; it does not await it and does not grant it any *decisive* force" (cited in Todorov 107).

Heteroglossic discourse, on the other hand, acknowledges "that there exists outside of it another consciousness, with the same rights, and capable of responding on an equal footing, another and equal *I*" (107). *Tell Me a Riddle*'s heteroglossia acknowledges the other consciousnesses that exist outside the text. As Meese indicates about similar strategies in *Silences, Tell Me a Riddle* activates its reader-subjects while subverting authorial domination; in the tradition of Bertolt Brecht's theater and Jean-Luc Godard's cinematic montage, it turns writer and readers into collaborators.

The two categories of Olsen's narrative/political strategy I have identified—her recording of heteroglossia and her reworking of relationships
among writer, text, and reader—constitute this essay's two major divisions.

In *Tell Me a Riddle*'s first story, "I Stand Here Ironing," Olsen begins her
recording of heteroglossia by exploring problems that fragment lives and
discourse and by experimenting with narrative forms that display that fragmentation. Emily, the daughter of the unnamed narrator, had been born into "the
pre-relief, pre-WPA world of the depression," and her father, no longer able
to "endure . . . sharing want" with the nineteen-year-old mother and child,
had left them when Emily was eight months old (10). The infant "was a
miracle to me," the narrator recalls, but when she had to work, she had no
choice but to leave Emily with "the woman downstairs to whom she was no
miracle at all" (10). This arrangement grieved both mother and child: "I
would start running as soon as I got off the streetcar, running up the stairs,"
the narrator remembers, and "when she saw me she would break into a
clogged weeping that could not be comforted, a weeping I can hear yet" (10–
11). Then came months of complete separation, while the child lived with
relatives. The price for reunion was Emily's spending days at "the kinds of
nurseries that [were] only parking places for children. . . . It was the only
place there was. It was the only way we could be together, the only way I
could hold a job" (11). Their situation improved with the presence of "a new
daddy" (12). Although the narrator still worked at wage-earning jobs, she was
more relaxed with her younger children than she had been with Emily: "it was
the face of joy, and not of care or tightness or worry I turned to them." But,
the narrator adds, by then it was "too late for Emily" (12).

The narrative is laced with references to the pressure of circumstance, the
limits on choice: "when is there time?"; "what cannot be helped" (9); "it was
the only way" (11); "We were poor and could not afford for her the soil of
easy growth" (20); "She is the child of her age, of depression, of war, of fear"
(20). Both mother and daughter have been damaged: while Emily expresses
fear and despair casually ("we'll all be atom-dead"), her mother suffers because "all that is in her [Emily] will not bloom" (20). All the narrator asks for
Emily is "enough left to live by" and the consciousness that "she is more than
this dress on the ironing board, helpless before the iron" (21).

The story includes two major discursive forms. The form that appears
through most of the story is indirect, circling, uncertain; it is heteroglossic.
The other form, which Olsen points out and discards in one paragraph near
the story's end, is direct, clipped, and assertive.[1] It is a version of the reductive dominant discourse contributing to the pressure of the circumstances in
which Emily and her mother struggle to survive. With these two forms of
discourse Olsen introduces issues that concern her in all the stories in *Tell Me
a Riddle:* language as power; dominant versus subversive modes of discourse;
heteroglossia.

The second major discursive form, the direct, is introduced by the narrator of "I Stand Here Ironing" in this way: "I will never total it all. I will

never come in to say: She was a child seldom smiled at. Her father left me before she was a year old. I had to work her first six years when there was work, or I sent her home and to his relatives. There were years she had care she hated" (20). What the narrator offers here is what she will not say and what she will not do. She will not "total"—sum up—Emily's life in a direct, linear, cause-and-effect way.

The other major discursive form—with its many modes of indirectness, false starts, and uncertainties—is signaled in the form of address at the beginning of the story. The narrator says, "I stand here ironing, and what you asked me moves tormented back and forth with the iron" (9). This "you" (never clearly identified, but likely one of Emily's high school teachers, a guidance counselor, or a social worker) is the ostensible audience to whom the narrator's discourse is directed. However, in this most indirect form of address, the entire story takes place in the mind of the narrator, who is speaking to herself as though rehearsing her discourse for the "you." We do not know whether this discourse ever passes from the silence of the mother's mind to the hearing of the audience (the teacher or counselor) for whom it is being rehearsed.

The narrator's discourse is persistently marked by indirectness, false starts, and uncertainties—the forms on which the narrator must rely as she looks back over her life with Emily: "Why do I put that first? I do not even know if it matters, or if it explains anything" (10); "In this and other ways she leaves her seal, I say aloud. And startle at my saying it. What do I mean? What did I start to gather together, to try and make coherent?" (18). These fitful "digressions" typify the movement of the story's first major discursive form. The user of that form, far from reducing her subjects to linear, cause-and-effect patterns, displays in multifaceted discourse her own complicated and ultimately irreducible forms of interdependence with her subjects. The form is heteroglossic; it is a "voice" made of many voices: caught in the memory of conflicts between Emily and her sister, Susan, "each one human, needing, demanding, hurting, taking," the mother says, "Susan telling jokes and riddles to company for applause while Emily sat silent (to say to me later; that was *my* riddle, Mother, I told it to Susan)" (16–17). As employed in this and other stories in the collection, heteroglossia is not solely a matter of multiple voices within or among cultures or subcultures; it is often the multiple and conflicting voices that make up one person. Olsen's displays of individual heteroglossia, the fragmenting of voices constituting a self and that self's interdependence with others, become one means by which her work offers alternatives to bourgeois individualism.

At the beginning of the story, the words of the unidentified teacher or counselor and the mother's reaction to those words create a complex intermingling of voices. The mother has been asked to assist in helping Emily: " 'I wish you would manage the time to come in and talk with me about your daughter. I'm sure you can help me understand her. She's a youngster who needs help and whom I'm deeply interested in helping.' " The next line of the story is " 'Who needs help.' " . . ." (9; ellipsis Olsen's). Who indeed? This entangling of the helpers and the helped, including the suggestion that the mother is being asked for the very aid she herself may need in order to assist Emily, is indicative of the ways in which the narrator's thinking and discourse proceed. She cannot, in language, fully demarcate herself from Emily or from those whose lives became entangled with Emily's in the past, such as an unsympathetic nursery school teacher: "And even without knowing, I knew. I knew the teacher that was evil because all these years it has curdled into my memory, the little boy hunched in the corner, her rasp, 'why aren't you outside, because Alvin hits you? that's no reason, go out, scaredy' " (11). Facing the incessant pressure of time and circumstance—"And when is there time to remember, to sift, to weigh, to estimate, to total?"—the narrator recognizes that multiple voices and memories constantly threaten to engulf her (9).

The nonlinear mode of discourse is so often replete with complexity of meaning that it risks falling into meaninglessness and the equivalent of silence. In this story that risk is most acute at moments when the mother cannot find the language to respond to Emily. While looking back over her life with Emily, the mother returns to times when she could respond to her daughter with nothing more than silence.

> There was a boy she loved painfully through two school semesters. Months later she told me how she had taken pennies from my purse to buy him candy. "Licorice was his favorite and I bought him some every day, but he still liked Jennifer better'n me. Why, Mommy?" The kind of question for which there is no answer (15–16).

On the night in which this story takes place the mother is remembering such details of Emily's life and instances of failed communication between mother and daughter. The cumulative details from the various stages of Emily's life and the crowding of voices force the narrator to say near the story's end: "because I have been dredging the past, and all that compounds a human being is so heavy and meaningful in me, I cannot bear it tonight" (20). A richness of meaning approximating meaninglessness and the equivalent of silence weighs on the mother when she says of Emily, "This is one of her communicative nights and she tells me everything and nothing as she fixes herself a plate of food" (19). Yet for the narrator a reliance on nonlinear discourse with its attendant hazards is not only a matter of what her circumstances have forced upon her. It is also a matter of choice.

The narrator must use nonlinear heteroglossic modes if her goal in telling Emily's story is, as she says it is, to "Let her [Emily] be." The complicated, conflicting stuff of which human beings are made can be discussed only nonreductively in nonlinear discourse, in a manner that has some chance of "letting them be." To adopt the dominant, linear, reductive mode of discourse is to usurp and control Emily, and it is to abandon the hope with which the story ends: the narrator's hope that Emily will know "that she is more than this dress on the ironing board, helpless before the iron" (20).

The two major discursive forms in "I Stand Here Ironing"—the indirect, uncertain, circling form, and the direct, clipped, assertive form—appear again in "Tell Me a Riddle," and, again, Olsen uses them to explore language as power; dominant versus subversive modes of discourse; and heteroglossia. The story begins with a battle between Eva and David, who have been married for 47 years, most of them spent in poverty. In the dialect of Russian-Jewish immigrants, they bitterly dispute whether to sell their home and move to a retirement cooperative operated by David's union. He craves company while Eva, after raising seven children, will not "exchange her solitude for anything. *Never again to be forced to move to the rhythms of others*" (76). David and Eva use a not-always-direct, but relentlessly assertive, and minimal form of discourse in their perpetual quarreling. We find that mode of discourse in their opening fray:

> "What do we need all this for?" he would ask loudly, for her hearing aid was turned down and the vacuum was shrilling. "Five rooms" (pushing the sofa so she could get into the corner) "furniture" (smoothing down the rug) "floors and surfaces to make work. Tell me why do we need it?" And he was glad he could ask in a scream.
> "Because I'm use't."
> "Because you're use't. This is a reason, Mrs. Word Miser? Used to can get unused!" (73).

They poke at each other with as few words as possible, using words not as instruments of communication but as weapons of combat and control. Further, each uses any available means to suppress the other's minimal discourse. She turns down her hearing aid and turns on the vacuum cleaner. He turns on the television "loud so he need not hear" (75).

The text only gradually reveals Eva's long-ago status as a revolutionary orator; only through fragments of dialogue and interior monologue do we learn that this obdurate, rancorous woman, who now wields power only by turning down her hearing aid, was once an orator in the 1905 Russian revolution. Models for Eva's revolutionary commitment included that of Olsen's own mother, Ida Lerner. Another was Seevya Dinkin, who shares "Riddle" 's dedication with Genya Gorelick.[2]

"Tell Me a Riddle" illuminates, as no polemic could, the terrible cost of a sexual division of labor. David, who has worked outside the home, has sustained a vitality and sociability. But he has lost the "holiest dreams" he and Eva shared in their radical youth, seems to accept American "progress," and would rather consume TV's version of "This Is Your Life" than reflect on his own (119; 83). Insulated at home, Eva has felt less pressure to assimilate, to compromise her values, and has preserved those dreams. But the many years of 18-hour days, of performing domestic tasks "with the desperate ingenuity of poverty" (years in which David "never scraped a carrot") have transformed her youthful capacity for engagement into a terrible need for solitude (Rosenfelt, "Divided" 19; *TMR* 74).

As Eva is dying she slips into the indirect discursive mode. After years of bitter silence, she begins to speak, sing, and recite incessantly. Fragments of memories and voices, suppressed during her years of marriage and motherhood, emerge as the old woman nears death. Eva, like the mother in "I Stand

Here Ironing," becomes an individual embodiment of heteroglossia. Eva had announced her desire for solitude, but ironically she returns in her reverie to the time when she was engaged with others in a revolutionary movement. She sings revolutionary songs from her youth and in a "gossamer" voice whispers fragments of speeches she had delivered in "a girl's voice of eloquence" half a century before (119). Her babble is a communal one; she becomes a vehicle for many voices.

Eva's experiences while dying may have been partly modeled on those of Ida Lerner. "In the winter of 1955," Olsen reports in *Mother to Daughter, Daughter to Mother,* "in her last weeks of life, my mother—so much of whose waking life had been a nightmare, that common everyday nightmare of hardship, limitation, longing; of baffling struggle to raise six children in a world hostile to human unfolding—my mother, dying of cancer, had beautiful dream-visions—in color." She envisioned three wise men, "magnificent in jewelled robes" of crimson, gold, and royal blue. The wise men asked to talk to her "of whys, of wisdom," but as they began to talk, "*she saw that they were not men, but women: That they were not dressed in jewelled robes, but in the coarse everyday shifts and shawls of the old country women of her childhood, their feet wrapped round and round with rags for lack of boots. . . .* And now it was many women, a babble" (261, 262). Together, the women sing a lullaby.

Like Ida Lerner, on her deathbed Eva becomes the human equivalent of a heteroglossic carnival site.

> *One by one they [the thousand various faces of age] streamed by and imprinted on her—and though the savage zest of their singing came voicelessly soft and distant, the faces still roared—the faces densened the air—chorded into*
>
> children-chants, mother-croons, singing of the chained love serenades, Beethoven storms, mad Lucia's scream, drunken joy-songs, keens for the dead, work-singing. . . (106).

Olsen blurs the distinction between high and popular culture in the diversity of cultural forms that sustain Eva: her beloved Chekhov, Balzac, Victor Hugo; Russian love songs; revolutionary songs; a "community sing" for elderly immigrants; and *Pan del Muerto,* a folk-art cookie for a dead child.

The barrage of voices and references that constitute Eva at her death return us to the danger I referred to in discussing "I Stand Here Ironing"— that multivocal, heteroglossic discourse may result in the equivalent of silence. Despite the danger, heteroglossia's cacophony, is preferable to the dominant discourse's reductive forms. As for Emily in "I Stand Here Ironing," what will "let Eva be" is heteroglossia. After years of living in silence and near silence, Eva emerges in heteroglossia. Yet in both stories the richness of meaning released in Emily's and Eva's heteroglossic utterances threaten to result in the equivalent of silence.

In *Tell Me a Riddle* mimicry provides examples of subversive, indirect modes of discourse jousting with dominant monolithic modes; however, in mimicry Olsen finds the occasion to examine hazards in marginalized discourse's competing with the dominant discourse. Like other forms of parody, mimicry comprises a powerful form of heteroglossia. Aimed against an official or monologic language, mimicry divides that system against itself. However, mimicry's ability to oppress the oppressor may be a snare for the mimic. To make her mother laugh, or out of the despair she felt about her isolation in the world, Emily, in "I Stand Here Ironing," imitates people and incidents from her school day. Eventually her gift for mimicry, pantomime, and comedy lead to first prize in her high school amateur show and requests to perform at other schools, colleges, and city- and state-wide competitions. However, her talent and achievement do not remedy her isolation: "Now suddenly she was Somebody, and as imprisoned in her difference as she had been in anonymity" (19). By exercising her parodic talent, Emily unwittingly exchanges one form of marginalization for another.

Like Emily, Whitey in "Hey Sailor, What Ship?" has a knack for mimicry, which he exhibits, for example, when telling Lennie about the union official who fined him: "(His [Whitey's] old fine talent for mimicry jutting through the blurred-together words)" (44). Whitey, a seaman being destroyed by alcoholism, is no less isolated than Emily in "I Stand Here Ironing." Lennie and Helen, who have been Whitey's friends and political comrades for years (Whitey saved Lennie's life during the 1934 Maritime Strike), and their three daughters are his only friends—indeed, the only people he can "be around . . . without having to pay" (43).[3]

Mimicry deals Whitey a fate similar to Emily's. However, an irony of "Hey Sailor, What Ship?" is that it is mimicry of the mimic, Whitey, that contributes to Whitey's fate. The family engages in an affectionate mimicking of the salty language that sets Whitey apart from their other acquaintances:

> Watch the language, Whitey, there's a gentleman present, says Helen. Finish your plate, Allie.
> [Whitey:] Thass right. Know who the gen'lmun is? I'm the gen'lmun. The world, says Marx, is divided into two classes. . . . [ellipsis Olsen's].
> Seafaring gen'lmun and shoreside bastards, choruses Lennie with him.
> Why, Daddy! says Jeannie.
> You're a mean ole bassard father, says Allie.
> Thass right, tell him off, urges Whitey. Hell with waitin' for glasses. Down the ol' hatch.
> *My* class is divided by marks, says Carol, giggling helplessly at her own joke, and anyway what about ladies? Where's *my* drink? Down the hatch (35).

Thus mimicry functions in "Hey Sailor, What Ship?" as one form that entices Whitey out of isolation and into the family, while simultaneously diminishing the importance of Whitey as "other." The behavior of the family in relation to Whitey, despite what seems to be their shared political beliefs and practice, becomes a microcosm for the dominant culture's behavior in relation to much marginalized discourse. Charmed by difference (the history of music in U.S. popular culture exemplifies the point), the mainstream culture co-opts the marginalized discourse, stripping it of its power as "difference," and diminishes its force in a process of homogenization. Olsen's references to mimicry in these stories comprise part of her running commentary on the power of dominant and subversive modes of discourse and the complications of identity that marginalized people and their discourses face.

In addition to mimicry, "Hey Sailor, What Ship?", like other stories collected in *Tell Me a Riddle,* manifests heteroglossia by incorporating genres that "further intensify its speech diversity in fresh ways" (Bakhtin, *Dialogic* 321). Although this strategy is not uncommon among fiction writers, Olsen employs it more than many. In "Hey Sailor, What Ship?" Olsen has inserted a valediction (because the story is a farewell to Whitey, this insertion becomes a valediction within a valediction). Whitey learned it as a boy from his first shipmate, and one of the children asks him to recite it. Originally delivered in 1896 by the Phillipine hero Jose Rizal before he was executed, it concludes:

> Little will matter, my country,
> That thou shouldst forget me.
> I shall be speech in thy ears, fragrance and color,
> Light and shout and loved song. . . .
>
> Where I go are no tyrants. . . (42).

Jose Rizal would have been an insurgent against both Spanish and American domination of the Philippines, and the recitation implicitly condemns American imperialism and the Cold War, at its height when Olsen wrote "Hey Sailor, What Ship?"

Whitey's recitation also eulogizes his (and Olsen's) youthful hopes for a socialist America, which have been snuffed out by Cold War strategists:

> Land I adore, farewell. . . .
> Our forfeited garden of Eden. . . .
>
> Vision I followed from afar,
> Desire that spurred on and consumed me,
> Beautiful it is to fall,
> That the vision may rise to fulfillment (41).

Moreover, the valediction associates Whitey, who has been destroyed as much by "*the death of the brotherhood*" as by alcoholism, with political martyrdom. Whitey, who has attempted to keep '30s militancy alive in a period of political reaction, feels estranged from the complacent younger seamen. "These kids," he complains to Lennie, "don't realize how we got what we got. Beginnin' to lose it, too." One "kid," who had overtime coming to him, "didn't even wanta beef about it" (44). As the ship's delegate, Whitey nevertheless took the grievance to the union, which had become a conservative, alien bureaucracy, and was fined for "not taking it [the grievance] up through proper channels" (44). The younger seamen also lack the sense of solidarity Whitey and Lennie experienced during the '30s: " 'Think anybody backed me up, Len?' . . . *Once, once an injury to one is an injury to all. Once, once they had to live for each other. And whoever came off the ship fat shared, because that was the only way of survival for all of them. . . . Now it was a dwindling few. . ."* (45). And, finally, because Whitey's efforts to stay sober have consistently failed and his health is rapidly deteriorating, Jose Rizal's valediction also functions as his own farewell address.

Yet there is a dimension to Whitey that cannot be explained in political or economic terms. Even in his youth, when both he and the Left were robust, Whitey was tormented by an emotional disorder that manifested itself in an inability to have sexual relations except when *"high with drink."* Many years later, at "the drunken end of his eight-months-sober try," Lennie and Helen hear a "torn-out-of-him confession" that the psychosexual problem persists, and likely, it will remain a riddle (44, 46). The story ends with its plaintive refrain—"Hey Sailor, what ship?"—which mourns the tragic waste of Whitey's life as well as suggests the disorientation, diminished options, and uncertainty of radicals in a period of right-wing ascendancy.

Both Whitey and Emily exemplify dangers in heteroglossic, subversive modes of discourse. Emily's and Whitey's individual talent allows each of them to joust with the dominant discourse. However, those individual talents, unlinked to other heteroglossic voices also intent upon jabbing at the dominant discourse, leave both Emily and Whitey without the supporting network of similar subversive voices. Without that support, they experience the dominant discourse's subsuming power and are returned to marginalized positions and forms of silence.

Mimicry and the two major forms of discourse—the direct and the indirect, and the risk that the cacophony of multivocal discourse may result in the equivalent of silence—play major roles in "O Yes." Helen, Lennie, and their daughters appear again in this story about the difficulty of sustaining a friendship across racial lines. Lennie and Helen's 12-year-old, Carol, is white; Parialee, her neighbor and closest friend from their earliest years, is African-American. "O Yes," which begins with Helen and Carol's attending Parialee's baptismal service, is permeable to the speech of "others"—songs by three church choirs; parishioners' shouts; Parialee's newly learned jivetalk; and Alva's African-American dialect. Carol, who has never before experienced the intense emotionalism that erupts during the service (chanting, shrieking, fainting), is a stranger in the world of an all-African-American congregation. Trapped in heteroglossia's cacophony, Carol falls into the silence of a near faint, and once again, an abundance of meaning approaches silence.

Yet, in the first of the story's two parts, a far more reductive and controlling mode of discourse—a form of "dialogue" that is both assertion and affirmation—presents itself as a counter to heteroglossia. In the dialogue's highly structured environment, the preacher takes the lead by making assertions that the congregation affirms. The dialogue includes the preacher's words, such as "And God is Powerful," and the congregation's response, *"O Yes"* and "I am so glad" (52, 54). The reductive and controlling mode of discourse in which the assertions are assigned to the figure of power, the preacher, and the affirmations to his followers, the congregation, replicates the structure of society outside the church. Exercising their role in the dialogue, the parishoners seem to be playing out the subservient parts African-Americans have so often been assigned within the society. Yet, within the church, heteroglossia persistently strains against the constraining mode of discourse. In "O Yes," as throughout *Tell Me a Riddle,* two major discursive forms—heteroglossia and, in this case, the countering assertion/affirmation dialogue—vie for power.

A complicated version of mimicry is prominent in "O Yes." What I identified earlier as a conventional assertion/affirmation structure placed in the midst of a swirling heteroglossia contains complex elements of a form of mimicry in which the preacher and congregation wittingly or unwittingly dramatize the roles of dominant and marginalized people, oppressor and oppressed. As the drama of the dialogue intensifies, it threatens to overpower heteroglossia by reducing it to the near-monological assertion/affirmation exchanges between a leader and followers. Much of that drama takes place in the sermon delivered at Parialee's baptismal service. The narrator tells us that the subject of the sermon is "the Nature of God. How God is long-suffering. Oh, how long he has suffered" (51). The narrator has shown us a version of the classic Christian mystery of incarnation: God as the maker of human beings who suffer and God as the human victim of suffering. This dual role of perpetrator and victim becomes central to the sermon-response's dialogic structure. Early in the sermon the preacher chants, "And God is Powerful," to which the congregation responds *"O Yes"* (52). Here, again, we find an assertion/affirmation structure in which the preacher assumes the lead in the dialogue by making assertions that the congregation, in its role as follower, responds to by affirming.

Other dimensions of the dialogue quickly emerge. The preacher, working the theme of the great judgment day, blows an imaginary trumpet and announces: "And the horn wakes up Adam, and Adam runs to wake up Eve, and Eve moans; Just one more minute, let me sleep, and Adam yells, Great Day, woman, don't you know it's the Great Day?" (53). The basic assertion/affirmation structure is still operating, but within that structure the preacher in godlike fashion now creates characters who in turn engage in their own dialogues. The scene becomes increasingly heteroglossic. Immediately after the created Adam's rousing call to a sleeping Eve ("Great Day, woman, don't you know it's the Great Day?"), one of the choirs responds, *"Great Day, Great Day"* (53). Is the choir responding to the voice of the created Adam or to the preacher? The answer is of little consequence. What is important here is that the structure of the assertion/affirmation dialogue has dictated conditions that the congregation follows. Whichever "leader," real or imaginary, they respond to in the course of the sermon, they persistently replicate their role as affirmers of the leader's assertion. Thus what emerges from this heteroglossic scene is a powerful counter to heteroglossia, a discursive structure that imposes unity and control by locking participants into predetermined traditional roles.

The force for unity within heteroglossia intensifies as the imaginary dimension of the dialogue escalates. The preacher moves from assertions about God and the creation of characters such as Adam and Eve to assuming the role of God, and with that move the form of his discourse shifts from assertion/affirmation to promise/affirmation. Having just asserted the multiple roles of God in relation to human beings (friend, father, way maker, door opener), the preacher proclaims: "I will put my Word in you and it is power. I will put my Truth in you and it is power." The response is "*O Yes*" (55). Soon after, the narrator says, "Powerful throbbing voices. Calling and answering to each other" (56). The narrator captures the vibrant force of the unity within heteroglossia when she says, "A single exultant lunge of shriek"(56).

What are we to make of this univocalizing of heteroglossia? The sexual implications that have been accumulating in this scene and that culminate in the orgasmic "single exultant lunge of shriek" invite an instructive digression into Mae Gwendolyn Henderson's discussion of an orgasmic "howl" in Toni Morrison's *Sula*. Henderson, who skillfully employs Bakhtinian analysis, observes of Sula's orgasmic cry: "The howl, signifying a prediscursive mode, thus becomes an act of self-reconstitution as well as an act of subversion or resistance to the 'network of signification' represented by the symbolic order. The 'high silence of orgasm' and the howl allow temporary retreats from or breaks in the dominant discourse" (33). The "single exultant lunge of shriek" has very similar functions in the church scene in "O Yes." The parishioners have repeatedly experienced the intense repetition of the constraining assertion/affirmation and promise/affirmation structures that mimic the dominant discourse of power to which the congregation members are subjected outside the church. The shriek becomes an act of "self-reconstitution" and, at the same time, a "subversion or resistance to the 'network of signification' " that constrains the parishioners.

Henderson argues persuasively that Sula's orgasmic howl occurs at the moment at which she is located "outside of the dominant discursive order" but also when she is poised to reenter and disrupt the discursive order. For Henderson, Sula's howl becomes a primary metaphor for African-American women writers whose objective is not "to move from margin to center, but to remain on the borders of discourse, speaking from the vantage point of the insider/outsider" (33, 36). This point of difficult balance is, I suggest, where Olsen places the African-American congregation at the moment of the "single exultant lunge of shriek."

But what more is there in the story to justify such a reading of this univocalizing of heteroglossia? Alva, Parialee's mother, will give us some indications. After Carol's near-faint, Alva blames herself for not having been more attentive to Carol's being brought into a situation she had no basis for understanding. Attempting to explain the situation to Carol after the fact, Alva says, " 'You not used to people letting go that way. . . . You not used to hearing what people keeps inside, Carol. You know how music can make you feel things? Glad or sad or like you can't sit still? That was religion music, Carol.' " Speaking of the congregation Alva says, " 'And they're home Carol, church is home. Maybe the only place they can feel how they feel and maybe let it come out. So they can go on. And it's all right' " (59–60). So we seem to have our answer. The univocalizing of heteroglossia is a shared singular escape of people who are trapped in multiple ways. They seem to choose to surrender the heteroglossia of their suffering to the univocal escape of the church/home. But is it "all right"?

The story's first section ends with an italicized rendering of what Alva did not say to Carol. This reverie—which remains silent, unspoken to Carol—stands as a response (like the earlier italicized responses of the congregation and the choirs) to an earlier series of the preacher's assertions. Earlier in the sermon the preacher proclaims: "He was your mother's rock. You father's mighty tower. And he gave us a little baby. A little baby to love." The congregation responds: "*I am so glad*" (54). Alva's silent reverie begins:

> *When I was carrying Parry and her father left me, and I fifteen years old, one thousand miles away from home, sin-sick and never really believing, as still I don't believe all, scorning, for what have it done to help, waiting there in the clinic and maybe sleeping, a voice called: Alva, Alva. So mournful and so sweet: Alva. Fear not, I have loved you from the foundation of the universe* (61).

Alva follows the voice "*into a world of light, multitudes singing,*" and the reverie ends: "*Free, free, I am so glad*" (61). The reverie's mixture of dream and reality parallels the mixture of the imaginary and the real in the sermon situation and seems to stand as Alva's singular response (not an affirmation) to the preacher's assertions in the sermon. But this is not a completely singular response, and it is not totally devoid of affirmation. When Alva acknowledges, "still I don't believe all," she locates herself, like Henderson's African-American female writer, both within and outside the church, inside yet resisting the univocality, outside yet resisting the conflation of the imaginary and the real. But we must remember that this is what Alva does *not* say to Carol, or to Helen, or as far as we know to anyone other than us. What is the force that creates this silence? Is it the circumstances of Alva's daily life? Is it the church?

We cannot begin to answer these questions without looking at the structure of the second part of the story. Just as Alva's reverie functions as a response to the sermon, the second part of the story stands as a response to the first part. In the second part, which takes place in the world of Helen and Len (or Lennie) and their daughters, Carol and Jeannie, a univocalizing force parallels that of the church in part one. In the second part the force against heteroglossia is the junior high school, which officially and unofficially attempts to separate Carol and Parialee, univocalizing Carol and other white students while shutting out Parialee and other African-American students. Because she is African-American, Parialee will not be tracked into Carol's accelerated classes; and even if she were initially admitted to them, the necessity to care for younger siblings while her mother works the four-to-twelve-thirty night shift would quickly put her behind in her studies. Carol is "college prep," whereas Parialee will likely not finish junior high, predicts Jeannie, a 17-year-old veteran of the public school system. According to Jeannie, "you have to watch everything, what you wear and how you wear it and who you eat lunch with and how much homework you do and how you act to the teacher and what you laugh at. . . . [ellipsis Olsen's] And run with your crowd" (63). Peer pressure is tremendous, and Carol and Parialee would be ostracized for attempting to be friends. Jeannie contrasts their "for real" working-class school with one in a nearby affluent neighborhood where it is fashionable for whites and African-Americans to be "buddies": ". . . three coloured kids and their father's a doctor or judge or something big wheel and one always gets elected President or head song girl or something to prove oh how we're democratic" (65).

The junior high school has its parallel to the preacher—the teacher, Miss Campbell (nicknamed "Rockface")—and in this parallel Olsen further suggests dangers in the monologic impulses within the church's heteroglossia. Godlike in the junior high school kingdom, the bigoted teacher has the power to decide whether Parialee can be trusted to take Carol's homework assignments to her when Carol has the mumps: "Does your mother work for Carol's mother?" Rockface asks Parialee. "Oh, you're neighbors! Very well, I'll send along a monitor to open Carol's locker but you're only to take these things I'm writing down, nothing else" (67). Like the preacher, Rockface has the power to make Parialee respond. In drill-master fashion, Rockface insists: "Now say after me: Miss Campbell is trusting me to be a good responsible girl. And go right to Carol's house. . . . Not stop anywhere on the way. Not lose anything. And only take. What's written on the list" (67). However, we know of this not because Parialee told Carol. The account of Rockface appears in a passage that parallels Alva's reverie—what she did not say to Carol. The passage in which Parialee accounts for Rockface appears in a section in which she has been talking to Carol, but the Rockface passage begins: *"But did not tell."* The knowledge we have of Rockface from Parialee is, like the knowledge we have of Alva's inner world, one more silence in Carol's world.

What are we to make of this chilling structural parallel between the worlds of the dominant and the marginalized, the oppressor and the oppressed? Certainly we must hear Olsen's warning that the marginalized imperil their identities by replicating, even through mimicry, structures of the dominant discourse. The African-American congregation risks imposing on itself the dominant culture's reductive and oppressive structures. But has the congregation yet succumbed? Perhaps not. Perhaps they as a collective, unlike the individuals Emily and Whitey, keep their identities apart from what they mimic (or in Whitey's case, what mimics him). Perhaps insofar as the assertion/affirmation structure (so dangerously reminiscent of the dominant discourse's reductive structures) remains embedded in a cacophonous atmosphere of heteroglossia, it remains a viable form of mimicry, and the African-American church maintains a delicate ecology of inside/outside with alternative structures and voices constantly checking and offsetting the structures of an oppressive discourse. Certainly the scene within the church approximates what Bakhtin identifies as heteroglossia in its fullest play—carnival—in which people's multiple voices play in, around, and against the dominant culture's hierarchical structures. Perhaps insofar as the African-American church remains a world about which Alva can say, "still I don't believe all," a world where she can be simultaneously inside and outside, it remains a dynamic social unit capable of resisting its own oppressive impulses.

Those readers who are strangers to the powerful culture of the African-American church cannot be sure how to assess that world and, like Carol, experience an abundance of meaning that approaches silence. In fact, Carol is a very useful point of reference for Olsen's readers. The story is a tangled web of explanations Carol never hears about historical circumstances that have enmeshed her. Carol hears neither Alva's reverie, which partly explains the phenomenon in the church, nor Parialee's account of Rockface. Further, as the story nears its end, Carol in desperation asks Helen a basic question, openly pleading for a response: " 'Mother, why did they sing and scream like that? At Parry's church?' " But in place of a response we find:

> *Emotion,* Helen thought of explaining, *a characteristic of the religion of all oppressed peoples, yes your very own great-grandparents*—thought of saying. And discarded.
> *Aren't you now, haven't you had feelings in yourself so strong they had to come out some way?* ("what howls restrained by decorum")—thought of saying. And discarded.
> Repeat Alva: *hope . . . every word out of their own life. A place to let go. And church is home.* And discarded.
> *The special history of the Negro people—history?—just you try living what must be lived every day*—thought of saying. And discarded.
> And said nothing (70).

Once more, Carol is met with silence.

We as readers may, like Carol, expect answers to our many questions about the disjunctures and potential connections among the lives and worlds of the story's characters. But Olsen, no more than Helen, supplies definitive answers. We are privileged to hear more than Carol hears, but Olsen does not answer our questions about how the lives and worlds might be connected. Is Helen's silence at the end of "O Yes" a failure in relation to her daughter? Is Olsen's silence in relation to us a failure of authorial responsibility?

To address these questions I turn to my discussion's second major division, Olsen's reworking of relationships among writer, text, and reader. Helen's silence provides insight into Olsen's designs on us as readers and our relationships to issues of dominant and marginalized people and their discourses. To return to Meese's previously cited observation, Olsen repeatedly "calls upon the reader to write the text—no longer her text, but occasioned by it and by the voices speaking through it" (110). Helen thinks but does not say: "*Better immersion than to live untouched*" (71). Structured immersion is what Olsen plans for us. Olsen demands that we not be passive receptors, but that we, in Bakhtinian terms, join in the heteroglossia. Olsen has skillfully structured textual gaps and developed strategies for readers' identifying with characters—structures and strategies that require readers to contribute to the emergence of heteroglossic meaning. In those gaps and moments of identification we are not given free rein as readers, but we are asked to act responsibly as members of a complex human community.

To observe Olsen's craft in teasing out our active participation, I return first to "Tell Me a Riddle." Eva craves solitude: *"Never again to be forced to move to the rhythms of others"* (76). And she is tired of the talk: " 'All my life around babblers. Enough!' " (82). Eva exercises her greatest control and feels triumphant when she manages to gain and maintain periods of silence. Olsen has given us a difficult kind of central character, one whose fierce desire for the silence she believes she has earned resists the telling of her story. We, as audience, are caught in the uncomfortable position of hearing the story of someone who wants her story left in silence. We are interlopers. We, like David, violate Eva's solitude and silence, and the narrator, seemingly torn between telling the story and honoring Eva's longing for silence, contributes to our discomfort.

The story's title and the presence of the phrase "tell me a riddle" in the story itself indicate sources of our uneasiness. In the story, the phrase "tell me a riddle" appears in the context of the "command performance." On the visit to daughter Vivi's, a visit Eva felt forced to make when she really wanted to go home, the narrator tells us very nearly from Eva's own perspective: "Attentive with the older children; sat through their performances (command performance; we command you to be the audience) . . ." (94). Here the traditional notion of "command performance" is reversed. It is not the performer who enacts her role by command; it is the audience who performs its role by command. Eva is trapped. She is once again at the mercy of others' needs and desires.

In her role as command audience, Eva "watched the children whoop after their grandfather who knew how to tickle, chuck, lift, toss, do tricks, tell secrets, make jokes, match riddle for riddle" (94). She watched David interact with the grandchildren in the expected ways, in all the ways in which she would not: "(Tell me a riddle, Grammy. I know no riddles, child)" (94). Eva, the command audience, plays her attentive role up to a point, but she does not fully meet expectations. To the command, "Tell me a riddle," she responds with a form of her prized silence, thwarting conventional expectations about grandparent-grandchild interactions.

Conventional expectations about interactions between us as audience and Eva and her story are also thwarted. We cannot be merely passive listeners to Eva's story. Whereas monologic discourse is, again, as Bakhtin asserts, "deaf to the other's response," even the title, "Tell Me a Riddle," signals the necessity of our response. From the moment we read the title, we are told to act: "Tell Me a Riddle." We expect to hear a story, but we are told to tell a riddle. We, like Eva, are a command audience, and we, like Eva, find ourselves responding with our own versions of silence. We, the command audience, have been identified with Eva, the command audience, and with her desire for silence. Again, we are put in the uncomfortable situation of wanting to be silent listeners to the story of someone who wants her story left in silence.

Why should we be submitted to this discomfort? On one level we are put in this position because of the narrator's sympathy with Eva's desires. Eva's is a story that needs to be told, yet the narrator sympathizes with Eva's hunger for silence. The compromise for the narrator is to disrupt our complacency as audience. We will hear the story, but not on our terms: We will hear the story as a command audience. What better way to force us to realize the complexity of Eva's situation than to force us into a position resembling Eva's experience as command audience? But there is another reason for our discomfort. As in *Yonnondio* and *Silences,* Olsen disrupts our passivity, demanding that we as readers share responsibility for completing Eva's story.

But how do we exercise our responsibility? We have some clues in David's response to Eva. To David it seemed that for 70 years she had hidden an "infinitely microscopic" tape recorder within her, "trapping every song, every melody, every word read, heard, and spoken" (118). She had caught and was now releasing all the discourse around her: " 'you who called others babbler and cunningly saved your words' " (119). But the harsh realization for David was that "she was playing back only what said nothing of him, of the children, of their intimate life together" (118). For David, the air is now filled with sound; yet that sound is the equivalent of silence. To him the danger referred to in my discussion of "I Stand Here Ironing"—that multivocal, heteroglossic discourse may result in the equivalent of silence—has become reality.

However, here we have a new perspective on the danger. The danger lies not in the discourse but in the audience. Because David hears nothing of Eva's life with him, the sounds become meaningless. His is an individualistic, self-centered response. But, crucially, what are these sounds to us as command audience? We have experienced the discomfort of being listeners to the story of one who does not want her story told, but now, at the end of her life, she speaks. If we identify with David's individualistic perspective, we will not understand Eva; her sounds will be the equivalent of silence. However, if we value Eva's identification with all human kind, we are an audience for whom Eva's last words have meaning.

Olsen aids us in valuing Eva's links to all humankind. One of those aids is a resuscitated David with whom we are invited to identify once he has remembered what he had long forgotten. Finally, David comes to a partial understanding of Eva's last words. When she brokenly repeats part of a favorite quotation from Victor Hugo, David remembers it, too, reciting scornfully: " 'in the twentieth century ignorance will be dead, dogma will be dead, war will be dead, and for all humankind one country—of fulfillment'? Hah!" (120). But Eva's feverish cantata finally awakens in the old man memories of his own youthful visions:

> Without warning, the bereavement and betrayal he had sheltered—
> compounded through the years—hidden even from himself—revealed itself,
>> uncoiled,
>> released,
>> *sprung*
> and with it the monstrous shapes of what had actually happened in the
> century (120).

David realizes with sudden clarity the full price of his assimilation into America's "apolitical" mainstream: " 'Lost, how much I lost' " (121). He and Eva "had believed so beautifully, so . . . falsely?" (122; ellipsis Olsen's):

> "Aaah, children," he said out loud, "how we believed, how we belonged."
> And he yearned to package for each of the children, the grandchildren, for
> everyone, *that joyous certainty, that sense of mattering, of moving and being*
> *moved, of being one and indivisible with the great of the past, with all that*
> *freed, ennobled.* Package it, stand on corners, in front of stadiums and on
> crowded beaches, knock on doors, give it as a fabled gift (122).

David also realizes that Eva's revolutionary faith did not die with his: "*Still she believed?* 'Eva!' he whispered. 'Still you believed? You lived by it? These Things Shall Be?' " (123). This story's epigraph, "These Things Shall Be," is the title of an old socialist hymn expressing hope for a future just society. Another riddle, then, is the puzzle of revolutionary consciousness: under what circumstances does it develop, dissipate? How does it sustain itself when confronted by "monstrous shapes"—the rise of fascism, two world wars, the extermination of six million Jews, the threat of global extinction?

The second aid Olsen provides us in valuing Eva's ties to all humankind is Eva's granddaughter, Jeannie (the same Jeannie of "Hey Sailor, What Ship?" and "O Yes," now in her twenties), to whom the legacy of resistance is passed on. Jeannie, who works as a visiting nurse and has a special political and artistic sensibility, cares for Eva in the last weeks of her life. " 'Like Lisa she is, your Jeannie,' " Eva whispers to Lennie and Helen, referring to the revolutionary who taught Eva to read more than 50 years before. It is at the end of the passage in which Eva compares Jeannie to Lisa that Eva says, " 'All that happens, one must try to understand' " (112, 113).

Those words comprise Eva's hope for Jeannie and Olsen's most basic demand on us as active readers. Recognizing the persistent threat of being so flooded with meaning that we may be faced with meaninglessness and the equivalent of silence, we must persist in the attempt to understand. In that attempt we must recognize the dangers of the bourgeois individualism into which we, like David, are constantly tempted to retreat. Olsen provides structures, such as the command audience structure I have discussed, to force us out of our passive individualistic roles as readers and to invite us into a web of interconnected, heteroglossic roles.[4] If we accept the invitation, we must do more than value Eva's identification with all humankind: we must remember if we have forgotten (the model of David) or learn if we have never known (the model of Jeannie) the complicated histories of worlds like those in which Eva lived and struggled. At the least, we are required to do our part in keeping alive the historical circumstances of oppressive czarist Russia and the connections among all oppressed groups. Eva and Olsen require us to learn the very histories to which America's "apolitical" mainstream would have us remain oblivious. With Jeannie, we are challenged to carry on Eva's legacy of resistance.

Olsen provides one further aid in valuing Eva's links to all humankind, an aid not limited to the collection's final story. The subject of motherhood so prominent in "I Stand Here Ironing," "O Yes," and "Tell Me a Riddle" provides a crucial reference point for our accepting a heteroglossia linking all humankind. Olsen has rightly referred to motherhood "as an almost taboo area; the last refuge of sexism . . . the least understood" and "last explored, tormentingly complex *core* of women's oppression." At the same time, Olsen believes that motherhood is, potentially, a source of "transport" for women, moving them beyond some of the constraints of individualism.[5] Responsible for what Olsen terms "the maintenance of life," mothers are often exposed to forms of heteroglossia, with their attendant benefits and hazards (*Silences* 34). In exploring the complexity of motherhood, Olsen renders versions of it that are "coiled, convoluted like an ear"—versions that may serve as models for the necessary hearing of heteroglossia.

I return to Helen's silence at the end of "O Yes." We can read Helen's silence as one of several textual comments on the limits of authority; indeed, it may have been through the experience of parenting that Olsen learned the limits of authorial control, which her texts so willingly concede. As an involved parent, one is forced to live intensely "in relation to," as the boundary between self and other is constantly negotiated. Such negotiating provides a model in which the ability to listen to constantly changing, heteroglossic voices is prized. When Carol asks, "why do I have to care?", the narrator tells us the following about Helen:

> Caressing, quieting.
> Thinking: *caring asks doing. It is a long baptism into the seas of human-kind, my daughter. Better immersion than to live untouched.* . . . [ellipsis Olsen's] *Yet how will you sustain?*
> *Why is it like it is?*
> Sheltering her daughter close, mourning the illusion of the embrace.
> *And why do I have to care?*
> While in her, her own need leapt and plunged for the place of strength that was not—where one could scream or sorrow while all knew and accepted, and gloved and loving hands waited to support and understand (71).

Although we risk being flooded by a multiplicity of meaning that approaches meaninglessness and the equivalent of silence, we as readers must submit to the "immersion," the "long baptism" that allows us to be the proper "ear" for the complexity of heteroglossia.

We have similar models at the end of "I Stand Here Ironing" and "Tell Me a Riddle." The mother listens to Emily on "one of her communicative nights . . . [when] she tells me everything and nothing" (19). The mother does not respond to Emily, but says to herself, to the teacher or counselor, and to us, "Let her be. So all that is in her will not bloom—but in how many does it? There is still enough left to live by" (20–21). In "Tell Me a Riddle" Jeannie, who has listened carefully to Eva's dying heteroglossia, is not actually a mother; but, like a mother, she is a caretaker, a nurturer, a listener.

However, Olsen asks more of us than listening. As Helen says to herself, *"caring asks doing."* In none of these models in *Tell Me a Riddle* is the mother figure a passive listener; rather, she is a listener responsive to heteroglossia. Even when multiple voices so overwhelm her that she is caught in silence (Emily's mother, Helen, Eva), she can sometimes caress or embrace, knowing the communicative power of such actions. As active readers, then, we are provided models of careful listening, leading to action. Olsen does not proscribe the field of political and social action that we as active readers might enter. However, she does demand that we work to understand the many voices of the oppressed. In "I Stand Here Ironing," the mother says of Emily, "Only help her to know," a command the dying Eva echoes: "All that happens, one must try to understand." These words comprise imperatives for us. And these mother figures, who live compassionately and interdependently in a multicultural and heteroglossic dynamic, become models for us as readers.

Olsen demands another, related form of action from her readers. In the collection, *Tell Me a Riddle,* we have been exposed to many moments in which characters sensitive to heteroglossia have been so inundated with complexity of meaning they have lapsed into silence. We have heard what the unnamed mother in "I Stand Here Ironing," Alva, Helen, and Eva have *not* been able to say to those most immediately connected to them. If the silence is perpetuated, these characters risk, as do Emily and Whitey, being subsumed by the dominant discourse. Olsen requires us, as readers of the complete collection, to hear the various oppressed voices and to make and articulate connections among them, connections the separate characters may not be able to see, or may only partially see. With such actions we become collaborators with Olsen in the democratizing enterprise of amplifying dominated and marginalized voices. We join her in a commitment to social change.

The "riddle" which Olsen's work challenges us to engage requires that we consider political activity not as something confined to a single class, party, gender, ethnic group, or cause, but as something undertaken within a kaleidoscopic social field and, simultaneously, within "the fibres of the self and in the hard practical substance of effective and continuing relationships" (Williams 212). Olsen's genuinely democratic content articulates itself in multivocal texts that prefigure postindividual cultural forms. In a sense, Olsen's sociopolitical vision has enabled her to write what cannot be written. *Tell Me a Riddle*'s form represents a *"pre-emergence,* active and pressing but not yet fully articulated, rather than the evident emergence which could be more confidently named" (Williams 126). With Virginia Woolf in "The Leaning Tower," Olsen's texts proclaim: "Literature is no one's private ground; literature is common ground" (125).

NOTES

1. For discussions of history of reading strategies and earlier defenses of indirect and figurational structures against schemes for linguistic reductionism, see Bartine.

2. In the edition of *Tell Me a Riddle* I have used for this essay, the title story is "for two of that generation, Seevya and Genya." In the 1989 edition, Olsen also dedicates

the story to her parents. Genya Gorelick had been a factory organizer in Morzyr, a famous orator, and the leading woman of the Jewish Workers' Alliance, the Bund of pre-revolutionary Russia. Her son, Al Richmond, has written about the role Gorelick played in the 1905 revolution, when she was just nineteen:

> . . . the 1905 revolution burst forth like the splendid realization of a dream, shaking the Czarist regime enough to loosen its most repressive restrictions, so that revolutionaries at last could address the public, not any more through the whispered word and the surreptitious leaflet but openly and directly in large assemblies. She discovered her gifts as a public orator. She was good, and in her best moments she was truly great (8; cited in Rosenfelt, "Divided" 19).

3. Olsen told me in an interview (11 July 1986, San Francisco) that she modeled Whitey partly on Filipino men she knew "in the movement" who hungered for contact with families at a time when U.S. immigration law kept Filipino women and children from entering the United States.

4. Patrocinio P. Schweickart outlines a promising model for reading based on a joining of reader-response theory and feminist theory. Her model contains some of the characteristics Olsen's writing demands of readers. Schweickart finds that feminist theory can move "beyond the individualistic models of [Wolfgang] Iser and of most reader-response critics" toward a "collective" model of reading. Describing the goal of that model, Schweickart observes that "the feminist reader hopes that other women will recognize themselves in her story, and join her in her struggle to transform the culture" (50, 51). It must be added that Olsen, like Schweikart, would have women and men "join her in her struggle to transform the culture."

5. *Silences* 202. For an enlightening discussion of *Tell Me a Riddle* in relation to other works dealing with motherhood, see Gardiner. Gardiner also suggests Jeannie's function as a model for readers when she notes that "at the end of the story, Jeannie has absorbed her grandmother's consciousness," allowing Eva to be "the agent of a revolutionary and trascendent ideal that can be passed from woman to woman, of a commitment to fully human values" (163).

WORKS CITED

Bakhtin, M. M. *The Dialogic Imagination.* Ed. Michael Holquist. Translated by Caryl Emerson and Michael Holquist. Austin: U of Texas P, 1981.

Bartine, David. *Early English Reading Theory: Origins of Current Debates.* Columbia: U of South Carolina P, 1989.

———. *Reading, Culture, and Criticism: 1820–1950.* Columbia: U of South Carolina P, 1992.

Eagleton, Terry. *Against the Grain, Essays 1975–1985.* London: Verso, 1986.

———. *Marxism and Literary Criticism.* Berkeley and Los Angeles: U of California P, 1976.

Gardiner, Judith Kegan. "A Wake for Mother: The Maternal Deathbed in Women's Fiction." *Feminist Studies* 4 (June 1978): 146–65.

Henderson, Mae Gwendolyn. "Speaking in Tongues: Dialogics, Dialectics, and the Black Woman Writer's Literary Tradition." *Changing Our Own Words: Essays on Criticism, Theory, and Writing by Black Women.* Ed. Cheryl A. Wall. New Brunswick: Rutgers UP, 1989.

Meese, Elizabeth A. *Crossing the Double-Cross: The Practice of Feminist Criticism.* Chapel Hill: U of North Carolina P, 1986.

Olsen, Tillie. *Mother to Daughter, Daughter to Mother.* Old Westbury: Feminist Press, 1984.

———. *Silences.* New York: Dell, 1978.

———. *Tell Me a Riddle.* 1961. New York: Dell, 1979.

Richmond, Al. *A Long View from the Left: Memoirs of an American Revolutionary.* New York: Dell, 1972.

Rosenfelt, Deborah. "Divided against Herself." *Moving On* April/May 1980: 15–23.

———. "From the Thirties: Tillie Olsen and the Radical Tradition." *Feminist Studies* 7 (Fall 1981): 371–406. Reprinted in Judith Newton and Deborah Rosenfelt, eds., *Feminist Criticism and Social Change: Sex, Class, and Race in Literature and Culture.* New York: Methuen, 1985. 216–48.

Schweickart, Patrocinio P. "Reading Ourselves: Toward a Feminist Theory of Reading." *Gender and Reading: Essays on Readers, Texts, and Contexts.* Eds. Elizabeth A. Flynn and Patrocinio P. Schweickart. Baltimore: Johns Hopkins UP, 1986.

Todorov, Tzvetan. *Mikhail Bakhtin: The Dialogical Principle.* Translated by Wlad Godzich. Minneapolis: U of Minnesota P, 1984.

Williams, Raymond. *Marxism and Literature.* Oxford: Oxford UP, 1977.

Woolf, Virginia. "The Leaning Tower." *The Moment and Other Essays.* London: Hogarth, 1952.

PART II

"Further Liftings of the Veil": Gender, Class, and Labor in Frances E. W. Harper's *Iola Leroy*

Carla L. Peterson

In conjunction with other recent critical movements, black feminist criticism has emphasized the extent to which the American literary tradition has worked to silence what it has deemed "minor" writing. One of the major goals of this scholarship has consequently been the recovery of nineteenth-century texts by African-American women that have been written out of literary history and thus lost to twentieth-century readers. Prominent among these has been Frances Ellen Watkins Harper's 1892 novel, *Iola Leroy*. To date, the recovery and critical appreciation of this novel have been undertaken primarily by scholars who, in reading according to familiar paradigms, have placed it within the context of sentimental culture and analyzed its heroine, Iola, as a revised "tragic mulatta" figure. In so doing, they have in turn silenced crucial aspects of the novel that are only now beginning to receive critical attention. In this essay, I join with those critics seeking to give voice to some of the silences that have been imposed on *Iola Leroy* by literary history and criticism as well as by an insufficiency of archival research. I also speculate on the extent to which our silences of interpretation might in fact be attributable to Harper's own silencing in her novel of certain problematical issues surrounding black self-representation in the post-Reconstruction era. Throughout, however, I remain mindful of the fact that textual silences can never fully be recovered and that interpretive readings are always partial.

In their analyses of *Iola Leroy*, feminist scholars such as Barbara Christian, Deborah McDowell, Elizabeth Ammons, and Claudia Tate have focused almost exclusively on Iola as the novel's light-skinned, well-bred "heroine," interpreting her as a propaganda tool designed to counter the dominant culture's degrading image of black women at the nadir and to prove their ability to participate in that culture's ideology of domesticity from which they had heretofore been excluded. From this point on, however, the critical arguments bifurcate. McDowell, for example, condemns the novel for reproducing intact the values of the hegemony, creating a white heroine in beigeface who embodies the nineteenth century's cult of true womanhood and thus lacks the black feminist political consciousness of such twentieth-century protagonists as Zora Neale Hurston's Janie or Alice Walker's Celie. Contextualizing the novel in its proper historical setting, Ammons, in contrast,

praises the novel as both a defiant attack against "white men's sexual exploitation of black women" (29) and an "overt political argument about black
women's right to sexual self-definition" (31), while Tate applauds its portrayal
of the racial uplift work performed by black middle-class women of the post-
Reconstruction period that politicizes domestic values and thus makes possible the realization of a "black, bourgeois female-heroic subjectivity" (106).

What is common to, and significant about, these discussions is the degree
to which they all privilege Iola in their tacit agreement with what Norma
Alarcón has seen as (white) feminism's tendency to interpret the female subject as an autonomous "unitary subject of knowledge and consciousness"
(365). Following such readings, the novel can then indeed be interpreted as a
narrative about the development of a "black, bourgeois female-heroic subjectivity" in which the presence of an elite "heroine" is taken for granted. As
John Ernest has recently noted: "Put most simply, uncritical assumptions
about sentimental conventions on the one hand and attempts to identify an
essentialist conception of black female identity on the other have caused many
to misjudge Harper's achievement" (498). Indeed, given such assumptions,
broader questions concerning the legacy of slave culture and the fate of the
black rural and urban subaltern classes in the postbellum era have been
slighted. It is only recently that critics such as Ernest and Marilyn Elkins—
and Hazel Carby before them—have begun to attend to such issues, focusing
in particular on the novel's depiction of the Southern black folk community
and its empowering culture during and after slavery and, to a lesser extent, on
the racial uplift program elaborated by the novel's elite.

If the critical marginalization of such issues in *Iola Leroy* may be attributable to the privileging of certain interpretive paradigms to the exclusion of
others, it is also due, I think, to our incomplete knowledge and understanding
of Harper's *oeuvre*. For the fact remains that much of Harper's writings still
lies buried and silenced in archives. As critics, we need to heed Abdul
JanMohamed's admonition that "archival work is essential to the critical
articulation of minority discourse" and that "theoretical and archival work of
minority culture must always be concurrent and mutually reinforcing" (8). We
also need to follow the lead of scholars like Frances Smith Foster whose
exemplary archival research has uncovered the existence of several fictional
texts written by Harper and published in the *Christian Recorder* between 1869
and 1889—namely, a series of short stories, entitled "Fancy Etchings" or
"Fancy Sketches," and three serialized novels, *Minnie's Sacrifice* (1869), *Sowing and Reaping* (1876–77), and *Trials and Triumphs* (1888–89). These texts
suggest not only Harper's commitment to working with fictional and novelistic forms as she shaped them to fit her political, social, and ideological ends,
but also her willingness openly to broach certain problematical issues—her
frustration with the antebellum convention of the tragic mulatta, her aspiration to create black male heroic characters, and her interest in addressing the
crucial dilemma of black labor in the urban North—that *Iola Leroy* approaches only indirectly or at the margins. Having recognized and named
these different kinds of silences, the question then remains what kind of

reading of Harper's novel can I offer to supplement those that literary criticism has already provided?

Harper's choice of title for her 1892 novel may well be significant in its difference from most of the titles of her earlier fiction as well as from those of other post-Reconstruction novels such as Sutton Griggs's *Imperium in Imperio,* Pauline Hopkins's *Contending Forces,* Charles Chesnutt's *The Marrow of Tradition,* or Paul Laurence Dunbar's *The Sport of the Gods.* For, unlike these titles that (with the exception of *Minnie's Sacrifice*) point to forces or events that are larger than the fate of any one individual, *Iola Leroy* deliberately foregrounds a single character and invites the reader to seek her out within its pages. Harper's decision thus to privilege Iola as a sentimental heroine might well have been part of that larger strategy of accommodation to audience already noted by Christian (203)—a strategy rejected by the other, more controversial, texts enumerated above. Indeed, in contrast to her *Christian Recorder* fiction, which was read by a primarily black audience, *Iola Leroy* was meant to appeal to a white readership as well; as Carby has noted, the novel was both reviewed and appreciated by the white press and went through three editions between 1892 and 1895 (xi–xii). Following Harper's own suggestive lead, then, feminist critics such as Christian and McDowell have assumed that Iola is the novel's central character, interpreting her as a late nineteenth-century reincarnation of the antebellum tragic mulatta figure and noting the close resemblance of her mother's story to that of Harriet Beecher Stowe's Cassy and William Wells Brown's Clotel (McDowell 300; Christian 203–04).

A contemporary review of Harper's novel published in the *A.M.E. Church Review* had already indicated its awareness of the racial and sexual politics of black literary production at the nadir and wondered about Harper's central use of the antebellum mulatta figure:

> The heroine is Iola Leroy, who, with womanly instinct, and Christian faith and courage, makes for herself a worthy name. Iola is a mulatto, and a slave, a thing not uncommon during those dark days of which our history can never be written. Some question the propriety of selecting a person so nearly white as Iola Leroy to establish the virtues of a colored woman; but this apparent error can be excused when we remember that Iola serves the double purpose of showing how the slave-owner enslaved those of his own flesh and blood, and also how even now, and in the North if you please, one drop of black blood in one's veins, when it is found out, immediately places a discount upon a person. Iola Leroy was considered a valuable accession to the business firm of Mr. Waterman, as well as to the one in New England, so long as they thought her to be of unmixed blood; but with the discovery of the new blood, all her better qualities vanished, and she with them (*AMECR* 9, 1893: 416–17).

Traditional interpretations have argued that as a "nearly white" character the tragic mulatta figure functioned as a socially acceptable literary device that enabled antebellum white abolitionist women to speak openly and sympathetically about the plight of the black female slave and perhaps even identify with her. Well before such twentieth-century critics as Karen Sanchez-Eppler and Hortense Spillers,[1] however, this nineteenth-century reviewer had already perceived the degree to which this convention equated whiteness and proper femininity, thereby erasing the blackness of the African-American woman who insisted upon her own virtue: "Some question the propriety of selecting a person so nearly white as Iola Leroy to establish the virtues of a colored woman."

Literary history has shown, however, that not even the tragic mulatta figure could allay America's anxiety over what constitutes blackness; the proliferation of such terms as *mulatto, quadroon,* and *octoroon* suggests the impossibility of defining that space in-between pure whiteness and pure blackness, and even of defining whiteness and blackness themselves. Furthermore, as Sanchez-Eppler has argued, antebellum tragic mulatta fiction was an intensely bodied form through which white women sought to displace their own sexual feelings (33). Replacing the seduction novel that had been imported from Europe to the United States in the late eighteenth century, the tragic mulatta plot became the site in which cultural fears over female sexuality were invested, in the process conflating the sexuality and blackness of its heroine. Such cultural anxieties over issues of race and sexuality could only be allayed by the sacrifice of the black woman. Thus, beneath its idealized surface, the tragic mulatta plot suggests just how insidious the "romantic" privatization of the heroine may become. Indeed, as a luxury commodity within the economic system of slavery, the mulatta may be retained by the slaveholder for his personal consumption; as the object of his gaze and desire, she renders female sexuality available; she legitimates the act of rape. Finally, however, she may at any moment be converted into capital and reinvested for the slaveholder's economic profit through her sale: "The slave-owner enslaved those of his own flesh and blood."[2]

Yet, as the *A.M.E. Church Review* critic was well aware, Harper's "error" in constructing Iola as a mulatta figure was only an "apparent" one, for the novel in fact tacitly works to deconstruct the antebellum tragic mulatta plot. First of all, as Carby has noted, Iola revises her mother's tragic mulatta story (76). Indeed, Marie's antebellum history, as related by Eugene Leroy and the narrator in chapters nine through twelve, suggests the degree to which she had allowed herself to be seduced by the romance of this story, falling in love with her master, marrying him, and accepting privatization. If, at her boarding school commencement exercises Marie had given a speech whose theme was "American Civilization, its Lights and Shadows" and in which she had pleaded "for those whose lips were sealed, but whose condition appealed to the mercy and justice of the Nation" (75), in marriage she has ceased to speak out publicly on issues of slavery. Accepting to keep her slave heritage a secret from her children, she is nonetheless reenslaved along with them at her husband's death. Unlike her mother, Iola refuses to be entrapped by the romantic elements of the tragic mulatta plot. She resists Dr. Gresham's vision of blacks that has led him to throw "a halo of romance . . . around . . . their misfortunes" (110) and to contemplate marriage to her in romantic terms: "All the manhood and chivalry of his nature rose in her behalf, and after carefully revolving the matter, he resolved to win her for his bride, bury her secret in his Northern home, and hide from his aristocratic relations all knowledge of her mournful past" (59–60).[3]

In refusing Dr. Gresham's marriage proposal, Iola chooses not only loyalty to race but to family and, most especially, to her mother. Beyond that, however, she also rejects the romance of the tragic mulatta plot and its attendant dangers of privatization. Finally, and perhaps most importantly, she resists a world view that is based on a separation of public and private spheres as evinced by Dr. Gresham's inability to comprehend the relationship between his desire to marry Iola and national race relations: " 'But, Iola, we have drifted far away from the question. No one has a right to interfere with our marriage if we do not infringe on the rights of others' " (234).

Harper's intimation of the limitations of Dr. Gresham's racial sensibilities is symbolically represented by the loss of his arm during the Civil War (144). While Iola can joyously proclaim to him in the aftermath of the war that she has been able to reconnect " 'the once-severed branches of our family' " (215), Gresham reveals himself unable fully to accept Iola's identification with blacks, her desire to participate in the public work of racial uplift and, even more broadly, the concept of black equality. Maintaining that the federal government cannot be expected to protect every black citizen from white mob violence, Gresham further asserts that power will always remain in the hands of whites: " 'I have too much faith in the inherent power of the white race to dread the competition of any other people under heaven' " (223). Thus, at the novel's end Iola enters instead into a marriage with Dr. Latimer in which both husband and wife are shown to be equally committed to the elevation of their race, Iola's privatization is no longer at issue, and public and private concerns neatly converge.

Such a rewriting of the tragic mulatta plot finds its antecedents in Harper's earlier serialized novel, *Minnie's Sacrifice*, in which the heroine, Minnie, and her lover, Louis, both products of a sexual relationship between master and slave woman, refuse to hide the secret of their birth and pass. Dedicating themselves to the elevation of their race, the two move from New England back to the South after the Civil War; and it is there that Minnie sacrifices her life to the reconstruction of her race. At the story's conclusion, the narrator openly expresses her contempt for those writers who remain bound to the conventional mulatta plot and asserts the superiority of a narrative plot in which the heroine refuses to forsake her race but insists rather on wedding private issues to public ones in order to aid in its uplift: "While some of the authors of the present day have been weaving their stories about white men marrying beautiful quadroon girls, who, in so doing were lost to us socially, I conceived of one of that same class to whom I gave a higher, holier destiny. . ." (*CR*, Sept. 11 1869).

If Harper found the antebellum plot that privatized the tragic mulatta unacceptable, she remained faced with the question of how fictionally to represent black women as public personae. To do so was highly problematic since the violence of postbellum racial politics—as illustrated by Minnie's fate—had, in Jacquelyn Dowd Hall's words, encouraged the black community's privatization of its women so that they might "escape white male supervision, devote their productive and reproductive powers to their own families, and protect themselves from sexual assault" (332). To achieve her ends, Harper first of all reconfigured her narrative presentation of the mulatta. Unlike antebellum writers such as William Wells Brown, for example, Harper undercut the legitimacy of this figure's sexualization by consistently refusing to allow the narrator's gaze to linger on Iola. Moreover, if Iola is initially presented to us from the perspective of the sexualized male gaze that emphasizes her lack of control over her own body—whether that of the slave Tom, the romantic Dr. Gresham, or the lascivious slave-catcher Bastine—the narrative increasingly deflects this male gaze. It is significant that, by the novel's end, it is Dr. Gresham alone whose gaze still insists on sexualizing her: "Dr. Gresham gazed upon her with unfeigned admiration, . . . he thought her superbly handsome" (214). Finally, toward the end of the narrative, Iola is doubled by her friend Lucille Delany, a pure black woman in whom "neither hair nor complexion show the least hint of blood admixture," and whom the narrator refuses to subject to the male gaze (199).

In developing the characters of Iola and Lucille, Harper sought to construct a feminist agenda that would deconstruct the dichotomy of public and private spheres and thus forge a space for black women's social activism in the Reconstruction era. As Tate has noted, one of Harper's primary goals in writing *Iola Leroy* was to define the role that black women were to play in the reconstruction of the race after the Civil War (106). Her solution was to encourage their involvement in different forms of educational and benevolent reform activities. Thus, Iola works to redeem her race, not by remaining by the hearth, but by mediating between private and public spheres within the black community—between home, church, and school. And Lucille becomes representative of the professional black woman who moves freely but with dignity in the public sphere of black education. In so doing, Harper underscored the increasing importance of black women in postbellum racial uplift efforts. Just as significantly, however, Iola and Lucille serve as vehicles for the narration of African-American institutional history—particularly that of church and school—in the Reconstruction era. Their activities are metonymic expressions of postbellum racial uplift efforts in the South and emphasize the extent to which these two characters are not unique heroines but part of a wider collective racial effort. Indeed, Iola's "private" quest for her mother at the war's end unfolds—and can only succeed—within the newly emergent organizational structures and networks of black Methodism in the South. And both Iola's and Lucille's teaching activities are emblematic of a much broader movement among black leaders to establish schools for the freedpeople independent of white control (Foner, *Reconstruction* 97).

Harper's central concern with the elevation of her race is made fully evident as the novel progresses and characters—both black and white—come together with increasing frequency to conduct a series of political discussions that culminate in a *conversazione* held by men and women of the black elite. In this scene, Harper's narrator carefully preserves the appearance of feminine decorum by restricting Iola's contribution to the topic of the "Education of Mothers" (253). Beneath this veneer of conventionality, however, a more subversive form of female discourse quietly emerges. Lucille, for example, is a highly active participant in all topics, speaking out in opposition to African emigration, commenting upon white dependency on black labor, and so forth. Furthermore, as Carby has noted, the characters' discourse is based largely on speeches that Harper herself delivered between 1875 and 1891 (Carby 85–88). It is of particular significance that not only Iola and Lucille but the male characters as well reproduce Harper's political discourse in their conversation. In an earlier debate between several of the black and white male characters, for example, both Rev. Carmicle and Dr. Latimer repeat portions of Harper's 1891 "Duty to Dependent Races" speech that seek to allay white fears of a black takeover and insist on the pacifism of the Negro race; and in the *conversazione* Professor Gradnor advances a theory of climate taken from this same speech while Rev. Carmicle reiterates Harper's analysis concerning "our people's condition in the South" excerpted from her "Colored Women in America" lecture. Through such a narrative dissemination of her own political discourse, Harper was seeking perhaps to mask the gendered origins of her characters' political discourse and thus accommodate any anxiety felt by the dominant culture, or even a segment of the black male elite, over the increased presence of black women in the public sphere of civic debate.

Emphasizing the twin realities of increased racial violence on the part of whites and the degraded condition of blacks as a result of slavery, the elite characters of *Iola Leroy* thus join together to debate those same political and social issues that were preoccupying the black leadership during the Reconstruction period: the advantages of African emigration over the claim of America as the Negro's homeland; the validity of theories of racial superiority; the education of black women; the rate of moral progress among the race; the importance of Christian values to achieve this moral progress. What is significant about these novelistic debates, however, is the relative silence of the elite over issues of black labor—that of both the peasant in the South and the urban worker in the North. Thus, if Rev. Carmicle commends the increase in educational opportunities among Southern rural blacks or frets about their lack of "home training," the only comment he makes about their economic condition is to note that "vast crops have been raised by free labor" (259, 258). Even more striking is the reluctance of the elite characters to give voice to the specific labor problems confronting black urban workers.

Indeed, it would seem that in seeking to write a version of Reconstruction history that would be acceptable to white and black readers alike Harper was faced with the dilemma not only of how to represent the black woman but the black subaltern as well. Given the state of race and labor relations at the nadir, Harper found herself contending with a silence that W. E. B. DuBois

would unmask and name ten years later as that "conspiracy of silence" surrounding the bodies and souls of black folk and the role they were to play in
the political economy of postbellum white America (*Souls* 204). This conspira-
torial silence between the dominant culture and the black elite, striving for
political, social, and economic equality amidst an ever-growing atmosphere of
racial hatred and violence, created a serious representational problem for
Harper: how to depict the labor conditions of the black peasantry and working class without offending the sensibilities of a readership composed both of
whites anxious to maintain their political and economic dominance, and of
blacks all too aware of the necessity of accommodating this white dominance.

In December 1872, newly returned to Philadelphia from a lengthy tour
through the South where she had been lecturing on issues of racial uplift,
Harper placed an advertisement in the *Christian Recorder* offering her services as a public speaker and promoting in particular a lecture entitled, in an
echo of Stowe's antebellum novel, "Life Among the Lowly" (*CR*, Dec. 11
1872). Harper herself was thus well acquainted with the emancipated slaves,
and her letters to William Still reflect a realistic appraisal of them. While
lauding their strength and vitality, and claiming that "the South is to be a great
theatre for the colored man's development and progress," she also detailed
the tremendous burden of the slave past on the freedpeople, "with its pain,
ignorance and low social condition": "Men talk about missionary work among
the heathen, but if any lover of Christ wants a field for civilizing work, here is
a field" (quoted in Still 768, 778, 773). In her speeches and letters the "lowly"
figure purely as the object of discourse, and thus for Harper the question
became whether fiction could perhaps serve as an enabling form that would
promote the emergence of a black subaltern subjectivity and allow this subaltern finally to speak.

Indeed, Harper's experimentation with fictional form in her short sketches,
poetry, and novels published during this period suggests her acute awareness of
the problems involved in the representation of "the lowly"—both the Southern
agricultural laborer and the Northern urban worker. The Southern black peasantry appears briefly and schematically toward the end of *Minnie's Sacrifice*
and is then portrayed more fully in the 1872 Aunt Chloe ballad poems that
inaugurate *Sketches from Southern Life*. These poems narrate the history of a
group of folk—Uncle Jacob, Jakey, and especially Aunt Chloe—from the dark
days of slavery, through the Civil War, to the Reconstruction period. This
history is conceptualized as a progressive one in which home and community
consistently function as a political locus from which the folk work collectively
to resist oppression, fight for freedom, and implement those social and political
rights gained in Reconstruction. The life of blacks living in the urban North—
fictionally termed the city of A.P., but most probably Philadelphia where
Harper had been living since 1871—is developed in both *Sowing and Reaping,*
a temperance novel that traces the fortunes of four sets of men and women
from different levels of black society whose personal relationships are severely
affected in one way or another by drink, and *Trials and Triumphs,* in which

issues of skilled black labor come to constellate around the figure of Mr. Thomas.

Much like the elite characters of *Iola Leroy* who refuse fully to debate the economic conditions of the Southern black peasantry, Harper as narrator seems to have been faced with a similar dilemma. Within the context of her novel, she attempted to solve the problem of how to represent the black peasantry to her post-Reconstruction readers by silencing the very harsh realities of its daily existence. She accomplished her goal in large part by situating the present of the novel in the Reconstruction rather than the post-Reconstruction era, as if such historical distancing could enable her to rewrite the course of African-American history. The novel's freed slaves—Aunt Linda, Salters, and Uncle Daniel—who buy the land of their masters and create a farming settlement, are already substantially prefigured in the earlier Reconstruction Aunt Chloe poems. As in these poems, Harper took great pains here to emphasize the many ways in which this folk community derives its strength and resourcefulness from its slave heritage. Oral traditions ensure community cohesiveness; folk religion is an empowering force; education is an important tool of social progress; women, finally, are seen as essential to the community's survival in their efforts to help the men acquire land and put their vote to good use. In fact, in her narrative representation of the political debates conducted by the folk, Harper's narrator allowed these to anticipate the *conversazione* of the elite and to propose a similar program of racial uplift, thereby providing living testimony that the black masses can raise themselves out of the degradation of slavery.

Such a portrayal of the black peasantry silences the extremely harsh conditions under which black agricultural workers lived in both the Reconstruction and post-Reconstruction periods. Eric Foner has shown how in the aftermath of the Civil War the freed slaves aspired to land ownership in the belief that it would grant them a necessary economic autonomy. Yet, while some did manage to buy land, most lacked the funds and so "entered the world of free labor as wage or share workers on land owned by whites" in which "their labor was bought and sold like any other commodity." Foner further points out that even land ownership does not automatically guarantee economic autonomy, for "where not accompanied by control of credit and access to markets, land reform can often be a 'hollow victory' " (*Reconstruction* 106, 109). Indeed, the historical reality of the postbellum period was that the majority of black farmers were enmeshed in a cycle of failure. Sharecropping and the crop lien system increasingly replaced farm ownership, effectively reducing the freedpeople to a new form of servitude. Cash crops rather than subsistence farming made the peasants dependent on world markets, resulting in devastation during the depressions caused by the drop in cotton prices in the 1870s and 1880s; and capitalism rendered even small farmers more susceptible to economic crises by forcing their dependency on the railroad system, mechanization, banks, and insurance companies. Finally, while such collective political movements as the Grange, the National Farmers Alliance, the Colored Farmers

National Alliance, and the Populist party did flourish during this period, ongoing racial tensions ultimately impeded any lasting cooperation between
black and white farmers.[4] The result was the creation of a black rural proletariat whose crushing poverty of body and soul was later to be portrayed by
DuBois in *The Souls of Black Folk.*

In her novel Harper as narrator also appears to collaborate with her elite
characters in that discursive "conspiracy of silence" surrounding the hardships suffered by the black urban worker. Indeed, the majority of the black
elite of this period clung to an antebellum racial uplift ideology that was
based on a fundamental miscomprehension of the newly emergent relations
of labor to capital and insisted on setting as its primary goals the achievement
of material wealth, middle-class respectability, and independent entrepreneu-
rial status.[5] Convinced that these goals could readily be attained through the
ballot, education, hard work, and frugality, this elite could not fully grasp the
harsh conditions of the black worker who, along with immigrant Europeans
and native whites, constituted an urban workforce whose labor the industrial
capitalist tapped at will. Perceived as incompetent to fulfill any but the most
menial tasks, black workers in particular were exploited by industrialists who
forced them to underbid their white competitors and transformed them into
an industrial reserve of strikebreakers. Moreover, despite the radical efforts
of such organizations as the Knights of Labor to create a brotherhood of all
working-class peoples based on cooperative labor, trade unionism in the post-
Reconstruction period was ultimately motivated by the racism of native white
and European-born workers, who feared economic competition by blacks,
and by its leadership, who promoted a divisive competitiveness in its differential treatment of workers and its wage system.[6]

In *Iola Leroy,* the Northern urban worker's body remains largely absent. It
does, however, appear briefly, cleansed and purified, in the figure of Iola
herself as she painstakingly searches for clerical work in the cities of the
North. Indeed, the *A.M.E. Church Review* critic who had wondered about
the appropriateness of Iola's near-whiteness to establish the virtue of black
women found even deeper significance in the text's inscription of African-
American labor problems on Iola's body. For Iola's mulaticity enabled
Harper's narrator to show "how even now, and in the North if you please, one
drop of black blood in one's veins, when it is found out, immediately places a
discount upon a person. Iola Leroy was considered a valuable accession to the
business firm . . . so long as they thought her to be of unmixed blood; but
with the discovery of the new blood, all her better qualities vanished. . . ." In
yet a final subversive revision of the conventional tragic mulatta plot, Iola's
function becomes that of resisting not only the sexual politics of a racist
society but also its discriminatory practices in the marketplace. Yet, even here
Harper withdrew from an explicit consideration of the implications of such a
plot. Iola secures a job at Mr. Cloten's store not through any significant
change in labor relations or policies but because of the higher moral conscience of her employer: " 'I feel, my dear,' said Mrs. Cloten, 'that what you
have done is a right step in the right direction, and I hope that other mer-

chants will do the same. We have numbers of business men, rich enough to afford themselves the luxury of a good conscience' " (212). At the novel's end, finally, the narrator chooses to pull Iola, along with all the other elite characters, back into the isolated security of the Southern black community.

Yet, there is one other character in *Iola Leroy* who is briefly and marginally positioned as a Northern urban worker, and that is Iola's uncle Robert Johnson. Indeed, I would argue that Robert in some sense rivals Iola as the novel's "center" and that Harper's portrayal of him is indicative of her aspirations to construct a black male fictional "hero." For, as I have been suggesting all along, despite the novel's title and the prominent place given to her as a tragic mulatta in critical discussions, Iola is not the single focal point of Harper's fiction. She is introduced to us as a character only in Tom's conversation in Chapter 5 and she becomes a physical presence only in Tom's deathbed scene in Chapter 8. Moreover, as Ammons has noted, Iola is often silent. But while Ammons links Iola's silence to her physical enslavement and argues that she learns to speak when free (31–32), I would suggest that even in the many debates conducted by both the peasantry and the elite, Iola speaks comparatively little. In contrast to the vocal Lucille Delany, it is primarily through her actions as nurse, schoolteacher, and loving daughter that Iola exemplifies the public work of black women in the 1890s.

It falls to Robert, then, to raise the all-important issue of leadership within the black community at the nadir. Like Iola, Robert is a mulatto but, unlike her, he has been born and bred in slavery. He is introduced to us in the very first lines of the novel as he and Tom engage in the "invented . . . phraseology" of the slaves' "market speech" and he responds to Tom's mysterious question with an equally mysterious answer (9, 7). Termed an "informant" by the narrator (7), Robert is in fact not destined to become a hero; instead, his function is to inform the reader, to introduce the reader to the different social groups that inhabit *Iola Leroy* and then to mediate between them, to recognize, comprehend, and bridge difference. Thus, in chapter after chapter at the beginning of the novel, it is Robert who invites us into the world of the slaves—on the Anderson plantation, at prayer meeting, in Uncle Daniel's cabin, in Gundover's woods—and who later reintroduces them to us, and to Iola as well, as freedpeople who have established their own independent farming community. Equally, it is Robert's decision to join the Union army that enables us to make the acquaintance of the Northern officers who are so sympathetic to the cause of the slave. And, finally, it is through Robert's friendship with the elite characters, Rev. Carmicle and Dr. Latimer, that these men are able to enter and participate in the novel's political debates.

Although born a slave, Robert nonetheless fully comprehends both white and black cultures, elite and subaltern classes, military officers and enlisted soldiers, and his function is to mediate between these disparate groups. In so doing, Robert achieves a "narrating" role as he mediates between story and reader, elucidating the racial politics of slavery and Reconstruction for Harper's audience. Thus, before the war Robert relies on his skills in literacy to mediate between the world of the slaves and that of their masters. During the war his near-whiteness gains Robert the trust and respect of the white officers, thereby allowing him to explain slave culture and the worldview of the black soldiers to them. Linked by blood ties to the black elite and by history to slave culture, Robert is the only character who after the war can move with total ease between the Southern farming community and the Northern urban elite; he is an active participant in the debates of both the elite characters and, unlike Iola, the black folk.

It is of particular significance, finally, that it is Robert who inaugurates the movement of the main characters North after the Civil War. Having moved to the city of P. (once again most probably Philadelphia), Robert convinces his mother, Marie, and Iola to join him there in order to establish a household together. It is also from this Northern urban site that the elite characters proceed to enter into the novel. Yet, if the city of P-- seems ostensibly to be the locus of intellectual debate, it is also, as we noted in connection with Iola, that of commercial labor; it is in P-- that Robert opens a hardware store where by his own account he is " 'doing a good business' " (183). In thus portraying Robert, Harper was seeking to construct for her readers a fictional version of the historical figure of the Southern freed slave who, having been taught a mechanical trade under slavery, moves North after the war in the hopes of sharing in the profits of national economic reconstruction. Harper's portrait of Robert, however, silences the very real hardships that confronted these black skilled workers and aspiring entrepreneurs.

Yet Harper had already explored some of these labor problems in several of her *Christian Recorder* fictional writings of the 1870s and 1880s, indicating the degree to which her political thought extends far beyond specifically women's issues to encompass a broad range of socioeconomic concerns. In the 1871 sketch "Opening the Gates," Harper's fictional spokesperson, Aunt Jane, had argued that " 'as we are shut out from workshops and other places of industrial departments, then there is greater reason why we should combine together to bring different trades and businesses within our reach. . .' " (*CR*, Oct. 28 1871). Her proposal is further developed in support of black entrepreneurship in one of the later "Fancy Sketches" as Jane's niece, Jenny, suggests that " 'colored men who possessed money' " should unite to build up " 'a cotton factory, could not this thing be effected among us by the power of combination?' " (*CR*, Jan. 15 1874). But it is in her 1888–89 short novel *Trials and Triumphs* that Harper actually created a male protagonist whose novelistic function it was to clarify questions of labor relations in the urban North to her black readership in a way that Robert Johnson does not.

Trials and Triumphs ostensibly centers around a young orphan girl, Annette, who is portrayed, in distinct contrast to the conventional mulatta figure, as physically unattractive and of a moody disposition; and its plot traces her education, aspirations to become a poet, and quest for romance which, after many trials, reaches a triumphant conclusion. Yet, one of the novel's most interesting characters is Mr. Thomas who, like Robert, dominates its first half only to fade away as the melodramatic love plot begins to take precedence. Thomas is introduced to us as Annette's former teacher who loses his job when the city of A.P. decides to integrate its student body but not its teaching staff. Looking for work, he analogizes himself in a telling metaphor to the " 'runaway slave who, when asked, "where is your pass?" raised his fist and said, "dem is my passes, and if I don't see an opening I will make one" ' " (*CR*, Oct. 11 1888). In so redirecting Thomas's economic fortunes, Harper revealed herself here to be more interested in exploring the dilemmas of the black skilled labor force than those of the professional class.

In the novel Thomas exhibits a remarkably acute understanding of United States labor relations. A freed slave who, like Robert, has learned a trade in slavery, he asserts "the right to sell my labor in any workship in this city same as the men of other nationalities, and to receive with them a fair day's wages for a fair day's work" (*CR*, Jan. 3 1889). His ability to do so is repeatedly hindered, however, by the competition mounted by cheap immigrant labor and the prejudice of the city's workers who successfully pressure their employers to deny blacks jobs. In a prescient speech, Thomas warns of the economic turmoil that will ensue as the " 'depressed laborer of the new South' " moves North into a workforce that refuses to allow him to compete on an equal basis with other workers (*CR*, Nov. 29 1888). Thomas eventually overcomes his trials and triumphs in his quest for "a fair day's wages for a fair day's work" through a combination of his own skill as a carpenter, his employer's concern for good workmanship, and his white co-workers self-interest in monetary gain. His concluding remarks reiterate, finally, the solution to black labor relations proposed earlier by the female characters of Harper's sketches—a recognition of the unity of interest among black workers and businessmen and the consequent need to establish a national labor bureau, " 'not as a charity among us, but as a business with capable and efficient men who will try to find out the different industries that will employ men irrespective of color and advertise and find steady and reliable colored men to fill them' " (*CR*, Jan. 3 1889).

In contrast, and perhaps because she was seeking to appeal to a broader audience, Harper pushed the portrayal and articulation of such labor issues to the margins of *Iola Leroy*. At the novel's end, Robert abruptly leaves the city of P-- to return with the newly married couples and the rest of the Johnson family to the South, where he buys a plantation and divides it into small lots to sell to "poor but thrifty laborers" (280). Such a conclusion forecloses the possibility of any further exploration of black urban labor and entrepreneurship in the North and reverts instead to the economic model of Southern homesteading. In reversing its geographic movement and returning the characters to the South, the novel also encloses them in an all-black community that is virtually self-sufficient.[7] Carby has interpreted such racial separation as a sign of black autonomy (93). I would suggest that it also signals Harper's retreat from any attempt as yet to construct a place for blacks within the political economy of the nation. Instead, the characters are made to follow a pattern of return migration, circling back to their Southern home place and the safety of a self-contained black community from which they may start anew the work of reconstruction.

On the level of character, however, one of the consequences of this retreat is that Robert's role as mediator becomes less necessary and less meaningful. Separated from white society and fully integrated into neither elite nor subaltern communities, Robert falls increasingly silent; for while he had been a vocal participant in the earlier discussions both with the black folk and the white professsional men, Dr. Gresham and Dr. Latrobe, he does not speak during the *conversazione*. Robert's increasing marginalization and silence in the novel thus underscore the poverty of debate over the place of African-Americans in the national political economy of postbellum America. As such, they also echo that very absence of black leadership in the early 1890s that would soon be filled by the coming to prominence of Booker T. Washington and W. E. B. DuBois.

NOTES

1. Sanchez-Eppler, 40, and Spillers, "Notes" 178.

2. For an earlier discussion of these points, see my article, "Black (Under)development," 9–10.

3. See also Young, 284, for comments about Gresham's self-perceived role as Iola's rescuer.

4. For a more extensive discussion of the condition of the black peasantry in the postbellum period, see Zinn 276–89.

5. For a more extensive discussion of the ideology of the black elite in the post-Reconstruction era, see Harris and Denhard 34; Meier and Rudwick 27–43.

6. For a more extensive discussion of blacks and the labor movement, see Philip Foner 26–67; Harris and Denhard 32–49; Meier and Rudwick 27–34.

7. Karla Holloway has argued that in contrast to *Our Nig*, *Iola Leroy* is more concerned with spiritual than with material values and that its fictional world deploys a sense of spatial freedom rather than constriction. My essay foregrounds the economic issues at the margins of the text and suggests that the novel's return movement South reflects a form of spatial constriction as well.

WORKS CITED

A.M.E. Church Review 9 (1893): 416–17.

Alarcón, Norma. "The Theoretical Subject(s) of *This Bridge Called My Back* and Anglo-American Feminism." *Making Faces, Making Soul*. Ed. Gloria Anzaldúa. San Francisco: Aunt Lute Foundation Books, 1990. 356–69.

Ammons, Elizabeth. *Conflicting Stories*. New York: Oxford UP, 1992.

Carby, Hazel V. *Reconstructing Womanhood*. New York: Oxford UP, 1987.

———. Ed. Introduction. *Iola Leroy, or Shadows Uplifted*. Boston: Beacon Press, 1987. ix–xxvi.

Christian, Barbara. "Shadows Uplifted." *Feminist Criticism and Social Change.* Eds. Judith Newton and Deborah Rosenfelt. New York: Methuen, 1985. 181–215.

Christian Recorder December 11, 1872.

DuBois, W. E. B. *The Souls of Black Folk.* New York: New American Library, 1969.

Elkins, Marilyn. "Reading Beyond the Conventions: A Look at Frances E. W. Harper's *Iola Leroy, or Shadows Uplifted." American Literary Realism* 22 (Winter 1990): 44–53.

Ernest, John. "From Mysteries to Histories: Cultural Pedagogy in Frances E. W. Harper's *Iola Leroy." American Literature* 64 (September 1992): 497–518.

Foner, Eric. *Reconstruction: America's Unfinished Revolution 1863–1877.* New York: Harper & Row, 1988.

Foner, Philip. *Organized Labor and the Black Worker.* New York: Prager, 1974.

Hall, Jacquelyn Dowd. " 'The Mind That Burns in Each Body': Women, Rape, and Racial Violence." *Powers of Desire: The Politics of Sexuality.* Eds. Ann Snitow, Christine Stansell, and Sharon Thompson. New York: Monthly Review Press, 1983. 328–49.

Harper, Frances E. W. *Iola Leroy, or Shadows Uplifted.* Boston: Beacon Press, 1987.

———. *Sketches of Southern Life.* Philadelphia: Merrihew and Son, Printers, 1872.

———. *Minnie's Sacrifice. Christian Recorder* 20 March 1869–25 September 1869.

———. "Opening the Gates." *Christian Recorder* 28 October 1871.

———. "Fancy Sketches." *Christian Recorder* 15 January 1874.

———. *Sowing and Reaping. Christian Recorder* 10 August 1876–8 February 1877.

———. *Trials and Triumphs. Christian Recorder* 4 October 1888–14 February 1889.

Harris, Abram, and Sterling Spero Denhard. *The Black Worker.* New York: Athaneum, 1968.

Holloway, Karla F. C. "Economies of Space: Markets and Marketability in *Our Nig* and *Iola Leroy." The (Other) American Traditions: Nineteenth-Century American Women Writers.* Ed. Joyce Warren. New Brunswick: Rutgers UP, 1992. 126–40.

JanMohamed, Abdul R., and David Lloyd. "Introduction." *Cultural Critique* 6 (1986): 5–12.

McDowell, Deborah. "The Changing Same: Generational Connections and Black Women Novelists." *New Literary History* 16 (1986): 281–302.

Meier, August, and Elliott Rudwick. "Attitudes of Negro Leaders Toward the American Labor Movement from the Civil War to World War I." *The Negro and the American Labor Movement.* Ed. Julius Jacobson. New York: Doubleday, 1968. 27–48.

Peterson, Carla L. "Capitalism, Black (Under)development, and the Production of the African-American Novel in the 1850s." *American Literary History,* 4 (Winter 1992): 559–83.

Sanchez-Eppler, Karen. "Bodily Bonds: The Intersecting Rhetorics of Feminism and Abolitionism." *Representations* 24 (Fall 1988): 28–59.

Spillers, Hortense. "Notes on an Alternative Model—Neither/Nor." *The Difference Within.* Eds. Elizabeth Meese and Alice Parker. Philadelphia: John Benjamins, 1989. 165–87.

Still, William. *The Underground Railroad.* Philadelphia: Porter and Coates, 1872.

Takaki, Ronald. *Iron Cages.* New York: Oxford UP, 1990.

Tate, Claudia. "Allegories of Black Female Desire; or, Rereading Nineteenth-Century Sentimental Narratives of Black Female Authority." *Changing Our Own Words.* Ed. Cheryl A. Wall. New Brunswick: Rutgers UP, 1989. 98–126.

Young, Elizabeth. "Warring Fictions: *Iola Leroy* and the Color of Gender." *American Literature* 64 (June 1992): 273–97.

Zinn, Howard. *A People's History of the United States.* New York: Harper & Row, 1980.

Attentive Silence in Joy Kogawa's *Obasan*

KING-KOK CHEUNG

> To the *issei,* honor and dignity is expressed through silence, the twig bending with the wind. . . . The *sansei* view silence as a dangerous kind of cooperation with the enemy.
>
> JOY KOGAWA, interview with Susan Yim (D8)[1]

Since the Civil Rights movement in the late 1960s, women and members of racial minorities have increasingly sworn off the silence imposed upon them by the dominant culture. Yet silence should also be given its due. Many Asian Americans, in their attempts to dispel the stereotype of the quiet and submissive Oriental, have either repressed or denied an important component of their heritage—the use of nonverbal expression. With many young Asian Americans turning against this aspect of their culture and non-Asians even less able to understand the allegedly "inscrutable" minority, it is not surprising that Joy Kogawa's *Obasan,* an autobiographical novel, has been subject to tendentious reviews. To Edith Milton the book is "a study in painful silence, in unquestioning but troubled obedience to the inevitable" (8); to David Low it is "clearly a novel about the importance of communication and the danger of keeping silent" (22); to Joyce Wayne it is "a tale of the submissive silence of the oppressed" (23). The resounding condemnation of silence reflects the bias of "translation" or of language itself which, as Paula Gunn Allen tells us, "embodies the unspoken assumptions and orientations of the culture it belongs to" (225). In English, *silence* is often the opposite of *speech, language,* or *expression.* The Chinese and Japanese character for *silence,* on the other hand, is antonymous to *noise, motion,* and *commotion.* In the United States silence is generally looked upon as passive; in China and Japan it traditionally signals pensiveness, alertness, and sensitivity.

These differences are too often eclipsed by a Eurocentric perspective to which even revisionist critics may succumb. As Chandra Mohanty has argued, much of Western feminist representation of oppressed "third world" women is pitted against the implicit self-representation of Western women as educated, liberated and, I might add, verbally assertive: "These distinctions are made on the basis of the privileging of a particular group as the norm or referent" (337). A similar norm frequently governs the assessment of racial minorities in North America. Marilyn Russell Rose, a sophisticated critic keenly aware of the danger of Orientalist discourse, nevertheless places inordinate blame on the victims in *Obasan:* " 'Orientalism' has been so internalized by this

Oriental minority, that their silence is an inadvertent bow to the occidental hegemony which legitimizes their abuse" ("Hawthorne" 293; see also Edward Said for a detailed discussion of Orientalism). Undeniably, nikkei have been subject to political exploitation, but to view their reticence as no more than the internalization of Occidental stereotypes is to tune out the "other" perceptions of silence in the novel. Countering Orientalism means challenging Western reduction or homogenization of Asian traits, but not necessarily denying or denouncing the traits themselves.

Situated on the crossroads of cultures, Kogawa in *Obasan* shows a mixed attitude toward both language and silence and reevaluates both in ways that undermine logocentrism. Certainly, language can liberate and heal, but it can also distort and hurt; and while silence may smother and obliterate, it can also minister, soothe, and communicate. The verbal restraint that informs Kogawa's theme and style manifests not only the particular anguish of voicelessness but also what Gayle Fujita describes as the narrator's specific nikkei legacy—"a nonverbal mode of apprehension summarized by the term 'attendance' " (34). Where Fujita subsumes several forms of reticence under the rubric "attendance," however, I find it necessary to distinguish among protective, stoic, and attentive silences, which Kogawa regards with varying attitudes. Kogawa also deplores negative manifestations of silence, such as political oppression through censorship and enforced invisibility, and the victims' repression.[2]

The thematics and poetics of silence are tightly interwoven. On the thematic level, the narrator negotiates between voicelessness and vociferousness, embodied respectively by her two aunts. The style of the novel likewise evinces a double heritage. The biblical injunction to "write the vision and make it plain"—advocated by one of the aunts—is soft-pedaled by the narrator's preference for indirection, a preference which sociologist Stanford Lyman associates with the nisei generally. Even as the narrator confronts the outrages committed during World War II, she resorts to elliptical devices, such as juvenile perspective, fragmented memories and reveries, devices which at once accentuate fictionality and proffer a "truth" that runs deeper than the official written records of the war years spliced into the novel. The gaps in the narrative demand from the reader a vigilance and receptivity that correspond to the narrator's attentiveness.

I

Kogawa bases *Obasan* on her own experiences during World War II and on letters, journals, and documents of the time.[3] After the Japanese attack on Pearl Harbor in December 1941, over 21,000 Canadians of Japanese ancestry (17,000 of whom were Canadian-born) were forced to leave their homes on the coast of British Columbia. They were sent first to Hastings Park in Vancouver and then to various ghost towns—hastily reconstituted by the wartime authorities—in the British Columbia interior. By 1944 Japanese Canadians who still remained in the British Columbia interior were made to choose between resettlement east of the Rockies or deportation to Japan—a country most of them had never seen. Unlike Japanese Americans, who could return to the West Coast after the war, Japanese Canadians were not allowed to return to British Columbia until 1949.

The novel is presented from the point of view of Naomi Nakane, a 36-year-old schoolteacher. It begins in 1972 when Naomi's Uncle Isamu is still alive in Granton, Alberta. A month later, Isamu dies and Naomi goes to comfort his widow Aunt Aya—the title character. *Obasan* is *Aunt* in Japanese, but it can also mean *woman* in general. The title thus implicitly "acknowledges the connectedness of all women's lives—Naomi, her mother, her two aunts" (Fujita 41). At Obasan's house Naomi finds a parcel from her Aunt Emily that contains wartime documents, letters, and Emily's own journal written between December 1941 and May 1942. (Many of Emily's letters of protest to the Canadian government are based on the real letters of Muriel Kitagawa, a Japanese-Canadian activist.) As Naomi sifts through the contents of this package, she reluctantly sinks into her own past. She recalls the uprooting and dissolution of her family during and after the war: her father died of tuberculosis; two of her grandparents died of physical and mental stress. Naomi and her older brother Stephen were brought up by Uncle Isamu and Obasan. Hovering over the tale is the riddle of what has happened to Naomi's mother, who acccompanied Grandma Kato (Naomi's maternal grandmother) to Japan on a visit shortly before the war, when Naomi was five. Only at the end of the book do Naomi and Stephen (and the reader) discover that their mother had been totally disfigured during the nuclear blast in Nagasaki and died a few years later. Before her death she requested Obasan and Uncle to spare her children the truth. The adults succeed all too well in keeping the secret; Naomi does not find out about her mother's fate for over thirty years.

The novel depicts Naomi's plight of not knowing and not being able to tell. Naomi has been speechless and withdrawn throughout childhood and adolescence—her quiet disposition tied to her mother's unexplained absence. As a girl she questions but receives no answer; as an adult she prefers to leave the question unspoken because she dreads knowing. As Magnusson has observed, "Naomi's individual drama is closely caught up in her linguistic anxiety, which comes to serve as a synecdoche for her estrangement—from others, from her cultural origins, from the absent mother who preoccupies her thoughts, from her past" (58).

In her quest for identity and for peace, Naomi is influenced by her two aunts' contrary responses to their harrowing experiences during the war. Obasan, the reticent aunt who raises Naomi, counsels her to forget and to forgive. Aunt Emily, the political activist, presses her to divulge the indignities endured by Japanese Canadians—to "write the vision and make it plain" (31). Emily brings to mind the Old Testament prophets who cry for justice; Obasan, the New Testament preaching of humility, forgiveness, and charity. But both sets of behavior also have roots in Japanese culture. As Michiko Lambertson points out, "There are two poles in the Japanese way

of thinking. One is a fatalistic attitude of acceptance, endurance, and sto-
icism and the other is a sense of justice, honour, and fair play" (94).
Obasan's attitude is as much Buddhist as Christian; she moves with equal
ease in Christian and Buddhist burial ceremonies, always ready with her
serving hands. Emily's activism, though ascribed to her Canadian schooling,
is also promoted in the Japanese tale, recounted in the novel, of Momotaro—the boy who defends his people valiantly against cruel bandits (see
Fujita 40). Naomi remarks:

> How different my two aunts are. One lives in sound, the other in stone.
> Obasan's language remains deeply underground but Aunt Emily, BA, MA, is
> a word warrior. She's a crusader, a little old grey-haired Mighty Mouse, a
> Bachelor of Advanced Activists and General Practitioner of Just Causes (32).

Naomi feels invaded by Emily's words and frustrated by Obasan's wordlessness. She undercuts Emily's polemics with irony and strains to hear Obasan's
inner speech.

II

> Unless the stone bursts with telling, unless the seed flowers with speech,
> there is in my life no living word. The sound I hear is only sound. White
> sound. Words, when they fall, are pock marks on the earth. They are
> hailstones seeking an underground stream.
>
> JOY KOGAWA, *Obasan*, prologue

Kogawa articulates her misgivings about language and history primarily
through Naomi. When Naomi receives Emily's package, filled with words, she
at first resists reading its contents and reopening old wounds: "What is past
recall is past pain" (45). Much as she tries to forget the past, however, it
continues to haunt her, as in one of her dreams: "We're trapped, Obasan and
I, by our memories of the dead—all our dead—those who refuse to bury
themselves" (26). The dream echoes an argument that took place years before
between Naomi and Emily:

> "Why not leave the dead to bury the dead?"
> "Dead?" she asked. "I'm not dead. You're not dead. Who's dead?"
> "But you can't fight the whole country," I said.
> "We are the country," she answered (42).

Western readers are likely to agree with Emily and to view Obasan and
Naomi as passive and timid. But the author's allegiance is much more complex. Although her novel acknowledges the need to retrace the past and the
importance of expression, it also exposes the many pitfalls of language (see
Goellnicht 291–94). To begin with, language is insidiously gendered so that
synonymous words, such as "spinster" and "bachelor," take on vastly different connotations. As Robin Lakoff has noted, "bachelor" is often used as a

compliment, but "spinster" is normally used pejoratively: "The metaphorical connotations of 'bachelor' generally suggest sexual freedom; of 'spinster,' puritanism or celibacy" (33). When Naomi is called a "spinster" by one of her students, she recalls Emily's objection to the epithet: "She says if we laundered the term properly she'd put it on, but it's too covered with cultural accretions for comfort" (8). Laden with time-honored prejudice, words as inherited have a way of perpetuating patriarchal ideology.

Kogawa in *Obasan* is far more concerned with racist rhetoric than with sexist language, however. As Donald Goellnicht points out, "Language shapes, rather than merely reflects, reality for both the victimizers and the victims, its manipulation resulting in empirical, concrete actions" (291). During the war the Canadian bureaucracy uses words to camouflage the most offensive actions against‚people of Japanese ancestry. Canadian-born citizens are dubbed "enemy aliens" (92); prison camps are dressed up as "Interior Housing Projects." Emily fumes, "With language like that you can disguise any crime" (34). Language becomes especially treacherous when abusive slurs and oppressive edicts pass for "news" and "laws" respectively. Emily says that the newspapers are printing "outright lies": "There was a picture of a young nisei boy with a metal lunch box and it said he was a spy with a radio transmitter" (85). The very reason given by the government for the evacuation—that the Japanese residents pose a security risk—begs the question, for "not a single charge of treason was laid against a Japanese Canadian" (Goellnicht 290).

Not only do white Canadian officials and nikkei citizens hold opposite views about the evacuation, members of Naomi's own family also diverge in their opinions. Where Aunt Emily wants to fight "fascist" Canada, Uncle and Obasan feel only "gratitude" to their adopted country (42). Even the perspective of one person may shift with time. Emily, who once "worshipped the Mounties" to the extent of brandishing their motto—*Maintiens le droit* [uphold the law]—is appalled by how rudely her erstwhile heroes treat her people during the war. Her former motto is translated literally into a sour question: "Maintain the right?" (100). Kogawa emphasizes that "facts" are often inseparable from interpretations, that even when intent to deceive is absent, language can only convey partial, often subjective, realities. The narrator observes her distance from her vociferous aunt: "For [Emily], the vision is the truth as she lives it. When she is called like Habakkuk to the witness stand, her testimony is to the light that shines in the lives of the nisei, in their desperation to prove themselves Canadian, in their tough and gentle spirit. The truth for me is more murky, shadowy and grey" (32).

Besides doubting the transparency of language, the narrator questions its efficacy. Naomi wonders whether anything tangible can come out of Emily's polemics:

> All of Aunt Emily's words, all her papers, the telegrams and petitions, are
> like scratchings in the barnyard, the evidence of much activity, scaly claws
> hard at work. But what good they do, I do not know—those little black

typewritten words—rain words, cloud droppings. They do not touch us
where we are planted here in Alberta. . . . The words are not made
flesh. . . . All my prayers disappear into space (189).

To Naomi, Emily's collections of data and didactic analysis are but so much
"noise" that hardly alleviate actual suffering or inspire redeeming vision. The
narrator wishes to find a verbal medium that can hold a listener without sound-
ing coercive or dogmatic, that can transform "white sound" into "living word."

III

> I do not wish to romanticize the Issei but to humbly and gratefully acknowl-
> edge what it was that shone with such deep energy through their lives—in
> their hands, in their silences.
>   Kogawa, preface to *Issei,* by Gordon Nakayama, 7

If skepticism about language and interrogation of majority consensus aligns
Kogawa with many a woman writer and postmodernist thinker, her ability to
project a spectrum of silence is, as Fujita suggests, traceable to her bicultural
heritage. To monitor this peculiar sensibility, one must avoid gliding over the
tonalities of silence in the novel, or seeing them all negatively as destructive.
The protagonist, to be sure, struggles against oppressive and inhibitive silence. She also feels divided about the protective and the stoic silence of the
issei which has sheltered her as a child but paralyzes her as an adult. She
continues nevertheless to cherish the communicative and attentive silence she
has learned from several female forerunners.

Oppressive silence in the novel takes both individual and collective forms,
inflicted on women and men alike. As a child Naomi was sexually abused by a
neighbor—Old Man Gower—who forbade her to tell of the violation: "Don't
tell your mother" (64).[4] Later, it is the Canadian government that harasses the
Japanese Canadians and suppresses the victims. Emily notes: "All cards and
letters are censored. . . . Not a word from the camps makes the papers. Everything is hushed up" (101). Naomi tells: "We are the despised rendered voice-
less, stripped of car, radio, camera and every means of communication" (111).

Not an uncommon reaction to suppression is repression on the part of the
victims. Instead of voicing anger at the subjugators, they seal their lips in
shame. Child Naomi, whose relationship with her mother has been one of
mutual trust, begins to nurse a secret that separates them after her molestation. Racial abuse similarly gags the victim. When Stephen is beaten up by
white boys, he refuses to tell Naomi what has caused his injury. Naomi intuits,
"Is he ashamed, as I was in Old Man Gower's bathroom?" (70). Rape, Erika
Gottlieb points out, is used here as "metaphor for any kind of violation" (45).
Like Stephen, many Japanese Canadians also refuse to speak about what
Rose calls their "political and spiritual rape" by the Canadian government
("Politics" 224). Naomi, for one, wishes to leave the past behind: "Crimes of

history . . . can stay in history" (41). Her attitude of acceptance is, however, ultimately complicit with social oppression: her self-imposed silence feeds the one imposed from without. Naomi nonetheless learns that she cannot bracket the past, not only because it is impossible to do so, but also because it is self-destructive. "If you cut any of [your history] off you're an amputee," Emily warns. "Don't deny the past. Remember everything. If you're bitter, be bitter. Cry it out! Scream!" (49–50).

What makes it especially difficult for Naomi to "scream" is her schooling in the protective and stoic silence of the issei, which she is gradually coming to regard with ambivalence. She appreciates the efforts of Mother and Obasan to create a soothing environment for the children. She recollects Mother's reassuring manner during a childhood crisis, after she tells her that a big white hen is pecking a batch of infant yellow chicks to death (an event that clearly foreshadows the pending interracial dynamics). Mother comes immediately to the rescue: "With swift deft fingers, Mother removes the live chicks first, placing them in her apron. All the while that she acts, there is calm efficiency in her face and she does not speak" (59). Obasan also exhibits serenity in the face of commotion. Even on the eve of the evacuation, "Aya is being very calm and she doesn't want any discussion in front of the kids. All she's told them is that they're going for a train ride" (108). An involuntary exodus is recast as a pleasant excursion—for the children's sake.

A point comes when such protective silence—a form of enforced innocence—infantilizes. Naomi, now an adult, is constantly frustrated by tight-lipped Obasan: "The greater my urgency to know, the thicker her silences have always been" (45). When Naomi asks her about the letters written in Japanese—letters describing the bombing in Nagasaki—Obasan produces instead an old photograph of Naomi and her mother, once more substituting a sweet image for harsh facts. Her silence can be as misleading as words.

The stoic silence of the issei is presented with a similar mixture of appreciation and criticism. The issei believe in quiet forbearance, in dignified silence. During the war they mustered enormous strength to swallow white prejudices, weather the ravages of the internment, and, above all, shelter the young as much as possible from physical and psychological harm. To the dominant culture their silence suggested passivity and weakness, and encouraged open season on them. Kogawa capsulates these divergent perceptions of silence in two successive images from nature: "We are the silences that speak from stone. . . . We disappear into the future undemanding as dew" (111–12). Stone connotes sturdiness, endurance, and impregnability; dew, by contrast, suggests fragility, evanescence, and vulnerability. Placed side by side, the two figures for silence reveal the complex attitude of the Japanese-Canadian narrator. She acknowledges the physical and inner strength of the issei: their sturdiness is a requisite to survival in taxing environments such as the ghost town of Slocan and the beet farm of Alberta. The silence exemplified by Uncle and Obasan attests at once to their strength of endurance and their power to forgive. At the same time, the narrator knows all too well that their magnanimity—redoubled by their Christian belief in turning the other cheek—lends itself to exploitation by the dominant culture. Like dew, they can become "wiped out."

Kogawa does not allow the negative implications of silence to engulf its positive manifestations, of which the most disarming is attentive silence. Fujita notes that attendance is instilled in Naomi since infancy, through the very decor of her prewar home: "Above my bed with the powdery blue patchwork quilt is a picture of a little girl with a book in her lap, looking up into a tree where a bird sits. One of the child's hands is half raised as she watches and listens, attending the bird" (52–53; cited in Fujita 38). The girl's heedfulness is significantly inseparable from her thoughtfulness and poised hand. Far from suggesting passivity, this form of silence entails both mental vigilance and physical readiness. Complementing the visual aids are the actual examples set by Grandma, Mother, and Obasan. They supply positive reinforcement for Naomi. Their "alert and accurate knowing" has left a lasting impression on her:

> When I am hungry, and before I can ask, there is food. If I am weary, every place is a bed. . . . A sweater covers me before there is any chill and if there is pain there is care simultaneously. If Grandma shifts uncomfortably, I bring her a cushion.
> "Yoku ki ga tsuku ne," Grandma responds. It is a statement in appreciation of sensitivity and appropriate gestures (56).[5]

There is neither explicit request nor open inquiry. At the point when her grandparents have been taken to the hospital and Obasan offers unspoken yet palpable solace, Naomi registers: "We must always honour the wishes of others before our own. . . . To try to meet one's own needs in spite of the wishes of others is to be "wagamama"—selfish and inconsiderate. Obasan teaches me not to be wagamama by always heeding everyone's needs. That is why she is waiting patiently beside me at the bridge" (128).

These instances trace attentive silence to a maternal tradition in Japanese culture. Naomi has learned it from Grandma, Mother, and her surrogate mother Obasan, all of whom have been raised in Japan. Yet it is also to be directed beyond one's kin, as is evident from what occurs on the train that takes Obasan and the children from British Columbia to Slocan. A young woman has given birth just before boarding, but she does not have a single baby item with her. Obasan quietly places in front of her a bundle that contains a towel and some fruit. Her kindness inspires another old woman to follow suit. Little Naomi, taking stock of these generous acts, is herself moved to charity: she notices her brother's unhappiness and slips a present (her favorite ball) into his pocket.

Grandma and Mother disappear from Naomi's life early on. The extant person, in whom the woe and wonder of silence converge, influencing Naomi into adulthood, is Obasan.[6] Kogawa has set her name as the title of the book because Obasan "is totally silent." "If we never really see Obasan," the author has stated, "she will always be oppressed" (Wayne 23). Kogawa realizes that Obasan's quiet fortitude makes her an easy target of subjugation, and she appeals openly to the reader to see Obasan and to hear "the silence that cannot speak" (epigraph). But she does not enjoin Obasan to emulate Emily. As readers, we must be wary of adopting the attitude of Stephen, who scorns Obasan's Japanese ways; or that of the chilling Mrs. Barker, whose "glance at Obasan is one of condescension" (224). Or we may be guilty of the very blindness that the author attempts to cure. Dismissing Obasan as a victim would legitimize her victimization.

The "world-traveling" advocated by María Lugones proves instructive here:

> Through traveling to other people's "worlds" we discover that there are "worlds" in which those who are the victims of arrogant perception are really subjects, lively beings, resistors, constructors of visions even though in the mainstream construction they are animated only by the arrogant perceiver and are pliable, foldable, file-awayable, classifiable (402).

The narrator herself, unlike Stephen and Mrs. Barker, never regards Obasan arrogantly. She does not view her through Eurocentric or even revisionist eyes: "Obasan . . . does not come from this clamourous climate. She does not dance to the multi-cultural piper's tune or respond to the racist's slur. She remains in a silent territory, defined by her serving hands" (226).[7] In portraying her aunt she pointedly departs from the view of silence as absence or as impotence. She divines unspoken meanings beneath Obasan's reticence and wishes to enter "the vault of her thoughts" (26). She textualizes the inaudible: "The language of her grief is silence. She has learned it well, its idioms, its nuances. Over the years, silence within her small body has grown large and powerful" (14). The quietest character in the novel, Obasan is also the most attentive. (She performs what Wordsworth in "Tintern Abbey" eulogizes as those "little, nameless, unremembered acts of kindness and of love.") One marked achievement of this novel is the finesse by which the author renders a wordless figure into an unforgettable character.

The destructive and enabling aspects of silence are recapitulated together in the climax of the novel. Naomi finally learns (from her grandma's letters) about her mother's disfigurement. Bewildered, she at first can only deplore her mother's protective silence: "Gentle Mother, we were lost together in our silences. Our wordlessness was our mutual destruction" (243). Yet almost in the same breath that remonstrates against protective silence the narrator is invoking attendance which, as Fujita observes, "supports Naomi in her moment of greatest need" (39). The act ushers in the process of healing: "Gradually the room grows still and it is as if I am back with Uncle again, listening and listening to the silent earth and the silent sky as I have done all my life. . . . Mother. I am listening. Assist me to hear you" (240).

In this receptive state she hears "the sigh of . . . remembered breath, a wordless word" (241). She is able to conjure up her mother's presence, and empathy restores the original bond: "Young Mother at Nagasaki, am I not also there?" (242). The communion continues:

> I am thinking that for a child there is no presence without flesh. But perhaps
> it is because I am no longer a child I can know your presence though you are
> not here. The letters tonight are skeletons. Bones only. But the earth still
> stirs with dormant blooms. Love flows through the roots of the trees by our
> graves (243).

Naomi breathes life into the verbal knowledge transmitted by the letters
("bones only") by means of a nonverbal mode of apprehension. Her ability to
grasp an absent presence through imaginative empathy is fostered by her
sedulous heedfulness. She finally discovers the key to the cryptic epigraph:
"To attend its voice, I can hear it say, is to embrace its absence."

IV

> Beneath the grass the speaking dreams and beneath the dreams is a
> sensate sea.
>
> *Obasan,* prologue

Attuned to the contradictory potential of both language and silence, Kogawa
uses multivocal discourses to articulate the manifold nature of reality and
employs a number of elliptical devices to harness the power of the unspoken.
The polyglossia of *Obasan* has often been noted (see Merivale 68; Goellnicht
294). Here I would call attention to the author's muted rhetoric, to her way of
punctuating words with silences. Kogawa deploys fables and dreams to spin a
web of associations, of verbal and emotional echoes. She alerts us to the
associative impact of words through Naomi's response to the honorific
"Nesan" in Emily's journal:

> The sight of the word . . . cuts into me with a peculiar sensation of pain and
> tenderness. It means "older sister," and was what Aunt Emily always called
> Mother. Grandma Kato also called Mother "Nesan" from time to time
> especially if she was talking to Aunt Emily. I remember one time I called
> Mother "Nesan" and Grandma Kato laughed and laughed (46).

The word agitates Naomi not because of its denotative meaning but because
of its connections with her mother and grandmother, with a time too blissful
for memory. Of all the words in Emily's journals this one steals its way most
readily into Naomi's heart.

Shattered imagery pervades Naomi's own reminiscences, described at one
point as "fragments of fragments," as "segments of stories" (53); at another as
"dream images" (112). The reader must attend to the unarticulated linkages
and piece together the broken parts; meaning permeates the spaces between
what is said. A simple fable may set off a rippling effect. Fujita has shown that
"attendance is clearly linked to . . . the story of Momotaro" (38), which
Naomi is told as a child. The tale also reverberates poignantly in Naomi's own
life. It is at the sight of Obasan that Naomi recalls "the old woman of many
Japanese legends" (54) and the fable about a boy who emerges from a peach,

to the delight of an old childless couple. When Momotaro grows up, he travels to a neighboring island to fight bandits; he wins the battle and brings honor to his aged foster parents. The plot is simple enough, yet each detail summoned by the narrator elicits in the reader a response to what has not been stated. The joy of the old couple at the sight of Momotaro has parallels in Naomi's own happy prewar childhood when all the adults lavish love and attention on her, when simply "by existing a child is delight" (55). The description of the day when Momotaro must leave his parents to go on the long and perilous journey also has analogues in Naomi's experience. Both the sadness of separation and the suppression of that emotion are delicately sketched:

> The time comes when Momotaro must go and silence falls like feathers of snow all over the rice-paper hut. Inside, the hands are slow. Grandmother kneels at the table forming round rice balls, pressing the sticky rice together with her moist fingertips. She wraps them in a small square cloth and, holding them before her in her cupped hands, she offers him the lunch for his journey. There are no tears and no touch. Grandfather and Grandmother are careful, as he goes, not to weight his pack with their sorrow.
>
> Alone in the misty mountains once more, the old folks wait (56).

This speaking picture prefigures several scenes of farewell in *Obasan:* that of Mother and Grandmother Kato when they leave for Japan, that of Father when he leaves Slocan, that of Grandpa and Grandma Nakane when they leave for the hospital, and that of Stephen when he leaves for Toronto. No tears are shed on any of these occasions. And few words. Unlike Momotaro, none of these leave-takers returns.

It is with respect to Obasan, who is now "older than the grandmother [Naomi] knew as a child, older than any person [she knows] today" (54), that the fable has multiple bearings. Obasan and Uncle are also a childless couple. When Obasan becomes the guardian aunt of Stephen and Naomi, she too treats them as her own offspring. The couple's love for Momotaro is expressed neither in words nor by touch, but through the slow movement of the old woman's hands; Obasan is similarly "defined by her serving hands." The couple's considerate silence resonates in the actions of Mother, Grandpa, Uncle, and Obasan, all of whom try to shield Stephen and Naomi from grief.

But there is a contrasting analogue. The rice balls offered by the old woman to Momotaro directly evoke a scene on the train. Obasan offers Stephen a rice ball. "Not that kind of food," Stephen sulks, rejecting her offer (115). The episode foreshadows Stephen's rejection of everything Japanese, including his own foster mother, who "mends and remends his old socks and shirts which he never wears and sets the table with food which he often does not eat" (215). He ends up avoiding Obasan altogether: "Stephen, unable to bear the density of her inner retreat and the rebuke he felt in her silences, fled to the ends of the earth" (14). On the day of his departure, Naomi thinks with pride of her brother as "Momotaro going off to conquer the world" (214). But the motivation of his long journey is a far cry from that of Momotaro's. He may obtain laurels in the musical world (for he becomes a concert pianist), but bringing honor to his aged foster parents could not be further from his mind. Stephen, who is "always uncomfortable when anything is 'too Japanese' " (217), has missed a point succinctly enunciated by Emily: "Momotaro is a Canadian story. We're Canadian, aren't we? Everything a Canadian does is Canadian" (57).[8]

Finally, the lonely waiting of the legendary grandparents foreshadows Naomi's own pain of anticipating her mother's return: "What matters to my five-year-old mind is not the reason that she is required to leave, but the stillness of waiting. . . . After a while, the stillness is so much with me that it takes the form of a shadow which grows and surrounds me like air. Time solidifies, ossifies the waiting into molecules of stone, dark microscopic planets that swirl through the universe of my body waiting for light and the morning" (66). Naomi, being little at the time, is finding it much more difficult than do the old couple to heed the needs of others before one's own: "My great-grandmother [who is very ill] has need of my mother. Does my mother have need of me? In what market-place of the universe are the bargains made that have traded my need for my great-grandmother's?" (67). This child must come to attendance the hard way.

Kogawa thus captures in less than half a page a montage of emotions that the characters hide from each other and traces such self-restraint to a formative childhood tale. The author herself has learned the lesson well. Her evocative style provides a counterpoint to the dry official papers and Emily's effusive rhetoric. The reader must probe beneath the surface of the lapidary prose to catch the inexpressible.

Kogawa also conveys the deflected emotions of the narrator—who "never spoke" as a child (57)—through "speaking dreams." Three in particular mark Naomi's growth. The child is waylaid by a recurrent nightmare after her encounters with Old Man Gower: "In my childhood dreams, the mountain yawns apart as the chasm spreads. My mother is on one side of the rift. I am on the other. We cannot reach each other. My legs are being sawn in half" (64–65). The dream conveys the sense of physical mutilation experienced by the victim and her resulting psychological alienation from her mother. We are told in the following chapter that it is "around this time that Mother disappears" (66). For good. The successive placement of Naomi's nightmare and her mother's disappearance suggests that the child connects her sexual arousal with her mother's departure: "She feels that her abandonment by Mother must be punishment for her unmentionable offence, her fall from innocence" (Gottlieb 46).

That the victim is plagued by guilt and shame is further signified in another nightmare that recurs even after Naomi has turned adult. In this dream three beautiful oriental women, captured and guarded by several British soldiers, lie naked in a muddy road. When one of the three—"stretched between hatred and lust"—tries to seduce the soldiers, they make a sport of shooting at the women's toes and feet. Naomi writes: "The soldiers could not be won. Dread and a deathly loathing cut through the women" (62). The dream, which couples sexual overtones with punishment and underlines the victims' self-contempt, takes us into the dreamer's tormented psyche.

The most instructive dream—one that alludes to the "Grand Inquisitor" in Dostoyevsky's *Brothers Karamazov*—occurs just before Naomi finally learns about her mother's ordeal in Nagasaki. In her dream the Grand Inquisitor (who resembles Old Man Gower) is prying open her eyes and her mother's mouth.

> His demand to know was both a judgement and a refusal to hear. The more he questioned [Mother], the more he was her accuser and murderer. The more he killed her, the deeper her silence became. What the Grand Inquisitor has never learned is that the avenues of speech are the avenues of silence. *To hear my mother, to attend her speech, to attend the sound of stone, he must first become silent.* Only when he enters her abandonment will he be released from his own (228; my emphasis).

Western hierarchical opposition of speech and silence are here reconfigured. It dawns on Naomi that by her incessant questioning she has unwittingly assumed the role of the Grand Inquisitor, who seeks to extort an answer from her mother. She now asks herself, "Did I doubt her love? Am I her accuser?" (228). The dream prompts Naomi to recognize her "culpability . . . [through] a deliberate attendance" (Fujita 39) and to enter her mother's suffering. At the point Naomi decides to give up her "inquisition," to have faith in her mother's love for her despite the apparent desertion, she learns the truth. The avenues of silence do coincide with the avenues of speech.

These dreams hark back to the various forms of silence discussed earlier. The first dream plays out what Naomi is forbidden to tell. The second traces her repression to childhood shame and guilt. The third yields a parable counseling attentive silence. The victims in the first two dreams concentrate on their own torments; in the last Naomi sees her mother as a fellow sufferer. Once she has ceased to focus on her own vulnerability, she becomes aware of her mother's ordeal; she sees she has been *wagamama*—guilty of making self-centered demands. In noticing and placing another's need alongside her own, in remaining solicitous of others despite her own buried grief, Naomi is being true to her Japanese upbringing and faithful to the example of Obasan. Paradoxically, it is through Naomi's willingness to "attend the sound of stone" that the "stone bursts open." In the next chapter she is apprised of the horror of Nagasaki. Staggering as it is, the knowledge frees Naomi from her years of gnawing doubt and unspeakable guilt.

V

> The reflection is rippling in the river—water and stone dancing.
> *Obasan* 247

The ending of *Obasan* enacts multiple reconciliations—between mother and daughter, past and present, death and life, and, above all, between the nonverbal and verbal modes of expression embodied in Obasan and Emily. Naomi learns about her mother's fate from Grandma Kato's letters, addressed to Grandpa Kato. The letters, as noted earlier, come across to her as "skeletons" unanimated by "love." And Naomi is wont to think of love in silent terms. "Did you not know that people hide their love / Like a flower that seems too precious to be picked?" she quotes a Chinese poem (228). This turn of thought accounts in part for her uneasiness about words. Grandma, too, apologizes for writing: "For the burden of these words, forgive me" (236).

But in fact the letters belie the binary opposition of stoical, protective, and considerate silence and self-lacerating or selfish telling. Grandma, whom Naomi remembers as "thin and tough, not given to melodrama or overstatement of any kind," describes the aftermath of the conflagration in an "outpouring" (234). Her letters show Naomi that jotting down unbearable thoughts, however excruciating at the time, can also release sorrow and help the writer "extricate herself from the grip of the past" (236). Such heartfelt expression is surely more salutary than the "vigil of silence" observed by Mother (236), whose protective silence has been long misinterpreted by Naomi as the absence of love, as evidence of abandonment. Ironically, it is through Grandma's presumably inconsiderate telling that Naomi learns of her grandmother's and mother's "deep love" (233).

For something other than deafening horror emerges from Grandma's letters. Through them Naomi learns that as soon as Grandma regains consciousness after the blast, she focuses wholeheartedly on rescuing her niece's two children: "At no point does Grandma Kato mention the injuries she herself must have sustained" (238). Mother, totally defaced and severely wounded, is found making a pyre for a dead baby. These examples of compassion in the face of atrocity provide an affirmative answer to Naomi's earlier questioning in her imaginary dialogue with Emily: "Greed, selfishness, and hatred remain as constant as the human condition, do they not? Or are you thinking that through lobbying and legislation, speech-making and story-telling, we can extricate ourselves from our foolish ways? Is there evidence for optimism? (199). Despite human shortcomings, Naomi can now break her silence by saying yes—there is evidence indeed.

Grandma's letters thus provide Naomi with both a personal reason ("extricate herself from the grip of the past") and a political reason (through "story-telling, we can extricate ourselves from our foolish ways") to write, to transform her personal silence and that of her family into words. Yet her (or Kogawa's) effectiveness as a "historian" lies precisely in her skepticism about historical authority. Naomi proceeds tentatively, insists that facts alone do not history make, and refuses to see things in terms of black and white. She traverses the historical landscape in slow motion and delivers a microscopic worm's eye view in terms of the muted sufferers. Her prose registers not only observable phenomena but emotional stirring unseen by the naked eye and unheard by the ordinary ear.

Toward the end of the novel, silence and speech are increasingly imaged as complementary rather than antithetical, as in Naomi's inspection of the two Japanese ideographs for the word *love:* "The first contained the root words 'heart' and 'hand' and 'action'—love as hands and heart in action together. The other ideograph, for 'passionate love,' was formed of 'heart,' 'to tell,' and 'a long thread' " (228). Love may take the form of Obasan's serving hands or Emily's (and Grandma's) passionate telling: "the heart declaring a long thread knotted to Obasan's twine, knotted to Aunt Emily's package" (228). The novel itself unwinds as a long thread that ties the variously strong women together.

Silence and words unite again figuratively in the lyrical ending of the novel, when Naomi decides to go to the coulee she and Uncle visited every year on the anniversary of the Nagasaki's bombing (though the reason for the pilgrimage was previously hidden from her). There she undergoes a symbolic baptism and enters a beatific vision: "Above the trees, the moon is a pure white stone. The reflection is rippling in the river—water and stone dancing. It's a quiet ballet, soundless as breath" (247). This epiphany, as Goellnicht observes, "holds in harmoniously negotiated tension the 'stone' of silence and the 'stream' of language" (297).

Such harmony infuses the style of the novel as well. In recollecting and recording the past, Naomi/Kogawa answers Emily's/Kitagawa's call for public expression. In writing a quiet book, one that is attentive to detail and images, and to nuances of feeling, expressed or repressed, the author also vindicates Obasan's silence. The most trenchant passages in the novel are not the expository and explosive entries reproduced from Emily's diary, but the pages of Naomi's understating prose. Kogawa suggests that open accusations and outspoken demands, while necessary, are insufficiently effective: thundering for justice will not alone solve any problem until people genuinely care. By heeding the poetry in the narrative, by witnessing the quiet strength of issei such as Obasan, the reader may well experience a change of heart.

Speaking of carpentry, Naomi observes: "There is a fundamental difference in Japanese workmanship—to pull with control rather than push with force" (24). Kogawa herself has carved a style that controls its force through the pull of silences.

NOTES

1. This essay is adapted from a chapter of my book *Articulate Silences. Hisaye Yamomoto, Maxine Hong Kingston, Joy Kogawa* (Cornell, 1993). A version of the essay was presented at the first MELUS Conference at U.C. Irvine (25 April 1987). Since then it has benefited from the insights of other critics: I am particularly indebted to Gayle Fujita for her explication of the "sensibility of silence," and to A. Lynne Magnusson and Donald C. Goellnicht for their analyses of Kogawa's ambivalence toward language. I would also like to thank Elaine Hedges and Shelley Fisher Fishkin for their suggestions.

Several terms appear frequently in the text. *Nikkei* refers to people of Japanese ancestry living outside Japan; *issei* (literally first generation), to Japanese immigrants; *nisei* (literally second generation), to children of the issei; *sansei* (literally third generation), to children of the nisei.

2. Though my essay stresses the positive uses of nonverbal behavior as a "corrective" to the prevailing critical trend, I do not mean to endorse all kinds of silences.

3. In real life Kogawa, one year older than the novel's narrator, Naomi, was six when her family was relocated. Her family, unlike Naomi's, was not separated: "Her minister father, mother and brother survived the relocation together and then moved to a small town in Alberta" (Yim D1).

4. Similar silencing after sexual molestation by a father figure occurs in Maya Angelou's *I Know Why the Caged Bird Sings* and Alice Walker's *The Color Purple*.

5. Fujita translates the Japanese words as follows: "You really notice/are aware/are attentive, aren't you?" (39). She notes that the phrase "looks back to the painting of the girl 'attending' the bird" (39).

6. Commenting on the limits and strengths of Obasan and on her influence on Naomi, Fujita writes: "Her steadfast love notwithstanding, she represents the inevitability of corrosion when silence means withheld knowledge. . . . But Obasan's destructive silence is part of a larger conception of her character as the embodiment of a vital *nikkei* culture including the positive use of silence exemplified by Naomi's attendance" (40). Erika Gottlieb similarly observes, "Powerful in her silence, Obasan is indeed in charge of 'life's infinite details,' as if the ball of string [she has] accumulated over the years would have somehow absorbed the wisdom and experience of those years themselves. . . . Struggling to overcome Obasan's silence, yet also inspired by its depth, Naomi has grappled with her task faithfully, unravelling her yarn in all its intricate patterns" (52).

7. Jeanne Wakatsuki Houston notes that Japanese Americans and white Americans frequently hold different attitudes about serving: "In my family, to serve another could be uplifting, a gracious gesture that elevated oneself. For many white Americans it seems that serving another is degrading, an indication of dependency or weakness in character, or a low place in the social ladder. To be ardently considerate is to be 'self-effacing' or apologetic" (20). The dominance of such an attitude perhaps explains why Obasan has so often been reproved by critics.

8. Emily herself, as Fujita has noted, exemplifies the spirit of Momotaro who, in the original Japanese tale, "leaves home to battle ogres" (38). Emily likewise travels all over Canada and the States to fight against injustice. However, in transferring Momotaro's courage to Emily, Kogawa has also redefined traditional heroism in accordance with the pacifist tenor of her novel. Instead of glorifying martial valor, she omits all descriptions of physical combats in Naomi's version of the fable. Just as Maxine Hong Kingston in *The Woman Warrior* transforms a swordswoman into a wordswoman, Kogawa turns Momotaro's physical combats into Emily's "paper battles" (189). The change allows women to enter the public arena without subscribing to the military ethos of patriarchal societies.

WORKS CITED

Allen, Paula Gunn. *The Sacred Hoop: Recovering the Feminine in American Indian Traditions*. Boston: Beacon, 1986.

Fujita, Gayle K. " 'To Attend the Sound of Stone': The Sensibility of Silence in *Obasan*." *MELUS* 12:3 (1985): 33–42.

Goellnicht, Donald C. "Minority History as Metafiction: Joy Kogawa's *Obasan.*" *Tulsa Studies in Women's Literature* (Fall 1989): 287–306.

Gottlieb, Erika. "The Riddle of Concentric Worlds in 'Obasan.' " *Canadian Literature* 109 (Summer 1986): 34–53.

Houston, Jeanne Wakatsuki. *Beyond Manzanar: Views of Asian-American Woman-hood.* Santa Barbara: Capra Press, 1985.

Kingston, Maxine Hong. *The Woman Warrior* [1976]. New York: Random House, Vintage edition, 1979.

Kitagawa, Muriel. *This Is My Own: Letters to Wes & Other Writings on Japanese Canadians, 1941–1948.* Ed. Roy Miki. Vancouver: Talonbooks, 1985.

Kogawa, Joy. *Obasan.* Toronto: Lester & Orpen Dennys, 1981. Boston: David R. Godine, 1982.

———. "Preface." *Issei: Stories of Japanese Canadian Pioneers.* Gordon G. Nakayama. Toronto: NC Press, 1984.

Lakoff, Robin. *Language and Woman's Place.* New York: Harper, 1975.

Lambertson, Michiko. Review of *Obasan,* by Joy Kogawa. *Canadian Woman Studies* 4:2 (1982): 94–95.

Low, David. Review of *Obasan,* by Joy Kogawa. *Bridge* 8:3 (1983): 22.

Lugones, María. "Playfulness, 'World'-Travelling, and Loving Perception." *Making Face, Making Soul/Haciendo Caras: Creative and Critical Perspectives by Women of Color.* Ed. Gloria Anzaldúa. San Francisco: Aunt Lute Foundation, 1990. 390–402.

Lyman, Stanford M. "Generation and Character: the Case of the Japanese Ameri-cans." *Roots: An Asian American Reader.* Ed. Amy Tachiki et al. Los Angeles: UCLA Asian American Studies Center, 1971. 48–71.

Magnusson, A. Lynne. "Language and Longing in Joy Kogawa's *Obasan.*" *Canadian Literature/Litterature Canadienne* 116 (Spring 1988): 58–66.

Merivale, Patricia. "Framed Voices: The Polyphonic Elegies of Hébert and Kogawa." *Canadian Literature/Litterature Canadienne* 116 (Spring 1988): 68–82.

Milton, Edith. Review of *Obasan,* by Joy Kogawa. *New York Times Book Review* 5 Sept. 1982: 8.

Mohanty, Chandra Talpade. "Under Western Eyes: Feminist Scholarship and Colonial Discourses." *Boundary* 2:12:3/13:1 (1984): 333–58.

Rose, Marilyn Russell. "Hawthorne's 'Custom House,' Said's *Orientalism* and Kogawa's *Obasan:* An Intertextual Reading of an Historical Fiction." *Dalhousie Review* 67:2/3 (1987): 286–96.

———. "Politics into Art: Kogawa's *Obasan* and the Rhetoric of Fiction." *Mosaic* 21 (Spring 1988): 215–26.

Said, Edward W. *Orientalism.* New York: Vintage-Random House, 1979.

Wayne, Joyce. "*Obasan:* Drama of Nisei Nightmare." *RIKKA* 8:2 (1981): 22–23.

Yim, Susan. "In a Hailstorm of Words." *Honolulu Star-Bulletin.* Evening Ed. 20 Sept. 1984: D1.

Northamerican Silences: History, Identity, and Witness in the Poetry of Gloria Anzaldúa, Cherríe Moraga, and Leslie Marmon Silko

KATE ADAMS

I have been told that a poet should be of his or her time. It is my feeling that the twentieth-century human condition demands a poetry of witness. This is not accomplished without certain difficulties; the inherited poetic limits the range of our work and determines the boundaries of what might be said. There is the question of metaphor, which moved Neruda to write, 'the blood of the children / flowed out onto the streets / like . . . like the blood of the children.' "

CAROLYN FORCHÉ

We who write are survivors. . . . For myself, "survivor" contains its other meaning: one who must bear witness for those who foundered; try to tell how and why it was that they, also worthy of life, did not survive. And pass on ways of surviving; and tell our chancy luck, our special circumstances.

TILLIE OLSEN[1]

Tillie Olsen's groundbreaking essays of the 1960s and 1970s, published together in *Silences,* mourn the losses to literature that result when a writer's individual life-circumstances deny her the means or opportunity to fully and freely practice her craft. These silences, as Olsen eloquently demonstrates, are legion, and each represents our loss. Some of these losses are irredeemable: the work, promised, of a promising writer, was stillborn, or never born at all. Other works are lost temporarily—perhaps only for a hundred years—and then returned to us through some "accident of history" like the one that put into the fifteen-year-old Tillie Olsen's hands a battered, bound, secondhand copy of the nineteenth-century *Atlantic Monthly* in which Rebecca Harding Davis's "Life in the Iron Mills" was first anonymously published (Olsen 117).

Yet individual circumstances and historical "accidents" themselves do not begin to account for the omissions of literary and cultural history. Some circumstances are not individual, but borne by classes, races, entire nations of people. Some losses are not local, but global; not accidental, but the inevitable result of hegemonic forces that privilege the artistic visions and sociocultural realities of, to name a few, men over women, Anglos over Chicanos, and Euro-American over Native American people. For the Northamerican woman of color, writing in the face of such forces means recognizing that her "silences" are, in some sense, *meant to be:* what Olsen has called "the overwhelmingness of the dominant" requires and depends on her silence; what Audre Lorde has called structures "defined by profit and linear power" actively discourage her coming to voice.[2]

A passage of Adrienne Rich's 1983 poem, "North American Time," evokes what is at stake as academic workers take on the prodigious task of unlearning and revising the paradigms that Northamerican writers of color have struggled against in conserving, continuing, and communicating their cultural heritages: "what I must engage / . . . is meant to break my heart and reduce me to silence."[3] Rich's line may help us appreciate the impediments to our hearing the woman of color whose literary history has been at best misunderstood and at worst decimated by the powerful forces of racism, sexism, and homophobia. The breaking of hearts, the reductions to silence: these are the circumstances inherited by the artist who struggles to affirm her existence unmediated by the voices of oppressive forces and informants; who means to be the speaking subject, the clear-eyed witness to her own oppression and the instrument of her own liberation.

This struggle informs the poetry of Gloria Anzaldúa, Cherríe Moraga, and Leslie Marmon Silko, three "witnesses" to the silencing forces of cultural and literary history, three poets pushing the traditional boundaries of the genre. First, each woman's work complicates our understanding of poetry's range and purpose by merging poetry with other literary forms and by bending the genre to serve revisionist literary and cultural agendas. Second, each poet's work—in its revisions of our inherited expectations of history, and in its emphatic reconstruction of repressed individual and cultural identities—tutors us in what has been lost, in what we will regain, and in what will be required of us if we attend to the voices we have become accustomed to rendering silent. To continue the work that will make the cultural history of the United States an honestly multicultural narrative, the academic worker must bear witness to the work of these witnesses, must risk her own voice to silence so as to attend to the voices that can help her hear.[4]

I

Gloria Anzaldúa's *Borderlands/La Frontera* (1987), Cherríe Moraga's *Loving in the War Years: lo que nunca pasó por sus labios* (1983), and Leslie Marmon Silko's *Storyteller* (1981)[5] are all texts engaged in building literary forms that can "overwhelm the dominant" or subvert it, or break the dominant open to diversity, to difference. Particularly all three works present poetry to American readers in novel ways.

The bulk of contemporary poetry usually enters the literary book market in one of two containers: the slim volume of poems by a single poet, most often published by a university or small press, and the thick anthology containing a few works by scores of poets, chosen by editors with various political, aesthetic, and pedagogic agendas, and published either by large commercial presses primarily for the college text market, or by smaller, marginal publishers whose audiences are often much more specialized and whose sales are modest. The slim volume usually contains ninety-odd pages of poetry, often accompanied by a brief biographical sketch focusing on the author's professional literary experience. Anthologies vary, but they usually contain a few pages of each poet's work and the same brief biographical sketch.[6] Readers of contemporary poetry, then, often read poetry within fairly formulaic, narrow contexts and containers; because of the effaced position of poetry among contemporary arts, readers do their reading in an atmosphere free of the kinds of critical apparatus that accompany other cultural products. Novels, movies, plays, even pieces of sculpture or painting are often presented to the public with more evaluative information floating around them than is available for poetry.

The books by the authors under discussion here present poetry to their readers in containers radically different from the slim volume and the thick anthology; here, readers confront poems that are contextualized by an informative net of materials surrounding or accompanying them. These materials reflect the content of the poetry itself, but are not identical to it. This "not-poetry" or "extrapoetic" material is a rich mix of things: an essay of lost or repressed cultural history, a photograph, a child's schoolbook, a community elder's memory, a recipe for nopalitos, a phone call from one's mother, a lullaby, a dream, a rage, a shout, a nightmare of invisible lies sifted through in daylight. Each author has made a book that, by the nature of what it contains, denies poetry as a discrete genre the purity or exclusivity that the slim volume, the anthology, and a great deal of academic discourse help to provide it. Each author challenges genre-restricted understandings of what the book of poems is or should be, and what cultural work such a book can or should do.

Hugo Achugar's essay "The Book of Poems as a Social Act" suggests alternative ways of imagining poetry's cultural work by revisioning the book of poems as object.[7] "The question of poetic production," he writes, "has been set, almost without exception, at the level of the individual poem, without taking into account its articulation within the book of poems" (651). Achugar uses the Spanish word *poemario* ("book of poems") for its connotations of wholeness, and asserts that a *poemario* must be read as more than the sum of its individual poems/parts. The critic must attend to the ways in which the book of poems "works as a social act" (654), emphasizing its power to do cultural work by recognizing and responding to "the verbal and social contexts external to the book itself" (652). Such a positioning enlarges the pool of possible questions we may ask of a specific poem: it helps us imagine the range or function of poetry's work in culture. Moraga, Anzaldúa, and Silko move beyond this expanded conception of the *poemario*'s work when they bring social, political, historical, and autobiographical information external to the poems inside the covers of their books, illustrating the importance of these informative nets to any reading of the poems themselves. In so doing, each author asserts that for her poetry to enact its cultural work, it must be accompanied by extrapoetic materials that will rescue from silence the knowledges that enable a full reading of the poetry.

For example, Leslie Silko first published many of the poems included in *Storyteller* in a slim volume of poetry called *Laguna Woman* (1974). Those early poems take on a new depth and significance when republished in the mixed-genre, autobiographical work *Storyteller,* where they are arranged among traditional stories rendered in verse, family sketches, short stories, and, most importantly, photographs—some of them one hundred years old— of three generations of Silko's family and neighbors as well as views of Laguna Village and the deserts, mountains, mesas, and strip mines that are part of it. Using them here, Silko takes these photographs out of the basket where they've lived in her family for years and places them among her rerenderings of her people's knowledge about themselves and the world. "It wasn't until I began this book," Silko writes on the first page of her text, "that I realized that the photographs in the Hopi basket / have a special relationship to the stories as I remember them. / The photographs are here because many of the stories can be traced in the photographs" (1).

Much is lost in the translation of oral literature to the printed page, as a neighbor of Silko's in Laguna Village points out when her grandchildren bring home a library book that includes a Silko poem based on a traditional story:

> "We all enjoyed it so much,
> but I was telling the children
> the way my grandpa used to tell it
> is longer."
> "Yes, that's the trouble with writing," I said.
> "You can't go on and on the way we do when we tell stories around here.
> People who aren't used to it get tired."
> "I remember Grandpa telling us that story—
> We would *really* laugh!
> He wouldn't begin until we gave him
> something real good to eat". . . (110).

Just as reading the story in the library book reminds the neighbor of her grandfather's original telling of it, Silko's use of photographs in *Storyteller* reminds her readers of the human and historical absences that written translations of oral literature represent.[8] This "trouble with writing" is mitigated somewhat by Silko's photographs. For example, the first long poem of *Storyteller* is interrupted by the reproduction of a family snapshot: an aging woman stands against a fence in silhouette, looking down at a girl about three years old who faces the camera. The woman's large figure dwarfs the child's; the woman's arm, outstretched as she leans on a fencepost, extends behind the child's small body in the left front foreground, protective and familiar. It is a portrait of Leslie Silko and her great-aunt Susie Reyes; the poem that it interrupts is itself a portrait of Aunt Susie, "a brilliant woman, a scholar / of her own making" (7), who was sent as a child to the Carlisle Indian School in Pennsylvania and attended Dickinson College before returning to Laguna. One of the first storytellers in Silko's life, Aunt Susie is also a transitional figure in the history of storytelling that Silko conserves in the making of this book. While Aunt Susie "had come to believe very much in books," she also was "of a generation, / the last generation here at Laguna" that was able to convey her culture's oral traditions, passing down "an entire culture / by word of mouth" (6). The "European intrusion" that had taken Laguna children away to the Indian schools threatened that tradition fundamentally, but in the figure of Aunt Susie, who "took time from her studies and writing" to listen to the young Silko "and tell me all that she knew" (4), the tradition is preserved. The poem-portrait ends with an acknowledgment of her aunt's legacy to Silko: "I write," Silko explains, "when I still hear / her voice as she tells the story" (7). This poem cannot adequately convey to us the voice that motivates Silko's writing; neither can the poems which follow it, rendering the stories that voice told into written verse. But joined with this photograph and the others throughout the text, the visual experience of the written literature is heightened, stretched, giving back to the printed *poemario* some of the multi-dimensionality of its oral roots. The photographs help us to imagine the storytellers' absent faces, voices, and personalities, so key, Silko intimates, to oral literature. They help preserve both poems and poet *in history* and *in community,* returned home to the ground, the cultural landscape that gave them birth.

Similarly, in Cherríe Moraga's *Loving in the War Years,* the extrapoetic is invited into the poem's space. In this text's mix of genres, the poem's work is continued beyond the poem's end by essay, confession, story, and dream. Metaphorical and thematic threads from the poems are taken up, elaborated, woven into the discourse of the essays; these threads' sources are traced in scraps of journal or dream. Dream, in fact, opens Moraga's book and provides her with its title. Beyond that, dream and Moraga's use of it stand in synecdochal relation to the function of genre-bending in the *poemario* as a whole, for dream-time interrupts the usual chronologies of narrative, and dream-image interrupts the calculations of expository analysis, asserting its own form of persuasive urgency. Dream is an interruption, yet at a deeper level it is also a continuation of consciousness. Just as the genre-mixing *poemarios* discussed here require an expansion of our understanding of what the "book of poems" is, dream can demand that consciousness elongate, expand, develop; that potentially threatening or revelatory information be incorporated into our reality.

Gloria Anzaldúa's work also pushes at the boundaries of the *poemario.* Originally Anzaldúa conceived *Borderlands/La Frontera* as a volume of poems prefaced by a ten-page prose introduction; that introduction, in its published form, grew beyond its conception ten times to become the predominantly prose first half of a volume of poems. *Borderlands/La Frontera* begins and ends with poetry, allows poetry to interrupt prose, to illuminate it, to introduce it; but the seven essays that appear at the beginning of the book are fundamental to any reading of the poetry: in them Anzaldúa provides some of the suppressed cultural history of the Mexican and Indian peoples of the Southwest that is prerequisite to our appreciation and understanding of her Northamerican experience and its rendering in verse. In these essays, laced with Aztec history and the lyrics of Mexican *corridos,* Anzaldúa elaborates a generations-deep, oppositional reading of the "nation-building" events of nineteenth-century Southwest history that might surprise the casual tourist at the Alamo. In this light, the Texas Republic is founded on acts of thieving intervention; the Tejano is an indigenous Aztec, pushed off the land; the border states of the United States symbolize "a space that was once national territory" and is now *"el otro México"*; and the undocumented workers moving north across what Anzaldúa calls "the open wound" of the U.S./Mexico border are enacting *"el retorno,"* the return of the Aztec-Chicano people to their homeland after centuries of displacement at the hands of Anglo conquerors (3,11). This land—Aztlan, *el valle de Tejas*—is a *living* presence in her work, and as Anzaldúa writes, "the me that has something in common with the trees and the rocks" (50) is at great pains in the poems and essays to understand contemporary Chicana existence in the context of this lost and suppressed cultural history.

II

Enacting *"el retorno,"* whether or not one has ever physically left one's homeplace, means countering the conqueror's histories with one's own. For both Anzaldúa and Silko, history begins and ends with an affirmation of the land as a living presence, an engagement with the earth that refuses hierarchies of ownership: poetry becomes an important vehicle for this work. In a trio of poems that open the second section of her book, Anzaldúa presents us with images of the profound alienation of the white man from the world of animal/nature/spirit. In "White Wing Season" and "Cervicide," Anzaldúa places the Chicana on a border, negotiating between the law of white power and the law of a living landscape to which her life is tied, to which she looks for the survival of those who depend upon her and are part of her. In both cases, the woman is forced to betray her balanced relation to the natural world in the face of the game warden's threat, the hunting party's bribe, and the intrusions they represent. In the third poem, "horse," an entire community is witness to the white power's destructiveness and more importantly to the white man's own blindness to that destruction. After *gringo* teenagers in a south Texas town have tortured a horse during a Saturday night drunk, the rich father of one tries to erase his son's crime with money while the local sheriff looks the other way. The *mexicanos* respond to the crime and to the attempted transaction of money for the animal's pain with faces "shut," with muttering, with shaking heads and averted eyes. The white man's worst crime is his innocent obliviousness to the levels of debt and division that his solution fails to address; his "open" face becomes a target for the poet's fantasy of retribution:

> Dead horse neighing in the night
> come thundering toward the open faces
> hooves iron-shod hurling lightning
> only it is red red in the moonlight
> in their sleep the *gringos* cry out
> the *mexicanos* mumble if you're Mexican
> you are born old (107).

Challenging the conqueror's history means countering the conqueror's central position in the stories he tells; it means refusing to capitulate to those stories by allowing them to silence one's own. Perhaps there is no poem that illustrates this better than Leslie Silko's, which begins

> Long time ago
> in the beginning
> there were no white people in this world
> there was nothing European.
> . . .
> This world was already complete
> even without white people.
> There was everything
> including witchery.

Indian witchery, in this poem of origins, creates white people in a moment of competitive hubris: at a gathering of witch people, the most gifted witch shows off, boasts that the stories he tells become real; and the story he spins is about "white skin people" across the sea "in caves of dark hills." These people "grow away from the earth" until "the world is a dead thing for them / the mountains and stones are not alive":

> They fear
> they fear the world
> They destroy what they fear.
> They fear themselves.
> . . .
> They will kill the things they fear
> all the animals
> the people will starve.
> . . .
> Stolen rivers and mountains
> the stolen land will eat their hearts
> and jerk their mouths from the Mother (130–37).

It is probably no accident that, in the pages of *Storyteller* and in the pages of Silko's 1977 novel *Ceremony* where this poem first appears, we find it printed in the exact center of each book, lending concrete, material emphasis to the poem's power to unseat and decenter the powerful witchery that permeates phrases like "age of discovery," "manifest destiny," "European contact," and "go west, young man."

III

The "overwhelmingness of the dominant" is subverted in this Silko poem; similarly Anzaldúa's poems of return to and embrace of the land and its inhabitants break long silences, countering the lies of racist and ethnocentric history with creative speech. But not all silences are imposed from outside the people, *la familia,* the tribe; not all silences are externally enforced: some silences originate from within the cultural group. Some group members must leave in order to speak. Certainly this is often true for the "mixed-blood" speaker, a position of great pain and promise in the work of these authors. "An accounting with all three cultures" that made her—"white, Mexican, and Indian" (22)—is the project of Anzaldúa's revisionary "new mestiza," and Silko and Moraga, mestizas themselves, replace the mixed-blood man or woman's outcast silence with potent speech as well. Gender, too, can exact one's silence: the mestiza is further silenced within the borders of sexist paradigms of identity, reinforced by external systems of oppression and internal cultural and religious traditions.[9] For Anzaldúa and Moraga, both lesbians, speaking their sexuality meant finding their way out of a false and constricting choice between ethnic and sexual identity, between the affirmations and restrictions represented by the homeplace and home culture.

"It is through a break with tradition," Norma Alarcón has written, "that self and culture can be radically reenvisioned and reinvented."[10] But for the lesbian woman of color, the break with heterosexual privilege that coming out represents can put her racial loyalty into question and her position within her ethnic community at risk. In the long essay that forms the theoretical center of *Loving in the War Years,* Cherríe Moraga elaborates this risk, drawing on the work of Alarcón and other Chicana feminists and retelling the legend of Malintzin/Tenepal, or Malinche, of Mexican history. "The woman who defies her role as subservient to her husband, father, brother, or son by taking control of her own sexual destiny," Moraga writes,

> is purported to be a "traitor to her race" by contributing to the "genocide" of her people—whether or not she has children. In short, even if the defiant woman is *not* a lesbian, she is purported to be one; for, like the lesbian in the Chicano imagination, she is *una Malanchista.* Like the Malinche of Mexican history, she is corrupted by foreign influences which threaten to destroy her people (113).

For Moraga, the Malinche myth has, perhaps, an added autobiographical resonance. The child of a brown mother who married her white father, Moraga's identity as mestiza and lesbian makes the theme of betrayal, so central to Chicano culture's traditional rendering of the Malinche story, particularly acute. "To write as a Chicana feminist lesbian, I am afraid of being mistaken, of being made an outsider again," Moraga writes. "I feel at times I am trying to bulldoze my way back into a people who forced me to leave them in the first place, who taught me to take my whiteness and run with it" (95).

The lesbian of color can thus find herself inhabiting a painful borderland: her sexuality complicates her relation to her community as it is defined by race, culture, and heterosexual privilege; and her race complicates her relation to a predominantly white lesbian/feminist community, whose ability to welcome her without silencing her is a function of its own willingness, too often limited, to confront internalized racist paradigms. But the "break with tradition" that Alarcón invokes and that the Chicana lesbian accomplishes in coming out is also an opportunity. For Moraga, whose Anglo father gave her a "passing" surname and access to the privileges of "La Guera," coming out is a process of renegotiating her relationship to the "brown in her," a process that consists of renegotiating her identities as writer, lover, and daughter.

"My lesbianism is the avenue through which I have learned the most about silence and oppression," Moraga wrote in 1979:

> I have, in many ways, denied the voice of my own brown mother—the brown in me. I have acclimated to the sound of a white language which, as my father represents it, does not speak to the . . . emotions which stem from the love of my mother (54–55).

In the poem, "It's the Poverty," Moraga sketches the complexities of her struggle against this internalized oppression, in which the status of writer, wielder of words, places her in a threatening borderland:

> *I lack imagination* you say.
> *No.* I lack language.
> The language to clarify
> My resistance to the literate.
> Words are a war to me.
> They threaten my family.
> To gain the word to describe the loss,
> I risk losing everything.
> I may create a monster,
> the word's length and body
> swelling up colorful and thrilling
> looming over my *mother,* characterized.
> Her voice in the distance
> *unintelligible   illiterate.*
> These are the monster's words (62–63).

The speaker addresses another writer whose relationship to the word, to the English language, is seemingly uncomplicated by vexing questions of identity (and who is therefore unable to see the speaker's complexity); for the speaker, however, the word is a threat, a barrier separating her from her mother. Being the mestiza, the border writer, means "resistance to the literate" and to "literature" insofar as that literature and its history is monolithic, rendering invisible or unintelligible Moraga's unique material, in this case her experience of her mother, her mother's experience, and their relation to two languages.

In other poems, the identities of "daughter," "writer," and "lesbian" are eroticized through the Spanish language of the mother's culture, and through the body of the mother herself. The poems "La Dulce Culpa," "What is Left," "The Pilgrimage," "The Slow Dance," and "Fear, A Love Poem," all articulate Moraga's claim to "the right to passion expressed in our own cultural tongue and movements" (136). This right, particularly the right to reclaim Spanish, becomes bound up in Moraga's text with the desire and tension playing between mother and daughter:

> I called up Berlitz today. . . . Paying for culture. When I was born between
> the legs of the best teacher I ever had (141).

Physical, spiritual, sexual, cultural birth "between the legs" of a woman is an omnipresent figure in *Loving in the War Years,* evoking the mother-daughter relationship in erotic, powerful language. In one poem, Moraga writes, "For you, mama, I have unclothed myself before a woman":

> Stretching my legs and imagination so open
> to feel my whole body cradled
> by the movement of her mouth, the mouth
> of her thighs rising and falling, her arms
> her kiss, all the parts of her open
> like lips moving, talking me into
> loving (140).

Lesbian desire and sexuality, which is "like lips moving, talking me into loving," becomes a type of the mother's language, which Moraga claims as a right.[11] But Moraga's lesbian desire, and her feminist politics which has at its center the love of the Chicana for herself, an "embrace . . . of the race of my mother" (94), is not unequivocally welcomed by the mother whose embrace of heterosexual privilege can become an abandonment of the lesbian daughter:

> I am a lesbian. I love women to the point of killing for us all. . . . My mother
> does not worry about me; she *fears* me. She fears the power of the life she
> helped to breathe into me. She fears the lessons she taught me will move
> into action. She fears I might be willing to die rather than settle for less than
> the best of loving (117).

The mother-daughter bond and lesbian desire become inseparable elements of a volatile revisioning of Chicana identity. At its center, Moraga reconfigures longing for the mother, for the mother-tongue, as the crucible-birthing of the Chicana lesbian-feminist. "Mama" writes Moraga, "I use you / like the belt / pressed inside your grip / seething for contact":

> I take
> what I know
> from you and want

to whip this world
into shape

. . .

I was not to raise an arm against you
But today
I promise you
I *will* fight back
Strip the belt from your hands
and take you
into
my arms (16).

The tension present in these lines—of leaving and return, of the forced exile and the stubborn reclamation, of a daughter's loyalty expressed in terms of sexual desire—is present as well, although in different form, in Anzaldúa's poem "Nopalitos" in *Borderlands/La Frontera* (112–13), in which the speaker's historical and sexual self-consciousness complicates her relationship to her homeplace and people ("though I'm part of their *comaraderia* / am one of them / I left and have been gone a long time"). It is present as well in Leslie Silko's portrait of her great aunt who was sent to Indian school, learned to revere books, yet remained able to teach her niece the oral traditions. It is the tension of the mestiza, the bridger of cultures and traditions, the traveler outward and the prodigal returned: changed, lined by the journey, a new woman.

IV

As *poemarios,* then, as social acts, these three books in their own specific and unique ways perform similar cultural work. They bear witness to the loss into silence of whole worlds of American experience. They bear witness to specific, particular, acts of oppression by which the dominant enforces these silences—means them to be. And they bear witness as well to particular acts of reconstruction that women of color advance on behalf of their own identity and their own history, sometimes against the resistance of both mainstream and marginalized cultural norms.

If the witness of these books breaks our hearts, if we are reduced to silence in the full presence of these Northamerican experiences, then our silence must lead us to a wider, deeper listening. When we lend our attention to these voices, we are not simply witness to the mestiza's resistance to the silencing of her history and identity; we are witnessing as well our own history reconstructed and the foundations of our identities challenged and changed. To lend "the life of our reading"—Olsen's phrase—to these texts is to reveal the screaming silences that the parochialisms of our own projects as academic and cultural workers too often represent. Too few books, Olsen writes, "are kept alive by critics or academics who could be doing so." Too many critics and academics, she continues, "tend to invoke the same dozen or so writers as if none else exist worthy of mention, or as if they've never troubled to read anyone else" (169–70); this is especially true when the writer's work comes from a culture, class, or tradition already underrepresented or invisible in the anthologies and reading lists.[12]

The real weight and profound revolutionary potential of multicultural challenges to the American literary canon as they are represented by these texts, if that potential is to become tangible and transformative, must be undergirded by our willingness to be changed by them. The debates about canons, curricula, and multiculturalism currently energizing academic conversations and scholarship challenge all academic workers to be open to the kind of transformative, sometimes terrifying, change that Native American poet Simon Ortiz evokes, when he suggests that before critics can truly evaluate indigenous American literatures, they "have to look at the underpinning, the structure of their own country, their own conscience":

> If the critic really looked at what Native America was and is today, [s]he would have to undo the construct that America according to Western civilization and its rationalizations is. . . . Fear is the real hindrance to criticism. It's not going to be just or rational unless self-directed questions are asked by critics.[13]

Such self-directed questions should inform our teaching and writing about the works of North American women of color, standing as a kind of witness not only to their presence in our classrooms but to the mountains of absence to which they testify as well. Texts like these by Anzaldúa, Moraga, and Silko lead us to the kind of silence that is prerequisite to our hearing new and vital voices on their own terms. Only then will the "constructs" that define dominant Northamerican narratives of history, literature, and philosophy, and the variety of our relationships to these constructs as academic workers, become truly open to challenge and change.

NOTES

1. The epigraphs are from Carolyn Forche's "El Salvador: An Aide-Memoire," *In Praise of What Persists,* ed. Stephen Berg, New York: Harper & Row, 1983: 107; and Tillie Olsen's *Silences,* New York: Delta/Seymour Lawrence, 1978: 39. All other references to *Silences* will be given in the text.

I'd like to thank Caroline Simpson and Shelli Booth Fowler, as well as the editors of this anthology, for helping me to understand all the questions that play at the edges of this essay.

2. "Poetry Is Not a Luxury," in *Sister Outsider,* Freedom, CA: The Crossing Press, 1894: 39. In another essay of the same volume, Lorde notes that such silences are the result of "institutionalized rejection of difference" and "an absolute necessity in a profit economy which needs outsiders as surplus people. As members of such an economy, we have all been programmed to respond to the human differences between us . . . in one of three ways: ignore it, and if that is not possible, copy it if we think it is

dominant, or destroy it if we think it's subordinate." See "Age, Race, Class, and Sex: Women Redefining Difference," 115.

3. *Your Native Land, Your Life,* New York: Norton & Norton, 1986: 33–36. In an earlier section of the poem, Rich writes "Poetry never stood a chance / of standing outside history." This line and the poem's title began much of the thinking that would become this paper.

4. The irony of calling both for the silence of academic workers and for their (vocal) commitment to efforts of cultural and historical revision does not escape me, but I speak of both because I believe the latter can only follow the former. The silence I call for from myself and other academic workers is not that born of oppressive circumstance but of choice and, I hope, an intelligent and open response to difference.

The work of literary criticism is noisy, voluble: we surround the literature we write about with analysis, exegesis, comparisons, flying buttresses of theory, reference, influence studies, etc. Because the canon of literature we study and the ethnic and cultural diversity of its authors and sources is changing rapidly, much more rapidly than the training or the diversity of literary critics themselves, we run the risk of surrounding new texts with interpretive frameworks that drown out rather than emphasize their unique music. Our essays become less a witness of their reality and more a kind of white noise distorting what they mean to transmit.

I interpret these texts and the cultures from which they arise from an outsider's perspective. What meaning I make of them I make within the limits of my own training, and with the help of the writers who made them and the academic workers who interpret before me, and, sometimes, from within the cultures these texts describe. But all of my interpretation has been, I think, most usefully preceded by a silence filled with attention to and observation of difference: the difference between myself and the woman who writes the texts I am witness to, as well as the difference between her purposes for writing and mine.

5. *Storyteller* was published by Seaver Books, an independent line distributed by Henry Holt & Company; it remained in print for several years before Holt dropped distribution for Seaver, and Seaver was picked up by Arcade Publishing (New York). The book is now published by Arcade and distributed by Little, Brown, with approximately 9,000 copies in distribution. *Loving in the War Years* is published by South End Press (Boston), the fourteen year-old publishing arm of the nonprofit Institute for Social and Cultural Change, an alternative media-projects consortium; with an original pressing of 10,000 copies, the book has nearly sold out and remains in print. *Borderlands/La Frontera* is published by The Aunt Lute Foundation, the nonprofit arm of the feminist publishing house Spinsters/Aunt Lute (San Francisco). Although *Borderlands,* Aunt Lute's first venture into bilingual publishing, has been enormously successful, selling over 11,000 copies, Aunt Lute was hard-pressed to find the funding to keep the book in stock, a common problem for small, undercapitalized feminist presses.

Any further references to these books will appear in the text.

6. I speak here of the marketing and packaging of poems in books, leaving aside the reception of single poems published in literary journals—although many of these journals function, I think, as ephemeral anthologies.

For a variety of opinions on the state of poetry's reception and publication in the United States, see Kate Adams, " 'Professionalizing' Poetry," *AND: Literary News, Reviews, and Interviews* 2.2 (1988): 6–9; Reginald Gibbons, "Who's Listening?" *Missouri Review* 7.1 (1983): 194–208; Barry Goldensohn, "Poetry Anthologies and the Canon," *Yale Review* 74 (1985):404–15; Donald Hall, "Poetry and Ambition," *Kenyon*

Review (1983): 89–104; "Is There, Currently, an American Poetry? A Symposium," *American Poetry* 4.2 (1987):2–40; "Interview with Ron Silliman," in *Alive and Writing,* ed. Larry McCaffery (University of Illinois Press, 1987):240–56; Reed Whittemore, *Poets and Anthologists* (Library of Congress, 1986).

7. Hugo Achugar, "The Book of Poems as a Social Act: Notes Toward an Interpretation of Contemporary Hispanic American Poetry," in *Marxism and the Interpretation of Culture,* eds. Cary Nelson and Lawrence Grossberg (Chicago: University of Illinois, 1988): 651–62. See also Cary Nelson's extraordinary *Repression and Recovery: Modern American Poetry and the Politics of Cultural Memory, 1910–1945* (University of Wisconsin Press, 1989), especially pp. 126–29.

8. My grasp of the differences between oral and written literature was enhanced by Paula Gunn Allen's "Bringing Home the Fact: Tradition and Continuity in the Imagination," *Recovering the Word: Essays on Native American Literature,* eds. Brian Swann and Arnold Krupat (Berkeley: University of California Press, 1987): 563–79. See also Bernard Hirsch, " 'The Telling Which Continues': Oral Tradition and the Written Word in Leslie Marmon Silko's *Storyteller,*" *American Indian Quarterly* 12 (1988): 1–26; Elaine Jahner, "The Novel and Oral Tradition: An Interview with Leslie Marmon Silko," *Book Forum* 5.3 (1981): 383–88.

9. For treatments of the impact of race, class, and gender studies on Chicana literature and criticism, see Norma Alarcón, "Chicana's Feminist Literature: A Re-Vision Through Malintzin/or Malinche: Putting Flesh Back on the Object," in *This Bridge Called My Back: Writings by Radical Women of Color,* eds. Gloria Anzaldúa and Cherríe Moraga (Watertown: Persephone Press, 1981) 182–89; Eliana Ortega and Nancy Saporta Sternbach, "At the Threshhold of the Unnamed: Latina Literary Discourse in the Eighties" in *Breaking Boundaries: Latina Writing and Critical Readings,* eds. Asuncion Horno-Delgado et al. (Amherst: University of Massachusetts Press, 1988) 2–23; Yvonne Yarbro-Bejarano, "Chicano Literature from a Chicana Feminist Perspective" in *Chicana Creativity and Criticism,* eds. Maria Hererra-Sobek and Helena Maria Viramontes (Houston: Arte Publico Press, 1989) 139–45.

10. Norma Alarcón, "Traddutora, Traditora: A Paradigmatic Figure of Chicano Feminism," in *Changing our Power: An Introduction to Women's Studies,* eds. Joe Whitehorse Cochran, Donna Langston, Carolyn Woodward (Dubuque, Iowa: Kendall-Hunt) 197. See also her "Making 'Familia' from Scratch: Split Subjectivities in the Work of Helena Maria Viramontes and Cherríe Moraga," in *Chicana Creativity and Criticism,* 147–59.

11. For another reading of this poem in the context of Moraga's imaging of the lesbian body, see Yvonne Yarbro-Bejarano's "Reclaiming the Lesbian Body: Cherríe Moraga's *Loving in the War Years,*" excerpted in *Out/Look* 12 (1991):74–79. See also her "Cherríe Moraga's *Giving up the Ghost:* The Representation of Female Desire," *Third Woman* 3.1,2 (1986): 113–20.

12. Two paragraphs later, speaking of the economics of the publishing industry, Olsen writes that "writers in a profit-making economy are an exploitable commodity whose works are products to be marketed, and are so judged and handled" (170). Yet academics, too, can exploit writers, for example when we assign xeroxed chapters of books published by small alternative and non-profit presses, robbing presses and poets of royalties and thereby contributing to their already uncertain and tenuous futures. Books published by small presses are fragile things, living brief lives in print, flashing up into availability for a few years and then guttering back into lostness.

On the other hand, academic orders can keep a book from a small press consistently available. Joan Pinkvoss, publisher of Gloria Anzaldúa, says that keeping

Borderlands/La Frontera available meant waiting out the first couple of years after its publication, before the book's importance was recognized and classroom orders became consistent.

13. "An Interview with Simon Ortiz," in *Winged Words: American Indian Writers Speak,* ed. Laura Coltelli (Lincoln: University of Nebraska Press, 1990) 115–16.

WORKS CITED

Achugar, Hugo. (1988). "The Book of Poems as a Social Act: Notes Toward an Interpretation of Contemporary Hispanic American Poetry." *Marxism and the Interpretation of Culture.* eds. Cary Nelson and Lawrence Grossberg. Urbana and Chicago: University of Illinois Press, pp. 651–62.

Adams, Kate. "Interview with Gloria Anzaldúa." Unpublished. April, 1990.

Alarcón, Norma. (1988). "Making 'Familia' from Scratch: Split Subjectivities in the Work of Helena María Viramontes and Cherríe Moraga." *Chicana Creativity and Criticism.* eds. Marie Hererra-Sobek and Helena María Viramontes. Houston: Arte-Publico Press, pp. 147–59.

———. (1988a). "Traddutora, Traditora: A Paradigmatic Figure of Chicano Feminism." *Changing Our Power: An Introduction to Women's Studies.* eds. Jo Whitehorse Cochran, Donna Langston, Carolyn Woodward. Dubuque, Iowa: Kendall-Hunt, pp. 195–203.

———. (1986). "Interview with Cherríe Moraga." *Third Woman* 3, 1/2: 127–34.

Allen, Paula Gunn. (1987). "Bringing Home the Fact: Tradition and Continuity in the Imagination." *Recovering the Word: Essays on Native American Literature.* eds. Brian Swann and Arnold Krupat. Berkeley: University of California Press, pp. 563–79.

Anzaldúa, Gloria (1987). *Borderlands/La Frontera.* San Francisco: Spinsters/Aunt Lute.

Baldwin, James (1961). "Faulkner and Desegregation." *Nobody Knows My Name.* New York: Dell, pp. 117–26.

Coltelli, Laura, ed. (1990). *Winged Words: American Indian Writers Speak.* Lincoln: University of Nebraska Press.

Forché, Carolyn. (1983). "El Salvador: An Aide-Memoire." *In Praise of What Persists.* ed., Stephen Berg. New York: Harper & Row, pp. 93–108.

Hirsch, Bernard A. (1988). " 'The Telling Which Continues': Oral Tradition and the Written Word in Leslie Marmon Silko's *Storyteller.*" *American Indian Quarterly* 12. 1–26.

Jahner, Elaine. (1981). "The Novel and Oral Tradition: An Interview with Leslie Marmon Silko." *Book Forum* 5, 3:383–88.

Moraga, Cherríe. (1983). *Loving in the War Years: lo que nunca pasó sus labios.* Boston: South End Press.

Olsen, Tillie. (1978;1989) *Silences.* New York: Delta/Seymour Lawrence.

Ortega, Eliana, and Nancy Saporta Sternbach. (1989). "At the Threshhold of the Unnamed: Latina Literary Discourse in the Eighties." *Breaking Boundaries: Latina Writing and Critical Readings.* eds. Asuncion Horno-Delgado et. al. Amherst: University of Massachusetts Press, pp. 2–23.

Rich, Adrienne. (1986). *Your Native Land, Your LIfe.* New York: Norton, pp. 33–36.

Silko, Leslie Marmon. (1981). *Storyteller.* New York: Seaver Books.

————. (1973). *Laguna Woman*. Greenfield Center, New York: Greenfield Review Press.

Sternbach, Nancy Saporta. (1989). " 'A Deep Racial Memory of Love': The Chicana Feminism of Cherrie Moraga." *Breaking Boundaries: Latina Writing and Critical Readings*. Amherst: University of Massachusetts Press, pp. 48–61.

Yarbro-Bejarno, Yvonne. (1988). "Chicana Literature from a Chicana Feminist Perspective." *Chicana Creativity and Criticism*. eds. Maria Hererra-Sobek and Helena Maria Viramontes. Houston: Arte Publico Press. pp. 139–45.

Silences in
Harriet "Linda Brent" Jacobs's
Incidents in the Life of a Slave Girl[1]

JOANNE M. BRAXTON
AND SHARON ZUBER

Tillie Olsen might well have included Harriet "Linda Brent" Jacobs in that category of writers she described in *Silences* as belonging to "a class, sex, color still marginalized in literature, and whose coming to voice at all against complex odds is exhausting achievement," had she been aware, when she wrote, of Jacobs's work. It was not until three years after *Silences* appeared, however, that a scholar was able to demonstrate conclusively that Jacobs's autobiographical slave narrative, *Incidents in the Life of a Slave Girl: Written by Herself* (1861), was, in fact, written by Jacobs herself, using the pseudonym "Linda Brent."[2] The book's author, as Jean Fagan Yellin established, was, indeed, a slave woman, a member of the most systematically silenced segment of antebellum America. Today we can understand Jacobs's book as a noteworthy example of a work by one of a sex, color, and caste marginalized in both nineteenth-century America and nineteenth-century American literature.

While critics have focused on such aspects of Jacobs's text as its authenticity, its importance to a tradition of black women's writing, its treatment of sexuality, and Jacobs's resistance as well as accomodation to some of the dictates of the cult of true womanhood and to some of the formal literary conventions of the sentimental novel form she employs, no one has yet fully examined the multiple and interrelated dimensions of silence as they operate both in Linda Brent's narrative and in Harriet Jacobs's construction of it. Michel Foucault has observed that while "silence and secrecy are a shelter for power, anchoring its prohibitions," they "also loosen its holds . . . making it possible to thwart it" (101). This essay will explore the ways in which Harriet Jacobs breaks through those silences imposed upon her as a slave, a woman, and a mother, and the ways in which, as an author, she appropriates silence to empower both her text and the character of "Linda Brent." *Incidents* is, in fact, both in its content and in its form, a complex series of negotiations between speech and silence.

The negotiations begin when, by taking up the pen in the first place, Jacobs breaks the silence of illiteracy imposed upon all slaves and becomes, both as author and as heroine of her text, a source of hope and inspiration.

But while her narrative breaks silence in this important way, it also inscribes silences of its own by incorporating the "not said" within the text. For the enslaved woman, silence becomes an instrument for the assertion of her personal and sexual autonomy. Jacobs's inscription of these silences of her own choosing—which often involves radically turning traditionally imposed silences to her own purposes—represents the supreme assertion of autonomy and requires that she subvert sexual and racial stereotypes. To inscribe these silences requires that she risk her reputation among those readers (including the Northern white women to whom she wants her book to appeal) who will find both her decisions, and her candor about her own sexual past, challenging to those claims to respectability that, as a free woman, she has now come to value. They require that she overcome conventional prejudices with the sheer power of her narrative art. Jacobs's achievement is closely linked to her ability to negotiate among these multiple layers of silence in her text.

The key silences that Harriet Jacobs breaks in her text are those surrounding the sexual and emotional abuse of slave women at the hands of their masters. While the cost of breaking these silences is great, the human cost of remaining silent is even greater. It is the thought of these abuses continuing unexposed that inspires Jacobs to take the risk. The story Jacobs tells is not just a story of oppression: it is a story of resistance. Whether resisting her master's will through "sass"[3] or through her own creative appropriation of the code of silence that the culture erected to contain and subdue women like herself, Linda Brent confounds the forces that would silence her and other slave mothers like her.

Jacobs begins her story, a combination of slave narrative and sentimental novel, with six-year-old Linda Brent's realization, on the death of her mother, that she is a slave. After suffering another death, that of her kind mistress, Linda Brent becomes the property of the daughter of Dr. Flint, a man who constantly harasses her sexually as well as mentally and emotionally. In order to escape Flint and to protect her children, Linda Brent spends almost seven years concealed in a three-foot-high garret above her grandmother's shed until she flees North where, ultimately, she is reunited with her children.

The most basic layer of silencing Jacobs confronts in her text is the silencing, with brute physical force, of slave women by the slaveholders who sexually exploit them. Linda learns early about the prohibition against slave mothers acknowledging the white fathers of their children:

> The secrets of slavery are concealed like those of the Inquisition. My master was, to my knowledge, the father of eleven slaves. But did the mothers dare to tell who was the father of their children? Did the other slaves dare to allude to it, except in whispers among themselves? No, indeed! They knew too well the terrible consequences (35).

When Flint's authority is challenged, he uses the slavetrader to silence slave mothers forever. The crime was not to have a mulatto child, but to speak of its father; a slave who dared name the child's father would be "delivered into the trader's hands" (13).

Even before Linda becomes a mother, Flint enjoins her not to speak about his sexual advances toward her. "Dr. Flint swore he would kill me if I was not as silent as the grave" (28). "I told him that I must and would apply to my grandmother for protection. He threatened me with death, and worse than death, if I made any complaint to her" (32).

Flint uses the threat of the slavetrader or the threat of death to guarantee silence about his sexual advances; he attempts to insure Linda's silence in other areas by hitting her. This strategy, however, sometimes fails. When Linda falls in love with a "young colored carpenter, a free born man" (37), she approaches Flint for approval to marry, knowing full well that "the husband of a slave has no power to protect her" (38). Flint asks her if she loves this man:

> "Yes, sir."
> "How dare you tell me so!" he exclaimed, in great wrath. After a slight pause, he added, "I supposed you thought more of yourself; that you felt above the insults of such puppies."
> I replied, "If he is a puppy I am a puppy, for we are both of the negro race. It is right and honorable for us to love each other. The man you call a puppy never insulted me, sir; and he would not love me if he did not believe me to be a virtuous woman" (38).

Infuriated, Flint strikes her. Brent responds with sass: "You have struck me for answering you honestly. How I despise you!" (39). Standing up to Flint with sass does not get Linda "killed on the spot"; instead it silences him for a time. She has, through direct speech, at least temporarily moved their conflict to an intellectual level, a battle of words, and "for a fortnight the doctor did not speak to me." However, "after a while he became weary of silence. I was sorry for it" (40). The struggle continued.

Eventually, in an act of independence, Linda takes a white lover, the "educated and eloquent" (54) Mr. Sands, by whom she has two children. Linda thwarts Flint's sexual aggression and assumes, on her own terms, the authority of womanhood, of motherhood. While she uses this new power to enrage and distract her tormentor ("I knew nothing would enrage Flint so much as to know that I favored another; and it was something to triumph over my tyrant even in that small way" (55), what galls Flint more than anything else is Brent's strict adherence to the code of silence about sexual relations that he had so assiduously tried to enforce when it involved himself. By twisting the unspoken rule about not revealing the identity of the white father of a slave child, Brent uses her very oppression as her protection. Flint's obsession with Brent's relationship with the child's white father allows her to assume a degree of power, shifting emotional control from master to slave. Like Harriet Jacobs, who keeps a silent space around her personal life by telling her story in the voice of Linda Brent, Brent protects herself through the assumption of the power of silence.

In her narrative, Jacobs also treats the implication of white women in the silence surrounding the sexual exploitation of slave women. White women participate in the silencing of black women while they are themselves silenced by the same patriarchal imperatives that oppress their black sisters. *Incidents* reveals the enforced quietude of the women of both races in the Old South, focusing readers' attention on the essentially patriarchal nature of the peculiar institution. The suppression of white women was necessary for the continued exploitation of black slave women and the perpetuation of the institution of chattel slavery. Unfortunately, white mistresses were slow to recognize the commonality of white and black women's oppression, and jealousy of slave women was the rule rather than the exception.

Even when the white women themselves were the owners of the slaves, they were powerless to prevent their husbands' or fathers' sexual abuse of slave women. Aided by the suffocating standards of Victorian womanhood, slaveholders like Dr. Flint were able to take possession, physically and sexually, of slaves owned by their wives and daughters, silencing the white women in the process. Linda Brent tells of a mistress who treated her inherited slaves humanely. When she married for love a man who had instead "resolved to marry for wealth," she stood powerless as her husband took control of her slaves (50). When one of these slaves became a mother by her new master, the mistress saw, in Jacobs's words "the likeness to her husband" (122) and "wept bitterly. She knew that her own husband had violated the purity she had so carefully inculcated" (51), but she was powerless to protect her slaves. Finally, the mistress is driven mad and dies, "glad to close her eyes on a life which had been made so wretched by the man she loved" (51).[4]

Linda Brent's own mistress or owner is, nominally at least, not Dr. Flint but his daughter Emily. But Dr. Flint slowly usurps his daughter's property, demands Linda's complete submission (sexually and otherwise) within his household, and vows that Linda "shall be my slave as long as I live" (109). When Emily marries, her new husband, Mr. Dodge, demands ownership of Brent. Power shifts from father to husband, reinforcing the white master's ability to silence women, both white and black.

Jacobs explores the theme of silence and silencing from other perspectives, as well. While male-authored slave narratives paint vivid pictures of the terrors of slavery, they do not usually emphasize depictions of the emotional abuse that often accompanied the physical tortures. For example, Frederick Douglass's response to his initiation into the horrors of slavery—the beating of his Aunt Hester—is to hide: "I was so terrified and horror-stricken at the sight, that I hid myself in a closet, and dared not venture out till long after the bloody transaction was over" (6). The self Douglass hides from his readers is an emotional, sexual self, reinforcing his narrative strategy to prove that he is an autonomous man.

Jacobs openly addresses the issue of emotional abuse by focusing on the question of whether slaves' silence, on emotional issues, was due to their lacking feelings, as their owners were wont to claim, or to their being afraid to express them. For example, when Mrs. Flint plans to have Jacobs's Aunt Nancy buried in the Flint family "burial-place," the minister reminds her that "perhaps Aunt Nancy's *mother* may have some choice as to where her remains shall be deposited." However, Jacobs goes on to say, "it had never occurred to Mrs. Flint that slaves could have any feelings" (146). In order to perpetuate the peculiar institution, slaveowners thought of slaves as a *tertium quid,* another order of being. From their perspective, the feelings of slaves went no deeper than their skin color. There were no outward scars or wounds to verify the slaves' invisible emotional abuse; therefore, it could be ignored.

Jacobs documents, from a distinctly female perspective, the internal suffering of slave women without minimizing the physical violence of slavery. (In Chapter 9, "Sketches of Neighboring Slaveholders," she reveals details of unmitigated torture, including the story about a slave named James who was screwed into a cotton gin, left to die, and eaten by rats.) One strength of Jacobs's narrative is the way she expands the definition of violence to include the invisible scarification resulting from severed relationships. Her reader can almost touch the scars of a slave mother's sorrow on New Year's Eve as "she sits on her cold cabin floor, watching the children who may all be torn from her the next morning" (16) at the auction block. Jacobs's unique perspective as a slave mother gives her the power to expose the often unseen, and unacknowledged, emotional violence of slavery.

If we look closely at two comparable passages from *The Narrative of the Life of Frederick Douglass* and *Incidents,* Jacobs's consciously gendered perspective is highlighted. In Chapter 1 of his narrative, Frederick Douglass recounts how "my mother and I were separated when I was but an infant," and he philosophizes that slave children were separated from their mothers in order to "hinder the development of the child's affection toward its mother, and to blunt and destroy the natural affection of the mother for the child" (48). Douglass's mother worked on a neighboring plantation about twelve miles away. At night, after working long hours in the field, she walked those twelve miles "through the darkness to share a morsel of food with her mulatto son and to reassure him that he is somebody's child" (Braxton 1). In Douglass's words, "She would lie down with me, and get me to sleep, but long before I waked she was gone." He notes that when he heard of his mother's death he "received the tidings . . . with much the same emotions I should have probably felt at the death of a stranger" (48–49).

Although we know little about Jacobs's mother, we know that Jacobs "grieved for her" at her death, when Jacobs was six years old. Much later, when she has become a mother herself and has been in hiding for several years, Jacobs laments that her children are "almost without memory of a mother," and she doubts whether Ellen or Benny "would have for me the natural affection that children feel for a parent" (139). Fear of the complete loss of this parental connection gives Jacobs the courage to risk seeing Ellen before she is sent to live with relatives of Mr. Sands, her white father. Brent leaves her garret hiding place and goes to the room in which she gave birth to her children. There she reaffirms her attachment to her child. That night Ellen

> nestled in my arms, and I had no inclination to slumber. The moments were too precious to lose any of them. . . .

> Before dawn they came to take me back to my den. I drew aside the
> window curtain, to take a last look of my child. The moonlight shone on her
> face, and I bent over her, as I had done years before, that wretched night
> when I ran away (140–41).

Frederick Douglass's mother probably looked through the moonlight,
with the same longing and love, at her sleeping child before she left him to
labor in the fields twelve miles away, but we were not seeing through her eyes.
Jacobs's version, a mother's version, of this horror of slavery exposes the
depth of the emotional abuse suffered in silence by slaves torn from their
family connections. Whereas Douglass's *Narrative* emphasizes the struggle for
literacy and autonomy, *Incidents in the Life of a Slave Girl* emphasizes another
dimension, one of caring and need and connection.[5] Jacobs reinscribes emotional depths that both the slaveholders and popular male authors of slave
narratives had "written out" of slave culture in part to conform to the
nineteenth-century ideal of what it meant to be a man.[6]

The problem of silence is also reflected in the author's relationship with
her audience. Like all African-American slave narrators, Jacobs was bur-
dened with the task of winning the attention of an audience of predominantly white, middle-class female readers. For several years after escaping to
the North, the future author of *Incidents* avoided speaking out publicly
about her life as a slave, but developed her voice in private correspondence
with her confidante, Rochester Quaker Amy Post. To Post she confided
pain-filled reflections on her sexual past and her personal conflict about
revealing that past. "When I first came North," Jacobs wrote, "I avoided the
Antislavery people as much as possible because I felt that I could not be
honest and tell them the whole truth."[7] As "the fallen woman," the outraged
mother feels a certain reticence about abandoning her newly gained respect
as a free woman and doing what respectable Victorian women didn't do—
talk about sex. Thus, paradoxically, we have Jacobs simultaneously silenced
by the dictates of the Cult of True Womanhood (as well as the literary
conventions of the sentimental novel form she's using) and compelled to
speak out because of moral obligation. Jacobs's audience is clearly delin-
eated in her "Preface" when she states that she "earnestly desire[s] to arouse
the women of the North to a realizing sense of the condition of two millions
of women at the South, still in bondage, suffering what I suffered, and most
of them far worse" (1).

By writing under the pseudonym Linda Brent and not naming herself
directly, Jacobs is able to break the silence regarding sexuality of the stereotypical True Woman, while at the same time keeping her identity and the
identity of her children a secret. Using the form of popular "women's literature" of the day, she turns weakness to her advantage. Here is the iron fist of
abolitionist rhetoric ("*Slavery is damnable!*" (23)) in the velvet glove of a
confessional, "poor Black slave mother's" narrative. This is exactly what
Hazel Carby talks about in *Reconstructing Womanhood* when she writes that
the "creation of Linda Brent was the terrain through which Jacobs had to

journey in order to reconstruct the meaning of her own life as a woman and mother" (50).

Arguing that Jacobs's narrative "be read as a crafted representation" through which Jacobs authenticates herself, Elizabeth Fox-Genovese in *Within the Plantation Household* suggests that this authentication is based on a "factual lie." She believes that "it stretches the limits of all credulity that Linda Brent actually eluded her master's sexual advances" and that Jacobs inscribes a silence, by way of a fabrication, for her Northern readers (392). Yet on another level, this "factual lie" is more than consideration for, or accommodation to, her white, upper-class, Victorian audience. Although one can believe that Jacobs was raped, was unable to resist the sexual advances of Dr. Flint's real-life counterpart, by constructing Linda Brent to resist Flint's advances, Jacobs has herself resisted the demoralization of rape. She has taken up the pen and crafted a self whose character refused to submit to one of the worst terrors for slave women—forced sex.

This resistance is played out in her use of literacy. Within the text of *Incidents,* Jacobs uses the paradox of literacy gained, then withheld by choice, to thwart Flint's sexual aggression. When Flint passes Linda suggestive notes, she states, "He knew that I could write, though he . . . failed to make me read his letters" (40). Thus she refuses to allow her quest for literacy to be perverted into a seduction, a quest ultimately realized in Jacobs's writing and publication of *Incidents.*[8]

A self-taught writer with few models other than the Bible, popular women's fiction, newspapers, and standard abolitionist tracts to emulate, Jacobs brought a powerful natural gift for language and structure to her writing. As she speaks out against the systematic silencing of black women in nineteenth-century America, Jacobs mounts a persuasive attack, as Jean Yellin has observed, not only on "the institution of chattel slavery with its supporting ideology of white racism," but on "traditional patriarchal institutions and ideologies" as well (xiii). Jacobs challenges both the male-dominated abolition movement and the nascent woman's rights movement by placing her own black and female experiences at the center of her narrative and by daring to break the silence surrounding the forbidden topics of the rape of slave women and the collusion of white mistresses in the sexual exploitation of their enslaved sisters. As she makes the experience of a black slave woman the central consciousness of her text, she fills in silences in coventional sentimental novels, in which all the women were white, as well as in traditional slave narratives, in which all the (narrating) slaves were male.

Acting as spokeswoman for the outraged black mother, still in bondage, Harriet "Linda Brent" Jacobs, like the biblical Jacob in her own reference, labored for seven years to gain the prize of buying her freedom only to be cheated of it. As Jacobs writes to Amy Post soon after a sympathetic Northern friend, Mrs. Willis, purchased her freedom,

> I thank you for your kind expressions in regard to my freedom; but the
> freedom I had before the money was paid was dearer to me. God gave me

that freedom; but man put God's image in the scales with the paltry sum of three hundred dollars. I served for my liberty as faithfully as Jacob served for Rachel. At the end, he had large possessions; but I was robbed of my victory; I was obliged to resign my crown, to rid myself of a tyrant" (204).

Jacobs feels that all of her work to gain her freedom is negated by the mistaken kindness of the friend who purchased her. Perhaps this explains, in part, her compulsion to extend and complete her act of rebellion by working, through the act of writing, to help the cause that would help free her slave sisters and their children. It may well be that this compulsion is what led her to break through the literary silence surrounding the sexual exploitation of slave women to strike her blow against the peculiar institution.

"[I]f silence is expressive of one's deep feeling," Harriet Jacobs once wrote Amy Post, "then in this way I ask you to receive the emotions of what my heart and pen cannot express."[9] Indeed, Jacobs's inscription within the text of *Incidents in the Life of a Slave Girl* of both her own use of silences and her own experience of being silenced are expressive of her deepest feelings. As an author Jacobs balances silencing with silence, coercion with passive resistance, lewdness with virtue, and racial and sexual stereotyping with a growing perception of her personal autonomy and power. Finding a public voice against the incredible odds faced by this former slave is indeed, as Tillie Olsen noted of those belonging to a sex, caste, and color still marginalized, an "exhausting achievement" (9).

NOTES

1. This essay came into being as a happy accident. Having begun to write it, I was asked to give its first version at the November 1990 meeting of the American Studies Association in New Orleans. Meanwhile, I had assigned the topic of "silence" to my American Studies graduate seminar in African-American Literature and Culture. The seminar was then reading Jacobs's autobiography. The students' ideas so enriched my thinking that I felt I could not legitimately appropriate them as part of my own work without giving them a voice. Accordingly, and in the spirit of cooperation, collaboration, and celebration I have found so prominent in the autobiographical tradition of black American women writers, I invited these four women, ranging in age from 20 to 60, to write the essay with me. I divided my class into teams who wrote and rewrote each other's work (and mine) under my supervision. One of these students, Sharon Zuber, a doctoral candidate in American Studies and an adjunct member of the English Department at the College of William and Mary, accompanied me to New Orleans and gave the paper with me, following a format where we alternately read from the work. She is now writing her own essay about her participation in this experiment. In the meantime, Sheryl Kingery, Kimberly Lankford, Elizabeth Scott, Sharon Zuber, and I wish to offer our shared process and the resulting essay as an example of noncompetitive, collaborative scholarship.

2. See Jean Fagan Yellin, "Written by Herself: Harriet Jacobs's Slave Narrative" in *American Literature,* Nov. 1981:53 (3), pp. 479–86. As Henry Louis Gates, Jr., has noted, "Few instances of scholarly inquiry have been more important to Afro-

American studies than has Yellin's." "Introduction," *The Classic Slave Narratives,* ed. Henry Louis Gates, Jr., New York: New American Library, 1987, p. xvii.

3. The concept of "sass" is more fully defined and analyzed in Braxton, *Black Women Writing Autobiography,* pp. 30–31, in which it is traced to its West African derivation which involves a "decoction" of sassy wood bark used "as an ordeal poison in the trial of accused witches. . ." (31). Thus, Linda uses "sass" as a linguistic weapon to "return a portion of the poison" that Dr. Flint has forced upon her and to preserve her separateness and self-esteem.

4. Jacobs's language often resembles that of the traditional sentimental novel. For more on Jacobs's use of sentimental novel conventions see Valerie Smith, " 'Loopholes of Retreat:' Architecture and Ideology in Harriet Jacobs's *Incidents in the Life of a Slave Girl,* in *Reading Black, Reading Feminist: A Critical Anthology,* ed. Henry Louis Gates, Jr., New York: Penguin Books, 1990, pp. 212–26. Smith sees Jacobs as inscribing "a subversive plot of empowerment beneath the more orthodox, public plot [of the sentimental novel] of weakness and vulnerability" (213). She recognizes that Jacobs "borrows heavily from the rhetoric of the sentimental novel" (213) and that "characters speak like literate, middle-class workers out of a romance" (222), but that by using "ellipses and ironies—linguistic narrow spaces," Jacobs expresses a black woman's experience—i.e., she conceals names of places and people who aided her escape to protect them; she is silent about her "continued relations with Sands and her own response to her second pregnancy," which Smith reads as "consigning to narrative silences those aspects of her own sexuality for which the [sentimental novel] genre does not allow," pointing up "an inadequacy of the form." On the whole, Smith sees the sentimental novel form as severely limiting (silencing) Jacobs in some ways, even while it allowed her to break silence by using a form her white readers could understand and respond to. She concludes that "in the ironies and silences and spaces of her book, [Jacobs] makes not-quite-adequate forms more truly her own" (225).

5. Carol Gilligan's "justice" and "care" perspectives, which define two distinct ways of looking at the world associated with but not limited to gender differences, provide a framework for this interpretation. In many male-authored slave narratives, the struggle for freedom and literacy is expressed primarily from a justice perspective in terms of linear movement toward autonomy or separateness. In contrast, the care perspective, which associates the final goal of maturation with connection and moral responsibility, moves toward home and family emanating from a center, a mother. Jacobs constructs a slave narrative written through a mother's eyes to emphasize the emotional scars and loss of connection.

6. There are, of course, some notable exceptions to this silence. In her discussion of Anna Julia Cooper, in " 'On the Threshold of Woman's Era': Lynching, Empire, and Sexuality in Black Feminist Theory," Hazel Carby indicates that Cooper "developed a complex analysis of social, political, and economic forces as being either distinctly masculine or feminine in their orientation and consequences" and "not dependent on biological distinction. Cooper made it clear in her application of such analyses that women could conform to masculinist attitudes and practices and men could display womanly virtues" (304). Cooper's analysis predates Gilligan by almost 100 years. Also, Henry Bibb's *Narrative of the Life and Adventures of Henry Bibb,* not covered in this paper, is the most striking example of a male-authored narrative that emphasizes the care perspective.

7. Jacobs also uses her hard-won literacy to deceive and confuse Flint by writing letters in her garret that a friend then mails from New York; three times he sets out to look for her, while she is still hidden in the "dark hole" that is both her prison and her

refuge. Flint "suppresses" one of these letters written to her grandmother, Aunt Marthy, who could neither read nor write, and substitutes his own. Unknown to him, Linda listens from her hiding place as Flint reads his altered letter to Aunt Marthy. "This was as good as comedy to me, who had heard it all" (130), the fugitive slave would later write in a chapter called "Competition and Cunning." Only Flint's arrogance makes possible the success of Linda's bold deception.

8. See Harriet A. Jacobs to Amy Post [1852?], IAPFP #84; BAP #676–78 (Letter 10). Quoted in Yellin's introduction to *Incidents in the Life of a Slave Girl,* xvii.

9. Harriet Jacobs to Amy Post, February 14, 1853, IAPFP #785; BAP #16: 0710–11. Quoted in Yellin's appendix to *Incidents in the Life of a Slave Girl,* 233–34.

WORKS CITED

Braxton, Joanne M. *Black Women Writing Autobiography; A Tradition Within a Tradition.* Philadelphia: Temple UP, 1989.

Carby, Hazel. " 'On the Threshold of Woman's Era': Lynching, Empire, and Sexuality in Black Feminist Theory." In *"Race," Writing and Difference.* Ed. Henry Louis Gates, Jr. Chicago: U of Chicago P, 1985.

———. *Reconstructing Womanhood: The Emergence of the Afro-American Woman Novelist.* New York: Oxford UP, 1987.

Douglass, Frederick. *Narrative of the Life of Frederick Douglass, An American Slave.* New York: Viking Penguin, 1988.

Foucault, Michel. *The History of Sexuality; Volume I: An Introduction.* New York: Vintage Books, 1990.

Fox-Genovese, Elizabeth. *Within the Plantation Household: Black and White Women of the Old South.* Chapel Hill: U of North Carolina P, 1988.

Gates, Henry Louis, Jr. "Introduction." *The Classic Slave Narratives.* Ed. Henry Louis Gates, Jr. New York: New American Library, 1987, p. xvii.

Gilligan, Carol. *In a Different Voice.* Cambridge, Mass: Harvard UP, 1983.

Jacobs, Harriet A. *Incidents in the Life of a Slave Girl; Written by Herself.* Ed. Jean Fagan Yellin. Cambridge: Harvard UP, 1987.

Olsen, Tillie. *Silences.* New York: Delacorte Press/Seymour Lawrence, 1978.

Smith, Valerie. " 'Loopholes of Retreat:' Architecture and Ideology in Harriet Jacobs' *Incidents in the Life of a Slave Girl.* In *Reading Black, Reading Feminist: A Critical Anthology.* Ed. Henry Louis Gates, Jr. New York: Penguin Books, 1990, pp. 212–26.

Yellin, Jean Fagan. "Written by Herself: Harriet Jacobs' Slave Narrative." *American Literature.* Nov. 1981:53 (3), pp. 479–86.

Women's Silence as a Ritual of Truth: A Study of Literary Expressions in Austen, Brontë, and Woolf

PATRICIA LAURENCE

Beginning with Tillie Olsen and continuing in the work of American and French feminist critics, silence in women has been viewed as the place of oppression, the mark of women's exclusion from the public spheres of life and from respresentation as speakers in a text. But it is time to recognize that there is a female tradition of writing beginning in the nineteenth century that invites us to reread certain paradigms of silence and expression. Knowing that women in certain times and places are unable to speak openly, the novelists Jane Austen, Charlotte Brontë, and Virginia Woolf narrate the inwardness of female listeners and observers in conventional frameworks in life and texts, inviting us to interpret their silences not as passivity, submission and oppression, but as an enlightened presence. The silences represent women's different ways of feeling and knowing—perhaps silences hiding fears, angers, taboo thoughts—as well as representing the available means of expression in particular historical and cultural circumstances. This female tradition, which is connected with the development of the novel and its ability to record inner life, replaces the speaking subject in the English novel with the observing, listening, thinking, dreaming female subject.

The brief survey of female characters that follows reveals that Jane Austen and Charlotte Brontë textualize an indirectness or muteness in women that in turn becomes a discourse of interiority and resistant silence in some of the female characters of Virginia Woolf. These resistant silences are sometimes "passive experiments": "To absent yourself—that is easier than to speak aloud. . . . It is worth watching very carefully to see what effect the experiment of absenting oneself has had—if any" (Woolf, *Three Guineas,* 135). This literary development from indirectness and evasiveness to overt and resistant silence moves further the feminist discourse on the narration and cultural and literary interpretation of silence. In a new turn in feminist criticism, the preservation of these female silences by female authors is noted, and in a reversal of the traditional notion of women's complicity with oppressive circumstances or cultural exclusion, such silences are viewed as a difference of view, an alternative code of "truth" or, sometimes, an expression of anger—the only kind that would be socially tolerated. Women's silence, that is to say, may be read as a strategy of resistance and choice—a ritual of truth.

The unsaid is of interest to many twentieth-century literary critics. Wolfgang Iser and Sanford Budick's recent collection of essays, *Languages of the Unsayable* (1989), testifies to this: "Once we have encountered the limits of the sayable, we must acknowledge the existence of 'unsayable things' and, by means of a language somehow formed on being silent, articulate that which cannot be grasped" (xii). In the tradition of Western culture, this language "somehow formed on being silent" acknowledges the inadequacies of language and the limits of interpretation. From this perspective, silence marks a lack or an absence—another revelation of the inadequacy of language to express life.

Female scholars, taking up the same topic, observe not the absence of women but their presence and struggle to find a voice with which to speak in the public realm—sometimes, ironically, through adopting a stance of silence. Women are socialized into ways of talking, and the development of a style of indirectness or tentativeness involves the learning of certain tones and intonations as well as vocabulary, as recognized by feminist linguists such as Sally McConnell-Ginet, who has written about "Intonation in a Man's World" (549). Because of exclusion from the public realm, some women, even today, are uneasy with male registers of expression and feeling. They lack spontaneity or fluency of expression in literature and life, and their silences—motivated more by their social position as women and the attendant psychological or cultural anxieties and taboos than by philosophical reflections on the inadequacies of language—are now being read according to a new tradition of interpretation. For example, the psychologists and sociologists Mary Belenky, Blythe Clinchy, Nancy Goldberger, and Jill Tarule have focused on women's different ways and expressions of "knowing" and "feeling"; the linguist Deborah Tannen has contextualized the different patterings of talk and silence in conversations between men and women; and the literary critic Janis Stout has directed attention to the strategies of reticence in Jane Austen, Katherine Ann Porter, Willa Cather, and Joan Didion. These female researchers reveal that *Logos* (the word) consists as much in feeling, knowing, and a kind of listening that allows things to come into presence as it does in speaking. They also remind us that expression consists of nonverbal signs, codes, and gestures as well as words (see also Laurence 1991).

These differing angles of vision suggest not one but many reasons for silence—linguistic, psychological, sociological, cultural, and historical—that these new readings excavate. Depending upon one's definition of reality, silences woven into the fabric of a woman's text can be an absence or a presence. If reality is perceived according to established partriarchal values, then women's silence, viewed from the outside, is a mark of absence and powerlessness, given women's modest expression in the public sphere until the twentieth century. If, however, the same silence is viewed from the inside, and women's experience and disposition of mind inform the standard of what is real, then women's silence can be viewed as a presence, and as a text, waiting to be read. Such a reading of women's silence differs from Elaine Showalter's assertion that "the holes in discourse, the blanks and gaps and silences are not the spaces where female consciousness reveals itself but the blinds of a 'prison-house' " (255–56). Showalter "underreads" women's silences in a text rather than "overreading . . . to unsettle the interpretive model" as Nancy Miller suggests (83). Such "overreading" of the narrative signs and silences represented by female authors, particularly in texts of the past, reveals the hidden psychic life and historical sense of women.

The emergence of semiotics, the study of signs, enables us to put words in their place. Words are signs, but they represent only one order of language among other kinds of nonverbal signs: punctuation, narrative spaces, bodily gestures. This essay then advances the notion that the difference between language and nonverbal, indirect signs in fiction and life amplifies a question posed by the critic Tzvetan Todorov:

> What is the place of linguistic signs among signs in general? So long as our consideration of meaning, value and communication is limited to verbal language alone, we remain inside a philosophy of language; only the shattering of the linguistic framework justifies the establishment of a semiotics (57).

Since speaking and language have been emphasized as subjects of analysis by poststructuralists and feminists, and by the Western literary tradition in general, there is a danger of losing sight of the resistance marked by women's cultural and textual indirectness of speech and silence: semiotics. Barbara Johnson warns of women who lose "self-resistance . . . as a source of insight and power rather than merely of powerlessness" (46). A silent woman, a nonspeaker in a text or life, has traditionally been viewed as powerless in the public and, sometimes, in the private sphere, or lacking in intelligence or expression. But as the anthropologist Shirley Ardener claims:

> Because the arena of public discourse tends to be characteristically male-dominated and the appropriate language registers have been "encoded" by males, women may be at a disadvantage when wishing to express matters of particular concern to them. Unless their views are presented in a form acceptable to men, and to women brought up in the male idiom, they will not be given a proper hearing (viii–ix).

In learning to read the indirectness of women's expression in the novels of Austen and Brontë and later, in the silences of Woolf, it is not my intention to valorize nonspeakers over speakers, but to use another value system and literary "code" to infuse their silences with different psychological and cultural meaning. As Annette Kolodny reminds us: "Insofar as literature is itself a social institution, so, too, reading is a highly socialized—or learned—activity" (10).

Silent yet knowing women listen, observe, think, and dream. Often they become the "knowing" and subjective centers of certain novels. The listening Fanny Price in Jane Austen's *Mansfield Park* and Anne Elliot in *Persuasion;* the thinking Jane Eyre in Charlotte Brontë's novel; the observing Mrs. Ramsay in Virginia Woolf's *To the Lighthouse,* and the dreaming Rachel in *The Voyage Out* and Rhoda in *The Waves* are characters created by female authors in dialogue with a reader who is expected to assume the same active and insightful "overreading" as the silent female characters themselves. Silences are narrated and marked in the text to represent the presence of women and are not a simple indexing of women's social positions. What we are learning to create then is a cultural dialogue with a silent woman, part of a rhetoric of silence. For as Aristotle reminds us: "Rhetoric may be defined as the faculty of observing in any given case the available means of expression" (Todorov 61). Given the "necessary indirectness" of women's speech referred to earlier, the most effective—and perhaps the only available—means of expression for women in certain historical circumstances may be metalinguistic and nonverbal signs. Such nonverbal signs, or silences, then invite the reader into the text to actively interpret the cultural dimension of a discourse constituted by signs and positions and, sometimes, by the body rather than by words.

The Listening Woman

"Power," Foucault states, "is always interactional." Despite the negative terms traditionally applied to the effects of power—"it 'excludes,' it 're-presses,' it 'censors,' it 'abstracts,' it 'masks,' it 'conceals' "—it, nevertheless, produces . . . rituals of truth" (*Discipline and Punish,* 194). A speaker and a listener together create a ritual of truth. In discourse, the speaker, in the Western tradition, has come to be viewed as the one who is in control; the listener, on the other hand, is viewed as passive and powerless—traditionally, the woman's position. Kierkegaard in his psychological novel, *Repetition,* challenges the simplicity of this view in observing that there is a power in listening or in not listening, as well as in speaking or in not speaking. Foucault complicates this notion of discourse in avowing that any such discourse involves at least two sides and that, indeed, there are many discourses of power involving the listener as well as the speaker. The novelist Jane Austen knows this, and she creates characters in her later novels—Fanny Price and Anne Elliot—who listen and observe more, in contrast to her clever talkers. Jane Bennett and Emma Woodhouse. J. F. Burrows, in his statistical analysis of the incidence of speaking and thinking in Austen's novels, reports that in both *Mansfield Park* and *Persuasion,* the characters' reflections are considerably larger than their spoken parts. His analysis reveals that Fanny of *Mansfield Park* speaks 6,117 words and thinks 15,418 words; Anne of *Persuasion* speaks 4,336 words and thinks 19,730; compared to Emma, the clever talker, who speaks 21,501 words and thinks 19,730. Such comparisons of conventional tags for external speaking or internal thinking, observing or listening, signal a shift in Austen's interest in "reflection," "observation," and "thinking," from the more "conversational" Emma to the plain, dominant heroines Anne Elliot and Fanny Price, who are actively quiet. Austen's movement toward the "unsaid" belies Virginia Woolf's speculation that had Jane Austen lived beyond forty-two years,

> she would have trusted less to dialogue and more to reflection to give us a knowledge of her characters. . . . She would have devised a method, clear and composed as ever, but deeper and more suggestive, for conveying not only what people say, but what they leave unsaid (*A Writer's Diary,* 148–49).

Indeed, in these later works, the reflection of Fanny and Anne is marked in narration. Fanny is described as a "quiet auditor of the whole" (*Mansfield Park,* 104), and Anne, similarly, as "a most attentive listener to the whole" (*Persuasion,* 34).

In examining Fanny's role in *Mansfield Park,* we discover that her "quiet listening" is as psychologically, morally, and discursively productive in the plot and vision of the novel as Edmund's "talk." Edmund appreciates Fanny's listening (if only as a spur for more of his own talk) as he unravels the complications of his waning relationship with Miss Crawford:

> "But Fanny,"—stopping her by taking her hand, and speaking low and seriously, "you know what all this means. You see how it is; and could tell me, perhaps better than I could tell you, how and why I am vexed. Let me talk to you a little. You are a kind, kind listener" (204).

Fanny, in the underrated position of a listener, contributes her silence to Edmund's talk. She lets things come into being, for she knows "what all this means . . . sees how it is; and could tell you . . . better than I could tell you" what is going on:

> Fanny, being always a very courteous listener, and often the only listener at hand, came in for the complaints and distresses of most of them. She knew that Mr. Yates was disappointed in Henry Crawford, that Tom Bertram spoke so quick he would be unintelligible, that Mrs. Grant spoilt everything by laughing, that Edmund was behind-hand with his part, and that it was misery to have anything to do with Mr. Rushworth, who was wanting a prompter to every speech (125).

Though Fanny has been read as passive or even "monstrous" by Nina Auerbach (218), this new reading, expanding on Marylea Mayersohn's earlier work, suggests that her observing and listening is not brooding or predatory but productive, for her listening often makes her a "knowing" center of consciousness in the novel. Her marked silences, which reveal that she "knew," are interwoven with the dialogue of others into a social and textual discourse that illustrates Derrida's notion of "*différance.*" Silence is necessary to talk: listening is necessary to speaking; we only know what a listener is because we have speakers. The meaning of talk or silence, or knowledge and ignorance, only exists in a network of differences.

The centrality of Fanny's consciousness, "the quiet auditor of the whole," and the connections she observes and makes motivate the plot. Despite her lack of background, breeding, and money, she "judged rightly" the theatrical,

"Lovers' Vows," (142). She is the moral center of the group of young people, refusing to participate in the "sin" of acting in the play or in wishing for the death of her uncle. She "knows" that Henry Crawford is a "sad flirt," accepts his absolute confidence with reservation, and relates to Miss Crawford that she had not

> been an inattentive observer of what was passing between him and some part of this family in the summer and the autumn. I was quiet, but I was not blind. I could not but see that Mr. Crawford allowed himself in gallantries that did mean nothing (275).

Fanny distrusts speech and glibness, as Woolf later distrusts, to some degree, male "phrase-makers" like Bernard in *The Waves*. Fanny, "though never a great talker, . . . was always more inclined to silence when feeling most strongly" (280). The glib Henry does not feel as deeply as Fanny, and after his pursuit is abandoned, and Edmund proposes, we are left with the image of Fanny and Edmund "always talking confidentially," though such conversations remain unrepresented in the novel.

Fanny listens carefully and quietly advises, revealing, we are told, what she "knows" in Austen's world of *Mansfield Park*. In Virginia Woolf's *The Voyage Out*, women's listening takes another turn. Here women outwardly observe the social convention of listening to men while being inwardly attentive to their own thoughts. Woolf overtly diminishes the talk of men by narrating what Austen left unsaid in Fanny while she "listened"—the inner thoughts of the ladies who "each . . . being after the fashion of their sex, highly trained in promoting men's talk without listening to it, could think—about the education of her children, about the use of fog sirens in an opera—without betraying herself" (17).

Such rituals of silence are constituted from a certain doubleness, for woman is at the same time, as Woolf states in *A Room of One's Own*, both an insider and an outsider of culture, both silent and a talk-producer. She is someone who is socially positioned to patiently listen to men yet uses the quiet space of listening, as in the above passage—her mind, after all, is her own—to create a space for herself in which to think.

In Woolf, not listening can often become subversive and resistant because we know what the character is thinking. The element of silence that Austen's Fanny supplies as a ready listener or observer is transformed a century later in Woolf's Lily Briscoe, who speculates about what would happen if women did not listen. At Mrs. Ramsay's dinner party in *To the Lighthouse*, Lily listens, but resists giving her sympathy to Charles Tansley:

> There is a code of behaviour, she knew, whose seventh article (it may be) says that on occasions of this sort it behooves the woman, whatever her own occupation may be, to go to the help of the young man opposite so that he may expose and relieve the thigh bones, the ribs, of his vanity, of his urgent desire to assist himself. . . . But how would it be, she thought, if neither of us did either of these things? (137).

The "code of behaviour" that Lily, like Fanny, has learned is that "it behooves the woman, whatever her occupation might be, to go to the help of the young man opposite." Empathy for the male must precede self-interest or "truth" of relations. Similarly, at the end of the novel, Mr. Ramsay, sighing, looking "skimpy, wispy," approaches Lily seeking sympathy. Woolf narrates the unspoken thoughts of Lily:

> All Lily wished was that this enormous flood of grief, this insatiable hunger for sympathy, this demand that she surrender herself up to him . . . should leave her . . . before it swept her down in its flow. . . . They stood there, isolated from the rest of the world. His immense self-pity, his demand for sympathy poured and spread itself in pools at her feet, and all she did, miserable sinner that she was, was to draw her skirts a little closer round her ankles, lest she should get wet. In complete silence she stood there, grasping her paint brush (228).

The anxious gesture of grasping the paint brush symbolizes Lily's holding on to her vision of herself as a painter as well as a resolve to achieve more sincere relations between the sexes. She does not want to be the angel of sympathy, but nevertheless, in the end, she praises Mr. Ramsay's boots, satisfying his need. Woolf reveals through Lily's interior monologue what she "knows" about men, rather than just observing, as Austen does, that Fanny does "know." We know what Fanny is, but not what she thinks, for her thoughts remain unrepresented in the text; in Woolf, however, we are privy to narrations of mind where nineteenth-century sentiment is transformed into twentieth-century psychology and, in this case, resistant reflection. Both authors present observing and thinking women, but Woolf more fully narrates and explores the inner life of women thinking, with a delicacy of language and a fluency of feeling rarely represented in the English novel. Lily Briscoe's articulated silences clearly express a more resistant stance, moving the reader to speculate upon the possibility of different kinds of relations between the sexes.

The Thinking Woman

Charlotte Brontë further develops the inner life hinted at in Austen's novels through the character of the silent, thinking, and observing Jane Eyre. Through her character's internal meditations, she increases the proportion of inner monologue in the novel, moving toward Woolf's experiment with psycho-narration. Brontë's characters do not learn the steps of the social dance to selfhood with the assistance of society, as Fanny Price and Anne Elliot do. In Brontë, a female tradition of silence emerges that is not social or ironic, as in Austen. Rather, it is an offshoot of a different literary and philosophical tradition: seventeenth-century religious or meditative poetry written mostly by men in dialogues between self and God (i.e., John Donne's *Holy Sonnets*). This tradition, transformed by Brontë—daughter, after all, of a vicar—becomes what I call the female prayer, with gender struggle replacing earlier religious dialogue.

In the soliloquies in *Jane Eyre,* we are presented not with the traditional struggle of man in embattled relation with God, but with a dialogue between a woman's self-interest (indicated by Jane's assertion—"I care for myself") in conflict with "conscience" and "reason" that cloak the interests of men—"Think of his misery." Jane, after discovering that Mr. Rochester has a wife in the attic, draws aside and meditates over the conflicts between reason and feeling:

> And while he spoke my very conscience and reason turned traitor against me, and charged me with crime in resisting him. They spoke almost as loud as Feeling; and that clamoured wildly. "Oh comply!" It said. "Think of his misery; think of his dangerous look, at his state when left alone; remember his headlong nature; consider the recklessness following on despair, soothe him; save him; love him; tell him you love him and will be his. Who in the world cares for you? or who will be injured by what you do? Still indomitable was the reply—"I care for myself . . . I will hold to the principles received by me when I was sane, and not mad—as I am now" (319).

Here Jane's own reason and conscience "turn traitor" against her as she articulates the embattled relation between her own self-interest and "saving" Mr. Rochester.

That she sticks to her resolve is important, but the above passage illustrates the substance of the new female prayer as an inner dialogue between female and male self-interest. Later that night, Jane has a dream in which a dialogue between self and a guardian mother occurs:

> "My daughter, flee temptation!"
> "Mother, I will!" (322).

Jane's inner struggle between sympathy for the man, Rochester, and the self-preservation of and sympathy towards herself—prompted by the motherly figure—surfaces in an unconscious moment in a dream. This nineteenth-century revelation of a woman's thinking through a female spirit only hints at the fantasia of the unconscious revealed later in the dreams of Woolf's Rachel and Rhoda.

Female Observers

Female thinkers and listeners—separated only for heuristic purposes in this essay—are knowing and intelligent women who become, according to Kierkegaard's categorization of observers, secret agents, and, perhaps, double agents:

> And when an observer fulfills his duties well, he [or she] is to be regarded as a secret agent in a higher service, for the observer's art is to expose what is hidden (135).

Women outwardly conform to social roles, but they develop strategies of silence and expression to resist these roles and to fulfill inner needs. They become "double," adopting, like other minorities, what Barbara Johnson describes as the "ability . . . to assume and articulate the incompatible forces involved in her own division. The sign of an authentic voice is thus not self-identity but self-difference" (164). Though the female observers in this section will be described in terms of what they "see" or "observe" rather than what they "hear" or "listen to" as in the previous discussion, they are yet another literary revelation of women who signal "knowing" through silent observations rather than talk. The discriminating, observing female "sees" different things than men, for as Martin Jay notes in a fascinating article on "the gaze," "what is in fact 'seen' is not a given, objective reality open to an innocent eye. Rather it is an epistemic field, constructed as much linguistically as visually" (182). What a woman sees is also socially constructed, and, in literature, women sometimes become the ultimate narrators of certain novels from which they are seemingly absent because they embody the unsaid of the narrative.

Virginia Woolf's interest in female observers leads to the development of a narrative strategy that enables her to narrate the silent resistances of women. Such characters are generally unrepresented in novels, not necessarily because they do not have words or ideas, but because authors may not believe that they have anything of value to say or because the narrative methods to reveal them have not yet been developed. Through the technique of "psychonarration" (Cohn 14), in which a narrator fuses with the consciousness of the character she narrates, the inner worlds of those who are socially inarticulate or unrepresented in the dialogue of the novel are presented. Woolf, acutely aware of the "unsaid" in life and society, found narrative methods, hinted at in Austen and Brontë, to express the selves of silent observers.

That there is power in the vantage point of an observer is a recognition that has evolved in the critics of consciousness: Martin Heidegger, Paul de Man, and Gaston Bachelard. Who could doubt it, reading Virginia Woolf reading Mrs. Ramsay reading Charles Tansley and her other guests:

> And why should that make Charles Tansley angry? He rushed in (all, thought Mrs. Ramsay, because Prue will not be nice to him) and denounced the Waverly novels when he knew nothing about it, nothing whatsoever, Mrs. Ramsay thought, observing him rather than listening to what he said. . . . At any rate, they were off again. Now she need not listen. It could not last, she knew, but at the moment her eyes were so clear that they seemed to go round the table unveiling each of these people, and their thoughts and their feelings, without effort like a light stealing under water so its ripples and the reed in it and the minnows balancing themselves, and the sudden silent trout are all lit up hanging, trembling. So she saw them; she heard them; but whatever they said had also this quality, as if what they said was like the movement of a trout when, at the same time, one can see the ripple and the gravel, something to the right, something to the left; and the whole is held together . . . now she said nothing (159–61).

The theory of mind suggested by the structure of the metaphors in this passage is one in which the mental processes of the observer are active and searching rather than inert and receptive: Mrs. Ramsay's "eyes . . . go round . . . unveiling . . . like a light stealing under water." We, as readers, participate in the illumination of the light of the mind in the act of silent observation. The mind is creating; it is a light; it is a lamp; it is almost an X ray, extending the metaphorical tradition of mind of the Romantic poets.

What is also interesting about Mrs. Ramsay is that, when thinking and observing, she seems to be suspended, absent from the spoken conversation of the dinner party that she is orchestrating, but present in the text through the narrative flow of her thoughts. The lady vanishes like the female subjects in the photographs of Kathy Grove, who are excised from expected settings, leaving us to reflect about the subversion of woman's conventional role. A woman's presence is marked in creating an empty space in a photograph or a silence in a text that invites reflection on cultural and artistic expectations and codes.

Female Dreamers

In creating the characters of Rhoda in *The Waves* and Rachel in *The Voyage Out,* Woolf adds another dimension to the female thinkers, observers, and listeners developed by Austen and Brontë who express themselves through indirectness, signs, gestures, and bodily expressions rather than words. In these novels, in addition to other forms of silence, Woolf creates expressions of the mind through the body. The bodies of Rachel in *The Voyage Out* and Rhoda in *The Waves* become the loci of techniques for maintaining silences as well as for expression. Bodily gestures and images are the means by which silence becomes externalized and visible to others.

Woolf adds to our cultural definitions of women, fashioning new modes of subjectivity in which we, as readers, are invited "to consult our own minds." She creates ways in which we can sense and experience the woman thinker or dreamer. In illuminating the "undiscovered countries that are then disclosed . . . when the lights of health go down" (*The Moment,* 9)—whether in common illness or in the delirium of Rachel's fever or Rhoda's dreams and hysteria—Woolf turns in her narration to the signs of the body. It is in the treatment of Rachel's sickness that we find some of the most vivid descriptions of the inner life:

> The sights were all concerned in some plot, some adventure, some escape. . . . Now they were on the sea; now they were on the tops of high towers; now they jumped; now they flew. But just as the crisis was about to happen, something invariably slipped in her brain, so that the whole effort had to begin again. The heat was suffocating. At last the faces went further away; she fell into a deep pool of sticky water, which eventually closed over her head. She saw nothing and heard nothing but a faint booming sound,

which was the sound of the sea rolling over her head . . . all her tormenters
thought that she was dead (341).

What makes this state so vivid is the flight of the body and the mind, the odd
angle of vision, the shifting symbols of water and towers, and the inseparabil-
ity of the external and internal "torment."

The enclosed space of the sickroom opens out into dreams of enclosure.
It is in the sick room—a room that is marginal to a house, a room that is
quarantined by Victorian society—that the body and the unconscious is
unleashed: the female imagination flourishes in this delirium. It is a room of
Rachel's own that holds creative possibilities important to her throughout
the novel because, in sickness and in health, it is a place where she estab-
lishes a reality, separate from social definitions, that no one else can enter. It
is here she plays the piano. It is a musical room; it is a narrative room; it is a
room of musical narration that contains Woolf's exciting descriptions of
women's subjective states that have the scent of disease as well as of health.
We, as readers, enter into rhythmic descriptions of strange chambers of
women's minds repressed during the daylight hours of society—the dreaming self.

Austen's valorization of the observant, listening Fanny Price and Anne
Elliot; Brontë's expression of the struggling, meditative thinker Jane Eyre; and
Woolf's poetic narration of the inner lives of Lily, Rachel, and Rhoda are moral
and literary gestures toward the silent woman. Though the listening and observing female characters in Austen and Brontë outwardly conform to traditional
female roles, their presence, gestures, and indirectness of expression subver-
sively hint at Woolf's more open narrative investigation of women's silence and
some of its more resistant social stances. Silence thus becomes for these characters a ritual of truth. By preserving their female characters' silence in the text as
a space to think, feel, dream, or observe, these authors preserve and develop
female insight into self and society from the nineteenth to the twentieth century. Silence is the space in narration where culture and feminine consciousness
do sometimes reveal themselves, if only we can learn to decipher the psychological and cultural meanings. Ideologically, we are trapped as critics if we cannot
shift the reading of silence in women from one of essence to one of position or
even, at times, choice.

WORKS CITED

Abrams, M. H. *The Mirror and the Lamp: Romantic Theory and the Critical Tradition.*
    New York: Oxford UP, 1953.
Ardener, Shirley, ed. *Perceiving Women.* London: Malaby Press, 1975.
Auerbach, Nina. "Jane Austen's Dangerous Charm: Feeling as One Ought About
    Fanny Price." *Women and Literature* 3 (1983).
Austen, Jane. *Mansfield Park.* Boston: Houghton Mifflin, 1814 Reprint, 1965.
———. *Persuasion.* London and New York: Oxford UP, 1818 Reprint, 1932.

Belenky, Mary, Blythe Clinchy, Nancy Goldberger, and Jill Tarule. *Women's Ways of Knowing*. New York: Basic Books, 1986.

Brontë, Charlotte, *Jane Eyre*. New York: New American Library, 1847 Reprint, 1960.

Burrows, John F. "Lively Measures." In *Computation into Criticism*. Oxford: Clarendon Press, 1987.

Cohn, Dorrit. *Transparent Minds*. Princeton: Princeton UP, 1978.

Derrida, Jacques. *Speech and Phenomena, and Other Essays on Husserl's Theory of Signs*. Translated by David B. Allison. Evanston: Northwestern UP, 1967.

Foucault, Michel. *Discipline and Punish: The Birth of a Prison*. Translated by Alan Sheridan. New York: Pantheon, 1977.

Iser, Wolfgang, and Sanford Budick, eds. *Languages of the Unsayable: The Play of Negativity in Literature and Literary Theory*. New York: Columbia UP, 1989.

Jay, Martin. "In the Empire of the Gaze." In David Couzens Hoy, ed. *Foucault: A Critical Reader*. Oxford: Blackwell, 1986.

Johnson, Barbara. "Nothing Fails Like Success." In *Deconstructive Criticism: Directions*. SCE Reports 8 (1980): 9–10.

———. *The Critical Difference: Essays in the Contemporary Rhetoric of Reading*. Baltimore: Johns Hopkins UP, 1981.

Kierkegaard, Søren. *Repetition*. Translated and edited by Howard U. Hong and Edna H. Hong. Princeton: Princeton UP, 1983.

Kolodny, Annette. "Dancing Through the Minefields." In Elaine Showalter, ed., *New Feminist Criticism: Essays on Women, Literature and Theory*. New York: Pantheon, 1985.

Kristeva, Julia. *The Kristeva Reader*. Ed. Toril Moi. New York: Columbia UP, 1991.

Laurence, Patricia. *The Reading of Silence: Virginia Woolf in the English Tradition*. Stanford: Stanford UP, 1991.

Marks, Elaine, and Isabelle de Courtivon, eds. *New French Feminisms*. Amherst: U of Massachusetts P, 1980.

McConnell-Ginet, Sally. "Intonation in a Man's World." *Signs: Journal of Women in Culture and Society,* 3, 3 (Spring 1978): 541–49.

Meyersohn, Marylea, "What Fanny Knew." In Janet Todd, ed. *Jane Austen: New Perspectives*. New York: Holmes Meier, 1983.

Miller, Nancy. *Subject to Change*. New York: Columbia UP, 1988.

Olsen, Tillie. *Silences*. New York: Delacorte Press, 1978.

Showalter, Elaine, "Feminist Critics in the Wilderness." In *New Feminist Criticism: Essays on Women, Literature and Theory*. Ed. Showalter. New York: Pantheon, 1985.

Stout, Janice. *Strategies of Reticence*. Charlottesville and London: UP of Virginia, 1990.

Tannen, Deborah. *You Just Don't Understand: Women and Men in Conversation*. New York: Ballantine Books, 1990.

Todorov, Tzvetan. *Theories of the Symbol*. Translated by Catherine Porter. Ithaca: Cornell UP, 1982.

Woolf, Virginia. *A Writer's Diary*. Ed. Leonard Woolf. New York: Harcourt Brace Jovanovich, 1953.

———. *The Voyage Out*. New York: Harcourt Brace Jovanovich, 1915.

———. *The Waves*. New York: Harcourt Brace Jovanovich, 1931.

———. *Three Guineas*. New York: Harcourt Brace Jovanovich, 1938.

———. *To the Lighthouse*. New York: Harcourt Brace Jovanovich, 1927.

———. *The Moment*. London: Hogarth Press, 1947.

Reading Feminist Readings: Recuperative Reading and the Silent Heroine of Feminist Criticism

Carla Kaplan

I pulled and she shook. I shook and she pulled, and before morning we had peeled off yards of that paper.

CHARLOTTE PERKINS GILMAN, "The Yellow Wallpaper"

Silent Heroines and Recuperative Feminism

Nothing less than our sanity and survival is at stake in the issue of what we read.

JUDITH FETTERLEY

Thirty years ago, Tillie Olsen presented a passionate case for feminist criticism as a corrective to cultural silencing. Delineating the "unnatural" silences characteristic of all creative endeavor but particularly definitive of women's writing, Olsen described

> the unnatural thwarting of what struggles to come into being, but cannot . . . *hidden* silences; work aborted, deferred, denied—hidden by the work which does come to fruition . . . censorship silences . . . the silences where the lives never came to writing. Among these, the mute inglorious Miltons: those whose waking hours are all struggle for existence; the barely educated; the illiterate; women. Their silence the silence of centuries as to how life was, is, for most of humanity.

In describing women's silences, Olsen built on an already established feminist tradition, drawing on Virginia Woolf's explorations of women's silence and its material conditions. Women, Woolf wrote, dine on "prunes and custard" (Woolf, *Room* 18) rather than the "partridges and wine" (23) that invigorate (male) thinking and conversation; have served, for "centuries as looking glasses . . . reflecting the figure of man at twice its natural size;" (35); are the subjects of literature and history but rarely its authors. Discouraged where men are encouraged, when women did write it was often defensively, in

168

forms not suited to them, with a "lack of tradition" and "a scarcity and inadequacy of tools" (80).

Since the appearance of Olsen's *Silences,* feminist criticism has continued to build on this recuperative paradigm of recovering lost, silenced, misunderstood, or devalued women's voices. Attempting to map the "infinitely obscure lives" and works of silenced women (Woolf, *Room* 93), the task of feminist criticism seemed to lie in three connected fields: (1) exposing the mechanisms of cultural silencing; (2) revaluing dismissed or ignored women's writing; and (3) recovering alternative forms of women's creative expression.[1] "There is a whole literature to be reestimated, revalued," Olsen wrote. "Others now forgotten, obscured, ignored, will live again for us" (44).[2]

Much of the now-classic feminist criticism of the seventies and early eighties took its political imperative from the need to write women back into what Adrienne Rich famously described as the "book of myths / in which / our names do not appear."[3] If revision was "an act of survival" (35), criticism was coming to be understood as an act of salvation. I do not think it is simply the vantage point of historical hindsight (nor, to speak autobiographically, a younger feminist's idealistic nostalgia for missed moments) that lends so much criticism of the seventies and eighties[4] its aura of shared mission and purpose. There is something heroic—often self-consciously so—about much of the criticism of this period, the sense of being involved in struggles which, to quote Rich again, "help to change the lives of women whose gifts—and whose very being—continue to be thwarted and silenced."[5] "As women," Rich concluded, "we have our work cut out for us" (49).

The rescue of thwarted, silenced, marginalized women, from history or from critical traditions, women like Lilith or Medusa, H. D.'s Helen, Judy Grahn's "common" women, Freud's (or better feminism's) Dora, Woolf's Judith Shakespeare, gave to feminist criticism what I would call its archeological imperative: "the recovery and cultivation," as Patrocinio Schweickart put it in 1986, "of women's culture." It also often imparted much of the sense of the heroic, the image of misunderstood, abandoned, neglected women, finally rescued and released by their stronger, bolder daughters, and the belief that the work of feminist criticism, in Schweickart's words again, is a "heartwarming task: that of recovering, articulating, and elaborating positive expressions of women's point of view, of celebrating the survival of this point of view in spite of the formidable forces that have ranged against it" (51).

Just as Schweickart's celebratory rhetoric may strike an anachronistic note today, the recuperative paradigm itself, with its concerns for women's "voices" and female "experience," its grounding in sameness and identification, and its rendering of feminism as generational bonding must seem even more dated. How, after all, can Olsen's gynocritical project of reclamation and tradition-building on behalf of women possibly be squared with the poststructural argument that categorical appeals to or on behalf of "woman" or "women" undermine a viable feminist politics because "woman" is a "regulatory fiction" that reifies existing structures of domination?[6] As Elaine

Hedges writes, "the poststructuralist project to problematize and displace identity is difficult to reconcile with the feminist project to reclaim it" (1992, 380). What place is there, finally, in what has become, for many, a postidentitarian, postidentificatory feminism for an enterprise tacitly founded on both identity and identification?

Throughout the seventies and early eighties, many feminists rested fairly comfortably with a politics of identification. Indeed, identifying with other women seemed to be not only possible but also an important ethical commitment, a way, as Rich put it, of ensuring "accountability." But in the wake of poststructural challenges to "identity," "experience," authentic "voice," the "author," and "woman," and perhaps even more importantly, in the wake of challenges posed by lesbians and women of color to the exclusionary practices inscribed within white American feminism's putative unity and homogeneity,[7] the sorts of assumptions to which Olsen, Woolf, or Rich's "revisionary rereading"[8] seem to subscribe may appear theoretically single-minded.

In a recent retrospective, Ann Rosalind Jones argues that the practice of consciousness-raising and its concomitant ethics of listening and "empathetic analysis" formed the basis for the particular hermeneutic feminist literary criticism developed. "It's certain," she compellingly argues, "that the phonocentric emphasis in American feminist criticism, the celebration of the 'real woman's voice,' came partly out of the consciousness-raising process: we wanted to speak, we constructed occasions to speak, we heard ourselves quavering out difficult sentences, we waited to hear a supportive response" (69). The recuperative paradigm deeply inscribed these cultural practices and their ethics.

"Nonetheless," Jones adds, "there were crucial silences in that group. We were all white, all middle-class, and all (at least at the moment) heterosexual" (68). The relationship between speech, silence, and a sense of sameness is complicated here. The very silences Jones laments were also partly responsible, she implies, for the feelings of safety and solidarity that empowered these women's speech. They felt comfortable, surrounded by others like themselves, able to identify with one another, sure of a sympathetic response.

Consciousness-raising, as Jones is quick to point out, was hardly "permanent." Its collapse, in fact, as a privileged cultural practice corresponded with the challenges I have mentioned above, with an increasing awareness of the exclusionary politics of American feminist "sisterhood," and with attempts to open feminist circles up to a proliferation of feminisms, to turn from simple solidarity to coalition politics and new, more complex understandings of identity politics.

But the recuperative paradigm hardly died in consciousness-raising's wake. Should it have? Citing a tendency toward critical self-celebration, reliance on the problematic categories mentioned above ("experience," "identity," "voice," and "identification" in particular), and a sentimentalizing self-understanding of "women's culture," many critics, no doubt, would say yes.

But while it is clear that essentialism and identification are shaky grounds for feminist theory and politics, it is not so clear that recuperation need ground itself in either. In fact, a critique of identification and identificatory politics, as I hope to show later in this essay, can be as enabling to the important work of recuperating women's literature as disabling.

And there should be no doubt that recuperation is still important work. In fact, it is perhaps most important, today, to the very groups of women—lesbians and women of color in particular—who are likely to challenge its identificatory premises. Much of the initial tradition-building work of locating, reevaluating, and reprinting women's texts (work that fueled so much of white American feminism through the seventies and early eighties) is still under way for the writing of lesbians and women of color. Olsen's concern for "hidden silences, work aborted, deferred, denied—hidden," for "censorship silences," for "the silences where the lives never came to writing" still very much obtains, as Alice Walker suggests in a 1974 essay on recuperating black women's texts.

Alluding to Woolf's incarnation of "a witch being ducked, of a woman possessed by devils, of a wise woman selling herbs, or even of a very remarkable man who had a mother" as signs of "a lost novelist, a suppressed poet, of some mute and inglorious Jane Austen, some Emily Brontë who dashed her brains out on the moor or mopped and mowed about the highways crazed with the torture her gift had put her to" (50–51), Walker figures black female artists as "Crazy Saints . . . crazy, loony, pitiful women . . . our mothers and grandmothers" who "saw visions no one could understand . . . driven to a numb and bleeding madness by the springs of creativity in them for which there was no release" (232–33).

Those who did find release, Walker writes, did so in "wild and unlikely places": cooking, gardening, sewing, church singing, the blues. So when we look for their "texts," Walker writes, we must learn to look "close" and "low" (239). Walker describes a quilt, made by "an anonymous black woman in Alabama, a hundred years ago":

> Though it follows no known pattern of quilt-making, and though it is made of bits and pieces of worthless rags, it is obviously the work of a person of powerful imagination and deep spiritual feeling. . . . If we could locate this "anonymous black woman from Alabama," she would turn out to be one of our grandmothers—an artist who left her mark in the only materials she could afford and in the only medium her position in society allowed her to use (239).

Walker's use of "we" here, her fusion, on the one hand, of white and black feminist traditions and her specification, on the other, of other black women as her knowing, sympathetic, identifying audience, reminds us of some of the problems seemingly embedded within the recuperative enterprise. Whose enterprise should this recovery of "Crazy Saints" be? Whose grandmother is Walker locating? And who is equipped to recognize her text and hear her voice? Is such recognition, for Walker, a simple matter of categorical identity: of being black and female, for example? Or is such recognition contingent upon some uncategorically defined set of skills, upon what Sally Munt, for example, describes as lesbian readers' particular ability to read both "between the lines [and] from the margins"? (xiii).

To take up some of these questions, I want to begin with examples of feminist literary history that work from the recuperative paradigm I have associated with Olsen, Woolf, and Rich and that exemplify some of the uses to which recuperative readings may be put and the premises upon which they may depend. In the last two sections I will turn to three of the most recuperated and privileged stories in the feminist canon. There I will deploy the recuperative paradigm, in a sense against itself to suggest new readings of these already often-read stories and to seek a recuperative practice based on a new paradigm that, as I will argue in conclusion, both complicates the recuperative enterprise and takes it in new directions. Rather than pronounce what has comprised the core of so much feminist work to date a theoretically, historically, or culturally bankrupt enterprise, I hope to contribute to its revitalization by suggesting new paradigms less dependent upon what Helena Michie calls the idioms of the "therapeutic," the "utopian," and the "familial". In my view, the legacy of recuperative, revisionary strategies remains an invaluable set of analytical tools.[9] The problem, in fact, may not be an overapplication of these methods but, in some instances (including texts we might think of as already completely over-read), a failure to apply them thoroughly *enough*.

"Fantastic Collaboration" and the Politics of Identification: The Heroics of Identificatory Reading

Once begun, liberation and identification are irreversible.

PAULA TREICHLER

In 1984, discussing the critical recuperation of Sappho, Susan Gubar advanced the notion of "fantastic collaboration" as an antidote to the Bloomian "anxiety of influence" with which nonfeminist writers (and implicitly readers) confront the precursors of their literary tradition. "Fantastic collaboration," as Gubar explains it, is an apt description of feminist recuperation: the construction of what one critic (somewhat derisively) calls "imaginary feminism" (Haney-Peritz 270): the effort to recover and resuscitate lost voices, to make them speak again, to restore them to their own meanings and values, to establish those reconstructed values as a new foundation for modern women.

Not surprisingly, this recuperative paradigm has had a particularly strong purchase on feminist literary history, which cannot help but be concerned with silences, absences, double messages, and palimpsestic texts. For reasons that are less self-evident, however, it is often taken for granted that the feminist literary historian is necessarily a "fantastic collaborator" and necessarily understands both her own work and the work she recuperates in counter-

Bloomian terms. I am not suggesting that Bloom's model in fact offers feminism a better purchase on intertextuality than these feminist alternatives. On the contrary, I am asking why identity, Bloom's persistent critical problematic, remains the central category and concern of feminist literary historical revisions. To put it more tendentiously: if Bloom's rigidly Oedipal narrative of intertextual "warfare" strikes a reductive and narrowly historical note with feminist scholars, what sort of alternative is the typical counter-narrative that reads women's intertextuality as a pre-Oedipal family romance of nurturance, support, and collaboration?

It is perhaps not surprising that Gubar would formulate her conception of "fantastic collaboration" in implicitly anti-Bloomian terms, since the influential theory of intertextuality she and Sandra Gilbert develop in *The Madwoman in the Attic* takes its point of departure from Bloom's theory of "heroic warfare," or "a literary Oedipal struggle," in which a writer becomes great "by somehow invalidating his poetic father" in "fierce power struggles" (48). By contrast, Gilbert and Gubar argue, the woman writer, "the daughter of too few mothers," could not afford such battles (although for her too they are part of creation). Hence, she suffers from an "anxiety of authorship" (51, 48). Rather than replicate the male writers' battles by attempting to overthrow her female precursors, the woman writer, Gilbert and Gubar argue, turns to other women as allies in a literary battle she wages not with them, but against her Oedipal *fathers*. The "female precursor . . . far from representing a threatening force to be denied or killed, proves by example that a revolt against patriarchal literary authority is possible" (49).

In this influential rereading of literary history, Gilbert and Gubar establish a pattern that is taken up again and again in subsequent feminist revisions of intertextuality and literary history. An initial delineation of a historically grounded difference—the difference between men's and women's cultural relation to writing and publicity, in this case—gives way to an ahistorical assumption of identicality and identification among the members of the newly reconstructed group: women writers, for example. This pattern is particularly pronounced in the work of other feminist literary historians who work, like Gilbert and Gubar, from an anti-Bloomian poetics of intertextuality.

Elaine Showalter's recent work repeats this pattern in the context of another refutation of Bloomian internecine textual warfare:

> To a striking degree, American women writers have rejected the Oedipal metaphors of murderous "originality" set out as literary paradigms in Harold Bloom's *Anxiety of Influence;* the patricidal struggle defined by Bloom and exemplified in the careers of male American writers has no matricidal equivalent, no echo of denial, parody, exile. Instead, Alice Walker proclaims, "each writer writes the missing parts to the other writer's story" (1991, 174).

Showalter's reference to Walker here is striking, particularly in its erasure— in the name of broader feminist affinities—of Walker's racial solidarities. The reference to Walker is striking not only as an appeal to authorization, but also because it is repeated by so many other feminist critics, white and black.

Christine Froula's "The Daughter's Seduction: Sexual Violence and Literary History" (1986), for example, begins with the cultural silencing that makes for woman's lack of "freedom to tell her stories" (622). In her search for a "radical cure of the hysterical cultural text that entangles both women and men" (633), Froula turns to the work of Maya Angelou and Alice Walker, work which she reads as a kind of allegory for the act of critical recuperation in which she herself is engaged. Angelou's "powerful memoir," Froula writes, "*rescues* the child's voice . . . by telling the prohibited story" (637, emphasis mine). *The Color Purple* Froula considers an even "more powerful cure" of "one daughter's hysterical silence" (637) and Celie a "hero . . . who recreates the universe by telling her story to the world" (644).

A politics of identification grounds Walker's novel as well as Froula's essay. As Froula points out, Celie's "identification" with other women—her mother, Sofia, Shug, and Mary Agnes—"saves her from silence" (638), presumably as an identification with Celie can "save," "cure," or "rescue" the reader or critic. But Celie's identification is identification with a difference. Rather than simply identifying with Sofia and Shug, Celie begins to understand her own needs and desires when she perceives her own difference from these other women, understanding that she was not a fighter (like Sofia), not attracted to men (like Shug), not bold (like both), and without the luxury of "somebody to run to." This sense of her own difference underlies both Celie's aggression toward Sofia ("beat her," Celie tells Harpo) and her desire for Shug. These differences, moreover, make it easier, not harder, for other women to help Celie.

The Color Purple, in short, cautions against identification as much as it seems to promote it. The novel's cautionary representations of women's differences suggest that it may be a mistake to read Walker's view of literary history—"each writer writes the missing parts to the other writer's story"—as a transhistorical (or ahistorical) "fantastic collaboration," or Walker herself as the "cure" for critical silence, including the critical silences in white feminist criticism about black women's history.[10]

Let me turn now to another influential essay of feminist literary history, this one by Deborah McDowell, to consider how its politics of identification, specifically oriented to particular historical and racial contingencies, address these pitfalls of the recuperative paradigm. Like Froula, McDowell depends upon Walker's claim that "each writer writes the missing parts to the other writer's story" to establish the particular ethos of her vision of "fantastic collaboration." In " 'The Changing Same': Generational Connections and Black Women Novelists" (1987), McDowell demonstrates how Iola in Frances Harper's *Iola Leroy* and Celie in Walker's *The Color Purple* both break cultural silences. Like Froula, McDowell views Celie as an allegory for her own feminist practice, a heroine who reincarnates earlier, silenced women, giving them life and voice. A "revisionist mission," she writes, is the "common center" (93) of black women's literature.

The black woman writer's relationship to her black female precursors, McDowell contends, "begins with thinking back through and reclaiming her female ancestors" (104). This process, she argues, is collaborative and nonconflictual:

> Bloom's linear theory of the Oedipal war between literary fathers and sons does not obtain among black women writers, many of whom reverently acknowledge their debts to their literary foremothers. Unlike Bloom, I see literary influence, to borrow from Julia Kristeva, in the intertextual sense, each text in dialogue with all previous texts, transforming and retaining narrative patterns and strategies in endless possibility. The pattern of literary influence . . . is also distinct from that among black men . . . [characterized by] formal relations . . . [which are] largely adversarial and parodic . . . therein lies a fundamental distinction between Afro-American male and female literary traditions (107).

Yet McDowell is also skeptical of this revisionary narrative. Interestingly enough, McDowell challenges the "revisionist mission" as an inherently limited project. "The impulse [to revise stereotypes and correct (mis)representations] is at once the greatest strength and the greatest weakness," of early women's texts, she writes. "It results without exception in the creation of static, disembodied, larger-than-life characters" (95).

Although McDowell narrows the scope of her identificatory poetics to black women and generates her vision of their collaborative, intertextual dynamics from a concrete set of historical particulars, there is, nonetheless, a tension within her essay between a generalized, identificatory politics and a critique of the politics of identification. In constructing her own poetics of black women's intertextuality along the counter-Bloomian lines I quote above, McDowell repeats the pattern found in both Showalter and Froula's arguments, whereby an initial gesture of differentiation—black women's literary history as opposed to black men's or white women's—gives way to presumptions from which differences and conflict seem suddenly to fade. In this sense, McDowell's intertextual "dialogue" also idealizes a romantic "imaginary feminism." I am not opposing gestures of utopianism, per se. In fact, utopian projections of sisterhood, solidarity, unity, and identification are underrated by those who overlook the *proleptic* as opposed to representational power of such idealisms. Nonetheless, the positivist notion of historical progress implicit in all three of these accounts can only lead to a new literary historical impasse by occluding, finally, all those texts that fail to fit the new paradigm and its collaborative, sisterly, dialogic ethics.

One claim for Bloom's importance to feminist theory has been that his "theory of influence" subverted the "static notion of a fixed or knowable text" (Kolodny 149) and thereby opened the way for a recognition of what Barbara Herrnstein Smith would later call "contingencies of value." But feminism hardly needed to depend on Bloom to make this point, as Kolodny's own work demonstrates. It is principally Bloom's heroics, I suspect, that have proved seductive. If Bloom's critic, by misreading, cannot help but be a Poet, the feminist critic, by "revisionary rereading" cannot help but be a fantastic collaborator, cannot help but "write the missing parts to the other writer's story." This narrative replaces the battleground with a friendly women's book-store and yet leaves Bloom's romance of great heroes intact. A romantic conception of literary tradition, in short, offers no clearer explanation (short of the same gender-essentialism that marks Bloom's psychodynamics of textu-ality) of the conditions of changing reception it takes as its starting point than does an agonistic, antagonistic one.

A positivist self-understanding of critical intervention or "collaboration" as a kind of cultural heroics was not, interestingly enough, a feature of Gilbert and Gubar's original polemic with Bloom, although no other American femi-nists have perhaps been so badly caricatured as advocates of illusory and essentialistic notions of sameness and identification.[11] On Gilbert and Gubar's account, it was not the modern critic's sympathetic or collaborative "rescue" of precursor texts that defined feminism's heroics. Instead, they located hero-ism in the efforts those precursors made to resist cultural silencing and leave a legacy, however coded and disguised it sometimes may have been. "If contem-porary women do now attempt the pen with energy and authority," they wrote, "they are able to do so *only because* their eighteenth- and nineteenth-century foremothers struggled in isolation that felt like illness, alienation that felt like madness, obscurity that felt like paralysis" (*Madwoman*, 151).

With a turn to privileging the vantage point of the contemporary critic, however, what was still a somewhat open question for Gilbert and Gubar—namely, how to narrate a story of conflict and discontinuity as well as collabo-ration and continuity—became codified, by and large, into a set of prescrip-tive ethics drawn from object-relations theory to shape a literary history that could elide difference in favor of a chain of mother-daughter identity and indebtedness. While grounded in the crucial insight that "unreadability . . . [is] historically contingent" (Haney-Peritz 269), identification-based models of feminist reading often ended up taking for granted that the modern reader had a kind of epistemological privilege that was not only, implicitly, impossi-ble for other readers, but that also gave her, in the metaphorics and rhetorics of many accounts, a maternal relation to the texts she recuperated.

This is not to say that there isn't much that is heroic about the recuperative enterprise, the legacy of reading and rewriting silence inherited from Olsen, Woolf, Rich, Walker, and others. But the rhetoric of heroism that often attaches itself to this enterprise should strike, I think, a cautionary note. Susan Lanser suggests that a reading politics of identification turns women's texts into self-indulgent mirrors that operate to fill a "need to isolate and validate a particular female experience, a particular relationship between reader and writer, and a particular notion of subjectivity as base for the writing and reading of (women's) texts. . . . Although—or because—we have read . . . over and over, we may have stopped short and our readings . . . may have reduced the text's complicity to what we need most: our own image reflected back to us" (419–20).[12] Building on Lanser's concern for critical mirrorings and self-celebration, I would suggest that particularly in those texts that are most often taken to mirror the practice of feminist criticism itself, the construction of textual mirrors may actually obscure the critical self-reflection they are meant, presumably, to provide.

(Re)reading (Over)reading: Identification in "The Yellow Wallpaper," "A Jury of Her Peers," and "The Blank Page"

Irresistible metaphorics

NANCY K. MILLER, 1986

In turning to three of the most overread stories in the feminist canon, I want to begin with the problem of "overreading" itself: a strategy for reading between the lines, deciphering silence, decoding double-talk and filling in gaps to correct and compensate for the double silence of repressed expression and critical misunderstanding that we might identify with all revisionary, recuperative work. "Overreading," Nancy K. Miller writes, "self-consciously responds to the appeal of the abyss" (87). It reads women's writing "as if it had never been read" (83).

It is impossible, of course, to read "The Yellow Wallpaper," "A Jury of Her Peers," and "The Blank Page" as if they had never been read. Instead, I want to begin by reading the history of feminist readings of these stories, focusing in particular on the way these stories served as allegories for feminist criticism and fantastic collaboration. The narrator of "The Yellow Wallpaper" frees the woman trapped in the paper by learning to overread her "repellant," "uncertain," "outrageous," "lurid," "irritating," "isolated," "pointless," "defiant," "torturing," "strangled" text. The storyteller in "The Blank Page" has been trained as an overreader. She knows how to "hear the voice of silence" and to ensure that "silence will speak" (1419). The two women in "A Jury of Her Peers" find themselves reluctant, but unavoidable, overreaders. They "*understand*" a woman's text that the men in the story are unable to see and they "*know*" that to read and recognize it is itself a subversive activity.

Each of these stories, in depicting a woman reader's unraveling of a mute and coded female "text," suggests both patriarchy's stake in silencing women and the need to expose and challenge such silencing. As such, these stories allegorize overreading and offer feminist criticism an "irresistible metaphorics" for its own imperatives. "American feminist criticism has constituted its terms," Lanser has recently argued, through stories like "The Yellow Wallpaper" (415). It is, Gilbert and Gubar argue, "a paradigmatic tale . . . of female confinement and escape . . . *the* story that all literary women would tell if they could speak their 'speechless woe.' " As Elaine Hedges puts it, "rediscovering lost women writers, reclaiming the experience of anonymous women, reexamining the image of women in literature, and rereading texts in order to discern and appreciate female symbol systems—many of the major approaches that have characterized feminist literary criticism in the past decade have . . . found generous validation in the text of 'A Jury of Her Peers.' The story has become a paradigmatic one for feminist criticism" (1986, 89–90). "For feminist critics of American literature," Elaine Showalter adds, " 'A Jury of Her Peers' has been taken since the mid-1970s as a metaphor for feminist reading itself" (146). As a representation of "the voice of silence" (149) and the imperative to ensure that "silence will speak" (1419), "The Blank Page" also provides a paradigm and mirror for feminist (over)reading and fantastic collaboration.

Although these stories provide a paradigm of feminist criticism as fantastic collaboration, they also suggest why such collaboration *is* fantastic, or fantasmatic. They both practice and parody feminist recuperation. Each warns against the very politics it seems to endorse, suggesting dangers, impasses, and problems inherent in any "fantastic collaboration" grounded in a politics of identification. Following a rehearsal of their standard feminist reading, then, my recuperation will seek out their critiques, rather than their representations, of the enterprise of fantastic collaboration.

Identification, Fetterley argues, accounts for the feminist "pleasure of the text" of "The Yellow Wallpaper." "It provides the woman reader with the gratification of discovering, recovering, and validating her own experience" (154). Even critics who see the narrator's identification as limiting or dangerous tend, along with Fetterley, to see the feminist paradigms encoded in this story in terms of problems and possibilities of identification.

"The Yellow Wallpaper" describes the constraints of "the sociocultural situation confronting women in the late nineteenth century," (Golden 9).[13] Denied "work," "society," "stimulus," imagination, writing, or conversation, although writing, she says, is "a great relief to my mind" (24), the protagonist of "The Yellow Wallpaper" initially defies prohibitions by writing in secret. But "having to be so sly about it, or else meet with heavy opposition" (25) eventually proves too exhausting. "The effort," she declares, "is getting to be greater than the relief" (32).

Denied all other outlets, she becomes obsessed with the wallpaper in her room, a pattern she originally finds "repellant, almost revolting" (26), but which comes to resemble a woman behind bars. As she transfers her passion for communication and recognition to this woman, she becomes a devoted reader, or overreader. And as she does so, she finds that "life is very much more exciting now than it used to be" (35).[14]

Her reading observes certain fundamental precepts: that women's voices may appear in surprising texts (quilts, gardens, wallpaper, blankness); that women write between the lines of dominant discourses, hiding subversive "patterns" behind more acceptable ones ("this wallpaper has a kind of sub-pattern in a different shade" (30)); that such palimpsests demand specially trained and sympathetic readers (feminists who know how to [over]read); and that women's silence, blankness, or absence must be translated back into visibility or audibility by a reader who is reader and rewriter both.

The narrator's impulse was originally compensatory, a substitute for other "work" and a hedge against boredom. But reading quickly develops its own urgency: saving the woman trapped in the suffocating wallpaper. The more willing the narrator is to see behind the dominant pattern, the more "the woman behind it is as plain as she can be" and the more clearly the dominant "pattern" becomes "bars" (34). From that point on, both are committed to fantastic collaboration and the narrator devotes all her energy to unburying this coded female text.

The work of collaboration should strike a familiar note with those who remember the agonizing exhilaration of the stages of consciousness-raising. First, the recognition of the violence of oppression: "she is all the time trying to climb through," "but nobody could climb through that pattern—it strangles so; I think that is why it has so many heads. They get through, and then the pattern strangles them off and turns them upside down, and makes their eyes white!" (38). Second, the danger of denial and the need to resist it: "if those heads were covered or taken off it [the wallpaper] would not be half so bad" (38). Third, a commitment to a new vision, one that changes everything: "I can see her out of every one of my windows!" (38). And fourth, an altered, sometimes obsessive, sense of the whole: instead of blaming the victim for her own oppression—"I don't blame her a bit" (38)—the narrator becomes increasingly alienated from and hostile to anyone who seems to have any part, however passive, in perpetuating the trap: "it does not do to trust people too much" (39).

As the narrator moves closer and closer to liberating this trapped figure, her actions seem to be motivated by sisterly affection. "As soon as it was moonlight and that poor thing began to crawl and shake the pattern, I got up and ran to help her. I pulled and she shook, I shook and she pulled, and before morning we had peeled off yards of that paper" (39).

But sisterly identification is also associated with madness. "The narrator," Hedges argues, "both does and does not identify with the creeping women who surround her in her hallucinations" (131). To identify completely would be to become what the repressive woman-hating society wants her to be: creeping, hidden, inarticulate, helpless. She wants, as Hedges points out, both to liberate and to destroy this "tragic product of her society" (131). Haney-Peritz also observes that identifying with the woman in the wallpaper means identifying with precisely the representation of woman that the narrator seeks to resist. "The narrator's identification with the wallpaper's shadow-woman seems to have turned her into the woman of John's dreams, for not only did the shadow woman first appear while John was sleeping, but the narrator also suspects that when all is said and done, she is what John really desires, the secret he would reveal if he were given the opportunity to do so" (268). Yet, although the narrator's madness, as Hedges puts it, can "be read as a victory or a defeat" (326) and in many ways "the heroine . . . is destroyed," (132), this is nonetheless read as a heroic story. The narrator, at whatever personal sacrifice, succeeds in passing on another woman's story, giving voice to what the dominant culture would keep silent and therefore, as Froula might say, curing both herself and other women. "Born of an hallucination," Catherine Golden writes, "her identification leads the narrator to free herself from the restrictive pattern of her own society and this liberation is conveyed on paper through her pronoun choice . . . [the] fusion of identity with the subtext of the wallpaper" (302).

But a heroic reading of the narrator's chilling sacrifice leaves important aspects of the reader-heroine relationship unexamined. The narrator's reading not only represents but also parodies critical interpretation as a dangerous practice. Her madness raises the question so often at issue in scholarly debates: has she, like many an anxiety-ridden scholar, simply invented—or imagined—her topic so as to have something to work on? Gilman provides a brilliant depiction of feeling mocked by one's subject of analysis: "It [the paper] is dull enough to confuse the eye in following, pronounced enough to constantly irritate and provoke study, and when you follow the lame uncertain curves for a little distance they suddenly commit suicide—plunge off at outrageous angles, destroy themselves in unheard of contradictions" (26) . . . all those strangled heads and bulbous eyes and waddling fungus growths just shriek with derision!" (40). And she also paints a painfully funny parody of the narrator's inability to "sleep much at night" (but sleeping "a good deal in the daytime,") as her obsession with her subject grows and the deadline by which she must either complete her research or resign herself to failure approaches. Her determination "that nobody shall find out but myself!" (35) captures a classic moment of scholarly possessiveness, paranoia, and jealousy. "I don't want anybody to get that woman out at night but myself," she reports. She resolves that "no person touches this paper but me—not *alive!*" (40); "there are things in that paper that nobody knows but me, or ever will" (32). Like most critics, she wants to "astonish" her intended audience and, like many, she will do violence to her subject, if necessary, to control it: "I've got a rope up here . . . if that woman does get out, and tries to get away, I can tie her!" (40). I take this parody as a serious warning about the dangers of the feminist overreading the story so vividly portrays. The reader—even if she sacrifices her "self" for her subject—is not necessarily more of a hero than John, the narrator's husband, or Jennie, his sister. The subject of all this heroics—the trapped woman—may find herself as imperiled and entrapped by her reader's own obsessions as she is rescued or released by them.

"A Jury of Her Peers" raises many of the same caveats about the potential hazards of the overreading it depicts. The "text" in question, as in "The Yellow Wallpaper," is a woman herself: Minnie Foster in this case, in jail for the murder of her husband. As the story opens, the sheriff and county attorney are trying to find (read) the "motive" for the crime, without evidence of which, they fear, the jury may not convict. The kitchen is filled with motive and evidence that the men are unable to read.

> "You're convinced there was nothing important here?" the county attorney asked the sheriff. "Nothing that would—point to any motive?" The sheriff too looked all around, as if to re-convince himself. "Nothing here but kitchen things," he said, with a little laugh for the insignificance of kitchen things.

Whereas the men fail to (over)read any meaning in "kitchen things," these insignificant kitchen things reveal to Mrs. Peters and Mrs. Hale the bleakness of Minnie Foster's life.

Mrs. Hale is quick to read the kitchen as a set of signs:

> Her eye was held by a bucket of sugar on a low shelf. The cover was off the wooden bucket, and beside it was a paper bag—half full. . . . Her eye was caught by a dish-towel in the middle of the kitchen table. Slowly she moved toward the table. One half of it was wiped clean, the other half was messy. Her eyes made a slow, almost unwilling turn to the bucket of sugar and the half-empty bag beside it. Things begun—and not finished" (378).

The more they look around the kitchen, the more evidence Mrs. Peters and Mrs. Hale discern. Most tellingly, they discover Minnie Foster's quilting, an unmistakable sign of both her determination to create and of aggression towards her husband:

> Mrs. Hale was looking at the fine, even sewing, and preoccupied with thoughts of the woman who had done that sewing, when she heard the sheriff's wife say, in a queer tone:
> "Why, look at this one."
> She turned to take the block held out to her.
> "The sewing," said Mrs. Peters, in a troubled way. "All the rest of them have been so nice and even—but—this one. Why it looks as if she didn't know what she was about!"
> . . . Martha Hale now scrutinized that piece, compared it with the dainty, accurate sewing of the other blocks. The difference was startling. Holding this block made her feel queer, as if the distracted thoughts of the woman who had perhaps turned to it to try and quiet herself were communicating themselves to her (873–74).

After they discover the evidence of anger, they immediately find its motive: Minnie Foster's pet canary, its neck wrung, evidently by Mr. Foster. Minnie, the sheriff's wife remembers, was "kind of like a bird herself. Real sweet and pretty, but kind of timid and—fluttery. How—she—did—change."

What is thoroughly obscure to the men is painfully clear to the women. "Why do you and I *understand?* Why do we *know*—what we know this minute?" (384) Mrs. Peters asks. Given their experiences, *as women,* Glaspell implies, they cannot help but understand. And they not only sympathize but collaborate. As soon as Mrs. Hale finds the tell-tale evidence that might convict Minnie Foster, she moves to erase it:

> A moment Mrs. Hale sat there, her hands folded over that sewing which was so unlike all the rest of the sewing. Then she had pulled a knot and drawn the threads.
> "Oh, what are you doing, Mrs. Hale?" asked the sheriff's wife, startled.
> "Just pulling out a stitch or two that's not sewed very good," said Mrs. Hale, mildly.

> "I don't think we ought to touch things," Mrs. Peters said, a little help-
> lessly.
> "I'll just finish up this end," answered Mrs. Hale, still in that mild,
> matter-of-fact fashion.
> She threaded a needle and started to replace bad sewing with good. For
> a little while she sewed in silence.

Mrs. Hale sews in silence; she literally sews silence into the text, replacing
Minnie Foster's talking stitches with safer, speechless ones.

As with "The Yellow Wallpaper," this rendition of female overreading is
generally read prescriptively, as a program meant for women readers to
follow. But overreading endangers Minnie Foster as surely as it recognizes
her. Saying nothing, it turns out, *refusing* to create a "revisionary rereading"
is the only way to try and save Minnie Foster. Her story must be left silent
and untold. The actions that are called for here—pulling the tell-tale quilt
stitches and hiding the dead bird "that would make certain the conviction of
the other woman"—are ones that hide Minnie Foster's story. In fact,
overreading appears here as an ethically suspect attempt to compensate for
the more important actions these women failed to take. Reading correctly
but doing nothing—materially and practically—to change Minnie's story is
worse than irresponsible. It is criminal. " 'Oh, I *wish* I'd come over here
once in a while!' she [Mrs. Hale] cried. 'That was a crime! That was a crime!
Who's going to punish that?' " (384).[15] Identifying with Minnie Foster unravels the feminist subtext behind all three women's lives, but it does not give
them a feminist politics of social transformation.

"The Blank Page" also contains a trapped heroine, and for her, as for
Minnie Foster, reading comes too late to liberate her. The story begins with a
Carmelite order of nuns in the mountains of Portugal who produce, preserve,
and exhibit the blood-stained bridal sheets of royal princesses. Among these
"portraits" is one "canvas" before which "the story-tellers . . . draw their veils
over their faces and are dumb." Before this canvas, "the old princesses of
Portugal—worldly wise, dutiful, long-suffering queens, wives, and mothers—
and their noble old playmates, bridesmaids and maids-of-honor have most
often stood still. [Here] . . . old and young nuns, with the Mother Abbess
herself, sink into deepest thought" (1423). This canvas is blank, an anonymous, unstained sheet of framed white linen, "snow white from corner to
corner," which the convent sisters, with "eternal and unswerving loyalty"
have included along with the others in their gallery.

As Susan Gubar has suggested, where an unsympathetic reader would
see emptiness and silence, the women who come to the gallery are
prototypical overreaders. They recuperate a multiplicity of meanings from
the blank canvas: perhaps she ran away or renounced sexuality, perhaps
she was not a virgin when she married, perhaps she was rejected by the
prince. Perhaps she died or was killed before the marriage could be con-
summated. The very absence of a story, Gubar argues, makes this sheet so
subversive. "The resistance of the princess," she writes, "allows for self-

expression; for she makes her statement by not writing what she is expected to write" (89).

Although it might seem that this story presents overreading and recuperation in a positive light, the most precious, revered, protected and coveted "subject" in this story is not this heroine's text at all. Paradoxically, it is silence itself that is most revered. "Who," asks the "old coffee-brown, black veiled woman who made her living by telling stories" (1418)

> tells a finer tale than any of us? Silence does. And where does one read a deeper tale than upon the most perfectly printed page of the most precious book? Upon the blank page. When a royal and gallant pen, in the moment of its highest inspiration, has written down its tale with the rarest ink of all—where, then, may one read a still deeper, sweeter, merrier and more cruel tale than that? Upon the blank page (1419).

This affirmation of silence is double-valenced. It affirms the importance of later, recuperative readers. But it also suggests, as did "The Yellow Wallpaper" and "A Jury of Her Peers," that trying to tell silence's story may be a presumptuous, even hazardous endeavor. Silence gives the critic/reader her reason for being. For this reason, in part, it is to be preserved and guarded rather than rewritten and revised.

Ecstatic Excavation

> The reading of women's texts by women might have been and might still be eroticized.
>
> JUDITH FETTERLEY

Susan Gubar, like Fetterley, has suggested that for certain writers, revisionary rereading is a "euphoric coupling in which the other is bound to the self as a lover" ("Sapphistries," 95) and that the practice of feminist recuperation or "excavation" is a potentially erotic one.[16] Although Gubar investigates this erotics only where there is manifest lesbian content, the formulation suggests that feminist classics might be read not only for their politics of identification, but also for their textual erotics, that the fantastic collaboration feminist readers often seek might be what Gubar calls an "ecstatic excavation" (95).[17]

In suggesting a homoerotic reading of these stories, I risk accusations of appropriating lesbianism as a merely metaphorical sign for nonlesbian sorority. Let me begin, then, with what I hope will be the less controversial strand of my thesis: that each of these stories, insofar as it invites our collaboration, asks us to collaborate in a critique of what one critic calls "heteronormativity," a resistance to compulsory heterosexuality that we might call "heterocritical" if not explicitly queer.[18]

"The Yellow Wallpaper" depicts a woman's imprisonment in a bedroom.

Although she seeks "work," "society and stimulus," air and exercise, her husband locks her in, "shut[s] the window" (25), forbids exercise, and laughs at her. "One expects that in a marriage" (24). The narrator longs, at first, for a room of her own "downstairs that opened on the piazza and had roses all over the window and such pretty old-fashioned chintz hangings!" But recognizing that she seeks to shut him out, "John would not hear of it. He said there was only one window and *not room for two beds,* and no near room for him if he took another" (my italics, 26). Beds loom large in this story. The room in which the narrator has been confined contains a "great immovable bed" nailed down to the floor and contrasted with the nonthreatening single bed of the "pretty" room downstairs. At one point, in her effort to get to the woman in the wallpaper, the narrator tries to move the bed in her room but finds that "this bed will *not* move! I tried to lift and push it until I was lame, and then I got so angry I bit off a little piece at one corner—but it hurt my teeth" (40). At another point in the story she describes the "great bedstead" as "fairly gnawed" from frustration and fury (40). As the signifier and the site of her sexual relationship with her husband the bed is a logical, if ineffectual, outlet for her rage.

Her husband, John, is not alone in compelling heterosexuality. He is joined by the narrator's brother who "is also a physician, and also of high standing, and he says the same thing" (25), and by other doctors, like Weir Mitchell. "But I don't want to go there at all. I had a friend *who was in his hands once,* and she says he is just like John and my brother, only more so!" (30, my italics). As the narrator's attention and longing increasingly turn toward the woman in the wallpaper, she becomes a parody of John, a possessive and jealous lover who doesn't "want anybody to get that woman out at night but myself" (38); "If that woman gets out and tries to get away, I can tie her!"; "I am determined that nobody shall find it out but myself!" (35). And John, of course, is the obstacle to her attainment of this love object. She wants to be free of him: "I wish he would take another room!" (38). As gatekeeper and policeman for patriarchy, he becomes simply the malevolent, generic "that man" who locks her in and, in effect, locks the other woman out.

"A Jury of Her Peers" investigates compulsory heterosexuality through depictions of gendered justice and reading. Toward the end of the story, the county attorney declines to scrutinize the things Mrs. Hale and Mrs. Peters have set aside to bring to Mrs. Foster in jail, remarking that "Mrs. Peters doesn't need supervising" because, as a sheriff's wife, she is "married to the law" (385). His comment echoes his earlier remark, in answer to the sheriff's question of whether " 'anything Mrs. Peters does'll be all right' ": " 'of course Mrs. Peters is one of us' " (376). What Mrs. Peters comes to recognize, however, is that "*the* law" is *their* law and she is *not* "one of them." Destroying evidence to save Mrs. Foster is an act of resistance to collaborating with "the law."

Minnie Foster's crime is explicitly connected to compulsory heterosexuality. She kills her husband in bed, reversing the symbolism by which she has been "tied" to his bed and "killed" in their marriage. Even her claim to have slept right through the murder—because she was on the "inside" of the bed and "didn't wake up" (374)—defamiliarizes compulsory heterosexuality and renders it both comic and absurd.

The story is filled with male violence and gender antagonism. The men make fun of the women for their interest in "trifles." They deride Mrs. Foster's homemaking. The women bristle at their ridicule and bitterly defend Minnie Foster against their cruel jibes. Cruelties abound to animals as well as women. Minnie Foster's bird's neck has been broken and Mrs. Peters remembers something that happened when she was a girl: " 'my kitten—there was a boy took a hatchet and before my eyes—before I could get there—' she covered her face an instant. 'If they hadn't held me back I would have'—she caught herself, looked upstairs where footsteps were heard, and finished weakly—'hurt him' " (383).

In this context, when the women decide that the key crime is not Minnie Foster's murder of her husband, not even his oppression of Minnie Foster, but rather *their* abandonment of her to him (letting "her die for lack of life"), they deliberately step outside of the signifying system of compulsory heterosexuality, a system that depends upon making women's ties to one another incidental and insignificant. Ending the story with the women's pun on Mrs. Foster's quilting, "we call it—knot it" (385), stresses this move outside, this refusal of complicity in the oppression of another woman or the administration of male justice.

This resistance to compulsory heterosexuality and discovery of sororal alternatives to it are perhaps even more explicit in "The Blank Page." What the other two stories imply through tropes of beds, justice, the law, and retribution, "The Blank Page" articulates through a plot that directly ironizes and undermines heteronormativity. Exhibiting the bloodstained sheets as testimony to the consummation of royal marriages, the convent sisters seem complicit with a social order that demands virginity from the women it exchanges between men. But placing a blank sheet "in the midst of the long row" demonstrates both the possibility and the cultural denial of alternatives. The story's convent setting (often the *only* choice available to women who sought to resist marriage) reinforces this counternarrative.

Storytelling itself is linked to resisting heterosexuality. The narrator's storytelling, like Scheherezade's, avoids both male sexuality and death, which it thereby links. Her stories began as responses to male seduction narratives: "tales of a red rose, two smooth lily buds, and four silky, supple, deadly entwining snakes" (1418–19). And storytelling was taught to her as a refuge from male sexuality: "it was my Mother's mother, *the black-eyed dancer, the often-embraced,* who in the end—wrinkled like a winter apple and crouching beneath the mercy of the veil—took upon herself to teach me the art of storytelling" (1419). Telling her story as she does to a "sweet lady and gentleman" slyly introduces dissonance into the romantic dyad, suggesting to the woman in particular that there are cultural signs which may not be evident to her but which she might well contemplate.

"The Blank Page," moreover, embeds a story of female love within its

narrative of resistance to heterosexual marriage. A "very old highborn spinster" who had "once, a long time ago, been playmate, friend and maid-of-
honor to a young princess of Portugal" (1422) comes to the gallery as a "loyal
friend and confidante" to "sigh" and remember. Her story demonstrates how
"old playmates" and friends, once they become "bridesmaids and maids-of-
honor," are often left alone, abandoned to their memories and nostalgia:

> Slowly, slowly a row of recollections passes through the small, venerable,
> skull-like head under its mantilla of black lace, and it nods to them in
> amicable recognition. The loyal friend and confidante looks back upon the
> young bride's elevated married life with the elected royal consort. She takes
> stock of happy events and disappointments—coronations and jubilees, court
> intrigues and wars, the birth of heirs to the throne, the alliances of younger
> generations of princes and princesses, the rise or decline of dynasties. The
> old lady will remember how once, from the markings on the canvas, omens
> were drawn; now she will be able to compare the fulfillment to the omen,
> sighing a little and smiling a little (1422).

As a reader, the spinster serves to reflect the story's own implied reader,
suggesting that desire may be as much a foundation for recuperation as
identification.

   In each of these three stories, the reader is asked not so much to collaborate by identifying with victimization and silencing, but rather, to collaborate
by desiring, or at least by identifying with the desire for other women. Collaboration in each story hinges upon and embraces an erotically charged, passionate connection between women: the narrator and the woman behind the
wallpaper, the abandoned spinster's longing for her long-gone princess-friend,
even Mrs. Peters and Mrs. Hale's moments of ecstatic merger with the absent
Minnie Foster.

   Is (re)reading these longings for merger, fusion, and contact as more than
identification a case of "conflat[ing] identification and desire"? (Mayne 181).
In a recent critique of the "representation of lesbianism within feminist
theory" (257), Teresa de Lauretis faults feminism for such collapses. In much
feminist theory, she argues, there is a "sweeping of lesbian sexuality and
desire under the rug of sisterhood, female friendship, and the now popular
theme of 'the mother-daughter bond.' In all three parts of the rug, what is in
question is not desire, but identification" (258). Drawing on psychoanalytic
categories to draw out the stakes of this "confusion," De Lauretis argues that
"the distinction between object-libido and narcissistic or ego-libido is crucial
here, for one is sexual and has to do with desire, *wanting to have* (*the object*),
the other is desexualized and has to do with narcissistic identification, *wanting
to be or be like* or seeing oneself as (the object)" (my italics, 260). De Lauretis
warns against blurring this distinction and thereby contributing to a tendency
to both de-eroticize writing and, at the same time, to erase lesbian representation altogether. But blurring this distinction, as these stories so deftly demonstrate, can also work, quite productively, to generate the very visibility De
Lauretis has in mind. In all three of these texts a collapse or blurring of the

dynamics of identification and desire works to suggest a homoerotic subtext that distinguishing more carefully between identification and desire might obscure.

In a recent analysis of conceptions of homo- and heterosexualities, Michael Warner pursues De Lauretis's objective of undermining "the heterosexual social contract" (1990, 20) and opening a space for lesbian (or gay) representation by taking the reverse of De Lauretis's position and arguing for a breakdown of the strict distinction between identification and desire, a complication of identification with desire. Warner argues that heterosexuality retains its normative, naturalized status by maintaining the fiction that "gender amount[s] to alterity" (193). Recognizing the dynamic interconnectedness of identification and desire, Warner argues, undermines this fiction and, finally, the illusion that "the difference between hetero- and homosexualities" is "a difference between sexualities of otherness and sameness" (200).

While this is not the place to enter into the complexities of this debate for either psychoanalytic or gay theory, blurring the line between identification and desire allows these stories to open themselves up to a different paradigm of reading than the prescriptive ethos of sameness and identification often found in recuperative criticism. An exclusive focus on identificatory reading oversimplifies the "collaborations" these texts project between themselves and their readers. By the same token, a posture of heroic "rescue" obscures what may be the critic's own erotic investments in the texts she recuperates. Acknowledging desire as well as identification in the dynamic of textual recuperation helps to foreground the fact, as is so clear in "The Yellow Wallpaper" and "The Blank Page," that no reading has access to *the* meaning of the story and that all readings are stories of readerly desire. The integration of desire (which does not demand sameness) into a literary politics of identification (which does) allows for difference as well as sameness, for disidentification and conflict as well as collaboration and cure. It reminds us that we need not, as Hedges argues, be always "pursuing and finding in the text, as the narrator does in the wallpaper, only our own image reflected back" (1992, 324). Finally, foregrounding desire as part of the recuperative process mitigates against some of the more solipsistic, self-celebratory dangers of the recuperative paradigm. Insofar as the critic recuperating a woman's text identifies its heroine or its author *as herself,* she rescues not another woman, but an aspect of her own being. If the other woman can only be seen—and saved—insofar as she represents a version of the self, a self with whom we identify, then perhaps we *can* only save, liberate, or help ourselves, one of the messages of 90s-style self-help ideology which I would be particularly loath to see feminism adopt.

None of these emendations solves the limits of the recuperative paradigm. On the contrary, foregrounding desire may be an effective way to keep those limits more clearly in view. The need to use recuperative strategies to move beyond recuperation was Woolf's message in what may well be the most famous instance of feminist recuperation: her influential evocation of Judith

Shakespeare. Judith Shakespeare's true recuperation, Woolf insisted, could never be effected by interpretive intervention, readerly identification, *or* critical desire. Judith Shakespeare "would come," Woolf wrote, only "*if* we worked for her . . . as for her coming without that preparation, without that effort on our part, without that determination that when she is born again she will find it possible to live and write her poetry, that we cannot expect, for that would be impossible" (118).

Opening the recuperative paradigm up to desire as well as identification provides for a larger, and to my mind a more interesting, set of readings. It preserves a set of analytical tools crucial to a critical social vision and its concomitant transformations. That such strategies might, however, perform that transformative work on their own remains, as Woolf, Gilman, Glaspell, and Dinesen suggest, "impossible." A conscious blurring of the lines between desire and identification is not an answer to feminism's "crisis of identity" any more than it is a solution to all of the impasses of the recuperative paradigm. But it may help rebut the poststructural challenge that speaking as or to "women" necessarily reifies the cultural construction of gender difference. Allowing ourselves to speak to our *desires* for "women," including our desires for affiliation, identification, solidarity, and dialogue, recognizes that categorical appeals need not name a "reality" we accept as fixed or immutable but can, instead, speak to the constructions within which we live even as we point to something beyond them.

NOTES

I thank Ann Ardis, John Brenkman, Nina Miller, and Louise Yelin for their comments on an earlier draft of this essay.

1. Nancy Miller writes of these last two as "two simultaneously compensatory gestures: the archaeological act of recovering 'lost' women writers and the reconstructive act of establishing a parallel tradition." See her "Emphasis Added: Plots and Plausibilities in Women's Fiction."

2. And only a few years later Olsen was to record her satisfaction that this call was being answered: "five years later (1976), it is unmistakable that out of the sense of wrong has come substantial yields for literature: its enlargement and vivification through reclamation of obscured writers and intensified rereading of classic ones; an enhancement and deepening of literary scholarship, criticism, and theory" (181).

3. See her poem "Diving into the Wreck" for a working out not only of the need for recuperation and recovery, but also of the difficulties and dangers of a recuperative enterprise in which saving one's self cannot be divorced from saving and being dependent upon others, living and dead, historical and material, male and female.

4. Patricia Spacks's *The Female Imagination,* Elaine Showalter's *A Literature of Their Own,* and "Feminist Criticism in the Wilderness," Ellen Moers's *Literary Women,* Barbara Smith's "Toward a Black Feminist Criticism," Judith Fetterley's *The Resisting Reader,* Sandra Gilbert and Susan Gubar's *The Madwoman in the Attic* and *Shakespeare's Sisters,* Annette Kolodny's "A Map for Rereading: Or, Gender and the Interpretation of Literary Texts" and "Dancing through the Minefield," Deborah E. McDowell's

"New Directions for Black Feminist Criticism," Rachel Blau du Plessis's "For the Etrus-cans," Bonnie Zimmerman's "What Has Never Been: An Overview of Lesbian Feminist Criticism," Nancy K. Miller's "Emphasis Added: Plots and Plausibilities in Women's Fiction," and Alicia Ostriker's "The Thieves of Language: Women Poets and Revision-ist Mythmaking," to name a few.

5. Susan Gubar, for example, concludes her classic essay on "The Blank Page," by talking about her "own sense of excitement at engaging in such a task" (93) and it is with almost religious reverence that she speaks of "how attentive and patient we must be before the blank page to perceive genuinely new and sustaining scripts" (93).

Elaine Hedges writes that "as Rich said in 1971, and as we believed, " 'hearing our wordless or negated experiences affirmed' in literature could have 'visible effects on women's lives' " (1992, 328).

6. The phrase "regulatory fiction" is Judith Butler's (1990, 3). See also Linda Alcoff, Jane Flax, Diana Fuss, Sandra Harding, Julia Kristeva, Denise Riley, and Monique Wittig. On the "identity crisis" in feminist theory, see also my "The Lan-guage of Crisis in Feminist Theory," *Turning the Century: New Directions in Feminist Criticism.*

7. The wealth of this material is too vast to permit enumeration, but early classics that challenged white, heterosexual, monolithic feminisms can be found collected in *The Powers of Desire,* ed. Ann Snitow, et al., *Pleasure and Danger,* ed. Carole S. Vance, the special lesbian issue of *Signs, Home Girls,* ed. Barbara Smith, *This Bridge Called My Back,* ed. Cherríe Moraga and Gloria Anzaldúa, *All the Women are White, All the Blacks Are Men, But Some of Us Are Brave; Black Women's Studies,* ed. Gloria Hull, et al.

8. The phrase is Annette Kolodny's. See her "A Map for Rereading: Or, Gender and the Interpretation of Literary Texts."

9. Jane Marcus makes a similar point in "Daughters of Anger/Material Girls: Con/textualizing Feminist Criticism." I thank Jane for bringing her essay to my atten-tion after my own was completed.

10. On the racial politics of Froula's essay, see also Ann Ardis, "The White Daugh-ter's Seduction."

11. See particularly Toril Moi's critical, and I think inaccurate, assessment of Gil-bert and Gubar in *Sexual/Textual Politics.*

12. Not everyone, of course, would concede that this is an automatically or neces-sarily bankrupt operation. Carolyn Heilbrun, for example, writes that "in decon-structing literature and life, we ourselves becomes novelists, making fictions out of the texts, and lives, other women have left us." This is, she writes, "one of the most appealing characteristics of feminist criticism" (291).

13. There is a particularly rich tradition of criticism on "The Yellow Wallpaper." Much of it has been recently collected, along with interesting background materials, in *The Captive Imagination,* ed. Catherine Golden.

14. "The narrator," Annette Kolodny notes, "progressively gives up the attempt to *record* her reality and instead begins to *read* it" (156). Or as Paula Treichler puts it, "the more the wallpaper comes alive, the less inclined is the narrator to write in her journal—'dead paper' " (194).

"Blocked from expressing herself *on* paper," Judith Fetterley observes, she seeks to express herself *through* paper. Literally, she converts the wall*paper* into her text. . . . Indeed, one might argue that the narrator overinterprets the wallpaper, the one stimulus in her immediate environment, as a reaction against this sensory deprivation."

She "engages," Susan Lanser writes, "in a form of feminist interpretation when she tries to read the paper on her wall" (418).

Somewhat less sympathetically, Mary Jacobus has argued that the narrator's "is a case of hysterical (over)reading" (279).

15. A different version of this discussion of "A Jury of Her Peers" appears in "The Language of Crisis in Feminist Theory," where I discuss these three stories in a different context.

16. On feminist "collaboration" between the woman writer and reader as an erotically charged, homoerotic "seduction," see also Jane Marcus, "Sapphistry: Narration as Lesbian Seduction in *A Room of One's Own.*"

17. It is surprising, given the intriguing rhetorics of normativity at play in all three of these texts, that lesbian readings have not, to my knowledge, previously been suggested. Even as we guard against anachronistic attributions, it is hard not to mark the ways these stories incorporate words like "gay" and "queer" in the service of defining and marking out the normative. The third sentence of "The Yellow Wallpaper," for example, reads: "still I will proudly declare that there is something queer about it" (924). And "A Jury of Her Peers" repeats the word "queer" no less than nine times. Minnie Foster looks "queer;" holding Minnie's quilt block makes Mrs. Hale "feel queer" as the other woman seems to move into her and speak through her; and Mrs. Peters, as she comes to sympathize more and more with Minnie Foster, begins speaking in a "queer" voice. Dinesen's startling description (which in 1957 carried the same homosexual connotations it does now) in "The Blank Page" of the women's procession and pilgrimage to the portrait gallery as "both sacred and secretly gay" (1421) seems pointedly double-voiced. Indeed, without the double meaning of "gay," this sentence is virtually meaningless, since this pilgrimage is anything but celebratory. It is a somber, self-reflective, often mournful journey for the women who undertake it.

By 1917 when "A Jury of Her Peers" was published, "queer" was already in common, if not widespread, usage as a term for homosexual men. "Gay" acquired its double meaning in America at least as early as the 1920s, where it appears along with "queer" in such novels as *The Scarlet Pansy.* On the use of the term "queer" before the 1920s, see George Chauncy's brilliant essay, "Christian Brotherhood or Sexual Perversion? Homosexual Identities and the Construction of Sexual Boundaries in the World War I Era." I am grateful to Nina Miller, Gary Schmidgall, Joseph Wittreich, and Michael Warner for their generous help in my (unsuccessful) attempt to fix the exact dates when these terms first came into common American usage. As far as I have been able to determine, this important work still remains to be done.

18. On compulsory heterosexuality, see Rich (1980). The phrase "heteronormativity" is Michael Warner's.

WORKS CITED

Alcoff, Linda. "Cultural Feminism Versus Poststructuralism: The Identity Crisis in Feminist Theory." *Signs* (Spring 1988) 13:3.

Ardis, Ann. "The White Daughter's Seduction: Christine Froula's Family Romance of Canon-Formation." Unpublished ms.

Bernheimer, Charles, ed. *In Dora's Case: Freud—Hysteria—Feminism*. New York: Columbia, 1985.

Bloom, Harold. *The Anxiety of Influence: A Theory of Poetry*. New York, 1973.

Butler, Judith. "Gender Trouble, Feminist Theory, and Psychoanalytic Discourse." *Feminism/Postmodernism*, ed. Linda J. Nicholson. New York: Routledge, 1990.

———. *Gender Trouble: Feminism and the Subversion of Identity*. New York: Routledge, 1991.

Chauncy, George, Jr. "Christian Brotherhood or Sexual Perversion? Homosexual Identities and the Construction of Sexual Boundaries in the World War I Era." In *Hidden from History: Reclaiming the Gay & Lesbian Past*. Ed. Martin Duberman, Martha Vicinus, and George Chauncy, Jr. New York: Meridian, 1990, pp. 294–317.

Chodorow, Nancy. *The Reproduction of Mothering: Psychoanalysis and the Sociology of Gender*. Berkeley: U of California P, 1978.

Dinesen, Isak. "The Blank Page." *The Last Tales*. New York: 1957. Rpt. in *The Norton Anthology of Literature by Women*. Ed. Sandra M. Gilbert and Susan Gubar. New York: W. W. Norton, 1985, pp. 1418–23.

Du Plessis, Rachel Blau. "For the Etruscans." Rpt. in *The New Feminist Criticism*. Ed. Elaine Showalter. New York: Pantheon, 1985.

Fetterley, Judith. "Reading About Reading: 'A Jury of Her Peers,' 'The Murders in the Rue Morgue,' and 'The Yellow Wallpaper.' " In *Gender and Reading: Essays on Readers, Texts, and Contexts*. Ed. Elizabeth A. Flynn and Patrocinio Schweickart. Baltimore: Johns Hopkins UP, 1986.

———. *The Resisting Reader: A Feminist Approach to American Fiction*. Bloomington: Indiana UP, 1978.

Flax, Jane. *Thinking Fragments: Psychoanalysis, Feminism, and Postmodernism in the Contemporary West*. Berkeley: U of California P, 1990.

Froula, Christine. "The Daughter's Seduction: Sexual Violence and Literary History." *Signs* (Summer 1986), 11(4): 621–44.

Fuss, Diana. *Essentially Speaking: Feminism, Nature and Difference*. New York: Routledge, 1989.

Gilbert, Sandra M., and Susan Gubar. *The Madwoman in the Attic: The Woman Writer and the Nineteenth-Century Literary Imagination*. New Haven: Yale UP, 1979.

Gilbert, Sandra M., and Susan Gubar, eds. *Shakespeare's Sisters: Feminist Essays on Women Poets*. Bloomington: Indiana UP, 1979.

Gilligan, Carol. *In a Different Voice: Psychological Theory and Women's Development*. Cambridge: Harvard UP, 1982.

Gilman, Charlotte Perkins, "The Yellow Wallpaper." *New England Magazine* (May 1892). Rpt. in *The Captive Imagination: A Casebook on The Yellow Wallpaper*. Ed. Catherine Golden. New York: The Feminist Press, 1992.

Glaspell, Susan. "A Jury of Her Peers." *Everyweek* (March 5, 1917). Rpt. in *Images of Women in Literature*. Ed. Mary Anne Ferguson. Boston: Houghton Mifflin, 1973.

Golden, Catherine, ed. *The Captive Imagination: A Casebook on "The Yellow Wallpaper."* New York: The Feminist Press, 1992.

———. "One Hundred Years of Reading 'The Yellow Wallpaper.' " In *The Captive Imagination*, pp. 1–23.

———. "The Writing of 'The Yellow Wallpaper': A Double Palimpsest." In *The Captive Imagination*, pp. 296–306.

Grahn, Judy. *The Common Woman*. Poem. Oakland: Women's Press Collective, n.d.

Gubar, Susan, " 'The Blank Page' and the Issue of Female Creativity." In *Writing and Sexual Difference*. Ed. Elizabeth Abel. Chicago: U of Chicago P, 1982, pp. 73–93.

———. "Sapphistries." In *The Lesbian Issue: Essays from Signs*. Ed. Estelle B. Freedman, Barbara C. Gelpi, Susan L. Johnson, and Kathleen M. Weston. Chicago: U of Chicago P, 1985, pp. 91–110.

Haney-Peritz, Janice. "Monumental Feminism and Literature's Ancestral House: Another Look at 'The Yellow Wallpaper.' " *Women's Studies* (1986), 12:2, 113–28. Reprinted in *The Captive Imagination*, ed. Golden.

Harding, Sandra. "The Instability of the Analytical Categories of Feminist Theory." *Signs* (Summer 1986): 11(4).

Hedges, Elaine R. "Afterword" to *The Yellow Wallpaper*. New York: The Feminist Press, 1973. Reprinted in *The Captive Imagination: A Casebook on "The Yellow Wallpaper."* Ed. Catherine Golden. New York: The Feminist Press, 1992, pp. 123–36.

———. "Small Things Reconsidered: Susan Glaspell's 'A Jury of Her Peers.' " *Women's Studies* (1986), 12: 89–110.

———. " 'Out at Last'? 'The Yellow Wallpaper' after Two Decades of Feminist Criticism." In *The Captive Imagination: A Casebook on The Yellow Wallpaper*. Ed. Catherine Golden. New York: The Feminist Press, 1992, pp. 319–33.

Heilbrun, Carolyn G. "Critical Response II: A Response to *Writing and Sexual Difference*." In *Writing and Sexual Difference*. Ed. Elizabeth Abel. Chicago: U of Chicago P, 1982, pp. 291–97.

Henderson, Mae Gwendolyn, "Speaking in Tongues: Dialogics, Dialectics, and the Black Woman Writer's Literary Tradition." *Changing Our Words: Essays on Criticism, Theory and Writing by Black Women*. Ed. Cheryl A. Wall. New Brunswick: Rutgers, 1989. Reprinted in *Reading Black, Reading Feminist*, ed. Henry Louis Gates, Jr. New York: Meridian, 1990, pp. 116–42.

Hull, Gloria T., Patricia Bell Scott, and Barbara Smith. *All the Women are White, All the Blacks Are Men, But Some of Us Are Brave: Black Women's Studies*. New York: The Feminist Press, 1982.

Jacobus, Mary. "An Unnecessary Maze of Sign Reading." *Reading Women: Essays in Feminist Criticism*. New York: Columbia UP. Report in *The Captive Imagination*, pp. 277–95.

Jones, Ann Rosalind. "Imaginary Gardens with Real Frogs in Them: Feminist Euphoria and the Franco-American Divide, 1976–88." *Changing Subjects: The Making of Feminist Literary Criticism*. Ed. Coppelia Kahn and Gayle Greene. London: Routledge, 1992.

Kaplan, Carla. "The Language of Crisis in Feminist Theory." *Turning the Century: New Directions in Feminist Criticism*. Ed. Glynis Carr. Lewisburg: Bucknell Review Press, 1992.

Kennard, Jean. "Convention Coverage or How to Read Your Own Life." *New Literary History* (1981), 13:1, 69–88. Reprinted in *The Captive Imagination*, ed. Golden.

Kolodny, Annette. "Dancing Through the Minefield: Some Observations of the Theory, Practice, and Politics of a Feminist Literary Criticism." *Feminist Studies* (Spring 1980), 6.

———. "A Map for Rereading: Or, Gender and the Interpretation of Literary Texts." *New Literary History* (1980), 11:3. Reprinted in *The Captive Imagination*, ed. Golden, pp. 149–67.

———. "Turning the Lens on 'The Panther Captivity': A Feminist Exercise in Practical Criticism." In *Writing and Sexual Difference.* Ed. Elizabeth Abel. Chicago: U of Chicago P, 1982, pp. 159–75.

Kristeva, Julia. "Woman Can Never Be Defined." *New French Feminisms.* Ed. Elaine Marks and Isabelle de Courtivron. New York: Schocken, 1981.

Lanser, Susan S. "Feminist Criticism, 'The Yellow Wallpaper,' and the Politics of Color in America." *Feminist Studies* (Fall 1989), 15:3, pp. 415–41.

Lauretis, Teresa de. "Sexual Indifference and Lesbian Representation." *Performing Feminisms: Feminist Critical Theory and Theatre.* Ed. Sue-Ellen Case. Baltimore: Johns Hopkins UP, 1990, pp. 17–39.

———. "Film and the Visible." In *How Do I Look?: Queer Film and Video.* Ed. Bad Object-Choices. Seattle: Bay Press, 1991, pp. 223–76.

Marcus, Jane. "Daughters of Anger/Material Girls: Con/textualizing Feminist Criticism," *Women's Studies* (1988) 15:281–308.

———. "Sapphistry: Narration as Lesbian Seduction in *A Room of One's Own.*" In *Virginia Woolf and the Languages of Patriarchy.* Bloomington: Indiana UP, 1987, pp. 163–87.

Mayne, Judith. "A Parallax View of Lesbian Authorship." In *Inside/Out: Lesbian Theories, Gay Theories.* Ed. Diana Fuss. New York: Routledge, 1991.

McDowell, Deborah E. " 'The Changing Same': Generational Connections and Black Women Novelists." *New Literary History* (1987), 18: 281–302. Reprinted in *Reading Black, Reading Feminist,* ed. Henry Louis Gates, Jr. New York: Meridian, 1990, pp. 91–115.

———. "New Directions for Black Feminist Criticism," *Black American Literature Forum* 14(1980). Reprinted in *The New Feminist Criticism: Essays on Women, Literature, and Theory,* ed. Elaine Showalter. New York: Pantheon, 1985.

Michie, Helena. *Sororophobia.* New York: Oxford UP, 1992.

Miller, Nancy K. "Emphasis Added: Plots and Plausibilities in Women's Fiction." *PMLA* (Jan. 1981), 96:1. Reprinted in *Subject to Change: Reading Feminist Writing.* New York: Columbia, 1988.

———. "Arachnologies: The Woman, The Text, and the Critic." *The Poetics of Gender.* Ed. Nancy K. Miller. New York: Columbia UP, 1986. Reprinted in *Subject to Change: Reading Feminist Writing.* New York: Columbia UP, 1988.

Modleski, Tania. *Feminism Without Women: Culture and Criticism in a 'Postfeminist' Age.* New York: Routledge, 1991.

Moers, Ellen. *Literary Women: The Great Writers.* Garden City: Doubleday, 1976.

Moi, Toril. *Sexual/Textual Politics: Feminist Literary Theory.* New York: Methuen, 1985.

Moraga, Cherríe and Gloria Anzaldúa, eds. *This Bridge Called My Back: Writings By Radical Women of Color.* Watertown, Mass.: Persephone Press, 1981.

Munt, Sally, ed. *New Lesbian Criticism: Literary and Cultural Readings.* New York: Columbia UP, 1992.

Olsen, Tillie. *Silences.* New York: Delacorte, 1978.

Ostriker, Alicia S. "The Thieves of Language: Women Poets and Revisionist Mythmaking." *Stealing the Language. The Emergence of Women's Poetry in America.* Boston: Beacon, 1986.

Rich, Adrienne. "Diving into the Wreck." *Diving into the Wreck: Poems, 1971–1972.* New York: W. W. Norton, 1973.

———. "When We Dead Awaken: Writing as Re-Vision." *College English* (Oct., 1972), 34:1. Reprinted in *On Lies, Secrets, and Silence: Selected Prose, 1966–1978.* New York: W. W. Norton, 1979, pp. 33–49.

————. "Compulsory Heterosexuality and Lesbian Existence." *Signs* (1980) 5:4, pp. 631–60.

Riley, Denise. *Am I That Name? Feminism and the Category of 'Women' in History.* New York: Macmillan, 1988.

Schweickart, Patrocinio. "Reading Ourselves: Toward a Feminist Theory of Reading." *Gender and Reading: Essays on Readers, Texts, Contexts.* Ed. Elizabeth A. Flynn and Patrocinio P. Schweickart. Baltimore: Johns Hopkins UP, 1986.

Showalter, Elaine. *Sister's Choice: Tradition and Change in American Women's Writing.* New York: Oxford UP, 1991.

————. *A Literature of Their Own: British Women Novelists from Brontë to Lessing.* Princeton: Princeton UP, 1977.

Smith, Barbara. "Toward a Black Feminist Criticism." *The New Feminist Criticism: Essays on Women, Literature, Theory.* Ed. Elaine Showalter. New York: Pantheon, 1985.

————. Ed. *Home Girls: A Black Feminist Anthology.* New York: Persephone Press, 1983.

Smith, Barbara Herrnstein. "Contingencies of Value." *Critical Inquiry,* (Sept. 1983) 10:1.

Snitow, Ann, Christine Stansell, and Sharon Thomson, eds. *Powers of Desire: The Politics of Sexuality.* New York: Monthly Review Press, 1983.

Spacks, Patricia. *The Female Imagination.* New York: Knopf, 1975.

The Lesbian Issue. Signs (Summer 1984) 9. Later reprinted (with additions) as *The Lesbian Issue: Essays From Signs,* ed. Estelle B. Freedman, Barbara C. Gelpi, Susan L. Johnson, and Kathleen M. Weston. Chicago: U of Chicago P, 1985.

Treichler, Paula A. "Escaping the Sentence: Diagnosis and Discourse in 'The Yellow Wallpaper.' " *Feminist Issues in Literary Scholarship.* Ed. Shari Benstock. Bloomington: Indiana UP, pp. 62–78. Reprinted in *The Captive Imagination,* ed. Golden, pp. 191–210.

Vance, Carole S., ed. *Pleasure and Danger: Exploring Female Sexuality.* New York: Monthly Review Press, 1983.

Walker, Alice. "In Search of Our Mother's Gardens." *Ms.* (May 1974). Reprinted in *In Search of our Mother's Gardens.* New York: Harcourt, Brace, Jovanovich, 1983, pp. 231–43.

Warner, Michael. "Homo-Narcissism; or, Heterosexuality." *Engendering Men: The Question of Male Feminist Criticism.* Ed. Joseph A. Boone and Michael Cadden (Routledge, 1990).

Wittig, Monique. "One is Not Born a Woman." *Feminist Issues* (Winter 1981) 7:4.

Woolf, Virginia. *A Room of One's Own.* New York: Harcourt, Brace, & World, 1929.

————. *The Pargiters: The Novel-Essay Portion of "The Years."* Ed. Mitchell A. Leaska. New York: Harcourt, Brace, & World, 1978.

Zimmerman, Bonnie. "What Has Never Been: An Overview of Lesbian Feminist Criticism." *Feminist Studies* 7.3 (1981). Reprinted in *The New Feminist Criticism,* ed. Showalter, pp. 200–224.

PART III

Silent Parenting in the Academy[1]

CONSTANCE COINER

FOR BARBARA SNYDER

Tillie Olsen's *Tell Me a Riddle* and *Silences* are virtually unique in American literature for their uncompromising look at the anguish of women who must choose between having children and the need to carry on other serious work. In the 1970s, when many feminists forewent or delayed childbearing, *Silences* dared to raise the issue of responsibility for children, an issue that has become, in my view, the crucible for the women's movement. In raising this issue, Olsen entered what in *Silences* she termed "an almost taboo area; the last refuge of sexism" (202). Today, over a decade since the publication of *Silences*, responsibility for children *remains* the last refuge of sexism, the Achilles heel of the women's movement. Even the women whom the movement has most helped to advance, its educated professionals, have with a sense of *déjà vu* felt that old shock of sudden recognition, that familiar "click": equal opportunity vanishes around the issue of who will take care of the kids.

As a person attempting to parent within the academy, I have experienced such "clicks," as the following anecdotes will show. When I was a graduate student and my daughter, Ana, was a newborn, I received a note from Tillie Olsen on one of those scraps of paper that are her trademark. "Thieve all the time you can for Ana" was all it said, but I have hung on to that scrap of permission to love my child while working my way into a profession that is often incompatible with the needs of children and parents.

When I completed my Ph.D. and went on the job market in 1987, the professor responsible for shepherding candidates through the job search advised me to replace the message on my answering machine that included Ana's cheery, four-year-old voice. "And I wouldn't let her answer the phone 'til this shootin' match is over," he added ominously. With misgivings, I complied with his instructions. But Ana, who was proud of her newly-acquired phone-answering skills, was not to be silenced. Unexpectedly, at eight a.m. one Saturday morning, the phone rang. Forgetting about the time difference between the east and west coasts, I relented and allowed Ana to answer, believing that only my mother would call at such an early hour. Ana put down the phone receiver, screeching, "Mommy, Mommy, it's the University of Transylvania!"[2] In the seconds before I spoke to the chair of the University of Pennsylvania's search committee, I saw my fledgling career as a minefield.

I took a job as an assistant professor at SUNY-Binghamton, partly because I was assured that my daughter would have access to its highly re-

197

garded campus preschool and kindergarten. I was thinking short- and long-run: In a pleasant setting very near her parents' offices, my child would enjoy a smooth transition into our new life; and the preschool, which enrolls children from the age of two on, would later provide care for a possible second child. As it turned out, the preschool had overenrolled, anticipating atrophy in enrollment that didn't occur, and my daughter wasn't admitted. I went immediately to the public elementary school, where the principal told me that the kindergarten Ana would attend ended at 10:30 a.m. Having had my expectations affected by 16 years in what *Sixty Minutes* dubbed the People's Republic of Santa Monica, California, I asked, "And what provisions are made for children after 10:30?" "Oh, their mothers come and pick them up," he offered with a shrug. "What about *parents* who work outside the home?" I said, emphasizing "parents" through gritted teeth. "Oh, they get babysitters," he replied ("family day-care providers" had not yet found its way into this principal's lexicon). "Maybe you could run an ad for a babysitter in the *Pennysaver*," he added, referring to the local throwaway newspaper.

A final anecdote has to do with my attempt to prepare a talk that my university's Women's Center asked me to give about combining parenting with my profession. (The Women's Center's request came during my first semester at the University, when I was developing two courses for the first time and writing three papers to be presented at professional conventions. During that semester I confessed my exhaustion to a colleague's wife, who with good intentions tried to reassure me that my experience was not unusual: "Oh, how well I remember George [not his real name] when he was at your stage in his career. He worked round-the-clock. The boys and I never saw him.") I brainstormed at the computer the night before the event, managing at least to come up with what I considered a clever title (a quote from Rosa Luxemburg, below), but some family obligation—I don't remember what—interrupted my work, and, out of necessity, I ended up speaking extemporaneously. All that I produced in that thwarted brainstorming session was the following computer printout:

Title: "Ach, I know of No Formula to Write You for Being Human"

Can you combine parenting with professoring? Yes. Well, maybe.

If you get a job at a research institution, you'll have to live three-and-a-half lives:
Mother Life = one life
Teaching Life = one life
Publishing   = one life
Maintaining a Home (hopefully sharing that responsibility equally with another adult) = half-a-life

If you get a job at a "teaching institution," you'll have to live only two-and-a-half lives—unless you're employed by a school that is increasing publication requirements while maintaining heavy teaching loads:
Mother Life   = one life

Teaching Life = one life
Maintaining a Home = half-a-life

I would try to . . .

The material circumstances of a mother's life—one that is, as Olsen has put it, "instantly interruptable"—prevented my getting any further (18).

Prior to the contemporary women's movement, many male professors produced while their wives enabled them to do so without distractions. A professorship was often a two-person operation, with two people, in different ways, supporting one career. Olsen contributed valuably to an unmasking of this hidden labor that often supports intellectual production. *Silences* foregrounded domestic labor and especially child care, which may be the most invisible, the most "naturalized" labor of all. One of many memorable passages from *Silences* describes what Edmund Wilson's second wife, Elena, provided him daily: "tea on a tray for his 'elevenses'; absolute silence in his working hours, and good meals at appropriate intervals" (221).

Although some of us have moved beyond the world of Mr. and Mrs. Wilson, the academic profession, in its structure and expectations, does not reflect the reality of our post-housewife era. The academy assumes a freedom from responsibility for maintaining a home and family that, for many academic women (and for some of our male allies), simply does not exist. The profession is still defined by the assumption that we have at our disposal what *Silences* terms "the essential angel," someone responsible "for daily living, for the maintenance of life" (34). And because few in positions of power *acknowledge* that assumption—probably because most of them have been insulated from family responsibilities—it is all the more insidious, all the more difficult to confront.

Moreover, although the academic profession is no longer the province primarily of the gentlemanly leisured class, we daily experience remnants of that empire, including a polite code of silence about certain topics. One of the unspoken requirements for tenure is for junior faculty to appear to be coping well with their myriad responsibilities. At faculty meetings and social gatherings, it behooves us to look relaxed and on top of things rather than frenzied, fatigued, malcontent. We have to prove that we're "one of them." It's a Catch-22: The people in the profession most likely to need parental leave and child care are often the same people expected to be on their best behavior. Most of the pretenure faculty I know believe that they would jeopardize tenure by making demands—or simply by admitting the truth about the quality of their lives. Yet it's time for people to be honest about the tremendous emotional cost of women's—and men's—professional advances. And unless we radically change the structure of the academic career and what Arlie Hochschild terms "its imperial relation to the family," it will be difficult for mothers "to move up in careers and for men to move into the family" ("Clockwork" 48). Both women and men will live less than full lives.

Before proceeding, I must enter a three-part caveat: First, the spirit of *Silences* would have me underscore that nonacademic parents employed at universities experience pressures, too. Many academic departments depend heavily on administrative assistants and staff members—mostly women, many of them parents—who, as much as their academic counterparts, deserve parental leave, on-campus child care, flextime, etc. We must organize within the academy, building alliances and unions with other university employees such as clerical, maintenance, and food-service workers. As Carl Freedman argues, "a great many reified myths will be dissolved or eroded when teachers, whose labor is predominantly mental, bargain and picket alongside those who sweep classroom floors and serve food in university cafeterias. To think of ourselves as workers at all is, indeed, in itself a powerful demystification of the ideology of professionalism. . ." (81). Second, in this essay "family" refers to nontraditional as well as traditional configurations, including partners of the same or opposite sex in living arrangements approximating marital partnerships. Third, I want to acknowledge that feminist agendas in the early 1970s, including those of women operating within professional academic organizations, addressed a number of the points I'll raise. With the ensuing discussion, I hope to remind the academy that some problems identified by feminists over twenty years ago have not been resolved and are still urgent.

I begin by surveying attempts, including those within the Modern Language Association (MLA) and the American Studies Association (ASA) during the last 25 years, to address feminist concerns that bear on problems of parenting within the academy. While I will refer often to efforts by people within these two organizations, I recognize that members of other professional academic organizations have addressed problems of parenting in the academy, and I intend my discussion and recommendations to apply to the academy as a whole, not simply to disciplines associated with the MLA and ASA.

At the Business Meeting of the 1969 MLA Convention, Florence Howe, Chair of the newly established Commission on the Status of Women in the Profession, which had been charged to "investigate 'discriminatory practices' in order to *assure* 'equitable standards,' " issued the Commission's preliminary report ("The 1969 Business Meeting" 645). The report made a series of recommendations, including some pertaining to parenting in the academy (e.g., the establishment of university supported, parent-controlled day-care centers). Ellen Cantarow, also working toward equity for women within the profession, had urged the MLA Resolutions Committee to bring several resolutions to that same meeting. As part of the March 1970 *MLA Newsletter,* these resolutions—with accompanying explanations written by Cantarow, Lillian Robinson, and Jacqueline Tunberg—were sent, among other resolutions, to the MLA membership (31,607 in that year) for a vote. Each resolution received over 4000 votes, which, when compared to returns on MLA mail ballots in other years, represents a very good response.

One resolution, approved by a close vote of 2246 to 2149, urged the establishment of day-care centers on college and university campuses. "These centers," the explanation read, "should be institutionally-funded, parent-controlled, staffed by both men and women, and open to children from the age of six weeks on, whose parents are students, teachers, employees, or neighbors of the institution" ("The 1969 Business Meeting" 651). Another critically important resolution—for paid maternity and parental leave for both men and women—failed in a close vote (2026 to 2321).

These resolutions were situated among others designed to improve the economic and professional status of women and the overall quality of life in the academy. In overwhelmingly positive responses, members voted to urge universities to overturn anti-nepotism rules (3526 to 754); to allow flexibility in faculty appointments, facilitating transitions between part- and full-time positions (3368 to 821); and to provide women employees with benefits, such as health and retirement, equal to those of men (3900 to 178). In another overwhelmingly favorable vote, members requested the *PMLA* and *MLA Newsletter* to provide space for women's professional concerns (3268 to 922).

MLA members also passed the resolution to exhort universities to call for the repeal of all state laws regulating contraception, abortion, and voluntary sterilization and to press university medical centers to offer free birth control information and devices (2304 to 2057). And members passed the resolution to "urge that the position of women, the conventions of love, courtship, and marriage, and the stereotypes involving women be made the subjects of courses and scholarship in the humanities" (2866 to 1270; "The 1969 Business Meeting" 651). A resolution to give preference to women, including women of color, in hiring, promotion, and tenure was defeated (1639 to 2767).

In summary, of the nine resolutions related to women and to family-care issues, seven were passed and two rejected. Thus, in 1970, a majority of voting MLA members supported significant institutional reform. But as readers of this essay know only too well, some of these reforms—such as the establishing of campus day-care centers—have not yet been widely implemented, over 20 years after they were originally endorsed.

In 1984–85 Tey Diana Rebolledo, a member of the MLA Commission on the Status of Women, reviewed parenting leave policies for some 50 academic institutions as well as the then-current literature on parenting leave policies within both the academy and private industry. By conducting this review, Rebolledo hoped to assist universities in developing codified parental leave policies. Her report is one indication that the 1970 MLA resolutions drawn up by Cantarow, Robinson, and Tunberg had not made sufficient impact on university administrations. According to Rebolledo's report, many universities lacked formal policies, relying instead on administrators' discretion. As she pointed out, these ad hoc policies allow administrators to be lenient in some cases and not in others. Many institutions had only "sick" leave for mothers, with no paternal leave. While some institutions provided full pay and benefits for up to three months, others allowed only a leave of absence without pay. Professor Rebolledo left the Women's Commission not long after completing this report, and, unfortunately, the MLA neither published the report nor pursued the project.[3]

In 1972 an 18-month-old ad hoc committee, the American Studies Association Women's Committee, became a permanent part of the Association and began to address issues pertaining to the lives of women and families within the academy. Recommendation for the permanent status of the Committee was one of many resolutions that year that signaled the ASA's growing sensitivity to pro-family concerns. In a report compiled by the Women's Committee of the ASA, "Personal Lives and Professional Careers: The Uneasy Balance" (1988), Linda Kerber, ASA President from 1988–89, discusses the 1972 resolutions. They centered on "structural and ethical" issues concerning equal treatment of women and men within the academy, in the ASA itself, and on the editorial board of the *American Quarterly,* the Association's journal (29). There were resolutions that dealt with child care, pregnancy leave, parental leave (for men as well as women), and options in the pace of career advancement. The resolutions also opposed nepotism policies and encouraged universities to include women's studies courses in their curricula. Moreover, they called for equity in faculty recruitment, hiring, salary, and promotion; in graduate student admissions; and in the awarding of grants and fellowships. The concerns of the ASA Women's Committee resembled those of the MLA Commission on the Status of Women; thus, there was a consistent effort to promote reform by the women's organizations of these two major academic associations.

In the 1988 survey and report of the ASA's Women's Committee, Kerber described the results of the 1972 ASA push for reforms, and that description also applies to the results of the earlier MLA attempts:

> Here we are nearly twenty years later, and on the face of it, much of this agenda is apparently accomplished. Anti-nepotism policies have indeed fallen; sex-biased questions have been removed from the hiring process, women's studies courses are widely available, women have for several years composed a majority of the ASA Council and serve in official capacities throughout the Association; three of the last four Gabriel Dissertation Prize recipients have been women. The academy is a considerably more decent, more open, more ethical institution (30).

In a foreword to that same report, Lois Banner, ASA President from 1986–88, noted, "By the mid 1980s issues raised by the [ASA] women's committee in earlier years seemed to have been addressed to the point that the question was raised of whether or not the organization needed a women's committee" (i). It would seem, then, that attention to "structural and ethical" issues had produced some satisfying results.

The value of these reforms in the last 20 years should not be underestimated. Yet, as Kerber noted in the afterword to the Women's Committee's report, "Academic women continue to find themselves uncomfortable in the academy" (30). Undoubtedly, some of that discomfort reflects the fact that "structural and ethical" reforms, while broadly successful, have not been equally realized in all institutions. However, for some women the discomfort stems significantly from work-family conflict, as the survey and report of the ASA's Women's Committee reveals. The report comments on the importance of the unexpected questions that emerged at the end of one 1985 ASA Convention session, at which Lois Banner and Annette Kolodny had presented papers: ". . . a number of younger women remained in the room. They had very pointed questions for the participants regarding their careers: when they rested, how they avoided 'burn out,' what they did about competing responsibilities in their professional and personal lives" (1). Recognition of these deeply felt work-family conflicts contributed significantly to the creation of the ASA survey.

To explore these and related questions, Banner, Kolodny, Lillian Schlissel, and Mary Kelley constructed a questionnaire that was mailed in 1986 to 1100 women in the ASA and to 1,831 women in the Organization of American Historians. The questionnaire was also sent to a random group of 200 male members of the ASA. Women in the ASA returned 23 percent or 238 questionnaires; women in the OAH returned 13 percent or 199; the ASA men returned 30 percent or 67. Respondents talked about stress they and their families experienced, burn-out and anxiety, and problems of survival in the professional marketplace. In an afterword to the report, Kerber describes what the Women's Committee received—on paper and in crowded sessions at both the ASA and OAH Conventions: "outpourings of anxiety, frustration, and despair that are not unlike what we heard 20 years ago, in those early attempts to articulate an agenda for political change" (30).

I attended the emotionally charged ASA Convention session in which the questionnaire responses were discussed, and Kerber's word "outpourings" is apt. People couldn't wait to speak; some exploded. As Banner insists in her foreword to the questionnaire report, "This is not just a document produced by numbers of discontented women: it speaks truths about the *nature of modern professionalism*" (my emphasis). "We all decry the rigors of the academic life," Banner continues, "but few of us do much to change the contours of a system rooted in capitalist competition and male hierarchy. . . . [B]oth men and women need to recreate the academic workplace so that it becomes a humane alternative to corporate America, not merely a replica of its negative features" (i–ii). The issue of parenting within the academy, then, is only one element—albeit a crucial one—in a more general dialogue about our profession that ought to take place, as Banner rightly insists, "in open convention forums and in public department colloquia, not just fugitively over beers late at night or privately in the security of individual offices" (ii).

The constructors of the ASA survey created an alternative to typical questionnaires that attempt to gather "objective," quantifiable information by translating respondents' concerns into a limited set of categories. While nonobjective questionnaires are not a feminist invention, Banner, Kolodny, Schlissel, and Kelley put into practice forms of language that many feminist theorists view as welcome alternatives to the dominant modes of communication. One description of a feminist exploration of communication appears in Nadya Aisenberg and Mona Harrington's *Women of Academe: Outsiders in the Sacred Grove:*

[That exploration] has from the beginning been communal, advanced by exchanges of insight, a conversational discourse, open to—indeed, dependent on—contributions in unfinished form. And it is also dependent on attentive listening—women's ancient skill, here used not to take direction from others but to join with others in defining new directions. In short, the language of feminist exploration is inevitably probing and tentative, and the participants in the exchange, therefore, have little choice but to abjure precision and fluency if they are to contribute (81).

Aisenberg and Harrington's experiences interviewing 25 tenured women and 37 women deflected from the tenure track confirmed for them the value of alternative modes of gathering information about the complexity of people's lives.

One set of questions in the ASA questionnaire and the summary of responses to it exemplify the survey's open-endedness, a feminist exploration that "encouraged respondents to follow the issues wherever they might lead" (1):

Are you aware of any clear directions, turns, major career determinations in your life? What initiated new starts? personal crises? departures from old life patterns? Were there individuals, role models, or mentors attached to these turning points? Was the women's movement, in any of its facets or complexities, a causative factor in any of your decisions about career, family configuration or other personal choices? (9).

The questionnaire's constructors viewed this set of questions as "a deliberate risk. . . . It was the most difficult to evaluate but provided the richest source of insights. It was precisely the disorder of responses that has proved most rewarding; often they led in directions that were not predictable" (9). I will focus on only one part of the summary of responses to the questions above, that which deals with the "picture of the academic profession":

Most of all, there is a startling picture of the academic profession that emerges. Where academia has been considered relatively secure, offering not wealth but stability, sometimes gentility, a profession suited for the talents of trained women, the picture that is now drawn seems little different from that of corporate America, where advancement is tied to geographic relocation. To be successful, an academic must be highly competitive and productive as well as highly mobile. Women who have attained their doctoral degrees by the application of enormous energy and determination and who have attained significant reputation by their scholarship and publication, are often stalled short of the top of the profession by family constraints that keep them less able to move aggressively from campus to campus (15).

We should be guided by insights from the ASA report "Personal Lives and Professional Careers: The Uneasy Balance" as we address the problems of acquiring information about how people perceive their lives in relation to the university and sharing that information with all concerned, including academic administrations. In that ASA report, we should be alert to Regina Morantz-Sanchez's warning about modern professions' (including the academic profession's) constraining dependence on scientific models of rationality, impartiality, and objectivity and their attendant forms of communication. To be involved in the daily "maintenance of life," to borrow Olsen's terms, is to recognize that these scientific models are dangerously inadequate to the task of understanding and communicating life's contingencies. Alternatives to these models are being pursued in feminist scholarship, but the discoveries of feminist language theory must be infused into the *day-to-day* operations of the university, modifying the forms of communication on which the academic world still relies. The ASA questionnaire stands as one attempt toward such infusion. Far too often, the questionnaires many of us have received from our university administrations and professional organizations silence rather than solicit information by posing reductive questions (often requiring "yes" or "no" answers or quantifiable responses) inadequate to the complexities of our experiences. And yet, many of us participate willingly in such requests for information when, for the sake of understanding the complex problems of parenting in the academy, we should be creating alternatives to the dominant modes of communication.

While we work toward radically improved forms of communication to assess the full range of needs for institutional reform, we can already identify a few of our most pressing needs. One is to broaden our definition of "parenting" to include caring for sick or disabled relatives and for aging parents, a rapidly expanding population. Between 1960 and 1980 the number of people in the United States 65 or older grew by 54 percent (Preston 44). According to a *Family and Medical Leave Act Fact Sheet* issued in February 1991 by the American Association of University Women,

> the federal government estimates that by 2025, Americans over 65 will make up 40 percent of the dependent care population. Women today are part of the "sandwich generation"—many have responsibility for the care of both children and elderly parents. Women in prime earning years (35–64) are especially vulnerable as they are more likely to have both kinds of dependents . . . (n. p.).

MIT's Committee on Family and Work learned from a 1989 survey that between 15 and 20 percent of faculty and staff had had significant responsibility for an adult dependent at some point during the five years prior to the Committee's survey. Kathy Luneau Simons's essay about the Committee's findings, "Beyond Campus Child Care: Supporting University Families," notes that "there was widespread interest in a variety of services related to adult dependent care" (65). In the population as a whole, those providing primary care for adult dependents, like those providing primary care for children, are disproportionately women. In many cases, women care for their husbands' parents as well as their own. Like the "mommy track," a career path in which women must forgo promotion in order to have time for their children, "the daughter track" is a growing phenomenon. As Simons effectively argues, our vision must extend beyond child care to reach other pro-family services as well, including elder care.

Another pressing need is a close examination of the "picture of the academic profession" that emerged from the responses to the ASA questionnaire. We must recognize that the academy has adopted some of the negative features of the traditional corporate model, such as competition as the unquestioned norm; the assumption that every worker has a wife functioning as a homemaker; and the assumption that promotion is linked to mobility, despite the hardships such uprooting often causes family members. While we cannot expect competition to disappear from the academy, we can modify the profession so that it is more responsive to families' needs.

Whether universities are doing more or less than corporations to develop pro-family policies and services remains an open question, my research suggests. One useful comparison has been made by Ellen Galinsky and Peter Stein, with the help of Judy David. They conducted interviews in ten organizations recognized as leaders in employing scientists. Five were major universities—MIT, Stanford, Berkeley, Harvard, and the University of Texas at Austin. Five were corporations that the universities regard as their competitors in the hiring of scientists—IBM, Merck, Digital Equipment Company, Johnson & Johnson, and AT&T (Bell Labs). Although the study's results are too detailed to summarize here, Galinsky and Stein report that "there has been a rapid expansion in the attention given to [pro-family] issues in both the universities and the corporations." For example, "all ten organizations interviewed are involved in helping employees with child care in a variety of ways" (19).[4]

Two studies conducted by the Hewitt Associates using identical categories provide another point of comparison between the academic and corporate worlds. For a *Special Report* published by the College and University Personnel Association (April 15, 1991), Hewitt Associates surveyed the work and family benefits offered to faculty and staff of 35 colleges and universities. Hewitt Associates also surveyed those benefits as offered by 837 businesses (*Work and Family Benefits Provided by Major U.S. Employers*, 1990).[5] Although it appears from these two studies that universities are doing at least as much in most pro-family categories as corporations, Ellen Galinsky—currently co-president of the Families and Work Institute, a New York City-based nonprofit research group—believes that parents of young children fare worse in the academic world than in the corporate world because corporations have a more flexible career path without the academy's probationary period followed by the "up or out" tenure decision. Parents who aren't promoted in corporations because they have family responsibilities, Galinsky observes, can still "paddle in place."[6]

In a growing number of corporations, employees responsible for children are allowed to do more than "paddle in place." A *New York Times* article (January 28, 1990) discusses several women who have been able to avoid the "mommy track." One mother, an audit manager, moved to part-time with her company's assurance that "she is still on the track to make partner" (Deutsch). Another mother, an engineer, had been on a mornings-only schedule since the birth of her first child in 1986 and was promoted in 1989 while pregnant with her second child (29). The same *Times* article details the Johnson and Johnson

Family Plan, one of the most progressive in the country, which includes a nationwide resource and referral system for child care and elder care; a year's family-care leave, with full benefits and a promise of reemployment for anyone who has to care for a child, a spouse, or a parent; pre-tax treatment for dollars spent on dependent care; training to sensitize supervisors to the need for balancing work and family; two child-care centers, one at the company's headquarters and another at an as-yet-unspecified location; and benefits that will pay some of the cost of adopting a child. The *Times* quoted Johnson and Johnson's vice-president for human resources: "One of the ways to get and keep [good employees] is to help them fulfill their family responsibilities" (29).

Another "family-friendly" employer, IBM, inaugurated programs in 1988 that the company hopes will attract and retain workers, particularly women trying to juggle the demands of work and family. These programs include an increase in flextime; work at home; an elder-care resource and referral service; and permitting many employees to take up to a three-year leave without interruption in company-paid benefits (Swoboda 8E; Galinsky and Stein 20). In a *Harvard Business Review* "Special Report" (March–April 1986), Dana E. Friedman, currently co-president of the Families and Work Institute, described how some companies have dealt with absenteeism associated with sick children. In San Jose, California, Hewlett-Packard and Levi Strauss cooperatively installed a 15-bed infirmary attached to a child care center. Other companies contract with services that provide trained nurses for all-day care in the child's home. The 3M Company, for example, pays 70 percent of the cost for in-home nursing services offered by the Children's Hospital in St. Paul (29). With Ellen Galinsky and Carol Hernandez, Friedman has also compiled *The Corporate Reference Guide to Work-Family Programs*, which surveys 188 corporations and includes a "family-friendly" index.[7]

But "family-friendly" employers, while growing in number, remain exceptional: "In 1988, out of approximately six million companies in the U.S., only 4,150 provided child care assistance to their employees."[8] And consider this telling revelation, from Arlie Hochschild:

> Among top-rated employers listed in *The Hundred Best Companies to Work For in America,* many offer country-club membership, first-class air travel, and million-dollar fitness centers. Only a handful offer job sharing, flextime, or part-time work. Not one provides on-site day care and only three offer child care deductions—Control Data, Polaroid, and Honeywell are exceptions (*Shift* 269).

Such definitions of "best" send one scurrying to *Working Mother* magazine's sixth annual ranking of family-friendly companies, which appeared in the October 1991 issue. Eighty-five companies made the 1991 list (up from 75 in 1990), ranging from titans such as Johnson & Johnson, Procter & Gamble, and Eastman Kodak to smaller businesses such as Ben & Jerry's Ice Cream of Vermont and Neuville Industries, a North Carolina sock manufacturer. Academics at institutions experiencing cutbacks and state budget crises— and at this moment that includes many of us—should arm ourselves with the information that the programs and benefits designed to support these companies' working parents "not only escaped the [recession's] ax, they have literally exploded" ("Magazine" 7B). "Given these difficult times, you would have expected to see real cutbacks [in pro-family policies]," commented Susan Seliger, associate publisher-editor of *Working Mother* and inaugurator of the annual ranking. "These are the latest innovations and you'd think they'd be the first things to go," Seliger added, but "they haven't been" ("Magazine" 7B).

Perhaps the single most valuable resource regarding universities and child care is *Campus Child Care Issues and Practices: A Collection of Conference Presentations, 1975–1987,* edited by Carol R. Keyes and Ruth E. Cook.[9] Its foreword rightly asserts, "Every higher education administrator in America needs to read this volume" (viii). As stated in its preface, this guide examines campus child care "in relation to the national picture"; provides "a sampling of particular designs in operation at specific colleges and universities across the country"; describes "how to start a center conceptually, practically, and financially, with some specific examples of different start-up approaches"; discusses "how centers relate to the teaching, service and research mission of institutions of higher education"; and supplies bibliographic resources (Keyes and Cook xi).

Our task, however, is not to compare the pro-family policies of universities and corporations merely to see "who's winning." Rather, we must investigate the most progressive programs in both worlds in order to learn about creative, humane, and cost-effective responses to families' needs and to share that information—with administrators at our "home" institutions, in union meetings, with colleagues at other universities, and within our professional organizations.

The following is my mushrooming list of recommendations for changing the academy's practices to acknowledge broadly defined parenting needs. This list reflects my desires and those of many others. I provide examples of significant pro-family innovations within a few universities.[10]

1. Establish a national clearinghouse for collecting and disseminating information about colleges and universities' pro-family policies (or lack thereof). This information would then be available to all institutions wanting to model their policies on peer institutions, to all major professional organizations, and to all job candidates. Currently, since no such central clearinghouse exists, colleges and universities must conduct their own surveys of peer institutions, such as the Johns Hopkins' survey (June 1990) and the Yale survey of selected private universities (October 1990), referred to below.

2. Fund adequate *paid* maternity leave. In 1990 Rena Cheskis-Gold, a demographer in Yale University's Office of Institutional Research, surveyed 11 private universities, including the eight Ivy League institutions, regarding their maternity leave, parenting leave, and adjusted tenure period policies. (At many of the institutions, the parenting leave is also available for the adoption of a child or for the care of a sick spouse or relative.) Paid maternity

leave is treated as a "disability" and ranges from six weeks to six months. At most of these institutions, long-term disability leave is available if needed.

3. Fund adequate *paid* parental leave. The Yale report reveals that none of the universities surveyed provided paid parental leave beyond the maternity leave. One school had no formal policy. The others provided unpaid leaves, ranging from 13 weeks to two years; all but one of these schools make the leave available to both men and women.

4. Offer family-related services and benefits to nontraditional families, including partners of the same or opposite sex in living arrangements approximating marital partnerships. Universities should listen to voices such as the following that appeared in a 1989 MIT survey of its faculty, staff, and graduate students:

> "I suspect that there are many more of us in the MIT community than you are aware of . . . who are homosexual and who are sustaining relationships that do not conform to standard notions of 'family' and 'household' " (*Report,* Part II, 13) [response from an academic staff member].

> "I would like to see more recognition for people that do not choose to marry but form stable households" (*Report,* Part II, 15) [response from a research staff member].

> I would like my [lesbian] spouse (of over 7 years) to be able to have library privileges, access to athletic and other facilities, Blue Cross/Blue Shield coverage like any other spouse. I would like to have my newborn son be recognized in the same way as my daughter, even though he resulted from my spouse's pregnancy and she [the daughter] from mine. . . . The issue of insurance is particularly important because denial forces most [one-sex] couples to be double income households. . . . If MIT is sincere about their antidiscrimination policy, it will recognize families like mine in some official way and treat us fairly, and when Massachusetts law limits the ability to be fair, it will actively be involved in correcting the offending laws" (*Report,* Part I, 25) [response from a graduate student].

> I endorse the recommendation of the MIT ad hoc Committee on Family and Work (November 7, 1990): "MIT should use a broader concept of family in defining family privileges and benefits. . . . We recommend that MIT move towards a policy in which benefits available to the spouse or child of an employee are also available to a partner in a relationship approximating marriage, or to a dependent child for whom the employee has a responsibility approximating guardianship, adoption or step-parenthood" (*Report,* Part I, 13).

5. Provide adequate, subsidized child care on or close to campus that will accommodate all preschool children, including infants as well as children with disabilities or special needs. In her 1991 article, "Beyond Campus Child Care: Supporting University Families," Kathy Luneau Simons reports on a model program at MIT. According to Simons, MIT has a campus nursery school with full-day care, a second child-care center off-campus that includes infant and toddler care, a summer day-camp for school-age children, a Child Care Office

to coordinate independent day care homes, referral services covering a range of family needs, and a reimbursement account plan, which allows employees to meet qualifying dependent care expenses using pre-tax earnings (58). MIT's Child Care Office also arranges numerous free-of-charge parenting support groups and workshops.

One of the five child-care programs at Stanford University serves as another model. Since its inception in 1970, it has been a "parent-participation" center. Governed by a board composed of parents as well as teachers, the center accommodates 225 children, including infants, toddlers, and preschoolers. For a few hours each week, one parent of a child enrolled in the center must "co-op," to use the facility's colloquialism, by working alongside the child's teacher. One parent of an infant or toddler must "co-op" for five hours per week (the maximum), with the option of "buying out of" three of those hours if necessary; a parent of a preschooler enrolled full-time must participate for only eight hours per month, due to the higher ratio of children to adults in this age group. Parental participation results in a special supportive relationship between families and the center.[11] Neither MIT nor Stanford subsidizes the tuition of their child care programs, although both universities provide buildings, playground space, and maintenance.

A model subsidized child care program is in place at Ohio State University, where funding comes from fees paid by parents on a sliding scale, the university's general fund, the university hospitals, Title XX (a federal government funding program that provides money for low-income parents to meet their child-care needs), the U.S. Department of Agriculture, and the provost's office. Unfortunately, the waiting list for this program has more than one thousand names, which represents a minimum 18-month waiting period.[12]

The University of Maine provides an unusual model program, "a public-private partnership" among the university, corporations, and a hospital.[13]

6. Establish child-care training programs and referral services to put university families in touch with community home-day-care providers. As reported in *The Chronicle of Higher Education* (February 17, 1988), Ohio State University, faced with a long waiting list for its campus child care center, undertook such a training and referral service. In the three years prior to the *Chronicle* report, the University had given some 30 home-day-care providers 40 hours of free training. In return, the providers had given university families "first crack at any openings" (Mangan A-14).

7. Establish reimbursement account plans that allow employees to pay child-care expenses using pre-tax earnings. Dependent care reimbursement accounts comprise the most prevalent pro-family policy. For example, all the 14 schools included in the 1990 Johns Hopkins University Peer University Survey on Family Issues provide reimbursement accounts for dependent care.

8. Expand work-study programs (programs in which university students are employed by their university) to contribute to child care. SUNY-Binghamton, for example, employs work-study students as teachers' aides in its campus preschool.

9. Involve the community's elderly in campus child care on a voluntary or paid basis. The City College of San Francisco has established an Intergenerational Program "aimed at providing qualified day-care workers to a field plagued by high turnover because of low pay." Clara Starr, the supervisor of City College's child care education department, says about their recruiting older people to the child-care field: "Older workers are more experienced, patient and miss work less often" The Intergenerational Program includes 10 weeks of classes in early childhood education and safety, along with internships at child care centers. It is one of five such programs operating nationally that were started by the University of Pittsburgh with money from the Sears Roebuck Foundation (Jacobus 7).

10. Allow faculty members with primary responsibility for a young child to stop the tenure clock temporarily. The University of California system, for example, has established this policy (one year for the birth or adoption of a child, or for caring for a child five years old or younger). Stop-the-tenure-clock, however, should be only one of several policies to support academic parents, because delaying tenure review, at institutions requiring extensive publishing for promotion, can give illusory rather than real support. If parents aren't also given temporary leave from responsibilities such as teaching, advising, and committee work, they won't have time to be productive scholars. (Partly for this reason, the American Association of University Professors, while supporting parental leaves from academic duties, opposes adjusted tenure periods.)

11. Create half- and three-quarter-time tenure track positions.

12. Permit tenure-track job-sharing. This arrangement should be allowable for a "team" of two parents from separate families as well as a couple who have had a child together. As reported in *The Chronicle of Higher Education* (December 14, 1988), two assistant professors in Carnegie-Mellon's History Department teach in alternate semesters and draw a single salary. The married couple also shares responsibility for their young daughter. The two plan to "continue to share the teaching position if they both earn tenure, or one will take it over." The chair of the History Department, who "is pleased with the arrangement," says the History Department benefits from "two scholars, two research strengths, and double the contribution" ('*In*' Box A-11). However, Liliane Floge, a sociologist who with Carolyn Rodriguez conducted research on job-sharing, reported to me that currently only approximately 14 percent of U.S. campuses make job-sharing available.[14]

13. Permit early sabbaticals for infant care, as proposed by Andrew Cherlin, a sociology professor at Johns Hopkins (*The Chronicle of Higher Education*, November 22, 1989). As Cherlin recognizes, "the biological clock and the tenure clock tick away in unison." He suggests that the sabbatical be offered to male and female parents on the usual terms—full pay for one semester or half pay for two. "In effect, the first sabbatical would be borrowed and used a few years early," Cherlin reasons. "The only significant cost—one semester's pay—would be incurred when someone who had taken an advance

sabbatical was later denied tenure" (B2). I would add to Cherlin's suggestion that these early sabbaticals should *not* be used as a substitute for paid maternity/parental leave.

14. Formally recognize that faculty members with primary responsibility for child care may have slower career tracks. Lotte Bailyn recommends the availability of two different career ladders, the one with which we're familiar and one which "defines a different career curve, one that rises more slowly but eventually may end up at the same point, though at a later stage in life" (55). While I worry that the slower track might become "the mommy track," with real power residing with those who take the traditional route, we should nevertheless explore alternatives in career pace.

15. Schedule meetings and colloquia when parents can attend. Meetings that can't be scheduled for the noon hour should be scheduled to end by four-thirty, when possible.

16. Schedule major conventions at times that don't conflict with family-oriented holidays (for example, the MLA Convention now falls between Christmas and New Year's; and schedulers of the ASA Convention, which usually takes place in late October or early November, should try to avoid coinciding with Halloween).

17. Become leading public advocates for federally sponsored child care and parental leave.

18. In the interest of parents and nonparents alike, be creative about dual-career recruitment and hiring among university employees to eliminate long commutes and, in some cases, the expense and stress of maintaining two households. Commuter relationships can be especially difficult for parents of young children and can subvert efforts to share child care equitably. Universities can also help partners of university employees find employment in the community. As reported in *On Campus With Women* (Winter 1989), the Office of Affirmative Action at Oregon State University has established an assistance program for dual-career couples, the Family Employment Program. One of the program's objectives is to help the spouses of faculty find employment (7).

Although the following recommendations refer specifically to the MLA, they can apply as well to other academic associations.

19. The MLA Committee on Careers should modify the preconvention workshops on the job search to include some reference to parenting-related issues—e.g., caution candidates who have or hope to have children to be vigilant about various universities' policies regarding parenting and child care.

20. The MLA Committee on Careers should revise the MLA *Career Guide* to reflect the reality that an increasing number of candidates for academic positions—female and male—are or hope to be significantly involved parents. The MLA *Career Guide* already includes advice to candidates about questions to ask search committees as well as advice to search committees about what to tell candidates. Those sections of the *Guide* should be aug-

mented to advise candidates to inquire about possible parental leave, on-campus child care, stop-the-tenure-clock policies, etc., and to advise search committees to provide such information routinely.

21. Unless a national clearinghouse such as the one recommended in proposal #1, above, is established, the MLA Committee on Careers should annually survey universities about their pro-family policies. An address and phone number for access to that information should be published in the *MLA Newsletter* and the MLA *Career Guide.*

22. The MLA should form a committee concerned with practical ways of infusing discoveries in feminist language theory into the day-to-day operations of the university. This committee should arrange special forums at the annual MLA Convention to foster public discussion about this project. This committee should also be responsible for developing alternative questionnaire models for administrations to circulate among faculty and staff and for the MLA to distribute to its membership.

23. The MLA should publish, in one volume, a collection of the various equity studies (including the Rebolledo study) it has sponsored in the last 20 years. Such a collection would reveal what has been called for in the past, would allow us to measure past recommendations against present realities, and would be suggestive for future efforts.

Enacting these recommendations requires mobilizing according to a slogan Olsen has often repeated to me: "Educate, organize, agitate." Such mobilizing is generally more familiar to political activists than to most academics. But, to return to Carl Freedman's terms, we must demystify the ideology of professionalism, recognizing ourselves as workers even though our labor is primarily intellectual. If these recommendations seem a mere "wishlist," we should recall that many reforms we now take for granted, such as the eight-hour day and the vote for women, once seemed fanciful, too. And we should keep in mind that the United States has less maternity and parental leave, less subsidized child care, and less job flexibility than any other industrialized country. As Ruth Sidel points out,

> It is often said that there is no money to truly make the U.S. a "kinder, gentler nation," but we must remember that the U.S. spends $300 billion annually on arms, the U.S. Congress has approved the Bush administration's savings and loan bailout proposal that will cost nearly $160 billion over the next ten years, and the U.S. has one of the lowest tax rates, particularly for the wealthy, in the industrialized world (231).

The National Commission of Working Women projects that "by the year 2000, 80 percent of women in their prime childbearing years (between 25 and 44) will be in the labor force" (Mercer n. p.). Especially in light of such projections, the care of young children and the well-being of their parents should be a national as well as an employer concern.

Universities are needed in the fight for government-subsidized pro-family policies. "Child care is a family's fourth largest expense, after housing, food, and taxes. The annual cost of care for one child ranges between $2,400 and $9,000 in urban areas, with the average about $3,400 per child. Costs for infant care are even higher" (Mercer n. p.). In 1972 Richard Nixon vetoed legislation that would have established a national child-care program to provide free day care for poor families and subsidized day care for middle-income parents. In his veto message to Congress, Nixon said that the $2.1 billion-a-year plan demonstrated "fiscal irresponsibility, administrative unworkability, and family-weakening implications" (cited in Thorman, v). "Between 1977 and 1986 direct federal outlays for child care programs, which benefited mainly poor and low-income families, declined nearly 25 percent" (Mercer n. p.).

Those seeking to establish a national pro-family policy saw some progress in October and November 1991, when the Senate and House approved the Family and Medical Leave Act (FMLA). This modest bill, which would affect only five percent of all businesses and forty percent of all workers, requires employers with more than 50 employees to provide up to 12 weeks of unpaid, job-protected leave per year for a birth or adoption or for the serious illness of an employee or an immediate family member (health insurance continues throughout the leave period).

In March 1991 a study commissioned by the Small Business Administration, which surveyed business executives in 10,000 small companies (approximately one-third responded to the survey), attempted to determine the fiscal impact on those firms of providing family leave. The survey found the expense of permanently replacing an employee to be significantly *greater* than the cost of granting a worker a family leave. Thus the FMLA would likely reduce costs to business.[15] In May 1991 the Families and Work Institute released a four-state survey showing that state laws requiring employers to provide unpaid leave for new parents "have proven easy and inexpensive to implement." The three-year survey was conducted in Minnesota, Oregon, Rhode Island, and Wisconsin, states that passed parental leave laws in the 1980s. The survey found that

> 91 percent of employers reported no difficulty with implementation of the new laws. . . . As Representative Marge Roukema (Republican-New Jersey), a key supporter of the FMLA, remarked, "Slowly, but surely, the arguments of the paid business lobby [against the FMLA] are being discredited" (AAUW, *Action,* June 1991, 3–4).

Moreover, according to a *Wall Street Journal*/NBC public opinion poll released in July 1990, 71 percent of Americans support the FMLA (AAUW, *Action,* January 1991, 2).

Despite such evidence, and despite the fact that a version of the FMLA is already in place in 125 other countries, President Bush promises to veto the bill. And the 253 to 177 House vote leaves supporters 34 votes short of a veto-proof majority. In a comment made before the vote, Patricia Schroeder expressed my view: "We're a long way from where we'd like to be."

In the struggle for government-subsidized child care, we're also a long way from where we'd like to be. Without adequate government funds for child care, it is likely that child care providers—in some ways our most important educators—will continue to rank in the lowest 10 percent of U.S. wage earners. "In 1988, the median salary for center-based providers was $9,724" annually. "For those in family day care, it was $4,800. More than 40 percent of full-time child care workers earn less than five dollars an hour." Indeed, "child care workers earn less than animal caretakers [and] parking lot attendants." These low wages comprise a women's as well as a workers' issue: of the "approximately three million people employed as child care providers in the United States, more than 96 percent are women." Low wages are the primary cause of high turnover rates (between 35 and 60 percent a year) among child care workers, although "lack of respect, difficult working conditions, low staff morale, and employee burn out also contribute to high turnover among providers." Moreover, many center-based providers do not receive benefits: "Only one-third to one-half receive health insurance; about one-third are not paid for overtime; many do not receive paid vacations; fewer than one in five has a retirement plan" (Mercer n. p.).

Action on the twenty-three recommendations listed above, and others like them, is especially important for academic parents who do not have the financial means to employ household maintenance and extensive child care services. As academia has expanded to include women and people of color, it has also become more inclusive in relation to class origin. Not all academics enjoy the cushion that inherited money or the income from a spouse's more lucrative profession has traditionally provided and still provides for some. In contrast, professions such as medicine and law, while at least as demanding as the academic profession, are usually remunerative enough to fund services that ease the difficulties of maintaining a home and family.

Sociologist Jessie Bernard's valuable and frequently cited study, *Academic Women* (1964), is by now something of a classic. But the work's blindness to issues of class is evident. Bernard concludes her book with brief autobiographical accounts by three academic women who, in the author's words, "illustrate the wave of the future" and "show us what is possible. . . . To talented young women contemplating the paths open to them, these stories should be revealing" (231). They are indeed revealing, but in some ways that Bernard did not anticipate.

The first case involves a woman who was part of a husband-wife team in science. Her schedule (not her husband's) changed abruptly with the birth of their children. In her own words, the woman "didn't work officially" for six months after the birth of her first child; eventually she returned to work on a "half or three quarter time" basis. The woman "managed four months at home" after the birth of her second child (presumably, her husband's income could adequately support the family) and then went back to part-time research (232–33). The second case exemplifying "the wave of the future" also involves an academic team. When this couple's child was born, they resolved potential work-family conflict by hiring a live-in nanny. The third case describes a mother of three in the final stages of a Ph.D. program. Commenting on the length of time it had taken her to complete her degree ("ten years instead of six or seven"), she says: ". . . it never disturbed me to have to write down '9th year graduate student' on my registration, because I didn't care if I made a living or not (I had a husband to support me) and my attraction to the field was motivated primarily by interest" (238). She was able to maintain her household, she acknowledges, because she "acquired a devoted retinue of [four] helpers," including a "cleaning lady, who [took] four buses" to get to the house; a person who came in the late afternoon about four times a week and helped with dinner and the children's baths; an "expert typist"; and a remarkably accommodating person who arrived every morning, made the beds, did the dishes and laundry, "and then disappear[ed]" (238–39). This disappearing angel bears a remarkable resemblance to Olsen's "essential angel," whose invisible labor *Silences* insists we recognize.

What emerges from these three autobiographical accounts is a picture of unusual financial comfort. In two of the cases, the families lived for extended periods on one income. Even though Bernard was writing during a time of economic prosperity in the United States, she unselfconsciously assumed that professors belong to an economic elite. Yet some academics—especially in their careers' early stages, years that often coincide with the time when their children are young—have difficulty living on what they earn and cannot afford to replace a wife's unpaid labor with the paid labor of a live-in nanny or "a devoted retinue of helpers," even if they might be willing to do so. Therefore, if solutions to problems of parenting in the profession are available only to those with access to inherited money or to income from a spouse's more lucrative profession, the careers of mothers belonging, by birth or marriage, to an elite class are far more likely to flourish than those of women of lesser means. Gender inequality in the academy will have been countered, then, partly by a reliance on class privilege.[16] This "wave of the future," to repeat Bernard's term, is hardly in the spirit of *Silences,* a text vitally concerned with class issues. While the hidden injuries and cushions of class are not about to disappear from the academy, paid maternity and parental leaves, subsidized child care, and other pro-family policies would help to democratize the profession.

Over 20 years ago, Ellen Cantarow rightly observed: "Women professionals must think more than twice not only about when to have children, but about whether to have them at all. . . . Many women professionals who have succeeded in their careers have in fact chosen to lop off a whole area of their lives, as men are never forced to do" ("Ballot" 5). Some women academics make a cruel compromise and have one child rather than the two (or more) they truly desire, recognizing the hard truth in Alice Walker's words: ". . . with one [child] you can move. . . . With more than one you're a sitting duck" (363).

Women entered the academic profession in significant numbers in the 1970s and 1980s, at a time when the profession's demands (for tenure, for example) rose in inverse proportion to the dwindling number of jobs. Partly because of the glutted market, the profession could dictate terms to us. During the coming two decades, however (despite the current budget-crisis epi-

demic), power may shift somewhat within the academy. If the predicted short-
ages resulting from mass retirement and a shrinking pool of Ph.D. candidates
actually occur, the profession may have to attend more sensitively to quality-
of-life issues in order to attract faculty.

Some universities have already recognized that the availability of campus
child care can be useful in recruiting and retention. Pamla Boulton, Director
of the University of Wisconsin-Milwaukee Child Care Center, reports that she
is receiving "more calls from deans on campus who are doing recruiting. . . .
Many want information about the center to include in a packet; other calls
come from candidates who want to see the center while they are interviewing.
Some candidates 'won't take the job unless there is a child care guarantee' "
(cited in McKenna 8). Judith Fountain, Director of Dependent Care Services
at Ohio State University, says her university's day care center serves as a
" 'seduction tool,' not a recruitment tool, because there is a two-year waiting
list. 'I know by individual stories,' she adds, 'that it is a retention tool' " (cited
in McKenna 8). The time may be ripe to reintroduce more forcefully some of
our concerns to the profession. Arlie Hochschild has rightly argued:

> If we are to bring more women into the university at every level, we shall
> have to do something more extreme than most affirmative action plans have
> imagined: change the present entente between the university and its service
> agency, the family. If we change this, we also introduce into academe some
> of the values formerly the separate specialty of women. We leaven the ethos
> of "making it" with another ethos of caretaking and cooperation ("Clock-
> work" 78).

If the academy acts on pro-family concerns, it will begin to move away from
the negative characteristics of the corporate model and toward a profession
not only *possible* for mothers but more humane for everyone.

The university's failure, thus far, to depart significantly from the negative
characteristics of the corporate model adds to the difficulty our students, the
next generation of workers and professionals, have envisioning humane alternatives for their own lives—something other than an individual "sprint for
consumer goods" (Sidel 224). In Ruth Sidel's interviews with young women
between the ages of 12 and 25 (many of them in college, some planning to go
to college), she documented what many of us hear—in horror—from our
female students: the conviction that they can and must make it on their own,
independent of cooperative networks and supporting services. While most of
Sidel's interviewees planned to combine working and parenting, "virtually
none . . . raised issues such as day care, parental leave, or the need to encourage the wider society to provide services for them and their children" (214).
Our students need to realize, as Sidel points out, that "women cannot make it
alone any more than men ever have" (241). Unfortunately, I cannot challenge
my students' individualism by pointing to the university community as an
alternative model. The university is, to borrow sociologist Lewis Coser's
term, "a greedy institution."[17]

I teach courses in American literature at a university that with some justification considers itself a "public ivy." Many of our undergraduates have SAT scores and GPA's that make them eligible for ivies and other expensive private schools, but for financial reasons they attend a state university. The student body is comprised largely of "pre-something's"—pre-law, pre-medicine, pre-graduate school. As a companion-piece to Charlotte Perkins Gilman's *The Yellow Wallpaper,* I require these "pre-something" students to read the epilogue to Sylvia Ann Hewlett's *A Lesser Life: The Myth of Women's Liberation in America.* The epilogue describes a reunion that Hewlett organized in 1984 for the female students she had known well as a teacher at Barnard from 1974 to 1981. "The first topic these women gravitated toward," Hewlett reports, "was how to combine careers with children" (384). These economically privileged, highly educated, and professionally successful women, who "at eighteen and twenty . . . truly felt the world was at their feet," expressed despair in the face of overwhelming family-work conflict (400).

Depending on their gender, my students respond to the epilogue in dramatically different ways: the females—many struck for the first time that combining their career aspirations with parenting might be at best difficult, at worst impossible—echo the anxiety expressed by the women at the reunion. But almost unanimously, males consider this a "women's issue." Both the male and female students who feel that they will eventually want children continue to want them after reading the epilogue, but only the females voice concern that they may have to lower their career aspirations in order to be parents. I suspect that the males have yet to hear (or take seriously) remarks such as the following two from professors responding to the 1989 MIT employee survey on family and work:

> I am on the daddy track, which is incompatible with the tenure track (*Report,* Part II, 9).

> Never see my wife, wouldn't recognize her if I did. Work. Family. Ain't no balance (*Report,* Part II, 8).

In my experience, students don't suggest that society redefine the demanding professions they hope to enter so that those professions no longer exact an enormous emotional price from men and women alike. Few students recognize our employers' or government's responsibility to parents and children. And none envisions parenthood combined with humanized careers supported by pro-family services and benefits. As educators, we fail our students if we do not help them to think creatively about these alternatives.

Many of my female students love the line from Alice Walker's well-known essay, "In Search of Our Mothers' Gardens," that describes our mothers and grandmothers as "moving to music not yet written" (232). That phrase seems to capture for them the quality of their own lives. But it is time we composed the music—not just privately, individually, and improvisationally, as many of us have been doing for years, but formally, publicly, institutionally. We owe it to ourselves, to our children, to the friendships we let die because we are insanely overworked. We owe it to our female students who are lowering their aspirations partly because they look at their role models and see horror shows—not because we aren't happy but because we're killing ourselves in the process of keeping all parts of ourselves alive. We owe it to our male students, who also stand to benefit if their careers allow them to be more involved in "the maintenance of [family] life." And finally, we owe it to "mothers" such as Tillie Olsen, a pioneer in raising the issue of silent parenting.

NOTES

1. A bit of the information in this essay, completed in 1991, is now dated. For example, I refer to President Bush's promise to veto the Family Medical and Leave Act, which President Clinton signed into law February 9, 1993, to take effect six months from that date.

This essay was, for me, a transgression of academic boundaries, and I couldn't have trespassed without help. First, I want to acknowledge gratefully Elaine Hedges's superb editing and steady encouragement. Carol R. Keyes, associate professor in the Department of Teaching and Early Childhood at Pace University and immediate past president of the National Coalition for Campus Child Care, commented on an early draft of the essay. She and Kathy Luneau Simons, an administrator in MIT's Child Care Office, were especially helpful and encouraging. Martha Noel Evans, the Modern Language Association's Director of Book Publications, responded enthusiastically to a nearly final version of the essay and kindly corrected inaccuracies in my discussion of the 1970 MLA resolutions regarding the equity of women and family-care issues; I'm deeply grateful for her investigative work and her sensitivity to such issues. I am also thankful to the following people, who talked with me about the issues, suggested other contacts, and/or sent me materials: Jill Bogard, Director of Library and Information Service at the American Council on Education; Rena Cheskis-Gold, Yale University's Office of Institutional Research; Sharon Congdon, Communications Department, the American Association of University Women (an organization, I should add, that lobbied from 1986 for passage of the Family and Medical Leave Act); Jean Dodson, Ohio State University Child Care Center; Liliane Floge, Assistant Provost, Gettysburg College; Lesley Lee Francis, the American Association of University Professors; Ellen Galinsky, Families and Work Institute; Nancy Golden, Director, Children's Center of the Stanford Community; Mary Kelley, Professor of History at Dartmouth College; Frank McArdle, Hewitt Associates; Lillian Robinson, Visiting Professor of English, University of Texas, Austin; Carrie Roy, National Commission on Working Women of Wider Opportunities for Women; Bernice Sandler, Executive Director, Project on the Status and Education of Women (in 1992 she will become a Senior Associate at the Center for Women Policy Studies); and Carol Zuses, MLA staff member. For Barbara Snyder, a virtuoso child care provider in the People's Republic of Santa Monica, this essay is small recompense.

2. The "University of Transylvania" is not to be confused with Transylvania College in Lexington, Kentucky.

3. Although I have not done so at other points in this essay, I feel I must provide an update here. In 1993, through the efforts of Sarah Webster Goodwin, with help from Naomi Miller and myself, the MLA Commission on the Status of Women in the Profession established a Subcommittee on Family Care Issues, chaired by Professor Goodwin. The Subcommittee published a call in the Spring 1993 *MLA Newsletter* for

information about universities' family leave policies. It organized a session on family-care issues for the 1993 MLA Convention and is planning a follow-up session for the 1994 Convention. The Subcommittee is investigating the difference in cost between the MLA's current dates for its annual convention (December 27–30) and the first week in January, a more convenient time for those with family responsibilities. The Subcommittee is also preparing a memorandum to urge the MLA Committee on Careers, in its preconvention workshops on the job search, to alert candidates to be vigilant about universities' policies regarding family-care issues. The memorandum will also urge the MLA Committee on Careers to augment the MLA *Career Guide* to advise candidates to inquire—and search committees to provide information—about possible parental leave, on-campus child care, stop-the-tenure-clock policies, etc. *Concerns,* the publication of the MLA's Women's Caucus, will publish a special issue (probably Spring 1995) on family-care issues, with contributions from several Subcommittee members. One of the Subcommittee's long-range goals is to publish an MLA Handbook on Family Care Issues for Administrators and Faculty that will address issues related to childbearing and child-care, domestic partners, and elder-care.

4. A more recent version of this essay appears as "The Impact of Human Resource Policies on Employees: Balancing Work/Family Life." *Journal of Family Issues* 11.4 (Dec. 1990): 368–83.

5. The Hewitt Associates found that 74 percent of the colleges and universities and 64 percent of the companies surveyed offer some kind of child care assistance to their employees. Of those that offer some kind of child care assistance, 38 percent of the colleges and universities and 9 percent of the companies sponsor a child care center. Thirty-nine percent of the colleges and universities and 41 percent of the companies providing some form of child care assistance offer resource and referral services. Ninety-two percent of the colleges and universities and 89 percent of the companies providing some form of child care assistance offer dependent care spending accounts, allowing employees to pay child care expenses using pre-tax earnings. An equal percentage of companies and colleges and universities offer flexible scheduling arrangements (54 percent). Of those offering flexible scheduling, the most common arrangements are flextime (63 percent of the colleges and universities, 67 percent of the companies) and part-time (53 percent of the colleges and universities and 67 percent of the companies). Twenty-six percent of the colleges and universities and 5 percent of the companies surveyed provide paid parental leave, while 48 percent of the colleges and universities and 44 percent of the companies surveyed provide unpaid parental leave. Thirty-two percent of the colleges and universities and 23 percent of the companies provide paid leave to employees to care for sick family members by allowing employees to use their own sick leave; 6 percent of the colleges and universities and 21 percent of the companies offer unpaid leave to care for sick family members. Elder care programs are emerging, with 54 percent of the colleges and universities and 32 percent of the companies providing some such assistance to their employees. The most common approach to elder care assistance is dependent care spending accounts, offered by 95 percent of the colleges and universities and 88 percent of the companies offering elder care assistance.

To receive a copy of the Hewitt Associates survey of 35 colleges and universities, contact: Mike Aitken, College and University Personnel Association, 1233 20th Street NW, Suite 503, Washington, D.C. 20036, (202) 429-0311, extension 21. Copies of the *Work and Family Benefits Provided by Major U.S. Employers in 1990* can be ordered for $25 from Diane Schuett, Hewitt Associates, 100 Half Day Road, Lincolnshire, Illinois 60069.

6. Telephone conversation, 11 June 1991.

7. Copies of this guide can be ordered from the Families and Work Institute, 330 Seventh Avenue, New York, New York 10001. See also Galinsky, Diane Hughes, and Judy David.

8. This figure appeared on a fact sheet produced by the National Commission on Working Women of Wider Opportunities for Women. The Commission, an excellent source for information on working women, is eager for its fact sheets to reach a wide audience. To obtain the fact sheets included in the Commission's "Women at Work" series and for permission to reproduce them, write to the Publications Manager, National Commission on Working Women, 1325 G. St., NW, Lower Level, Washington, D.C. 20005, (202) 737-5764.

9. This resource is available from the National Coalition for Campus Child Care, Inc., Box 258, Cascade, Wisconsin, 53011, (414) 528-7080. The Coalition "is an educational and professional membership organization devoted to promoting high-quality early child care and education programs on campus. The coalition seeks to create new child care options and alternatives in conjunction with academic departments, local communities, and state and national groups. The coalition holds an annual conference and mini-sessions and regional meetings around the country; publishes a conference collection, two journals, and occasional papers and booklets; and compiles local, state, and national reports on campus child care. Membership is open to directors, administrators, teachers, students, staff, and faculty groups in higher education" (Keyes 28).

10. Because I completed this essay in 1991, the university policies, programs, and reports I refer to in the following recommendations may now be somewhat dated. The importance of the recommendations themselves, however, has not diminished.

11. Telephone conversation with Nancy Golden, Director of the Center, 10 July 1991.

12. *On Campus With Women* 4; telephone conversation with Jean Dodson, Director of the Child Care Center, 11 July 1991.

13. Keyes 27. For brief descriptions of other innovative programs, see Keyes. And for a discussion of "characteristics of comprehensive campus child care," see Townley and Zeece.

14. These data, collected in 1989–90, are not yet published; telephone conversation, May 29, 1991. The Hewitt Associates survey of 35 colleges and universities reports that 54% (or 19 institutions) offer flexible scheduling; of those 19 schools, 21 percent permit job-sharing.

15. AAUW, *Action*, May 1991, 1. *Action Alert*, which monitors current Congressional activity and helps its readers "be more effective in the public policy process," is published monthly by the Program and Policy Department of the American Association of University Women. To subscribe to *Action Alert*, write to AAUW *Action Alert*, Subscriptions, P.O. Box 96793, Washington, DC 20090-6793.

16. I share Ruth Sidel's concern that immigrant women, as nannies and housekeepers, often sacrifice caring for their own children while making it possible for "our new" professionals to "have it all" (199).

17. See Coser's *Greedy Institutions: Patterns of Undivided Commitment.*

WORKS CITED

Aisenberg, Nadya, and Mona Harrington. *Women of Academe: Outsiders in the Sacred Grove.* Amherst: U of Massachusetts P, 1988.

American Association of University Women [AAUW], Program and Policy Department. *Action Alert.* Washington, D.C.: Jan. 1991, May 1991, June 1991.

———. *Family and Medical Leave Act Fact Sheet.* Washington, D.C.: Feb. 1991.

Bailyn, Lotte. "The Apprenticeship Model of Organizational Careers: A Response to Changes in the Relation between Work and Family." *Women in the Workplace.* Ed. Phyllis A. Wallace. Boston: Auburn, 1982.

"Ballot on Resolution." *MLA Newsletter* 2.2 (Mar. 1970): 3–7.

Banner, Lois, Eileen Boris, Mary Kelley, et al. *Personal Lives and Professional Careers: The Uneasy Balance.* Report of the Women's Committee of the American Studies Association. 1988.

———. Foreword. *Personal Lives and Professional Careers: The Uneasy Balance.* Report of the Women's Committee of the American Studies Association. 1988.

Bernard, Jessie. *Academic Women.* University Park: Pennsylvania State UP, 1964. New York: New American, 2nd ed. 1974.

Cherlin, Andrew. "Needed: Early Sabbaticals for Pregnancy and Infant Care." *The Chronicle of Higher Education* 22 Nov. 1989: B2.

Cheskis-Gold, Rena. *Faculty Maternity/Parenting/Child Care Leave Policies for Schools of Arts and Science at Selected Private Universities, October 1990.* Office of Institutional Research, Yale University.

Cobb, Sandra E. *The Johns Hopkins University Findings of Peer University Survey on Family Issues.* Office of the Vice President for Personnel Programs. 1990.

Coser, Lewis A. *Greedy Institutions: Patterns of Undivided Commitment.* New York: Free, 1974.

Deutsch, Claudia H. "Saying No to the 'Mommy Track.' " *New York Times* 28 Jan. 1990, sec. 3, part 2: 29.

Freedman, Carl. "Marxist Theory, Radical Pedagogy, and the Reification of Thought." *College English* Jan. 1987, 70–82.

Friedman, Dana E. "Special Report." *Harvard Business Review* Mar.–Apr. 1986: 28–34.

Galinsky, Ellen, Dana Friedman, and Carol Hernandez. *The Corporate Reference Guide to Work-Family Programs.* New York: Families and Work Institute, 1991.

Galinsky, Ellen, Diane Hughes, and Judy David. "Trends in Corporate Family-Supportive Policies." *Corporations, Businesses, and Families.* Ed. Roma S. Hanks and Marvin B. Sussman. New York: Hayworth, 1990.

Galinsky, Ellen, and Peter Stein. "Balancing Careers and Families: Research Findings and Industrial Responses," *Marriage, Family, and Scientific Careers: Institutional Policy versus Research Findings.* Proc. of a symposium. American Association for the Advancement of Science Annual Meeting. 16 Jan. 1989. San Francisco.

———. "The Impact of Human Resource Policies on Employees: Balancing Work/Family Life." *Journal of Family Issues* 11.4 (Dec. 1990): 368–83.

Hewitt Associates. *Special Report: Work and Family Benefits Provided by Colleges and Universities* (compiled for the College and University Personnel Association). 15 April 1991.

———. *Work and Family Benefits Provided by Major U.S. Employers in 1990, Based on Practices of 837 Employers.* 1990.

Hewlett, Sylvia Ann. *A Lesser Life: The Myth of Women's Liberation in America.* New York: William Morrow, 1986.

Hochschild, Arlie. "Inside the Clockwork of Male Careers." *Women and the Power to Change*. Ed. Florence Howe. New York: McGraw-Hill, 1975.

Hochschild, Arlie, with Anne Machung. *The Second Shift: Working Parents and the Revolution at Home*. New York: Viking, 1989.

'In' Box. The Chronicle of Higher Education 14 Dec. 1988: A11.

Jacobus, Patricia. "Day Care's Elderly Assets." *New York Times* 4 Aug. 1991, sec. 4A: 7.

Kerber, Linda, Afterword. *Personal Lives and Professional Careers: The Uneasy Balance*. Report of the Women's Committee of the American Studies Association. 1988.

Keyes, Carol R. "Multiple Missions: Campus Child Care Programs." *Academe: Bulletin of the American Association of University Professors* 76.1 (Jan.–Feb. 1990): 25–28.

Keyes, Carol R., and Ruth E. Cook, eds. *Campus Child Care Issues and Practices: A Collection of Conference Papers 1975–1987*. National Coalition for Campus Child Care, Inc., 1988.

"Magazine Notes an Increase in Family-friendly Companies." *Press & Sun Bulletin* [Binghamton, NY] 18 September 1991: 7B.

Mangan, Katherine S. "In Response to Growing Demand, Colleges Are Starting to Offer Child Care as Benefit for Their Employees." *The Chronicle of Higher Education* 17 Feb. 1988: A13–A14.

McKenna, Barbara. "Family-friendly Contracts." *On Campus* 11.1 (Sept.–Oct. 1991): 8–9.

Mercer, Elizabeth (researched by). *Women, Work and Child Care*. Fact Sheet. National Commission on Working Women of Wider Opportunities for Women. Washington, D.C. May 1989. n. p.

"Model Child Care Program at Ohio State U." *On Campus With Women* 19.1 (Summer 1989): 4–5.

Morantz-Sanchez, Regina. Commentary. *Personal Lives and Professional Careers: The Uneasy Balance*. Lois Banner, Eileen Boris, Mary Kelley, et al. Report of the Women's Committee of the American Studies Association. 1988.

"New Faculty Recruiting Tool: Spouse Assistance." *On Campus With Women* 18.3 (Winter 1989): 7.

"The 1969 Business-Meeting: Actions, and a Summary of Discussion." *PMLA* 85.3 (Sept. 1970): 644–54.

Olsen, Tillie. *Silences*. New York: Dell, 1978.

Preston, Samuel H. "Children and the Elderly in the U.S." *Scientific American* 251.6 (Dec. 1984): 44–49.

Rebolledo, Tey Diana. *Parenting Leave: Law, Policy and Practice*. Unpublished report of the MLA Commission on the Status of Women. 1985.

Report of the ad hoc Committee on Family and Work (Part I and Part II, separately pag.). MIT. 7 Nov. 1990.

Sidel, Ruth. *On Her Own: Growing Up in the Shadow of the American Dream*. New York: Penguin, 1990.

Simons, Kathy Luneau. "Beyond Campus Child Care: Supporting University Families." *Early Childhood Research Quarterly* 6.1 (March 1991): 57–68.

Swoboda, Frank. "Leave Policy Helps IBM Keep Employees." *Press and Sun Bulletin* [Binghamton, NY] 25 Dec. 1988: 8E–7E.

Thorman, George. *Day Care . . . an Emerging Crisis*. Springfield, Illinois: Charles C. Thomas, 1989.

Townley, Kim F., and Pauline Davey Zeece. "Managing the Mission: The Primary Challenge to Campus Child Care." *Early Childhood Research Quarterly* 6.1 (March 1991): 19–27.

Walker, Alice. "*One* Child of One's Own: A Meaningful Digression within the Work(s)." *In Search of Our Mothers' Gardens*. New York: Harcourt, 1983.

———. "In Search of Our Mothers' Gardens." *In Search of Our Mothers' Gardens*. New York: Harcourt, 1983.

"How Many of Us Can You Hold to Your Breast?": Mothering in the Academy

DIANA HUME GEORGE

> More than in any other human relationship, overwhelmingly more, motherhood means being constantly interruptible, responsive, responsible. Children need one *now*. . . . The very fact that these are real needs, that one feels them as one's own (love, not duty), that there is no one else responsible for these needs, gives them primacy. It is distraction, not meditation, that becomes habitual; interruption, not continuity.
>
> TILLIE OLSEN, *Silences* (18)

The Danger of the Different Voice

Several years ago at the final reading in a poetry series I organized, a colleague named John stood up and spoke movingly about the delights of the writing life for those of us gathered to celebrate it. We were all feeling like the close community of writers and listeners we were. John turned to me and proposed a toast: "To Diana, the mother of us all." It should have been one of those quiet high points of daily working life, and in some respects it was; but what I primarily felt was defensive resentment, and a desire to hit John with a blunt object. Hard.

The title of this essay comes from a poem one of my students—herself a mother and wife—wrote to me several years ago. Only Marlyn among my students at the time seemed to understand what they asked of me. She apologized on behalf of herself and others far younger. She knew I was mothering in the academy, and she sensed that it drained and silenced me as a person and as a writer. "But I can't help it," she said. "I was starved for knowledge and intellectual contact for so many years, and now I'm greedy. I'll take whatever I can get from you."

I read Marlyn's poem to my friend and colleague, Karen, with whom I have talked for twenty years. We have a shorthand, a code, a series of secrets about which we are silent, because most of our colleagues would regard them as more tiresome special pleading from women. I want to break that silence here.

In the wake of Tillie Olsen's ground-breaking discussion in the 1970s of the meanings of actual maternity for the woman artist, and the insights provided us by psychoanalytic studies such as Dorothy Dinnerstein's *The Mermaid and the Minotaur* (1976) and Nancy Chodorow's *The Reproduction of Mothering*

(1978), the cultural and individual consequences of mothering have become fundamentals that a generation of feminist academics know by heart. When we entered academe, we did so with premonitions of the price that would be exacted of us in the economy of our personal and professional balances; popular culture coined the term "superwoman" for those who chose to have it all and be it all.

Even the superwoman syndrome was at first predicated on a naive dichotomy between the demands of the personal and familial on the one hand, the professional and corporate on the other. So we set about trying to "feminize" the workplace, bringing to it the values of nurture and relationship. This, at least, was our desire. In education in particular, a recent body of literature on mentorship and learning models, much of it building on Carol Gilligan's *In a Different Voice* (1982), codifies that desire.

In *Profession 90,* the pedagogical annual of the Modern Language Association, Gail Griffin's essay, "Alma Mater," records her adventure researching the remarkable teaching career of a mid-nineteenth century woman named Lucinda Stone, who was for many years head of the "Female Department" of Kalamazoo College. Seeking out Stone in the college archives, Griffin found that student testimonials always referred to Stone's maternal qualities, even to her "mother love." Stone consciously adopted this role, stating that what she called the "motherheart" is "at the center of all true teaching" (Griffin 40–41).

Griffin situated her search for Stone in terms of her own professional identity. The academic woman must consciously be "analyzing and negotiating her position within academe itself, determining her relation to its assumptions and traditions, its ceremonies and values, most of which originated not only without her but in overt opposition to her . . ." (Griffin 38). Lucinda Stone presented a maternal model for teaching in which intellectual growth was clearly not sacrificed. Griffin confirms the values of the maternal teaching model, invoking Carol Gilligan's "different voice" that must be heard in education, speaking against specialization, competition, the obsession with product rather than process. Stone's "motherheart," Griffin says, can "speak for an ethic of care and encouragement whose aim is to teach not subjects but people and whose larger goal is to create an environment where human beings can grow in and toward the fullness of themselves" (Griffin 41).

Gilligan and her associates extended the implications of *In a Different Voice* in *Mapping the Moral Domain* (1988), which calls for a large-scale change in the perspective of American education. "To see self-sufficiency as the hallmark of maturity conveys a view of adult life that is at odds with the human condition, a view that cannot sustain the kinds of long-term commitments and involvements with other people that are necessary for raising and educating a child or for citizenship in a democratic society" (Gilligan, Ward, Taylor, xii). We must change education, Gilligan and her colleagues argue, to reflect a focus, fostered in and developed by women, on care considerations as opposed to justice structures. Separation, individuation, and autonomy need to be countered by concerns for responsiveness and relationship, which can together "cohere to form a world view or a way of constructing social reality, as well as a problem-solving strategy" (Gilligan xix–xx).

In *Erotic Reckonings,* a study of mentorship and apprenticeship between writers, Thomas Simmons uses Gilligan and others to point to the self-contradictory motives of traditional hierarchical theory on mentorship. The artist identified as mentor "takes on the mantle of power, instruction, and direction, even though he may attempt to wield it benignly. This mantle is a serpent: ultimately it constricts both the one who wears it and the one who admires it" (Simmons 25). He suggests that if personhood, rather than the intellectual tradition, is the focus of the mentor-apprentice configuration, then "a relationship may evolve which permits the exchange of intellectual knowledge without running serious risks of domination and submission" (Simmons 16).

Gilligan's and Simmons' are feminist arguments, ethically and personally attractive to me. I agree with their politics and their values. But the mantle of feminist "morality" itself is also a serpent. And living by the values I believe in does entail serious risks of domination and submission—risks ironically not for the apprentice's submission, but the mentor's own.

The renewed call for restructuring education to reflect the "care" model of mentoring and traditionally "female" ways of construing moral development is related to and follows from Dinnerstein's and Chodorow's earlier work on the need to vastly restructure our sexual arrangements. Dinnerstein's and Chodorow's theories place the burden for social transformation primarily on men. Both theorists call for fathers to share in primary parenting; both—to simplify their arguments—ask that men learn to do what has been regarded as women's work, that the male enter the nursery, the kitchen, the infant psyche, as nurturer. Ostensibly the call by Gilligan and her colleagues is to a subset of the patriarchy—the educational institution—to place greater emphasis on relationships, personhood, caregiving, nurture, mutuality. We know that such calls for action addressed to patriarchal institutions are all part of a feminist utopian literature, and that actual transformation occurs only sporadically and slowly, in individual lives more than in impersonal institutions.

In the earlier psychoanalytic studies, the *theory* was based on relieving women of burdens borne primarily or only by us. In the new mentoring and educational models, women are in effect asked to extend the work of mothering from the domestic to the professional sphere. Men are implicitly requested to join in this venture, of course, but whether or not they do so, the theory validates, even valorizes, the caregiving and relational model of teaching that is already primarily provided by women. We become, in practical terms, responsible for humanizing the academy. It's still women's work, and I see no end in sight. Having been called upon to be the Angel in the House by Victorian society, women are now called upon—by ourselves, by each other—to be the Angel in the Academy.

The pedagogical literature that exhorts us to reject the exclusive cultural emphasis on autonomy, individuation, and separation actually adds to those areas of our lives in which we bear the maternal burden. Validating the "different voice" can serve to silence those parts of us that are, of necessity, still attempting to come to grips with the overemphasis on relationship that makes many women unable to deal with boundary issues in the formation and maintenance of identity. Separation, individuation, and autonomy are indeed overemphasized in patriarchal theories of moral and psychic development, but as real women living and working in such a patriarchy we are already likely to lack adequate skills and strategies for maintaining separate identities. The overvaluation of the different voice can create enormous problems for many of us.

Profile of the Academic Mother

Near the beginning of Gail Griffin's essay is a beautiful articulation of the maternal trap. She and her female colleagues are asked to play academic mommy, which means "to do the housework; kiss the hurts and make them better; forgive everything; take on the wretched refuse, emotional and psychic, of academic life; play intercessor and softy . . ." (Griffin 41). Ah, I think as I read, there it is in print at last, a statement about this soul-draining phenomenon Karen and I, and a number of my female writing and teaching colleagues nationwide, have discussed in private. But by the end of the essay, with the example of Lucinda Stone to show it can be done, Griffin has fully embraced the maternal model, and exhorts me and all her readers to think it possible. Similarly, Gilligan and her research associates speak of bringing the web of relationship and the ethic of care into the academic setting.

To be concrete about this process I will return to introductory simplicities. If as college professors we are *in loco parentis* to our students, it is inevitable that we often become maternal and paternal figures. Older males become father figures; older women become mother figures. We all know this, but we are less aware of the consequences that often follow, for our students expect of us some subtly transmogrified forms of what they have learned to expect from their parents. And they expect vastly different things from mothers than from fathers.

Who are fathers, in the cultural sense? They are relatively remote figures who deserve respect and project a sense of authority. Middle-class white American children—most of the students I teach—expect from fathers relatively little in the way of personal presence, time devoted to individual contact. Who are mothers? They're the ones who are always there, always available, whose work is not as important as the fathers', who give their children infinite time, who heal wounds. They are the primary parents in the most literal sense. Infancy is still female dominated, and mothers are the entire world's first and primary caretakers of the young. Upper-middle-class white American feminism has hardly touched that global fact.

When students perceive a certain kind of female professor as a mother-figure, they expect, demand, and often get from such professors just what our culture has always expected, and continues to expect, from mothers. We become, as surely as if we were their mothers, towering imago figures onto which students project not only their personal expectations, but also the largely unconscious mixture of love for and rage against mothers characteristic of patriarchal arrangements (Dinnerstein 59–69). The drain of time, energy, and spirit creates a continuation of Olsen's maternal silence in a locale (the institution of higher education) and at a time (the dawn of what many are calling the postfeminist era) where we might naively assume it would have been escaped. The result is a continued muting of our words and works.

The women writers who do produce under these conditions pay tremendously high personal and professional prices. When a certain kind of woman writer becomes a professor, the pressures on her and the expectations she has of herself, and that her students (and often her colleagues) also share unconsciously, are very like the demands of motherhood that Tillie Olsen addressed in *Silences*. Ironically, many of the large number of writers in the academy are thus little removed from the jobs their mothers had raising small children in the heyday of the feminine mystique. These women are feminists. It doesn't matter. They appear powerfully autonomous. It's a lie.

Over the years, Karen and I have been mothers together watching our own and each other's children struggle and grow; and we have been teachers and writers together while we went to graduate school, earned our Ph.D.s, took our first academic jobs. While we were doing all of this—holding down our jobs, making our homes, being proper superwomen—we were also trying to write essays, poems, critical and creative books. We have indeed written some of our books, but far fewer than we have in us, and we have done it slowly and paid dearly for the privilege. Our silences have not been complete, not tragic, but they have been real.

The maternal trap is most likely to ensnare women professors who teach certain kinds of courses—creative writing, women's studies, psychology—in which students are not only learning new material but facing issues that challenge them to examine and perhaps change their lives, engaging them in the same kinds of recognition and transformation their women professors went through twenty years and more ago. Women's studies professors, for instance, become midwives to great transformations of spirit as well as of personal politics. The material is close, intense, and the line between course content and psychotherapy can become perilously thin. Increasing numbers of our students are older women who may make greater demands on their teachers, even if they also give greater returns on the investment than do typical younger students.

Psychology courses can create similar demands and expectations of the teacher, since the study of psychological development often causes students to apply what they are learning to their own lives. The psychology professor is often perceived as a clinician, which is in fact sometimes the case; students can assume that here will be found a sympathetic ear and an understanding of personal problems. However, psychology as a discipline also offers some protection against the maternal trap, because the professionalism associated with it and the rituals of the psychotherapeutic encounter are often honored by students; furthermore, psychology Ph.D.s are well aware of the pitfalls, have been trained to be wary, and often develop specific behaviors that guard against this professional hazard.

Another kind of course that encourages wholesale consumption of the professor in mothering in the academy is creative writing, which attracts students with many of the same characteristics as those who choose women's studies. Because this essay is primarily about the silences of women writers who are professors, about how the writing process gets derailed, I will concentrate on how writers who teach writing end up mothering their apprentices.

The woman professor's personality is probably just as important as her subject matter. I've known many women writers who know exactly how to avoid the trap. They know that their writing lives will be subverted if they allow mothering their students to engulf them, and they protect themselves in the knowledge that if they are to be real writers they must have singleness of vision and of purpose, must be in some sense selfish to obtain peace, privacy, opportunity for sustained concentration. "Wholly surrendered and dedicated lives," as Olsen wrote, "time as needed for the work; totality of self" (17).

If some women know how to avoid the trap, who are those who do not? They are the women who typically project qualities culturally perceived as maternal. They are open, warm, supportive, terrifically competent, strong. I think it's a safe generalization, and not a mean one, to say that a certain kind of female professor is perceived as more open or giving, more, yes, nurturing, than her typical male counterpart—and also more so than women who deliberately style themselves against the grain, who refuse to exhibit or embody traditional maternal and feminine qualities.

Writers Teaching Writing

Jane was troubled, depressed, sometimes suicidal, but also a fine student with a first-rate mind who never failed in her classroom responsibilities. She came to me to discuss her writing and reading of poetry. But here is where the thin line between teaching and counseling becomes a permeable membrane. Her poetry was intensely personal, about her bulimia among other things. As a workshop teacher, I encouraged her to explore the wounds, to dig deep, to write about what hurt—because that's what good teachers of writing do for their students if they're to be of any use: we help them to find their own material.

This is why creative writing teaching is a trap. You begin with the simple, sad premise that most literature of any merit is fearless, brave in its exploration of despair as well as of delight. The student tries writing sweet, light love poems, and the results are terrible. But when the same student explores the complexities of love, the ambivalence, the disappointment, the fear that engages hope, the writing is always better, stronger, more authentic.

So you encourage, support, nurture the process by which young writers— not all, but most—begin the difficult inward gaze. What they uncover sometimes frightens them, even frightens you. You are careful to caution them not to romanticize their pain, nor to confuse creativity and despair. You must do that continually. But you also have to caution them that any inward gaze, even any honest outward one, encounters human frailty and anxiety at every step; and someone must help them deal with that.

How does this link up with mothering? The psychotherapeutic situation, despite its institutionalized, hierarchical, and authoritarian aspects, involves empathetic listening, support, care-giving—all traditionally feminine activities. If one believes in a personal poetics, then the process by which the young writer personalizes the language becomes a kind of cultural feminization. One confides one's vision—troubled, ambiguous, intimate—to the page, much as one confides it to a trusted other.

When the trusted other, the teacher, is also an authority figure, the relationship is dangerously likely to become that of the child to the mother rather than the sister to the sibling, or the friend to the friend, or even the doctor (traditionally male) to the patient. This process has been enacted in my teaching life repeatedly over the years. Students turn me, slowly, inexorably, into a mother. I watch it happen. I participate. I did not decide to do this as a way of enacting any theory I believe in. It came to me—excuse the phrasing—naturally.

I try to guard against its more self-destructive aspects. Sometimes I partially succeed. The pull in this direction comes from them, but also from me. I am saying things that are maternal in function: be careful here, you will be okay, I'm right here beside you, don't be afraid. The developmental process for the young writer begins with a symbiotic dependency, and while autonomy may be the goal, as it is with parenting, the stages of bonding and separation must be enacted. Apprentice writers use training wheels, graduate to two-wheelers, walk to the store alone, stay out later, begin to discover who they are, need me less, grow up.

In the best-case scenario it happens this way, but the stages are filled with the many pitfalls of parenting. They need you now. They are enthralled with words, in love with language, growing in their own powers but asking for your constant feedback and approval, resenting your imposition of rules, forms, discipline. I have to write a sestina? (I have to be home by what time?) They show up at your office door when you don't have time, and they need you to read this poem now. If you do, your own time is sacrificed. If you don't, they resent you, and you have to engage in a parodic version of "quality time" later on, because they remember that their sibling rival poet got your time that day. You read *her* poem, and now you must read mine.

In one of the more extreme cases of this maternal dependency I have experienced, Maureen, an apprentice writer and daughter figure, had a mental breakdown. When she was hospitalized after a failed suicide attempt, she at first trusted neither her male nor her female doctors. She wanted to talk to me. Her female doctor, who had had her hospitalized against her will, became the punitive mother with whom she experienced negative transference, and I, who had given her only support, became the object of positive transference.

Two years later, she's fine, and has broken her dependencies on me and on others. Like Jane, she is someone I now regard as a friend. But what we went through on the way to this transformation was frightening, intense, too close—and based on patterns altogether too common in my professional life.

There Still Aren't Enough of Us

I say Maureen and Jane became independent women with whom I could form friendships; but I do not forget what happened with Joanne when I say this. It could happen with Jane, too, even though it appears for the moment to be deflected. Joanne was another of my poets, and like Jane, like most of my female students, she developed an intense relationship to me in part because of the paucity of other female figures of authority on whom to model herself, against whom to struggle, with whom to learn and grow.

After a long period—more than three years—of closeness to me, during which I supported her growing poetic development, she reacted against me intensely, saying she would not be perceived as my clone. If she had had more female mentors with whom to study, the fear of identification, of being perceived as the daughter of a powerful maternal and professional woman, would surely have been lessened. But she, like many others, has had only me, and while this situation may be extreme, I would guess that it's true for many young women, many exhausted teachers. I had experienced this stage of such relationships before, but this one was full of an anger that eventually bordered on rage.

Joanne could not tolerate my human frailties, could not allow me to be imperfect or weak or to behave stupidly. She began to select my frailties and hold them up to me for close inspection. She analyzed me coldly, meanly. Long after her graduation, she seemed to have outgrown this desire that I be perfect, this need to damn my common, obvious, glaring imperfections. We laughed together about her previous need to make me the perfect mother. She said it had all been so silly. But the next time she was confronted with one of my failings, she reverted to the daughter stage of the relationship with a force that stunned us both. She railed against me like a child having a showdown after years of repressed anguish toward the mother she has loved and failed, who has loved and failed her. It was all my fault, she concluded.

During an interlude in this diatribe, which still continues on and off, she takes a deep breath and says, Christ, I thought I was over all of that, I thought I didn't need you to be perfect any more, I thought it was fine with me if you were human, even ridiculous. Where is this coming from in me? But despite her degree of self-awareness, it happens all over again when she is angry. Finally she says it directly: if you're pathetic, if you're weak, if you're corrupt, then what hope is there for the rest of us? She means herself and other young women who have been my apprentices in the learning process. Because there is only one of me, I cannot, must not, fail.

Do these students experience similar feelings, including disappointment and anger, toward their male professor mentors? Perhaps, to some degree, they do. But a host of mitigating factors tends to keep such feelings repressed, and thus to spare most male mentors the time-consuming, draining emotional manifestations. In the middle-class paradigm, one may be angry with the father, may see his faults, but one does not tend to confront him with them until much later in life, if at all.

The distance and aura of authority surrounding and protecting the father insulates many male professors from even knowing about students' psychic baggage regarding them; and if a protegé is brave enough to force the issue, many males can effectively deflect it, reject it, refuse to engage it, get steely. Fear that the father will reject the child acts as an effective deterrent. Nor, as I have said, does one expect of the father what one does of the mother. Power, authority, rightness, yes—but not necessarily expressed affection, daily nurturance and support; and if one is female, one is not looking to the father for evidence that one's own life may be empowered in precisely the same way.

It is encouraging to find an occasional statement by a male professor who has thought about the dynamics of mentoring. In "On Men Mentoring Women: Then and Now," John Kronik, a professor at Cornell, writes about his male and female students of a generation ago. His male apprentices, says Kronik, have managed to "combine their personal and professional lives to their satisfaction without need for sacrifice or even compromise. Not so with the women," who have all been forced into a set of difficult choices (Kronik 55). Kronik wonders about the changes effected by the large numbers of women now available to students in their selection of mentors. Students can choose from almost as many women as men in Kronik's department at Cornell. It is clear that Kronik's mentoring process has been thoughtful and developmental. He has grown as a mentor, and even notes his own earlier sexism. The relationship with his female apprentices sounds reciprocal and relatively close; I found no indication that he was personally consumed or drained by his mentees, nor that they expected him to solve their problems.

Cornell is obviously exceptional in many respects, among them the proportion of available female mentors. While my own college of Penn State may be remarkable on the other end of the scale for how few such women are available to students in my sub-field it is nevertheless more typical than Cornell. It is still possible at my institution, for instance, for students to graduate without taking courses from more than three or four tenure-track women with Ph.D.s.

In my field at my college, I am quite simply the only female professor of senior rank whom students will encounter, and although this situation may be extreme, the pattern is still true nationally in many disciplines, even those in which women now earn a high percentage of the Ph.D.s. Such women have still not attained mass seniority. While there are many father figures among whom to distribute the intensities of the students' need to experience and transform fathering, there are relatively few mothers.

Here is an instance of how the dynamic works. My university's student evaluation forms included for years an item on "instructor availability outside of class." Although I rated very high on student evaluations in general, and have won my college's excellence in teaching award, I rated dismally low on this item. How could this be, since for many years I held more office hours than many of my colleagues, still see large numbers of students, am in fact exceptionally "available outside of class"?

While the typical student interview during office hours might take ten to fifteen minutes, my students often act wounded when I try to pry them out the door after half an hour, even an hour—which I must often do because there are others waiting. If I am not in my office when needy students happen by, if I give them an hour but they want three, then by their lights I have failed them, not been available to them. When I checked with male colleagues several years ago to find out how they rated on this questionnaire item, they indicated they did fine. If you expect only five minutes and you get ten, you're more than satisfied; if you want an hour and get only thirty minutes, you've been let down. A good mother is always there when you need her, and she gives you unlimited time.

Most of my students would not dream of confiding a personal problem to their male professors, but they think nothing of bringing such matters to me. Many of them would not fail in their work or miss a due date for a male professor when their lives are falling apart, but they will ask me for personal and extra consideration. They call me at home, they want me to give them time and love. And I do.

The Mothers Back Home

While it would be difficult to generalize with statistical validity on the basis of my own and other colleagues' experiences, I have gleaned impressions about the family backgrounds of typical college students that may be of use. I teach middle-class white students for the most part, so my population is shaped by both class and race considerations. Even within the narrow, limited sample of middle-class white American students, the family dynamics from which they emerge are various. Many will have been very close to their mothers and distant from their fathers; I have heard dozens of variations, from students of both working-class and professional backgrounds, on the traditional middle-class theme: distant, detached fathers who don't know their children very well, students who say they can't talk to their fathers about anything personal or intimate. Dad was always working, came home late, collapsed in front of the television or went straight to bed. Their mothers are the ones they call in crisis, the ones who send them packages at school, the ones they refer to most often. For these students, the need to find a woman at school who will provide them with some semblance of the nurture they are living apart from for the first time is clear, direct, obvious.

But this is by no means always the case. While it's the most common pattern, I have also encountered many students who describe family dynamics in exactly the opposite terms. They miss their fathers most. Their fathers are warm and nurturant, their mothers distant. In this case more anger is usually directed at the mothers; the ones with detached fathers are living within a traditional cultural pattern, and thus the fathers have not violated their expectations. But when the mothers are the distant or ungiving ones, the indication of resentment is clear. These students are seeking from a female parent figure not what they had at home and miss, but rather what they have never had. The result, though, is much the same: the hope and expectation of, the need for, nurture from a female mentor figure.

Interestingly, in both cases another pattern emerges, in which at least the female students are seeking an alternative to the lives they see their mothers live, most of whom, regardless of their personalities, are relatively powerless. While this would not necessarily be the case for students in well-endowed private schools, many of whom come from upper-middle-class and professional backgrounds, it is most certainly the case in many state university systems, where the bulk of the student body is composed of first-generation college students. In me they see what they imagine to be, and what is, in relative terms, a woman of power. They are attracted to that image of power, often eager, sometimes desperate, to internalize it as a possibility for themselves. "My mother, myself" is a frightening possibility for them, whereas "this other mother, myself," represents their hope for their own future transformations deeply enmeshed with what the promise of a college education means to them.

A Day in the Life of Silence

I am tired. I would like to get home and work on this article, for which I've already missed several deadlines. Today I have taught three classes, in two of which I did the kind of "mothering" I believe in. I also conducted a thesis conference with an angst-ridden young writer. I held office hours for my students during which they were piled knee deep outside my door. Each one wanted more time than I could give. I concluded business with only one of the seven students I saw today. The rest will be back. I ended my day with meetings on two key college committees where my presence is necessary in order to represent the concerns of women and minorities. It should not be necessary for me to be on so many such committees, but it is, and this is why.

Women are held to the same standard that men are to produce and perform—equal pay for equal work. But we know the pay is seldom equal, and neither is the work. Women writers in academe have to write as much, publish as much as men in order to make it through the hurdles, and men and women alike will hold them to this single, ostensibly equal standard in reviews for tenure and promotion. But when they have children at home, they will be working far harder than most of their male counterparts, will have less time and energy to devote to their work. And if their professional work is feminist, in either activist or research and publication terms, evaluation committees are likely to take it less seriously.

But what about the new paradigm in which many of the lucky ones of us live? What about the academic women writers who are married to feminist men, many of them also members of the academy? We are the privileged few with tenure, rank, decent salaries, and, it would appear, ample opportunity to do our writing—opportunity as ample, at any rate, as that afforded our male mates. If all of us in academe are newly overwhelmed with the multiple pressures on us, the burgeoning expectations from administrations and bureaucracy, at least male and female academics sharing the burdens of child care are equally disadvantaged, are we not?

No, we are not.

Let me tell you about the rest of my day.

John comes up behind me and says, "You weren't in your office when I came to see you today. I really want to talk to you." I turn to face him. I'm a tad raw. John is one of the students who's always saying this to me. "John, you didn't come during my office hours. I was there." I don't mention to him that if he'd shown up then, I probably wouldn't have had time to see him. "Yes, but I've stopped by to see you three times this week, and you're never there." I'm there a lot. I'm there specifically for students at all the times I list office hours.

But I didn't happen to be there when John came by, so that means I'm "never there." I don't exist for him apart from my function in his life, and if I'm not there when he happens by, that means I'm not available. I am supposed to be constantly and continually at his disposal, like a mother for small children. He is grumpy and pouty and whiny today. "You never give me any time," he adds. Perhaps I should send him to his dorm room and order him to take a nap until he's in better sorts.

"Look, John," I say, "I just spent forty-five minutes with you last week, and you say I'm never available? Be serious." "I am serious," he says, I needed at least an hour." This is an exact quote. And that's only the time he wanted from me last week, because the week before last I conferred with him for at least twenty minutes, and I give him ten minutes almost any time I run into him on campus. He hasn't got any idea how out of bounds expectations such as these are when he's just one of almost a hundred students for me this semester. Does this sound familiar?

I escape John and get to my car. Then I drive for an hour, because mine is one of the common arrangements in which the couple teaches at different colleges—in our case across state lines—and I'm the one with the heftier commute. I'm often sleepy during this drive, because it comes in the dark at the end of a long day, and often I'm supposed to be back at the office for a class or a meeting at eight the next morning. In the winter the drive sometimes takes an hour and a half.

When I get home the domestic obligations begin—the phone calls to my grown children, to aged parents. It's only for the past three years that I'm not coming home to a house full of our kids and their friends. My son now lives far away, but when I arrive home my daughter is there with my grandchild, three years old, full of energy and just waiting for some quality time with her Nana, who has papers to grade, this essay to work on, and a mate who hasn't seen her except in exhausted sleep for many days. Like John, but with infinitely more right to it, he's feeling kind of grumpy about that. Of course, my writing voice is silent this night, and for many nights to come. I draft the section of this article you're reading now about two months after all I've just described takes place. But I'm a writer, so I cast it in the present tense to lend it a sense of immediacy. I had many other things to say the night I was going to write it all down, but I've forgotten what they were.

A Decade in the Life of Silence

But I am not nearly as silent in print as my colleague and friend, Karen. Her story is in many respects another familiar one, and far worse than mine. After her marriage of many years ends, she raises her two daughters on her own— or, rather, she raised them on her own all along. Somehow she manages to return to college, commuting long distances for years to do it. When it's time for graduate school she drives in the opposite direction another seventy miles. We are in graduate school together, and throughout our Ph.D. studies I am aware that this woman has not only one of the finest minds I've ever encountered, but that she has important things to say, a worthy book—or three, or four—to write.

Her work is on the cutting edge of literary theory, but it is nearly impossible for her to get the silent uninterrupted peace necessary to read Derrida, to say nothing of the kind of concentrated energy it takes to write herself into the international conversation among theoreticians. She is also a fine poet, but she has no time for writing poems. Somehow she manages to write her dissertation, and to obtain a degree with distinction from one of the best graduate programs at that time in the country. But then, tied down by mothering and family obligations, she must take a temporary job at my own institution teaching freshman composition, which, with commuting and continued mothering, uses all her time and energy.

When a tenure-track position finally opens, she does not get it. The reason she is given is that surely such a job will bore her, given her sophisticated theoretical interests. We don't hire her, in other words, because her "overqualifications" translate into an apprehension that she won't be good at teaching basic writing courses, despite stunningly high student evaluations in teaching exactly those courses. If there were other, even less rational reasons she wasn't hired, you could perhaps guess what they were.

In the meantime she marries a feminist man who also teaches English, and goes to work on a year-by-year basis in the SUNY system where he is a full professor. Every year she suffers the anxiety of not knowing if she will be employed the following year. She is underpaid and overworked, of course, teaching seven sections of writing, both creative and composition. Her book languishes.

Her husband gets two well-earned sabbaticals to do his writing; she is not eligible for one, and for nearly ten years continues midwifing other people's writing while hers proceeds so slowly that her vita is nearly empty. Because she is a woman, a popular and charismatic professor, and teaches creative writing, she becomes a mother figure to many of her students. They swamp her office. They call her at home. They expect of her things they would never ask of her male counterparts. During this time, she is working to build a thriving program to help young writers.

After a number of years she is finally instated on the tenure track. She now has job security, and in the intervening years her children have grown up and moved away, though she still has her second husband's child at home. Somehow, and I still don't know how she did it, she finishes her book. She is slowed not only by these circumstances I have described, but by new developments in her field. The time it takes her to finish is increased because while she was silent, others have spoken, most, though not all of them, men with cushy jobs that involve less than half of the teaching she does.

Only I and two or three other people will ever know the contributions to theory she might have made, in addition to the ones she is now, belatedly, making. She expands her work, accommodates the changes that have taken place, gracefully acknowledges the work of other people. I have never heard her express the resentment I feel on her behalf. Her book is published now. Between its inception and its completion more than a decade of her silence has passed.

Why Do We Let This Happen To Us?

Why do many women professionals in the business of teaching and writing participate in, invite, become complicit in a dynamic that threatens not only their own productivity as writers, but sometimes their identities and their mental health? First, we have to admit the force of our own unconscious nostalgia for a definition of femininity that is attached to maternity. Many of us are not just conditioned by but believe in the web of relationships that Gilligan analyzed in *In a Different Voice*. This situation is not just the trap we're caught in; it reflects fundamental beliefs we may hold—feminist beliefs—about what it is to be most fully human, and certainly about what good teaching might accomplish. We contribute to this problem ourselves by projecting too much availability and maternal caring. Perhaps we need to be needed, and lead our students to become emotionally dependent upon us, else we would not permit and perpetuate this dependency.

Well, all right, perhaps. But if that's so, it's in response to personal and cultural mandates so old and deeply rooted that we could not erase the need without obliterating our deepest selves, our core sense of identity. We believe that it is right to conduct our lives much the way we do. We believe that the extremes that result from that conduct are not altogether our fault. The cultural and personal patterns that we enact, and to which we respond, are more than equalled by our students'—and often our colleagues'—similar expectations of us. That would be true even if we projected much less personal accessibility.

It's difficult to place constraints and limits on what happens when you open yourself to relatedness as a way of being in the world. Some of us, despite becoming feminists after we were fully adult, and certainly well after our basic sense of identity formation took place, find ourselves pulled back again to the self-destructive aspects of the need and the desire to nurture—the self-abnegating, self-erasing aspects of it, the ones in which our own ego boundaries are revealed as still tentative, delicate, fragile.

And it's entirely possible that we also suffer from a subtly pervasive sense of guilt for our individualism, our toughness, the ways in which we have failed to be good women in the traditional sense. If we are all, men and women alike, as Dinnerstein has said, full of rage against the all-powerful mother of infancy, if that mother is resented at the unconscious level for any separate existence from us, then we are likely to be most angry with ourselves for embodying the most extreme form of that separateness, most guilty about our fantasized failures to nurture our young.

Young people sense those permeable psychic boundaries, and are drawn to them. If what draws them to us first and foremost is their initial sense of our health, our autonomy, our completeness, our accomplishment, if they think they might learn from us how to acquire these things themselves, they also are drawn to the soft underbelly just below the surface of the strong skin of independent, individualistic resolve. Recently a young feminist writer, exasperated with her own self-erasure in relationship after relationship with men, said to me, "Why is it that I look around me and see the women I know putting their own personalities on hold for the duration of each love affair, and I think, you shouldn't be doing this, why are you letting this happen—and then I watch myself do the same thing over and over, even though I know better."

If she, a woman of twenty-three whose own mother is a strong feminist, who grew up as a second-generation feminist, is still struggling against cultural patterns of such tenacity and strength in the unconscious that they defeat her again and again, it is not hard to understand that we, her collective feminist and writerly mothers, should encounter repeatedly in ourselves the backsliding power of the repetition compulsion. We adopted feminism as latecomers to it in terms of the life process, adopted it consciously and politically. Many of us have not found our conscious resolve sufficient to protect us from the massive forces that pull us back toward models or mothering that are self-erasing.

And for many of us the enemy with outposts in our heads (Sally Kempton's phrase) is also our dearest, deepest lifelong friend, for we believe in the rightness of the web of relationship rather than the autonomous, hierarchical goals that we associate, rightly, with patriarchal structures. Perhaps the most destructive aspect of this other "reproduction of mothering" is the tendency among some women writers to let their protegés, their metaphorical children, do the work that they cannot do. Tillie Olsen reminded us of this powerfully in *Silences:* "Women are traditionally trained to place others' needs first, to feel these needs as their own (the 'infinite capacity'); their satisfaction to be in making it possible for others to use their abilities" (17).

Mothers have often lived vicariously through their children, contenting themselves with fostering accomplishment and creativity in others instead of in themselves. Our writing students give us an easy out for our maternal urge to live vicariously, to measure and define our creativity in terms of our enabling others to become creative. Our silence feeds on the speech of these important, often beloved others; our erasure is enabled by their inscription; their inscription is enabled by our erasure.

Other factors also feed into the decision to become mother-figures to our students. One way to deflect erotic energy between teachers and students is to displace it into the maternal model. All relationships of any substance contain variants on one or more of the fundamental patterns of relating first enacted in the nuclear family: mother-child, father-child, brother-sister, husband-wife. When I am choosing which possibility to build on in my relationship with students, the sibling model does not work because students need to have some confidence in my authority and knowledge in order to accept that they can learn through me; I turn to the sibling model later to transform the nature of the bond. (Returning older students sometimes offer exceptions to this rule of thumb.) I certainly cannot select the openly erotic model of husband and wife, the institutionalized form for the lover relationship. Instead I choose the safest paradigm, in which eroticism is repressed or sublimated.

For the most part, this is a highly successful strategy. When intimacy begins to build in teacher-student relationships, it is safer to let it be expressed in a maternal way. When the degree of closeness reaches the point where touch is appropriate, whether it's a supportive hand on the shoulder or a hug, I have clearly signaled students to receive the gesture much like the touch of a mother—and this has served me well at a number of potentially volatile human moments. The strategy protects me against the erotic pressures students can bring to bear on the relationship.

And let it be spoken in these times of appropriate concern about sexual harassment; it also protects them against vulnerabilities of my own that could turn into harmful action against them. The young are beautiful. Roethke, Larkin, Berryman, Wright, Lowell, Kinnell—most male academic poets have admitted in print the erotic power of young women over mortal, aging men. Women are not proof against these frailties, these delights, these opportunities for seduction and betrayal, and occasionally, even, for love. We all know academic marriages that began as teacher-student romances; my own mate was my former professor.

We all know the possibilities for abuse inherent in such situations. Almost any one of us, male or female, in the throes of a mid-life crisis, or feeling in love with love, or simply walking across a college campus anywhere in America in the spring, is able to be touched by desire for the young. When I was younger, the maternal model protected us because there wasn't enough distance between us in years; now it protects them, and me, because there is so much distance, and that, too, holds dangers. I'd rather be Mrs. Ramsey than Mrs. Robinson. But remember that Mrs. Ramsey was consumed by mothering.

"It's your own fault. You must like it this way or you'd change it." Both Karen's mate and mine have always said something like this to us when they tire of our exhaustion, when they become impatient waiting for us to be through mothering the world. They thought, after all, that we were done with our primary mothering when the kids moved out. Both of us have in the past been quietly angered by their accusation, in part because it's so unfair and in part because it's true.

Our mates are both feminists, both superb professors available to their students, rightly admired, respected even loved. They are not distant, remote, inaccessible. But it's not the same, and we don't know how to justify the difference. They get calls at home, help troubled students, give of their spiritual energy—but they do it judiciously, economically, carefully. They know how to protect their privacy and their time, and, quite simply, we do not.

What Can We Do About It?

Wholly surrendered and dedicated lives, time for the work, totality of absorption—this is a description of the conditions of the writing life, but also of motherhood. If women are traditionally trained to place others' needs first, feel these needs as their own, find their satisfaction in making it possible for others to use their abilities, many of us who ought by now to know better are still buying that debilitating lie.

What can be done about this? First, I think the issue needs to be talked about in public, in print, openly among us. Those of us with strategies that save our writing souls need to share ways to cope with those of us who aren't good at it. Because for the writing mother—that term to be interpreted as many ways as possible—our academic responsibilities will drain the writing life from us if we let it happen. Like mothers with children, we will continue to seek the hours of the night for our writing. We will pay again and again for every choice on our own behalf that we make. Wresting our writing from the fabric of our other lives, we become tired, we stay tired. I recognize and remember this tiredness. My children are now in their twenties, but I am still an infinitely interruptible, responsive, responsible mother, and my children are legion, and I am full of silence.

But not as silent as I used to be. I have bettered my writing circumstances, as has Karen. She made many shifts in her behavior before I did, and I learned from her partial, halting progress. At some point—she does not know exactly when, or what precipitated it—she began to believe in and act on, instead of merely to assert, her own need for autonomy. This belief was late in coming and did not occur until years after she had consciously adopted the politics of feminism. Desperation may have catalyzed this subtle transformation. She was exhausted and anxious for years, and eventually the anxiety became impossible to sustain. I suspect the same thing happened to me, though I still do not protect myself as effectively as I should.

Instructions for survival: without giving up the different voice that speaks of mutuality and the web of relationship in teaching and mentorship, listen for the syllables that are spoken by its serpent double, the Angel in the House.

Instead of being *more* accessible in response to demands that you're not available enough, be less available. You'll still be giving more than most professors do, and ironically, the students will complain very little more. Close your office door. Put a sign on it that reads "NOT NOW," and lists your available hours below it. If students knock anyway—and, stunningly, appallingly, some will—do not answer the door. It's hard. You can do it. If you must answer the door for some reason, open it only a crack and then do the hardest thing in the world: be cold. Be distant. Detached. Speak in the voice of the father. Permit yourself to sound as irritated as you feel. They will not die of it, nor will you.

Resign from several committees on which you are the token female. You'll be guilt-tripped for this, because your presence is so necessary. But they will find another female to take your place. In many cases, they will have to. The institution's tokenism, its lack of sufficient numbers of women at adequately high ranks, is not your problem, and you do not have to solve it, contrary to your feeling, and theirs, that you must.

Be prepared to be told not only by your students, but by your colleagues and possibly by administrators, that you are slacking off in your professional responsibilities. Be prepared to feel wrong in your heart. But if you're in this mess in the first place, you have always felt wrong and inadequate, whatever your public persona may convey. You've also felt used, exploited, and unappreciated—an unsavory, self-pitying, maternally martyred psychic dynamic. Listen only, for a while—five years at the very least—to the voice that knows you're going to collapse in the hall some day if you don't slow down. It's probably true. Your colleagues and students and administrators will get over your failures to nurture at all times. You will, after all, be becoming one of them, and if you're smart enough about it, your female invisibility will protect you, just as your feminist visibility threatened you. Shoot the enemy within. Go back and read Woolf. Strangle the Angel in the Academy as well as the one in the house. When she struggles to her feet, hit her again. You can comfort her later, on your own time, if you must—when you *have* your own time.

There's something important at stake here, and it's more than your writing, bigger even than your personal sanity. It has to do, ironically, with your function as role model and mother figure in the lives of your students. You worry about failing them, not helping them, not saving them. But do you really want to convey to them, by your own behavior, that this kind of nurturing is what women, even the strongest, most independent women they know (which you are) should do? Do you want them to think they can be writers if they do not claim their time and privacy? Do you want them to think they can be free women, whole people, if they allow others to run over their lives like bulldozers? Do you want to convey this to the young women for whom you represent possibility and change? Or to the young men you hope will know how to be whole, too? Do you want to help to create yet another generation of infantilized women who in turn infantilize men?

And do you want to say, by your behavior, that a good mother still is, as she has historically been, self-abnegating, interruptible, always conciliatory? Go ahead and mother them—but let them know that a good mother is a person who has important work to do in the world. You can best show them that by doing yours. You want to show them how to be writers? Go then and write. We can all participate in redefining and expanding mothering, and in separating it in part from nurturing, both to allow men and fathers to be nurturing and to allow women and mothers to be individuals. It's difficult when one of the sources of identity becomes the source of identity's diffusion and even its dissolution, but it must be done.

Yet however diligently we may work toward redefinitions, I believe strongly enough in the conservative power of the unconscious to think it unlikely that those of us who formed our identities prior to the modern feminist movement will be able utterly to obliterate the formative influences that are sometimes destructive to us. Ironically, feminist theory asks for institutionalized patriarchy to value qualities that are culturally feminine (nurture, relationship, caregiving, mutuality), and to give us a chance to develop qualities that are culturally masculine (individuation, autonomy). Such a program is not as paradoxical or self-contradictory as it might appear, but the project of such realignment cannot be accomplished easily or soon. We must learn to redress an individual imbalance while believing in and arguing for what looks like its opposite, but is really its complement. I am for accepting part of what I cannot change, and changing part of what I cannot accept.

Tillie Olsen foresaw the circumstances I have examined here. "More and more women writers in our century, primarily in the last two decades, are assuming as their right fullness of work *and* family life." But her belief and hope are tempered by what she knows about the power of the mothering paradigm. "I fear because almost certainly their work will be impeded, lessened, partial. For the fundamental situation remains unchanged" (32). While the circumstances she refers to are primarily those of juggling actual maternity and the writing or professional life, she would not be surprised at the degree to which we are also mothering in the academy. For those of us who are college teachers she had special advice. "Help create writers, perhaps among them yourselves" (45).

WORKS CITED

Chodorow, Nancy. *The Reproduction of Mothering: Psychoanalysis and the Sociology of Gender.* Berkeley: U of California P, 1978.

Dinnerstein, Dorothy. *The Mermaid and the Minotaur: Sexual Arrangements and Human Malaise.* New York: Harper & Row, 1976.

Gilligan, Carol. *In a Different Voice: Psychological Theory and Women's Development.* Cambridge: Harvard UP, 1982.

Gilligan, Carol, Janie Victoria Ward, and Jill McLean Taylor, with Betty Bardige, eds. *Mapping the Moral Domain: A Contribution of Women's Thinking to Psychological Theory and Education.* Cambridge: Harvard UP, 1988.

Griffin, Gail. "Alma Mater." *Profession 90:* 37–42. New York: Modern Language Association, 1990.

Kronik, John W. "On Men Mentoring Women: Then and Now." *Profession 90:* 52–57. New York: Modern Language Association, 1990.

Olsen, Tillie. *Silences.* New York: Delacorte Press/Seymour Lawrence, 1978.

Simmons, Thomas. *Erotic Reckonings: Mastery and Apprenticeship in the Work of Poets and Lovers.* Champaign: U of Illinois P, forthcoming.

Teaching From the Open Closet

REBECCA MARK

> For those of us (few in number, for the way is punishing), their kin and descendants who begin to emerge into a more flowered and rewarded use of ourselves in ways denied to them—and by our achievement bearing witness to what was (and still is) being lost, silenced.
>
> TILLIE OLSEN, *Silences,* ix

> A teacher is disinterested, yet he [sic] is very much a self, for he is a living embodiment of a world rather than an abstract social code or system of morality.
>
> MAURICE FRIEDMAN, *The Life of Dialogue,* 179

We have all heard the horror stories about gay faculty—the careers and lives destroyed by homophobia, the books, articles, and speeches lost, never written, published, or spoken. These are stories we have told and unfortunately will tell again. I am not interested in adding to them here. Instead I would like to explore the dynamic that occurs when gay and lesbian professors openly discuss their sexuality in the college classroom. When sexuality breaks through the institutional barriers and begins to speak its truth, the reverberations disrupt our most deeply rooted pedagogical assumptions. The presence of the living word, the body speaking, challenges the bases of the academy, not only the epistemological split between mind and body, but the theory that the transmission of knowledge can and should be an objective, abstract process.

As I begin this discussion, I would like to make several clarifying statements. First, I use the category "gay and lesbian professors" in the previous paragraph, not the inclusive "professors," because it is gays and lesbians who have, historically, been forced to make their disclosure of sexuality an act of "coming out." However, for a professor who defines him- or herself as heterosexual, to make coming out a conscious act would challenge not only student assumptions about sexuality, but the act of assuming itself. This kind of disclosure would shift the pedagogical terrain even more radically.

Second, this essay grows out of my own experience of coming out in the classroom and is not a prescriptive argument. I do not believe that all professors can, would want to, or even need to come out in front of their students. Third, the term "coming out" has many performative meanings. It is simultaneously the statement of a moment, and a continuous process. Because of the charged political nature of homosexuality, coming out is never simply personal disclosure, but instead a willingness to align oneself with a certain set of assumptions, stereotypes, inconsistencies, incoherences, irrationalities, and projections. Because of this bewildering confusion and profusion of meanings, beyond the statement "I am" is a lifetime of creating understanding of what "I am" means. With my family and those I love I take an active role in the life-time project. With students and in other political situations, I negotiate a space between statement and dialogue, encouraging the dialogue to go on beyond the sphere of my influence.

Each time I have come out in the classroom I have done so because I felt an urgent need to amend what I perceived as an extremely homophobic or closeted discussion of sexuality. I first came out in the classroom when I was teaching composition as a graduate student at Stanford University. Several students were leading an ill-informed discussion on homosexuality. I felt compelled to breathe some political fire and life experience into this deadening exchange. I came out again when I taught at St. Olaf College. The atmosphere for gay students at this religious midwest college was extremely oppressive, and I wanted to help the students create a more accepting atmosphere. At Tulane University, where I now teach, I have come out to students in individual classes and at campus-wide political events, once while teaching Audre Lorde's *Zami* and many times in response to David Duke's candidacy for senator.

I have never been fired for coming out. I have not lost promotions or raises or been publicly ridiculed. I have never had my tires slashed or my house spray painted as I have often feared. But I have been asked a question that alternately irritates and interests me: why do you feel you must come out? I feel irritated when I think that there would be no need for me to come out if we lived in an open-minded and open-hearted society. My "coming out" should be as uneventful as a statement of marriage would be for the heterosexual who asked me the question. When I am feeling more altruistic I answer simply and truthfully that my coming out has changed and probably will change the lives of many students, both those who identify as gay and those who do not. Last year I attended the second annual St. Olaf College "Walking Between Two Worlds Week," sponsored by the St. Olaf gay, lesbian, and bisexual association. Before I came out on that campus there was no gay and lesbian organization and very little support for alternative sexualities. My speech was the catalyst for students to come out and to begin to form a strong gay/lesbian/bisexual community, which has flourished long after my departure. My talk and the community response to the talk led professors to begin to teach tutorials and courses on sexuality. This dramatic change is all the evidence I need of the political, cultural, and human importance of coming out.

But my response and responsibility does not end here. The situation for gay faculty and students has not changed enough to make these success stories more than locally significant. In fact recently I attended the memorial service of a gay student who committed suicide. Whether he took his life because of the homophobia he faced I do not know, but I feel compelled to find answers for his death and his life. In order to make a more lasting impact, I and others who have had similar coming-out experiences must try to communicate why and how the specific dynamics of coming out make it a powerful and empowering pedagogical act. This type of work is especially critical as we face both a reactionary political environment that condones gay bashing and the supposedly radical anti-essentialism of current critical theory. Unless we theorize and validate coming out, its current unfashionable position may throw many people back into the closet of silence or indifference.

Recent work on sexuality by John Boswell, Judith Butler, Michael Moon, John D'Emilio, Estelle Freedman, David M. Halperin, John Jay Winkler, Ed Cohen, and Eve Kosofsky Sedgwick proves quite convincingly that, as Sedgwick states in *Epistemology of the Closet,* "it becomes truer and truer that the language of sexuality not only intersects with, but transforms, the other languages and relations by which we know" (3). What is still under debate is whether the statement of identity, coming out, enhances this transformation, or, by privileging identities over multiple and shifting alliances, makes us complicit within an established structural hierarchy. In a time when we are de-emphasizing essentialist and identity politics, one could easily argue that coming out at best makes no difference and at worst reduces the terms of discussion to personal disclosure or confession. As long as the professor makes sexuality an active, contested, and visible term in class dialogues, it might be thus argued, her statement of her own sexuality is irrelevant.

In a world free of power relations, where people who love, have sex with, and live with members of the same sex are guaranteed the same economic and political opportunities, the same social acceptance, where popular culture offers as many positive images of homosexuality as of heterosexuality, where we can candidly discuss sexuality in the classroom, we might be able to free ourselves from naming, but I think de-emphasizing the act of coming out at this moment in history is political suicide. De-emphasizing coming out in the classroom denies the epistemological and pedagogical power of the human presence and all that constitutes this presence—the body, the voice, the senses, the emotions. The desire to divorce sexuality from physical being ignores the simple fact that role models do change students' perceptions of themselves—that whom we learn from, how we learn, does help determine how and what we learn. This has always been part of the argument for affirmative action. From this institutional point of view, to diminish the importance of bodies, of experience, at the moment when bodies with different experiences are finally entering the academy, is suspicious at least. We can, however, keep our disclosures of experience from becoming reductive by expanding the way we think of identity. By making it a relational, pluralistic, rather than autonomous concept, we can begin to see coming out as much more of an exchange and much less of a confession.

In "Lesbian Desire As Social Change," Nett Hart reminds us that coming out is not simply a confessional moment.

> When a people disenfranchised within that existing system validates their
> own identity as a starting point for their world view, elemental change can
> happen because the structure through which reality is apprehended becomes
> fluid. For me, to be lesbian is elemental social action, not a metaphor, not an
> example, but social change itself (295).

Both Sedgwick's concept of society as the "relations by which we know" and
Hart's "structure through which reality is apprehended" allow for the possibility that social constructions of reality are pliable, "fluid"—not easily changed
but potentially changeable. Hart shifts lesbian identity from a static inalter-
able fact to a dynamic, relational possibility, from the frighteningly vulnerable
act of self-disclosure to the potentially creative process of questioning cultural
notions of self. Lesbian as idea, disconnected from lesbian body or experience, could never have this impact. But lesbian as identity isolated from all
other identities, unable to include subtle differences and developments,
would have little or no profound destabilizing effect either.

Shane Phelan in *Identity Politics: Lesbian Feminism and the Limits of
Community* reminds us of the role the university has played in demanding a
singular vision of self.

> Perhaps the most difficult place in which to celebrate difference is the acad-
> emy. The nature of theory has been to make connections, to tell grand
> stories that tie threads together. This has been evident at least since Plato's
> *Republic,* in which every animal, every person, manifests the degree of
> order and harmony that rules the polis. Until the advent of postmodernism,
> the aim of theoretical work was to smooth and connect, not to disrupt or
> disorient us. But people who are left out of the story know the price of such
> simple smoothing. . .(165).

By coming out in the academy we disturb the impulse toward unity, we disrupt
simple stereotypical categorizations, placing ourselves at the dynamic center
of this more relational, "porous" community; the act makes us, not more
isolated, as we are taught to fear, but infinitely more allied, and more human.
If we can show our students that *self* can include more than one set of terms,
then they and we can learn to exist in many communities simultaneously. We
can tolerate more than a monistic or dualistic existence.

Jacqueline Zita in "Lesbian Body Journeys," goes so far as to say that it is
often an initial statement of identity which makes nonessentialist, nonidentity
politics possible.

> Claiming any one identity is not a precondition for the unity of self, but at
> times a precondition for self-preservation. Claiming a lesbian identity often
> diffuses into difference, once its locations are made physical, real and lived
> (329).

The statement of lived experience, coming out, makes lesbianism, ethnic
difference, racial difference, "physical, real and lived," for those who hear us.
Without an initial statement of difference there can be no further exploration
of difference. If we all assume a general identity or nonidentity there can be
no "diffusion," or—a word I prefer—proliferation, of difference. Recogniz-

ing difference is dependent on speaking the details, and particularities, of felt, observed experience.

If there is one fact we have learned from the pedagogical experiments of the open classroom in the sixties, it is that as professors, even if we engage in nonhierarchical or feminist pedagogy, we still represent power within the space of the classroom. If, rather than trying to ignore or minimize this power, we recognize the complex interactions that constitute this power, name it as power, and embrace the potentially transformative elements of the pedagogical relationship, then our presence serves as the catalyst for action, rather than a demand for passive subservience. When we engage in a process such as coming out, we represent the possibility of asserting oneself into the dynamic center of cultural dialogue rather than assuming a victimized position on the margin. As we do this, while we do not change the grim realities of the social construction of gender and sexuality, we do for a moment, in this locality, create a space in which sexuality is less culturally codified and repressed than outside the classroom. While this may seem like a minor victory, this moment, this opening, may provide the necessary spark for the student's own coming out to begin. Here I do not necessarily mean coming out as gay and lesbian but coming out as a vocal, political, human being. If we minimize or ignore our power, we have underestimated the transformative nature of human contact, the imaginative ability of the human spirit to see beyond the system in which he or she has been playing a role.

Sarah Parmeter suggests in her essay "Four Good Reasons Why Every Lesbian Teacher Should Be Free to Come Out in the Classroom,"[1] that coming out allows for the possibility of a true multicultural debate within the classroom (50–55). Once the "secret," the most politically volatile, the most historically invisible identity is spoken, then other identities can emerge more easily. I might say that I am a lesbian and then go on to say that I am Jewish, Irish, middle class, etc. At another time and place one of these other identities might be more volatile or dangerous to speak than my lesbian identity. My experience of more than one identity will connect me with people from a multiplicity of experiences and allow me to cross barriers that initially seem insurmountable. As this process continues to invite rather than exclude identities, we will extend beyond race, class, sexuality, and ethnic origin into the less vocalized parameters of linguistic experience, childhood experience, body image, etc. Both the silenced name and the name proclaimed too loudly, to the exclusion of all others, make identity politics stagnant.

As Zita states, the initial statement of identity can lead to more detailed and exacting recognitions of difference. For example, a student who states, "I am Jewish, feminist, dyke," might not only connect with other dykes but with other Jews and other feminists, and as the dialogues and coming outs continue, she might find herself connecting with southerners, single mothers, adult children of holocaust survivors, etc. The act of stating difference, a seemingly exclusive act, is potentially inclusive, and potentially disruptive of assumed power relations, of concepts such as center-margin, inside-outside, and teacher-student.

When I came out at St. Olaf College in a chapel talk, I told the gathering of 1,500 students, faculty, and administrators how the pink triangle was used to identify and destroy homosexuals in Nazi Germany. At the end of the talk I asked all of the people in the audience who thought they could wear this triangle as the symbol of gay pride which it had become to step forward and take a triangle. The students had made only two hundred pink triangles, and in a matter of minutes they were gone. We could have given out hundreds more. All day long people were cutting up pink paper and making triangles, and when later that day I walked into the classroom to teach my course in modern American literature, all the students were wearing pink triangles. I was, needless to say, overwhelmed. The pink triangle was no longer a symbol of gay identity but of political alliance. There was, for a moment, no closet, no center, no margin.

Later I wondered whether these students had worn the triangle out of fear; whether they thought they might have received a lower grade if they didn't wear a pink triangle. I was concerned that my position of power was influencing their decision. But now I know that if my position did lead them to this decision, I have no regrets. Whatever their reason, the act itself had shifted their previous position. Once they had accepted that symbol as part of their identity, a departure from the norm had occurred that would reverberate for the rest of their lives.

For the next few weeks I heard many voices, some celebrating, some confused, some angry. But even the most disturbed students prefaced every comment with, "I respect what you said." The distinction between human respect for a gay person and trouble with the idea of homosexuality is the tension that human presence demands. As much as they wanted to dismiss the idea, they could not fully dismiss the person. I told them that I understood that some of them came from deeply religious families and that they had been taught to hate homosexuals, but I also reminded them that we live in a homophobic society and that, while I would not hold them solely responsible for their beliefs, I would encourage them to think again, to look at their assumptions.

While I took all their responses into consideration, I did not take care of them. If my presence as a lesbian presented them with a problem, it was not my responsibility to solve that problem. What they felt as ambiguity was the uncomfortable locus of change. Whenever I have come out in a class, I have encountered several students who spend hours searching for an answer to what they see as a direct contradiction between what their parents and pastors have taught them and what they are now perceiving and feeling. These searches, these journeys happen with or without my participation.

For the gay students my talk at St. Olaf's was a cause for celebration. Many felt elated, as if they had at last had their experience validated in the classroom. Most importantly, many came out themselves, in the student newspaper, in classes, to their parents, to professors. I asked one student to write her response for this essay.

When Rebecca came out to me, I suddenly had access to a very positive and healing lesbian image, a dyke who smiled and laughed, had friends, and had the strength to feel the pain of being gay in this society. She had voice and the internal power to walk in both worlds. . . . She was instrumental in my coming out to my friends and family, and eventually to all 1,500 people at St. Olaf College.[2]

I think this student's choice of "image" and "voice" and "laughter" emphasizes the degree to which my actual, bodily presence was important.

Inside these four walls that we call the academy, we have been taught that our acts of inclusion of women, African Americans, Asian Americans, Native Americans, Hispanics, etc., can be allowed, funded, "institutionalized" without seriously altering the institution itself. All of these movements toward inclusion have been seen by outsiders as acts of collusion, contributions to the grand story, opportunities for co-optation—an attempt to be part of the club—rather than what they really are: a disruption of the way we do business in this place of higher learning. We have been taught to assume that the institution, the old forms, can remain intact while we as "others" are "included" on the margin. Our voices can be held in the little spaces they call programs, minors, even majors, but which we call struggling, underfunded.

What the "they," who is often "we," do not realize is that the old institutional structures and pedagogical methods cannot contain the new epistemologies. The model of the classroom as a place where students will be socialized, calmed down, molded into good citizens, and prepared for business still exists, but the "inclusion" of new voices is causing a quiet upheaval that we can see today both in the reactionary response to "politically correct" teaching and the liberal attempt to pay more attention to issues of diversity. Both the reactionary response and the multicultural programming "band-aid" response refuse to acknowledge fully that change is occurring. However, the fervor of the debate indicates the power of the movement, a movement that demands above all else the return of bodies, sexualities, genders, emotions, and identities to education. As long as we keep discussion of race and sexuality disconnected from our physical and emotional experience, we can maintain an illusion of inclusion. But when we embrace physical and emotional experience, we make a connection between idea and body, between mind and body, heart and mind—a connection that directly challenges the basic tenets, the foundation, the *raison d'être* of the academy.

When I refer to the "return" of bodies, sexualities, genders, emotions, and identities, I should explain that while all of these have been present in the academy, they have only been allowed to exist in circumscribed, formulaic, restricted representations. In fact it is possible that our reluctance to name our own sexual identities might be related to how well we have learned that bodies and sexualities have very particular, confined places in our pursuit of knowledge. It is impossible to discuss the role of the body and sexuality in higher education without confronting the patriarchally established link between the female body and knowledge.

As the Eves and Pandoras, as the ones who would eat the apple, open the box and let loose the uncontrollable demons of carnal and emotional knowledge, women were, for hundreds of years, quite literally kept from entering the sacred groves and gardens of the university. However, while the "real" woman's body and sexuality were kept out of the institution, the woman as body was the subject of literary metaphor, artistic expression, psychological examination, and sociological conjecture. As Virginia Woolf writes in *A Room of One's Own*, "Why does Samuel Butler say, "Wise men never say what they think of women'? Wise men never say anything else . . ." (16). Woolf's observation reminds us that men depended on woman to be the screen on which they could project masculinist theories and fantasies. Woman's body, however, her physical presence, was a definite problem. When the portrait speaks, who is the artist?[3]

Woolf finds herself drawing a picture of a very angry professor as she reads the thousands of documents on women in the British Museum. "His expression suggested that he was laboring under some emotion that made him jab his pen on the paper as if he were killing some noxious insect as he wrote, but even when he had killed it that did not satisfy him; he must go on killing it; and even so, some cause for anger and irritation remained" (31). Until the establishment of women's colleges and the admission of women to previously all male colleges and universities, the only female body allowed to exist in the college classroom was the dead female body, the noxious insect pinned to a velvet board and romanticized into art—the aesthetic ideal. Even after being allowed into the college classroom, her body has been subdued, effaced, by the exclusion of her real experience from the content of the class. Until the advent of women's studies programs, she found herself the object of study rather than the agent of that study. Only the presence of real agents, of female faculty, of female historians and critics has begun to change this situation.

In "Toward A Woman-Centered University," Adrienne Rich reminds us that the sexuality that cannot be discussed in the rarefied atmosphere of the college classroom will find distorted expression in the offices and bedrooms of professors. "The eroticism of the father-daughter relationship resonates here, and romance and flirtation are invisibly present even where there is no actual seduction" (Rich 139). What we can begin to argue is that this silencing of sexuality is not an aberration in an otherwise enlightened system; it is the intentional silencing and exclusion of the female body and sexuality for which the institution was founded. Rich goes on to say:

> What we have at present is a man-centered university, a breeding ground not of humanism, but of masculine privilege. As women have gradually and reluctantly been admitted into the mainstream of higher education, they have been made participants in a system that prepares men to take up roles of power in a man-centered society, that asks questions and teaches "facts" generated by a male intellectual tradition and that both subtly and openly confirms men as the leaders and shakers of human destiny both within and outside academia (127).

Although Rich did not mention sexuality in this 1979 article, the roles of power that men are trained to take up are the roles of sexual as well as economic power. The facts generated by the male intellectual tradition are facts of male sexual dominance over women, of the dominance of heterosexuality over homosexuality, and of the inferiority of the female body to the male mind.

When a lesbian professor comes out in the classroom, she not only makes body, gender, sexuality, desire, and emotion legitimate subjects of discussion, but she questions the foundation of the institutional structure that has depended for its very existence on the systematic removal of these "others" from its dualistic epistemology. Her body and sexuality make themselves present in the space that has denied them. The act of relegating sexuality, women, and the body to the back halls of academia is equivalent to relegating homosexuality to the closet. Just as men projected fears of sex onto women, heterosexuals have projected fears of sex onto gay people. Homosexuality has become synonymous with sexual promiscuity, sexually transmitted disease, perversion, immorality, sexual abuse—the obviously poisonous tree of sin from which no one would be caught dead eating. Heterosexuality, on the other hand, has been allowed to remain pure and "untainted," sex sanctified and stagnated by marriage and procreation. By coming out, the professor makes heterosexuality as well as homosexuality a contested term, open for discussion.

Now, as "the body" makes its reappearance in academic dialogue and as feminists and scholars of African American and multicultural studies not only give "the body" a voice, but argue for the proliferation of bodies, of sexualities, of discourses, of truths, the relegation of homosexuality to the closet becomes increasingly impossible. It is the experience of the closet that has taught us the importance of discussing, living, and understanding sexuality. It is women and gay people and lesbians who understand and can give language to this subdued and silenced experience.

Unfortunately, most institutions would like sexuality of any kind to remain subdued and silenced. Those in authority in school systems from elementary through college have consistently seen homosexuals as capable and guilty of corrupting innocent children. In Lillian Hellman's *The Children's Hour*, when Mrs. Tilford discusses her accusation that Karen and Martha, the headmistresses of a girl's boarding school, are lesbians, she exclaims, "What they are may possibly be their own business. It becomes a great deal more than that when children are involved" (Hellman 49). Given the distortion, isolation, and repression of sexuality, it is not surprising that within the walls of educational institutions, homosexual teachers have been accused of sexual harassment of students at an alarming rate.[4] The myth of lesbians and gay men as child molesters has been one of the most damaging homophobic myths. Not supported by any statistical evidence, the specter of the homosexual teacher taking advantage of the young has haunted gay faculty. People have lost jobs, careers, and have taken their own lives because of these accusations. The statistics indicate that of the widespread cases of child sexual molestation and abuse in schools and sexual harassment on college campuses, the perpetrators are predominantly white heterosexual males. But the myth is much stronger than the truth, and the act of coming out brings any professor face to face with this angry and accusing ghost. The language of the attacks, which often includes the word "corruption," suggests that people fear that the schoolroom will be contaminated by the sexuality and body undeniably present in the figure of the gay teacher, that their sexuality will somehow "spill out" and "infect" their students. The presence of the AIDS virus in the gay community has only heightened this hysteria. Sexuality, like femininity, as a concept, as a theoretical pursuit, as a metaphor, is not nearly as threatening as the actual presence of lesbians and gay men.

The flip side of exaggeration of gay faculty's sexuality has been the denial of female faculty's sexuality, which has resulted in the stereotype of the spinster or the old maid school marm. The two identities, lesbian and teacher, do not have a happy or affirming history. The derogatory stereotypes of sexually oppressed, repressed, weird sisters, with their hair pulled tightly back immediately come to mind. The images equate single female teachers with lives of sacrifice, denial, and repression. Both stereotypes—the overly sexual and the sexually repressed—suggest something wrong: either too much or too little, not the norm.

The modern version of the school marm is the dyke/man-hater/feminist. This stereotype has been particularly successful in discrediting women's studies programs and in silencing lesbian students and faculty. At Tulane University, after reading Audre Lorde's *Zami*, I felt that I could only have a meaningful discussion of this book if I came out to my class. I was surprised to find that one of my best and brightest feminist students was upset. She expressed concern that now that I had come out no one would take me seriously.

> I didn't think it was a good idea for you to come out in class because I thought it would only serve to perpetuate people's stereotypes about all feminists being lesbians. When you decided to share information about your sexual preference with the whole class, I felt it would further cement the notion in the students' heads that feminism and feminist concerns are not applicable to the average heterosexual American woman. By further proclaiming your marginality I felt that, unfortunately, that would make it easier for both male and female students to rationalize dismissing the political concerns you raised during the semester as concerns that are only of consequence to lesbians and radicals.[5]

Although the actual experience of students discussing sexuality openly and finding new expressions and language for their own sexuality has since made her change her mind, I think this student articulates the feelings and fears of many students. One of my freshman students said recently, after interviewing a feminist, "She wasn't a flaming man-killer or anything." I love this quote because it combines flaming-faggot and man-killer in one sentence, conflating stereotypes of masculine and feminine, gay and lesbian. Adrienne Rich addresses this issue in "Toward a Woman-Centered University":

> Women in colleges where a women's studies program already exists, or where feminist courses are beginning to be taught, still are often made to feel that the "real" curriculum is the male-centered one; that women's studies are (like Third World studies) a "fad"; that feminist teachers are "unscholarly," "unprofessional," or "dykes" (136).

On the three campuses where I have taught, students have been wary of taking women's studies courses for fear their boyfriends or friends will think they are lesbians. While coming out does risk creating the impression that all feminists are lesbians, such as my student feared, not coming out won't make this impression go away. Silence only serves to let the misconceptions continue, unexamined and unchallenged. On the other hand, the discussions that can follow coming out may enable teachers and students to explore what is behind the stereotypes of the feminist professor—including a fear of women's autonomy and power. It might challenge them to think about why they think it would be so awful if all feminist professors were lesbians. But in order for this kind of open discussion to occur, heterosexual feminist professors must be willing to engage in their own forms of self-disclosure.

When I come out in a class, I am acutely aware of every gay-bashing event that has taken place on the campus on which I am speaking. I am acutely aware of the students who have been driven out for being gay, of the graffiti on the walls of the bathrooms, of the gay bashing in the fraternities. But for one powerful moment, I can allow my students to see my passion, to hear it, feel it. I choose the word passion very carefully. To place the terms pedagogy, homosexuality, and passion together is to open the gay Pandora's box. Passion, especially, in our Puritan society, evokes images of free love, lust, wanton sexual display, irrational outbursts, uncontrolled sexual eruptions—all the terms used to discredit the gay male community. The synonyms for *passion* in *Roget's Thesaurus* are desire, craze, interest, eloquence, sexual desire, zeal, emotion, excitement, distress, love, anger. These contradictory synonyms mirror our society's extreme ambivalence about the body, sexuality, and love, but they also suggest that passion is at the heart of all human existence. Passion at once represents being out of control, or "crazed," and some of the most admirable qualities we could expect from a human being: eloquence, interest, love. In fact, the antonyms for *passion* are "indifference" and "apathy," exactly the attitudes we dislike in our students.

For a lesbian to reclaim passion is also for her to see that the root of this word is a history of our own experience. In the *Oxford English Dictionary* the meanings for *passion* proceed as follows: 1. suffering; 2. the fact of being acted upon; 3. an affection of the mind; 4. a fit or mood marked by stress of feeling or abandonment to emotion; a transport of excited feeling; 5. amorous feeling, strong sexual affection. From suffering to being passive, to being acted on by a strong affection, to sexual desire, we as gay people who are emerging from the closet have known the whole journey, and in this journey and in the repetition of this journey we have known a fullness in our living.

The literature on feminist pedagogy reminds us of the kind of passionate environment we have been hoping to create in the classroom. This is not the open-classroom model of the sixties which, while it helped establish many useful precedents, tended to leave the relationship between teacher and student unclear. Instead, this is a model based on mutual respect and acknowledgement of the teacher's power and responsibility. The writers of *Women's Ways of Knowing* sum up by stating:

> We have argued in this book that educators can help women develop their own authentic voices if they emphasize connection over separation, understanding and acceptance over assessment, and collaboration over debate; if they accord respect to and allow time for the knowledge that emerges from firsthand experience; if instead of imposing their own expectation and arbitrary requirements, they encourage students to evolve their own patterns of work based on the problems they are pursuing. These are the lessons we have learned in listening to women's voices (229).

In this model the teacher must actively help, emphasize, accord respect, allow time for, and encourage. By coming out, the lesbian professor does not automatically create these conditions, but she can enhance and give form to otherwise abstract notions, such as how to develop one's own authentic voice, how to emphasize connection over separation, understanding and acceptance over assessment, and collaboration over debate. But coming out is not enough. One must come out with a clear theoretical understanding of the complex dynamic that exists between student and professor. Martin Buber's essay, "Education," still stands as one of the most ethical descriptions of this pedagogical dynamic.

> Because this human being exists: therefore he [sic] must be really there, really facing the child, not merely there in spirit. . . . if he has really gathered the child into his life then that subterranean dialogic, that steady potential presence of the one to the other is established, and endures. Then there is reality between them, there is mutuality.
>
> But this mutuality—that is what constitutes the peculiar nature of the relation in education—cannot be one of inclusion, . . . no other is in that regard like this, completely directed to one-sidedness, so that if it loses one-sidedness it loses essence (*Between Man and Man*, 98–99).

What is important in Buber's assessment is his understanding that the relationship of professor to student depends on the total presence of the professor but does not demand that the student include her professor's life in her perspective. I must have no investment in my students being able to empathize with my life, but I must be able to be inclusive of theirs; and to be inclusive I must not be afraid. I must have no fear of losing myself. This is a delicate balance, an act of love. I cannot be holding on to the secret of my sexuality, or my mind will be censoring, judging, second-guessing, not opening. On the other hand, as I come out, I can have no need for support from my students. I must be receiving this elsewhere.

The challenge to traditional pedagogy occurs precisely at this moment, the moment when the professor can stand before the class in his or her totality, proclaiming that no essence of human existence will be excluded in this space which they are creating together, that each human being will be able to bring his or her own reality to bear in the journey of discovery. In his analysis of Buber, Maurice Friedman develops this idea.

> Buber does indeed point a way out of both isolated individualism and the 'oppositeness' between the pupil and the teacher. He does so, however, not through any attempt to recapture organic wholeness in society, but through the dialogical relation in which the I and the Thou remain separate and really 'other' beings (*The Life of Dialogue,* 180).

The concept of the I and the Thou remaining separate and other echoes Zita's theory of the diffusion into difference and Phelan's call for a disruption and disorientation over connection and grand stories. Isolation, forced harmony, and even corruption or domination are impossible in an atmosphere of presence.

> A teacher is disinterested, yet he is very much a self, for he is a living embodiment of a world rather than an abstract social code or system of morality (*The Life of Dialogue,* 179).

Only by coming out can a gay teacher be a living embodiment of a world. If she is censoring herself, keeping her life secret, she is not expressing a real human existence. She cannot respond in the way Buber suggests the living situation of the classroom demands:

> In spite of all similarities every living situation has, like a new born child, a new face, that has never been before and will never come again. It demands of you a reaction which cannot be prepared beforehand. It demands nothing of what is past. It demands presence, responsibility; it demands you (*Between Man and Man,* 114).

When I am coming out to my students I am simply making my fullness as a human being present in the classroom so that they can recognize their own fullness.

Whether gayness is essential or not, whether it is biologically determined or socially determined, those of us who have lived in the closet have a different experience from those who lived in the room, and when we move into the room, the classroom, we are speaking with a voice that has known silence and a body that has known invisibility. It is our right, our responsibility, our power to speak the truths of that experience, and as we speak we validate this journey of human discovery. We validate all feeling bodies. We validate movement and changing definitions.

NOTES

1. Parmeter touches on most of the reasons I have heard and used myself when asked why lesbian professors should come out. Her four reasons are:

> 1. Coming out makes lesbian teachers more comfortable in the classroom because we know our students see us for who we are.
> 2. When lesbian teachers come out, straight students gain a new sensitivity to gay issues.
> 3. Coming out helps us create a culturally diverse classroom.
> 4. Coming out lets us create a home at the university for lesbian and gay students who might otherwise not have one (44–57).

2. Student, St. Olaf College, June, 1989.

3. The most ironic display of this fact occurred when female art students in the nineteenth century in Europe were not allowed to take life drawing classes because they would view the nude body, while their bodies had been projected onto the canvases of male artists for centuries. See Linda Nochlin, "Why Have There Been No Great Women Artists?" In *Art and Sexual Politics,* ed. Thomas B. Hess and Elizabeth Baker. Collier Macmillan: New York, 1973.

4. See abstracts of specific cases in Robert B. Marks Ridinger, *The Homosexual and Society: An Annotated Bibliography.* Westport, Conn.: Greenwood Press, 1990.

5. Student, Tulane University, February 10, 1991.

WORKS CITED

Belenky, Mary Field, Blythe McVicker Clinchy, Nancy Rule Goldberger, and Jill Mattuck. "Connected Teaching." In *Women's Ways of Knowing: The Development of Self, Voice, and Mind.* New York: Tarule Basic Books Inc., 1986.

Buber, Martin. *Between Man and Man.* Translated by Ronald Gregor Smith. London: Routledge and Kegan Paul, 1947.

Foucault, Michel. *The History of Sexuality: Volume I: An Introduction.* New York: Vintage Books, 1980

Friedman, Maurice. *The Life of Dialogue.* Chicago: U of Chicago P, 1976.

Hart, Nett. "Lesbian Desire as Social Change." Ed. Jeffner Allen. *Lesbian Philosophies and Cultures.* New York: State U of New York P, 1990.

Hellman, Lillian. "The Children's Hour." In *Six Plays by Lillian Hellman.* New York: Vintage Books, 1979.

Nochlin, Linda. "Why Have There Been No Great Women Artists." In *Art and Sexual Politics.* Ed. Thomas B. Hess and Elizabeth Baker. Collier Macmillan: New York, 1973.

Parmeter, Sarah-Hope. "Four Good Reasons Why Every Lesbian Teacher Should Be Free To Come Out in the Classroom." In *The Lesbian in Front of the Classroom.* Santa Cruz: Herbooks, 1988.

Phelan, Shane. *Identity Politics: Lesbian Feminism and the Limits of Community.* Philadelphia: Temple UP, 1989.

Rich, Adrienne. "Toward a Woman-Centered University." In *Lies, Secrets, and Silences.* New York: W. W. Norton, 1979.

Sedgwick, Eve Kosofsky. *Epistemology of the Closet*. Berkeley: U of California P, 1990.
Woolf, Virginia. *A Room of One's Own*. New York: Harcourt, Brace, Jovanovitch, 1929.
Zita, Jacqueline N. "Lesbian Body Journeys." Ed. Jeffner Allen. *Lesbian Philosophies and Cultures*. New York: State U of New York P, 1990.

Cognitive Desires: An Allegory of/for Chicana Critics

NORMA ALARCÓN

As I write this I cannot help but realize that it is 1992, the year of the quincentenary, marking the "encounter," as the Anglo-Spanish promoters call it, between Europeans and the indigenous in the Americas for whom it is more of an agonistic than celebrative occasion. Thus for those of us who continue to exist on the downside of the "encounter," remembrance is more the commemoration of a deadly collision that continues to kill and produce anger and grief in the context of multinational capitalist "development" and exploitation that carries over into institutions, even academic ones, in ways that we have yet to clarify. In my view, then, the academic allegory for Chicana critics refers to that woman of Mexican descent who claims the name Chicana, lives in the United States, may even be a descendant of natives or long-time residents, and, most importantly, refuses to forget that she is also the descendant of peoples, some of whose names have disappeared, who have been engaged in continuous conflict with state and institutional power structures that wish to repress the memory of the unsavory consequences of conquest, colonization, dislocation, discrimination, and their historical transformation. Though the allegory is one pertaining to an academic power structure, I would like to make the connection that the consequences of imperialisms and their multiple transformations are not only pertinent to the political economy but cognitive as well, for it is within academic institutions that knowledge production may be "recycled" into narratives that support the national(istic) status quo. Cognitive desire, then, is not just a "hunger of memory" that is subsumed by categories produced elsewhere, but a "hunger of memory" desirous of its own productive intervention in the retrieval and making of cognitive symbols and concepts that may help us apprehend our experience of the political economy in conjunction with jurisprudence, history, ethnography, and literary mediation. It is, after all, the conditions of the political economy, especially in the twentieth century, that have made migrants of many of us. Not just migrant workers in the agribusiness fields, but in many other enterprises of industrial development locally and globally, as well as the migration of peoples from third world areas to the Euro/American terrain.

To tell the tale, then, I will start out with an academic anecdote from the United States-Mexican border, a border on the verge of another radical transformation as the goundwork is already being laid out so that the North American Free Trade Agreement may kick into place.[1] A ground was prepared by the establishment of maquiladora shops starting in the early 1960s when the Chicano Movement (1965–1975) was just beginning, and Chicanas were struggling for self-defined positions within it and experiencing exclusion there as well as in the contemporary Women's Movement, whose own momentum was simultaneous with all of these events. Is it ironic coincidence that, simultaneous with the cry of liberation by Euro-American women and minority populations in the United States, the multinationals began the construction of shops whose workers are primarily women, not only on the United States-Mexican border but all over the globe? Certainly for the women working in the maquiladoras under polluted, life-threatening conditions, their quietist and exploited group history dovetails into global shifts in the political economy of the metropolis which places them in a contradictory double bind between necessity and economic "opportunity," which, given the unsafe working conditions, put them at risk. For me, there is a tenuous connection between women working in the actual border shops, who put their lives at risk, and Chicana critics who work an interstitial zone that is constantly on the move, given its structural displacements within the academy. That is, the latter displacements parallel those of the former and remain nonequivalent. Thus, though each lives within different economies of signifying circuits, "we" nevertheless share experiences of dislocation that contribute to cultural productions. Since the emergence of Chicana critics can be traced no further back than about 1965, applying the name retroactively is much like calling Sor Juana Inés de la Cruz a modern woman. Thus, the scenario on the border that opens up the allegory is a necessary step in the travails of the Chicana critic since it implicates both Mexicans and Anglo-Americans in the production of meaning for her. Such a critic, who could only take shape through this fabulous construction, is a paradigmatic woman of multiple incarnations. The construction aims to situate the Chicana critic in the locus of *la différend,* the site of a conflict, collision, or contest opposed to judicial litigation, or (constitutional) law, indeed opposed to anything that presupposes for its interpretation an inherent monological rationality. My contention is that heretofore the Chicana critic has not taken account of her insider/outsider/insider status with respect to multiple discourse structures, some of which cannot easily be translated into each other.[2] To pursue the nexus or intersectionality of the multiple discourse structures that surround the Chicana critic is in a sense to come to terms with the modes through which her disappearance is constantly promoted through the speech of others no matter how unintentional, and against which she struggles through counter- and disidentificatory discourses. In the process one may come to terms on theoretical grounds with how the speech of the bordershop worker may be drowned out, so that one may then ask the purposefully naive question, "Can the subaltern speak?"[3] The struggle is for histories actual and imaginary that give substance and provide an account of her position within culture and the political economy.

Scenario on the Border: (Dis)identifying the Players

At a recent conference in the Mexican border city of Tijuana, two women—as it happened, one Anglo-American and the other European—presented, sequentially, Spanish-language written papers on the same work—*Querido Diego, te abraza quiela* by the Mexican-Polish writer Elena Poniatowska. Poniatowska grew up speaking French and Spanish—French as the preferred language of the Polish aristocracy and Spanish as a result of her Mexican upbringing and education. The audience included Poniatowska herself, a handful of Chicanas—some of whom fully understood Spanish, others not—a few Anglo-American scholars who pursue Spanish-language literary studies, and local community women, who fully understood Spanish but not the interpretive apparatus. The rest of the audience were Mexican women who were literary scholars and intellectuals from the Colegio de México, a co-sponsor of the conference with the Colegio de la Frontera Norte. As you may anticipate, given the diverse social identities and their discursive formations, the potential for cross-purposed misdialogue and misrecognition was rife. I cannot pursue the ramifications for each player, but I will attempt them for Chicanas, most of whom were actually critics or writers. Theoretically the various players could, if they so desired, place themselves in the nodal point of *la différend*. However, I would guarantee a different outcome for each. It is my intention to be as impartial as possible, especially insofar as the Chicana critic does not have a "word to her name" except the proprietary claim to the term of recent recodification—Chicana.[4] On the other hand, to center the inquiry through the term Chicana already bespeaks bias. As such she is, like most women of color in the United States, a recent arrival on the stage of the Western critical (mostly male) tradition. This is not to say that she does not claim female ancestors; however, they cannot be said to exist at the interstice and intersection of the multiple discourses that give shape to the Modern and Postmodern, which cannot be assumed to be sequential either, but to be implicitly or explicitly interreferential.

On the San Diego-Tijuana border, the two speakers presented completely different interpretations of Quiela, the writer of the letters addressed to Diego (Rivera) that represent the fictive textualization of a historically real Russian-born artist's ill-fated romantic attachment to Diego Rivera. The Anglo-American critic interpreted the letters as an instance of the social production of female oppression based on the account given in the text of Quiela's experiences, which would ultimately silence her but for Poniatowska's intervention. The European critic interpreted the letters as an instance of the symbolic construction of femininity, a near-perfect sample of a quietist *écriture féminine*.[5] The first interpretation was motivated by a sociopolitical desire to demonstrate that Quiela's inequality, overdetermined gender identity, and experience are so negative that no sane woman should want to assume such a position, a calculated move to put the romantic in crisis and lead listeners to disidentification with Quiela. The second interpretation was motivated by an aestheticist textual desire to demonstrate Quiela's elegantly constructed pathos, a phallocratic production of femininity and its correlative embodiment. The first interpreter insisted on a heterosexist social referentiality that called for political positions beyond the text, while the second insisted on a self-referential (inter)textuality, which nonetheless appealed to the audience to share in the work's aesthetic pathos. The first was firmly embedded in the liberal self-other experiential paradigms of some Anglo-American bourgeois feminist theories which, though still historically interesting, are not complex enough to explain our diverse sociosymbolic formations, positionalities, or heterogenous histories; the second was embedded in French feminist appropriations of crosshatched Derridean-Lacanian deconstructive practices which, though also important theoretical contributions, remain a self-sufficient system, difficult to transpose and map onto sociosymbolic formations outside the bourgeois Eurocentric intellectual tradition, though the possibility of resonance with the non-European is not neccesarily precluded. The "new" feminist "identity politics" of women of color forged through a "politics of cultural difference" that have emerged and developed since World War II require multiple theoretical and paradigmatic conjunctions that only now are beginning to be addressed. However, I will elaborate this below as I return to the allegory of "the" Chicana critic who configures in part such conjunctions.

The interpreters, who were clearly fully invested in their respective positions, were unable to negotiate a passage between themselves, though they both had a clear claim to the literary discipline. When both finished, the silence in the room was stunning. Since neither the audience nor the presenters was forthcoming with questions or responses; Poniatowska herself was asked to comment on the interpretations of her work. Were those her intentions? Did either or both critics hit upon the meaning of the work? Poniatowska, who is the contemporary champion of the silenced in Mexico, in fact giving voice to a forgotten Russian artist, and who feels that if the sociopolitically oppressed are silenced someone must intervene for them, refused to comment on the grounds that the work in question is too close to her. The work was a vehicle for the exploration and displacement of one of her intimate personas. Since Chicanas had been explicitly invited to the conference with the aim of building bridges with Mexicanas, and one kept waiting for dialogue to take place, I for one wondered how it ever could under the circumstances. Further, if for argument's sake anyone was looking for some sort of Mexican social identity and experience in the work, or a Mexican interpretation of it, and she had asked, she would have been taken for a fool. The only things Mexican there were the border, constructed and reconstructed as it rubs against/with the United States; a large portion of the silenced audience who carried Mexican passports in case they wanted to cross to the United States; Chicanas who carried proper identification not so much to enter Mexico as to return to the United States; and Diego Rivera, the recipient of Quiela's letters. That is, texts and cultural productions may cross borders, but some people risk arrest without *señas de identidad* (signs of identity), to quote the title of a Spanish novel published in Franco's Spain. People may be more closely tied—whether they want to or not—to nationally conferred identities than some texts. The fact that one needs "signs of identity" should tip us off to the requirements of subordination to the nation-state that (non)citizens must comply with and the fact that the inside/outside/inside occupied by Chicanas is not just symbolic but sociopolitical as well, regardless of the documentation status, since the Immigration and Naturalization Service may not wait for it. Racism (or the particular historical constructions of Mexicanness) makes her subject to a constant demand for the production (proof) of "ethnic" identity and citizenship in both Mexico and the United States. Placing her in continuous movement from inside/outside/inside, as I have stated.

Since the interpreters had given us divergent interpretations of the sociosymbolic formation of femininity based not only on work widely recognized as Mexican, but based on letters addressed to a Mexican, to ask what any of it had to do with a Mexican identity and experience was to risk being seen as an ignorant déclassé given to excessive referential quibbling and maybe even essentializing, which ironically drew one nearer to the Anglo-American than the European with whom most of the Mexicanas sympathized, apparently because the former was too "aggressive" (read too "anti-men"). And yet there is that documentation required by law burning a hole in one's pocket and the knowledge that the aim of the conference was to clarify the proximity or overlap between Mexicanas and Chicanas through literature, our "medium," though apparently the organizers took the meaning of "magical" mediations as the primary meaning of medium. It became increasingly clear that there was no productive strategy for effecting the avowed goals of the Mexicanas, and frankly it reminded one of the National Women's Studies Association, where the organizers often feel that if you have a "caucus" you are participating. Here, if you had a Chicana literature panel that was participation. For me, however, this particular event marked the collapse of the enterprise. Indeed the major accomplishment was one that most Chicanas already knew of, and that was the marked class differences between us— Mexicanas and Chicanas. Also, it would appear that it was such class differences that might draw Chicanas closer to the Anglo-American who did not deny historical socioreferentiality, thus opening up the possibility of addressing class positions; while the taboo of referentiality in the other interpretive system made it impossible even to speak of Quiela and Poniatowska as entities formed through cultural emblems drawn from a different aesthetic.

Such recognized differences make a difference in the constellation and concatenation of texts and critical tools. As in the case of African American women, as Hortense Spillers notes, Chicanas "maintain no allegiances to a strategic formation of texts," which further draws them to a "logological" (textually Eurologocentric) feminist discourse. In fact the Euro-American "process of aligning with prior acts of the text [is] the subtle component of power that bars . . . women of color as a proper subject of inquiry from the various topics of contemporary feminist discourse."[6] That is, the Euro-American canon formations demand privileged priority over the inquiries of women of color, a fact which may lead to contradiction, contestation, deconstruction, resistance, disidentification, or the production of alternative discursive practices. My claim, however, goes further to include the critical speaker who is positioned by that "subtle component of power" as a nonspeaker (a silent subaltern) because the privileged linguistic practices cannot hear, translate, or transcode (with a residue of nonequivalence) what is said.

In any case, the disjunction between purported aims and expectations and the actual events contributed to the increasing gap between Mexicanas and Chicanas, which resulted in our marginalization and silence. We became spectators to a textual performative that claimed to incorporate us. Could it be that such interstices are potential sites for the actual productive and bridging dialogues? In this particular scenario the only speech possible was to remark on the discursive weave, which did not afford an opportunity for a positive Chicana intervention. Thus Chicanas were placed in a negative position whereby, if they had wanted to speak, it would have been to note their exclusion from an event that supposedly included them in the conference's goals, most certainly its title—*Mujer y literatura mexicana y chicana: Culturas en contacto.*[7] In the end, Poniatowska herself intervened by stating that when it came to feminist activism, the Mexicanas were *mosquitas muertas* (loosely translated, wallflowers), which angered her countrywomen no end. To this day, she told me recently, some of those who were there do not speak to her.

The exchange between Chicanas and Mexicanas does not appear at this time to be as extensive as one might expect. Bourgeois Mexicanas in general tend to find distasteful an identification with their "prole" kin, who are not *gente decente,* the "customary" epithet through which raced-class positions are segregated in Hispanic societies. Few upper-class Latin American women would admit to being a colleague to someone who could have been the household maid but for the grace of a monitoring education in the United States. And now the woman who could have been their maid talks back, often with a class-inflected speech, and has gone the way of many maids in Latin America, to the maquiladoras scattered all over the continent, and not just on the United States-Mexican border.

Speaking in Tongues: Cruising the Academy

Most Chicana critics are likely to come in contact with Anglo-American critics who have learned to pretend to some extent that this is a classless society where economic conditions heretofore, at least since World War II, have enabled a pretense that now begins to crumble.[8] Within the Anglo-American context, then, Chicana critics are often subtly but forcefully compelled to choose between the Anglo-American and the European interpreters characterized above. Moreover, it becomes increasingly apparent that there is an implicit "two-class theory" in the practitioners of the approaches, not so much because each is inherently of a different class so much as the fact that the Europeans recognize class divisions and the Anglo-Americans "bracket" them. It is often the institutionalized prerogative of both the Anglo-American and the European to decide where we belong, which may foreclose almost all possibilities for self-propelled inquiry on the part of Chicanas.

In effect, these maneuvers recall the old "add and stir" method that a previous generation of Euro-American feminists protested and have successfully contested, thus radically changing the "cognitive map" of feminism and Women's Studies. Since each practitioner of the critical discourses in question is more interested in strengthening her position than bridging the disparate discourses, there are no adequate sources to aid the observer/reader in negotiating, not necessarily resolving, their paradoxes and contradictions. Moreover, more often than not, our students are taught those positions in isolation from each other. If the Chicanas call for a change of critical discourse so that our text may be included in a more dialogized fashion than is possible within the containing "add and stir" method, we may be told to go to Ethnic Studies.

If there is an Ethnic/Chicano Studies Program and Chicanas take refuge there, we may be compelled to historicize (following a male-head-of-household genealogical story) and sociologize (quantitative empiricism) our text into the "raced masculine model" at the expense of whatever feminist insight we may have had, as there too there is an "add and stir" containment. If there is no Ethnic/Chicano Studies Program, a Chicana may get bounced around between the Spanish and English departments, where she may not be better off than before, since at this time it is a toss up as to who can silence most. The tendency of many departments is to neocolonize rather than enable critical thinking on her part, which would mean providing the pedagogical conditions for her speaking intervention and for exercising her interpretive agency. A Chicana critic may be inside studying and teaching, but outside the legitimate curricular mission of the department. If, as a feminist, she decides to insist on taking refuge in a Women's Studies Program, she may once again be faced with the cited interpreters of the text who are indeed sympathetic to her pathos and her unbelievable oppression. Yes, they'd be happy to take her text but not her, except as a seasonal worker. On the other hand, she may be glad to learn that her text is already in the curriculum—feminist sociology, anthropology, or regional history—all of which claim their own inherent rationality. Her feminist critical voice may be muted, but she is now (through the text) part of a guided international tour.

Indeed, taking the long view since the emergence of Chicana critics in the 1960s, after a decade or more of carrying "our text" around looking for a home for both of them, a Chicana critic may realize that she has become typed in one or both of two ways: (1) she is a minority woman narcissistically obsessed with herself through her text; (2) she is a wonderful resource. To employ some Marxist and Freudian vocabulary for a moment, in the first instance she is being so particularistic as to have no use-value; in the second instance she returns as a sample of the repressed and oppressed, and her use-value is theoretically reinstated. Thus, in the first instance she is erased from the scene even as her text accrues exchange value because pluralism and diversity are more simply satisfied with texts than with actual people. Since her text has acquired exchange value through the 1970s, in the 1980s another generation of Chicana critics emerges, even as the previous ones have disappeared. In the 1990s the successors of those from the 1970s and 1980s, plus a new crop of writers, are now often seasonally employed, joining the ranks of migrant/segmented, albeit intellectual, labor.

Aside from the fact that the successors have acquired a great deal more book knowledge, we may well wonder how our lot has changed from that of our parents or grandparents, who actually were migrant field or segmented manufacturing laborers. Successors should not completely despair, though, for at this juncture we have also acquired many kin in the Third World, where intellectuals travel around various schools and universities in order to make a living. This is not so much a misery-loves-company interpretation as perhaps a reminder that within the United States we are viewed in similar fashion to Third World intellectuals, inside/outside/inside, and it is worthwhile to investigate the ground of such views. Yet I do not speak of just any Third World intellectuals, as my discussion of Mexicanas should have demonstrated, but a genealogy of writers and thinkers who have been or are engaged in contestatory inquiry rather than sheer mimicry, though the latter should be identified as well. The Chicana critic is now, and perhaps has always been, positioned as a Third World intellectual, as are Mexicanas, and it was being inside the United States that has led her to (mis)recognize the position. That is, if upper-class Mexicanas favor "quietist" European interpretive theories over Anglo-American ones, which may align them away from Chicanas, through her status in the United States academy, the Chicana critic is repositioned as Third World intellectual, thus realigning her from another angle with the Mexicanas. In other words, boundary crossing has been largely a mental exercise because our *señas de identidad* are inappropriately embodied; that is, the very rage at our embodied history as Chicanas can find no adequate "inherently rational" (monological), in Spillers's terms "logological," discourse with which to sweep up the letters of her name. Moreover, the social contradictions at work cannot be easily overcome through symbolic representation at conferences.

If a Chicana critic has had time to meditate about her lot, she now realizes that the only thing she might have had was her version of the (socio) text, and not the text itself. It is plain to see, if she is still on the fringes of the academy, that the text she thought was hers may be claimed by everyone. Thus, without having read Saussure, Derrida, Foucault, Lacan, or even Marx, she has discovered that the text/signifier is a commodity, and almost from the beginning she was a "signifying problem" rather than a participant of the "political economy of the signifier." If for some bizarre reason she still harbors an attachment to her text, she now keeps it a secret, lest she once again show her déclassé status by identifying too closely with it—you, so the accusation went last time she mentioned her attachment, are essentializing, as the version of the text you've hung onto demonstrates. Essentializing is back, however, as the new journal *Differences* proclaims, so she can essentialize again, but she had better watch her mouth, for it is only permissible as a rhetorical strategy.[9] In fact, of course, many of use are déclassé, but it's best not to show it, except theoretically.

My no-win narrative of/for Chicana critics and our text is what Bateson, in *Steps To An Ecology Of Mind,* called the double-bind.[10] Since the term has been popularized, it is hard to remember that it is the kind of bind that actually produces psychosis. Most people, as Bateson notes, will do anything to escape the double-bind, or they risk psychosis, at which point psychoanalysis is of no use whatsoever. His solution for escaping the double-bind is to proceed to a higher epistemological or metanarrative ground; however, I think that one must discern and unravel the double-binds that cross our path, since our path is culturally, politically, and economically located such that we live out the double-binding *différend* effect, and such junctures help us identify contradictory practices that require transformation. Moreover, there is no "talk cure" for psychosis. By the time a person is indeed psychotic, a protective wall has been erected that no one can talk themselves through—neither the one "inside" nor the one "outside"—except that in the United States it is very difficult to tell what's inside and what's outside because we all share the same political boundary rights, or so we are told. Here again, we are in good company. Because of colonialism and the multinationals' international division of labor, a lot of the Third World cannot tell what's inside and what's outside either, as selected discourses, processes, and procedures cross borders with capitalist bureaucratic structures. As the Chicana poet Lorna D. Cervantes has remarked in conversation, criticism is not enough to assist us out of a critical situation, yet it is often necessary to its clarification.

Survivalists have had at least three options. The first is the Richard Rodríguez option, whereby one can affirm that "the child who learns to read about his nonliterate ancestors necessarily separates himself from their way of life."[11] Many people experience this as an incontrovertible force that calls for abandonment, as obviously he did. Today, paradoxically, he finds himself writing about the successor ancestors and makes his living writing about *los pobres*. They are, however, now at a safe distance as some reductive version of the nonliterate other. Thus, he preserves his psychic well-being by denying his metonymic relationship to the others while simultaneously affirming it through his brand of journalistic transliterations, and by offering us an oversimplified but coherent story. The second is the orthodox Marxist option, where we could join the generic class struggle and change the subject, or forget the subject as well as forget the raced cultural history of the group. This version of the déclassé has invited us to view the "marginalized" as some monolith without any clue with regard to the social formation or the conditions of our existence nor recognition of our protestations along the way. The third is the resource option already mentioned, except that in the late 1980s and probably in the decade ahead, some may obtain, as a result of the success of our differential text and pluralism, a nonmigratory position, albeit segmented. (The "segmentation" could be turned into a less fractured account if the academy in general were supportive of (feminist) cultural studies; however, the disciplined departmental investment continues to dominate.)

If past generations of Chicana critics still desire to stage a comeback, we may discover that our "essentializing" obsolescence has returned under a new market-commodified value that has opened up what Trinh T. Minh-ha calls "planned authenticity." She explains, "as a product of hegemony and a re-

markable counterpart of universal standardization, it constitutes an effica-
cious means of silencing the cry of racial oppression." That is to say, the
minoritized are granted voice as long as they speak as "authenticators" of
cultural experiences without pursuing the dialectical reconfiguration of knowledge production vis-a-vis the "other" (dominant). Anglo-Europeans now tell
us, "We no longer wish to erase your difference. We demand, on the contrary,
that you remember and assert it. At least, to a certain extent."[12] What extent?
Here again, the Chicana critic is on dangerous ground. How much difference
is enough? Let's say she decides to risk, and in the parlance of today take the
"window of opportunity" that has opened up to her. Since conferences today
are often clearly staged events, perhaps even "minoritizing" spectacles,
commodified shows, our older Chicana critic may coincide in the same panel
with her younger "sister"; the younger critic, unlike herself, has been
schooled in representation, thematization of othering, and textual difference
focusing on the constructed nature of identity, while the older critic may
continue to "essentialize" social difference. In a sense we are back in Tijuana,
though our critics are no longer Anglo-American or European. They are us,
and we find ourselves unable to speak with each other even in theory.

Moving On: Subjects-in-Process

In theory, the perils of this fabulous Chicana critic are endless because, as
Cornel West would say, a monitorized intellectual who tries to work with and
on the same terms as the dominant/dominating is always on the defensive or, I
would add, such an intellectual may already be bidding to occupy a dominant/
dominating pose.[13] In fact, our relationship to the hegemonic political economy, institutions, and the symbolic order has always been asymmetrical,
though we are purportedly assured juridical symmetry, i.e., equality. However, as Rosaura Sánchez points out, the terms of the boundaries can be
reduced or extended to include us or exclude us by processes and manipula-
tions beyond our control. At this juncture we all discover, as Sánchez suggests, that we do not possess much of our identity, difference, or experience
because some of these are fixed elsewhere; that is, they are not as self-
determined as one may pretend, but fixed by political and economic agendas
and stereotyping public policies as well as by texts.[14] Resistance through self-
determined identity formations, in effect, is a powerful force often doused by
official (legalistic) maneuvers, commodifying discourses, and the mass media,
which keep themselves busy producing, erasing, modifying, and transcoding
identities. Precisely because there is a continous drive for hegemonic containment toward a stasis that assures its control, resistance movements cannot
afford to let up the pressure. If some of this sounds familiar to theory buffs, I
want to emphasize that most of us learn this "in the flesh," as social movements continually testify. It is for this reason, for example, that the Chicana
poet Lorna D. Cervantes can say that (proto) deconstruction is the social
modus operandi—not just the textual theory—of the politically marginalized/

excluded, which, I would add, generates the "politics of difference" as initially sketched out by Audre Lorde.[15]

The desire for critical agency on the part of Chicana critics and writers presupposes subjects-in-process who construct provisional (self-determining) "identities"[16] that subsume a network of discursive and signifying practices and experiences imbricated in both the historical and imaginary shifting national borders of Mexico and the United States. A subject-insertion into such a geographical economy and politics presupposes not only specific historical sociosymbolic texts, but a situated contemporaneous horizon of meanings and intentions that swerve away from those produced and enunciated by Euro-Americans and Europeans, especially when the latter produce hegemonic structures and discourses of containment. Identity formations through differentially theorized experience—in this instance, through the term Chicana, thus signaling a historically raced/gendered/class position forged through the interstices of two nation-states—proposes a subject-in-process. Such a subject-in-process is desirous of self-determination, yet is "traversed through and through the world and by others. . . . It is the active and lucid agency that constantly reorganizes its contents, through the help of these same contents, that produces by means of a material and in relation to needs and ideas, all of which are themselves mixtures of what it has already found there before it and what it has produced itself."[17] Through the speaking critical subject-in-process, cultural production reintroduces what was there before in new and dynamic combinatory transculturations. A bi- or multiethnicized, raced, and gendered subject-in-process may be called upon to take up diverse subject positions that cannot be "unified" without double-binds and contradictions. Indeed, what binds the subject positions together is precisely the difference from the perceived hegemony. The contradictions between subject positions move the subject to recognize, reorganize, reconstruct, and exploit difference through political resistance and cultural productions, and to see herself "in-process."[18] It is not a matter of doing away with "the discourse of the other" (whomever or whatever the other, hegemonic or not, is) "because the other is in each case present in the activity that eliminates [it]."[19] The traces of a process of elimination (however unintended) may construct the subject as much as the efforts to incorporate. A critical subject-in-process who reorganizes "contents" upon the demands of the contingent historicopolitical moment may discover that it is in the inaugural transitional moment from being traversed to reconfiguration that the political intention, as well as the combinatory transculturating, takes place. Through such "moments," one can discover diverse cultural narrative formations, translations, and transcodifications that generate texts which are "hybrid" or "syncretic," and far from wanting to remain at rest in that taxonomy, make a bid for new discourse formations, bringing into view new subjects-in-process. In Gloria Anzaldúa's terms, these are the "borderlands"[20] through which the border "theory circuits" of geopolitics and critical allegories find resonance but the zones of figurations and conceptualizations remain nonequivalent. That is, the very contingent currents through which the geopolitical subject-in-process is dislocated, forced into (im)migration, will retain an irreducible difference that refuses to neatly correspond to the criticodiscursive dislocated subject-in-process.

It is my hope that through the writing of this essay, I have presented to the reader an exemplum, a practice, and a theory of the speaking subject-in-process, who in this instance stands in as a Chicana critic positioned in the interstice between nation-states.

NOTES

1. See Vicki L. Ruiz and Susan Tiano, eds. *Women on the U.S.-Mexico Border: Responses to Change.* Boston: Allen & Unwin, 1987; M. Patricia Fernández Kelly and Anna M. García, "Invisible Amidst the Glitter: Hispanic Women in the Southern California Electronics Industry," in A. Stathram, Eleanor M. Miller, and Hans O. Mauksch, eds. *The Worth of Women's Work: A Qualitative Synthesis.* New York: State U of New York P, 1988; 265–89.

2. Jean-François, Lyotard. *The Différend: Phrases in Dispute.* Trans. Georges Van den Abbeele. Minneapolis, U of Minnesota P, 1988; 9–10.

3. Allusion to Gayatri C. Spivak's "Can the Subaltern Speak?" In Cary Nelson and Lawrence Grossberg, eds. *Marxism and the Interpretation of Culture.* Urbana: U of Illinois P, 1988; 271–313.

4. See Norma Alarcón, "Chicana Feminism: In the Tracks of 'the' Native Woman," *Cultural Studies,* 4:3(1990), 248–56.

5. Toril Moi, *Sexual/Textual Politics: Feminist Literary Theory.* London: Methuen, 1985. By citing Moi, I do not mean to endorse her typology vis-à-vis the Anglo-Americans and the French, let alone her characterization of lesbians and U.S. women of color; rather, I refer the reader to a readily available bibliography.

6. Hortense Spillers, "Interstices: A Small Drama of Words," in Carole S. Vance, ed., *Pleasure and Danger: Exploring Female Sexuality.* London: Pandora, 1989; 80, 89.

7. The most recent anthology printed as a result of these conferences is Aralia López-González, Amelia Malagamba and Elena Urrutia, eds. *Mujer y literatura mexicana y chicana: Culturas en contacto, 2.* México: El Colegio de México/Colegio de la Frontera Norte, 1990.

8. Mike Davis, *Prisoners of the American Dream.* London: Verso, 1986.

9. See *Differences,* 1 (Summer 1989).

10. See Gregory Bateson, *Steps to an Ecology of Mind.* New York: Ballantine, 1972.

11. Richard Rodríguez, *Hunger of Memory: The Education of Richard Rodríguez.* New York: Bantam, 1988; 169.

12. Trinh T. Minh-ha, *Woman/Native/Other.* Bloomington: Indiana U P, 1989; 89.

13. Cornel West, "The Dilemma of the Black Intellectual," *Cultural Critique,* 1 (Fall 1985), 109–24.

14. Rosaura Sánchez, "Ethnicity, Ideology and Academia," *Cultural Studies,* 4:3(1990), 294–302.

15. Audre Lorde, "The Master's Tools Will Never Dismantle the Master's House," in Cherríe Moraga and Gloria Anzaldúa, eds. *This Bridge Called My Back: Writings by Radical Women of Color.* Boston: Persephone Press, 1981; 98–106.

16. Commenting on the shift that the notion of identity has undergone in women's discourses, Trinh T. Minh-ha claims in *Woman/Native/Other* that the shift does not lead to "a theory of female identity" but rather "to identity as points of re-departure of the critical processes by which I have come to understand how the personal—the ethnic me, the female me—is political" (p. 104).

17. Cornelius Castoriadis, *The Imaginary Institution of Society*. Translated by Kathleen Blamey. Cambridge: The MIT Press, 1987; 106.

18. The notion subject-in-process (on-trial/in-question) was first introduced by Julia Kristeva to refer to the double identitarian status of the speaking subject vis-a-vis the law on the one hand and, on the other, the transformative and unsettling movements she undergoes in writing, in culture, as agent vis-a-vis her place in the symbolic order. See, for example, *Desire in Language: A Semiotic Approach to Literature and Art*. Edited by Leon S. Roudiez. Translated by Thomas Gora, Alice Jardine, and Leon S. Roudiez. New York: Columbia U P, 1980; 17–19.

19. Castoriadis, 107.

20. Gloria Anzaldúa, *Borderlands/La Frontera: The New Mestiza*. San Francisco: Spinsters/Aunt Lute, 1987.

WORKS CITED

Alarcón, Norma. "Chicana Feminism: In the Tracks of 'the' Native Woman." *Cultural Studies* 4:3(1990), 248–56.

Anzaldúa, Gloria. *Borderlands/La Frontera: The New Mestiza*. San Francisco: Spinsters/Aunt Lute, 1987.

Bateson, Gregory. *Steps to an Ecology of Mind*. New York: Ballantine, 1972.

Castoriadis, Cornelius. *The Imaginary Institution of Society*. Translated by Kathleen Blamey. Cambridge: The MIT Press, 1987.

Davis, Mike. *Prisoners of the American Dream*. London: Verso, 1986.

Differences, 1 (Summer 1989).

Fernández-Kelly, M. Patricia, and Anna M. García. "Invisible Amidst the Glitter: Hispanic Women in the Southern California Electronics Industry." In A. Stathram, Eleanor M. Miller, and Hans O. Mauksch, eds., *The Worth of Women's Work: A Qualitative Synthesis*. New York: State U of New York P, 1988; 265–89.

Kristeva, Julia. *Desire in Language: A Semiotic Approach to Literature and Art*. Ed. Leon S. Roudiez. Translated by Thomas Gora, Alice Jardine, and Leon Roudiez. New York: Columbia UP, 1980.

López-González, Aralia, Amelia Malagamba, and Elena Urrutia, eds. *Mujer y literatura mexicana y chicana: Culturas en contacto, 2*. México: El Colegio de México/Colegio de la Frontera Norte, 1990.

Lorde, Audre. "The Master's Tools Will Never Dismantle the Master's House." In Cherríe Moraga and Gloria Anzaldúa, eds., *This Bridge Called My Back: Writings by Radical Women of Color*. Boston: Persephone Press, 1981, 98–106.

Lyotard, Jean-Françoise. *The Différend: Phrases in Dispute*. Translated by Georges Van den Abbeele. Minneapolis: U of Minnesota P, 1988.

Moi, Toril. *Sexual/Textual Politics: Feminist Literary Theory*. London: Methuen, 1985.

Poniatowska, Elena. *Querido Diego, te abraza quiela*. Mexico: Biblioteca Era, 1978.

Rodríguez, Richard. *Hunger of Memory: The Education of Richard Rodríguez*. New York: Bantam Books, 1988.

Ruiz, Vicki L., and Susan Tiano, eds. *Women on the U.S.—Mexico Border: Responses to Change.* Boston: Allen & Unwin, 1987.

Sánchez, Rosaura. "Ethnicity, Ideology and Academia." *Cultural Studies* 4:3(1990), 294–302.

Spillers, Hortense. "Interstices: A Small Drama of Words." In Carole S. Vance, ed., *Pleasure and Danger: Exploring Female Sexuality.* London: Pandora, 1989.

Spivak, Gayatri C. "Can the Subaltern Speak?" In Cary Nelson and Lawrence Grossberg, eds., *Marxism and the Interpretation of Culture.* Urbana: U of Illinois P, 1988; 271–313.

Trinh T. Minh-ha. *Woman/Native/Other.* Bloomington: Indiana UP, 1989.

West, Cornel. "The Dilemma of the Black Intellectual." *Cultural Critique,* 1 (Fall 1985), 109–24.

Silences in the In-Between: Feminist Women Critics and the Canon

JUDITH L. SENSIBAR AND
JUDITH BRYANT WITTENBERG

In an article entitled "Feminism and Faulkner: Second Thoughts," Minrose Gwin asked "whether feminists who do feminist criticism should do it with texts of canonical male writers" and, specifically, whether "we as feminist readers benefit from reading Faulkner" (Gwin 1991). While Gwin noted that her own 1990 study, *The Feminine and Faulkner,* read Faulkner as a writer who has much to teach us about the ways in which women are silenced and about the workings of power and dominance, she nevertheless questioned the "authenticity" of his female characters and concluded that feminist readers looking for depictions of female growth and development and for "authentic female subjectivity" must turn to the work of women writers. Gwin's provocative questions form the starting point of this essay. Although our conclusions differ from hers, we, too, as feminist critics who work on Faulkner, are pondering these questions in an attempt to come to terms with our own uneasiness as to whether we have—or ever will have—reconciled our feminism with the implications of having concentrated for more than a decade on a writer often regarded as one of the most misogynist figures among those creators of what Judith Fetterley calls "the masculine wilderness of the American novel" (viii). Any woman working on Faulkner—and the feminist woman Faulkner critic in particular—confronts a particularly vexing set of problems and doubts. We realize that many of these problems and doubts are similar to those faced by women working elsewhere in the challenging "masculine wilderness" of the American canon.[1]

Here we want to explore the persistent problems—in particular the various modes of silencing—confronted both by women critics in general and by feminist women critics who work in and on the male canon. As our evidence we draw on experiences—our own and those of other women scholars at colleges and universities in the United States whom we interviewed. We do not, however, by any means claim to speak for all women working on canonical male writers, and we are also aware of the hazards of seeming to essentialize a complex issue. Moreover, the two of us speaking here, like nearly all the others we interviewed and invoke, have in no profound sense been silenced and have no wish to claim victim status—we are tenured, promoted, and published—and we realize that many more female critical voices can now

be heard than in the fairly recent past. Nevertheless, at times we have faced
the prospect of silencing—of being silenced or of silencing ourselves. Often
we find ourselves tense, and not always in productive ways. We experience
this tension in our formal engagements with the fiction we critique, in our
classrooms, on both personal and ideological levels within the community of
Faulkner scholars, with feminists in the larger academic community, and
within our own predominantly white male departments. We do not always
proceed with certainty that our voices are being heard, or heard accurately.
Indeed, even to raise the issue of threatened silences is to experience uneasiness: there is the fear of appearing to complain unnecessarily; even worse, of
seeming to speak irrationally, *like a woman.*

Recognizing that our (separate and joint) predicaments have some facets
that are clearly visible and even quantifiable, others that are more subtle and
thus more difficult to articulate, we nonetheless feel it imperative to attempt
an elucidation, to speak from the somewhat murky realms in which we often
feel ourselves and our work to be positioned. To be sure, some of the murki-
ness of our particular positions arises from the nature of the work we have
done on Faulkner, some of which could be considered gender-neutral; it has
included psychoanalytic, textual, bibliographic, and source studies as well as
feminist criticism.[2] Yet we have increasingly realized that many of the challenges we face both externally and internally are not only gender-based but
are also confronted by other women who do comparable work.

The most apparent problem we and other feminists working on canonical
male writers confront is the threat of silencing from without. It may well be, as
some have argued, that feminist critics contribute creative tension to a primarily male community such as the Faulkner field, usefully providing voices that
speak difference. Yet it is equally true, as Gwin notes, that as women and as
feminists we are "inevitably positioned outside the dominant discourse of this
community" because "the politics of Faulkner criticism is male politics; the
discourse of Faulkner criticism is male discourse" (1991). The majority of
Faulkner critics are male, particularly those who publish regularly (approximately 75 percent of the Faulkner entries in three recent MLA bibliographies
[1987, 1988, 1989] were authored by men,[3] despite the numbers of women
working in the field, as evidenced by their membership in the Faulkner Society). The woman critic often has difficulty in finding both a language of her
own and a literal space in which to speak. One of our senior female colleagues
described the situation in extreme terms when she said, "There is no support
or encouragement for women or minorities in Faulkner studies." This situation is not unique to Faulkner criticism, as exemplified by a recent issue of
PMLA (106:2 [March 1991]), whose "Cluster on Modern Fiction" included
four articles by male critics on male writers, introduced by a man.

The implications of this silencing are practical as well as theoretical. Because, as Dale Bauer points out, critical communities exercise their power by
the threat of exclusion, and thus inclusion requires playing by the rules of the
dominant group (xi), the feminist critic has the likely potential of being an
outsider, completely or partially excluded when invitations to join panels or

editorial boards are extended. Thus, in the Faulkner field, although close to forty percent of the Faulkner Society (the membership of which includes virtually all scholars whose primary publications are on the author) are female, until 1993 the editor and entire editorial board of the *Faulkner Journal* have been male; women served as "editorial consultants." The individuals selected to reedit the Faulkner novels for Random House, for Library of America, or for the Norton critical editions, or to prepare the concordances and to publish the Faulkner letters and manuscript facsimiles are almost exclusively male.[4] Invitations to deliver papers at the annual week-long Faulkner conference held in his hometown of Oxford, Mississippi, go out each year to eight or nine scholars, rarely more than one of whom is a woman; other women win places on the program by submitting their papers to a competition. As of 1993, women occupied just 20 percent of the spaces on the program. And invitations to the biannual international Faulkner symposium held in such locations as Paris, Tokyo, Bonn, Rome, and Vienna are regularly issued to eight or nine American scholars, almost never more than one of them a woman. Under these circumstances, such invitations present a dilemma. To accept is to accede to tokenism; to decline is to be silenced.

Admittedly, both of us have received and accepted some of these token invitations. And the situation is to some degree a result of the fact that men dominated the field in the early years and then tended to support primarily male protegés. Still, the proportions are inappropriately skewed; in 1979, the year we both first published on Faulkner, about 30 percent of the Faulkner publications listed in the *MLA Bibliography* were by women, which might suggest that by 1991 30 percent of scholarly invitations would be issued to women. Obviously, this is not the case. These facts, especially considered in light of the increasing feminist activity and growing visibility of female Faulknerians during the past ten years, make clear that the gender proportions of these invitations should be reappraised by those in positions of authority. The relative exclusion of women scholars from the most public and privileged activities in the Faulkner field may be to some degree a matter of historical accident rather than a strategy consciously propagated, but it has become noticeable, and, for those women who have been excluded, both personally annoying and professionally deleterious. The relative lack of public recognition of women Faulkner critics eerily recalls that of women writers disclosed by Tillie Olsen's 1971 inventory, which revealed that although women were publishing about 20 percent of the books, only 8 percent of them were accorded recognition in book reviews, course lists, and anthologies (24, 28). Given the twenty-year time lapse, the increased number of women in graduate schools and in Faulkner studies, and the ascendancy of feminist criticism during those years, the situation in the Faulkner field seems particularly shocking.

Moreover, evidence of similar silencing is apparent elsewhere in American literary scholarship on male canonical authors: the gender composition of panels at the two Thoreau Society conferences held in the summer of 1991 was, at the first, merely one-tenth women, at the second, less than one-fifth; at the 1992 *Arizona Quarterly* Symposium on American Literature and Culture, one-fourth of the speakers were women; and just one woman was included among the speakers at the 1992 conference on Whitman. There are reports of attempts to make some events even more exclusionary; it has been said that the group planning the 1992 conference for the Society for the Study of Southern Literature proposed a program that included solely male-chaired panels discussing male writers, altering it only after objections from one member (a woman).

At the same time, however, efforts to provide a more typically balanced and gender-inclusive conference program can backfire. A woman who offered a revisionist assessment of James Agee's *Let Us Now Praise Famous Men* at a conference devoted to his work reports being assailed excessively for her irreverence. And a participant in the 1990 international conference on Hemingway (the twentieth-century American writer against whom perhaps even more charges of misogyny are leveled than against Faulkner) noted that, although the meeting represented "progress" in that one-third of the panels were devoted to gender issues in Hemingway and about half of the speakers were women, the predominantly male audience virulently attacked several papers presented by women because they saw them as maligning Hemingway. While some such reaction is predictable, this was reportedly extreme; moreover, versions of these verbal assaults continued at subsequent Hemingway meetings that academic year, apparently going well beyond the limits of acceptable conference dialogue. Clearly, in this realm, even progress has its penalties. Indeed, in their report on antifeminist harassment, the MLA Commission on the Status of Women in the Professions cites "heckling of feminists at conferences" as one of the most commonly reported forms of "silencing" or "intellectual harassment" (*Concerns*, 8).

Another form of exclusion, with distinct *ad feminam* overtones, has been practiced on some women scholars seeking access to the collections of male writers. Both of us have experienced moments that disturbingly reenact the memorable scene in Virginia Woolf's *A Room of One's Own* in which the female persona is denied admission to the Oxbridge library, waved back by a "silvery" gentleman. Some years ago one of us was turned away from the Thomas Hardy collection in Dorset by such a gentleman, despite having been preceded by the appropriate scholarly letters of introduction, additional copies of which were presented at the moment of attempted entry. In this case, it may have been that the combination of gender and nationality was simply too much for the guardian of the collection. More recently, the other of us had a similar experience is this country—too recent to write about at this time. We also know of another woman who, visiting a large collection while completing a biography of one of Faulkner's earliest advocates, was not informed by its male curator of the existence and availability of relevant unpublished materials, including early Faulkner letters, which the curator was then making exclusively available to a male scholar.[5] One senior woman scholar believes that this is a result of the fact that directors of major research libraries are almost all male and often exercise their authority by giving primary and sometimes exclusive access to other members of scholarly male networks.

In these differing ways, the feminist critic working on a canonical male writer tends to confront the muting, if not outright silencing, of her public voice. At the same time, because she has elected to ally herself, however marginally, with the predominantly white male scholarly community, her access to the emerging power structures of gynocriticism is also problematic. Feminist scholars who work on women writers have been publishing and editing the much-needed texts of previously lost or marginalized women, creating new anthologies of writing by women, and setting up panels and conferences that attempt to redefine and expand the canon and validate previously devalued genres such as sentimental poetry or narratives of community. Noting the ways in which the women who work exclusively on women writers have by now developed their own networks and communities, we who concentrate on male writers and also think of ourselves as feminists are vulnerable to feeling occasionally that we have located ourselves in an impossible middle zone between two theoretically and politically antithetical scholarly groups. Moreover, because of the gender politics involved, this constitutes more than simply nonalignment with one of the matrixes of power. One gynocritic queried a woman about a talk she had given on James Fenimore Cooper's representation of women and Indians in such a way as to make clear that the questioner believed it was simply not possible to offer critiques of a male author that are fully, credibly feminist. This response to the reading of Cooper echoes aspects of Josephine Donovan's assertion that "[t]he rank misogynism and racism which run through the moral text [of *Light in August*] make it impossible for me as a feminist and humanist to suspend disbelief and to accept the probabilities of Faulkner's fictional world" (606). At the same time, those of us attempting to retrieve Faulkner's female characters from marginalization or to explore beyond the charges of misogyny that are periodically leveled at Faulkner by figures ranging from Leslie Fiedler to Joyce Carol Oates sometimes find ourselves viewed as marginal by those in the larger critical community.

Awareness of such conditions provokes fundamental questions about the nature and purpose of our own work and thus about our scholarly identity. If some of the feminists who work on only female writers view askance those women who work on male writers as well, while the male community at least partially excludes them, we end by asking ourselves not only where we are but who we are. Moreover, the fact that an increasing number of men in the Faulkner field are now doing feminist critiques further complicates our questions—and our positions. Nearly half of the obviously feminist articles on Faulkner in the 1989 and 1990 MLA bibliographies were by men,[6] and while it may be cheering to see that male critics are finding intellectual rewards in feminist approaches, the tendency in past years for men to receive the lion's share of invitations to present papers and undertake projects leading to publication suggests that male feminists in the Faulkner field may ultimately prove to be more visible than female feminists, just as men have been in general. Some recent developments in Faulkner criticism lend credence to Elaine Showalter's 1983 assertion that "feminist ideas are much less threatening when they come from a man" (139).[7] A recent example appears in Frederick Crews's retrospective essay on the last ten years of Faulkner criticism, in which the only book-length feminist study discussed was a partially feminist critique by a male—John Duvall's *Faulkner's Marginal Couple*—while a fully feminist work by a female—Minrose Gwin's *The Feminine and Faulkner*—was ignored (47–52).

Not surprisingly, our pragmatic and far from complex solution to this uncomfortable situation is to periodically focus our critical attention on women writers. Both of us, more or less dedicated Faulknerians, have also explored critical questions centering on such American women writers as Sarah Orne Jewett, Edith Wharton, Ellen Glasgow, Nella Larsen, and Joan Williams, and we shall continue to do so, turning away intermittently from male canonical texts with a certain sense of relief. When we do so, we join other feminists engaged in retrieving such female figures from the margins to which they tend to be consigned and in this way expanding the canon. At the same time, we operate with a high degree of comfort, there being a much less complicated struggle to define ourselves in and against the text. All in all, the ideological merit of our undertakings in such moments is apparent, the scholarly identity crisis is resolved, and a sense of sisterhood with the writer and with other gynocritics is achieved.

Nonetheless, for the same reasons that within our own traditionally structured departments we think it is as important to alter from within as it is to ally ourselves and our work with that of the gynocritics, we will continue to teach elective courses that include those male writers such as Faulkner and Henry James whose novels we find so infinitely fascinating. Thus, along with offering gender-based courses such as Women in Literature and Women in Film, we also teach canonical courses such as American Literature Survey or American Realism with revised syllabi, and we offer graduate seminars on such topics as Sexual/Textual Politics in James, Wharton, and Glasgow or Faulkner: Feminism/Modernism. While we are stimulated by opportunities to teach courses that concentrate on feminist issues and female artists, we believe it is equally crucial to provide new perspectives on canonized male authors, to place them clearly in their cultural contexts, and to balance their texts with those by women and by men of color.

We have discovered, however, that proponents of the "classic canon" often find our decision to mainstream women writers in the curriculum more disruptive than a gynocritical approach. One of our colleagues recently defended his nearly all-male syllabus by arguing that "one woman writer is plenty in American Realism. [X] covers the others in her course on American Women Writers." Yet we see that our students' critical faculties are strengthened by the experience of juxtaposing the voices of canonized white male modernists with those of Zora Neale Hurston, Edith Wharton, Nella Larsen, Gertrude Stein, and Virginia Woolf. In relatively homogeneous and politically unsophisticated student populations like those we teach, such juxtapositions lead to direct confrontations with issues of race, class, and gender. We also cross-list all our mainstreamed courses in our Women's Studies programs, on whose advisory boards and faculty we serve. It is, however, an uneasy compromise, and here, as in our own research, we feel torn between what appear as rival claims of "equality" and "difference," between the desire to be scholars of the canon occupying the center on equal terms with men and the wish to be different, to avoid the center by concentrating on women and minority writers still largely seen as marginal despite the ongoing attempts to retrieve them from marginality.[8] Despite such inner conflicts, however, we believe that our own critical thinking is enriched by our continued engagement with the variously feminine, feminist, and hegemonic voices of all these novelists.

And we return continually to Faulkner, fascinated by the almost endless variety of intellectual challenges presented in and by his high modernist texts. But there we confront a different threat of silencing, more complicated and in some ways more hazardous than that presented by external factors such as limited numbers of speaking invitations or curtailed access to collections—the threat from within.

The conceptual and moral questions that Faulkner's fiction raises are often painful for a feminist. For example, a member of the audience at the 1991 American Literature Association panel on Faulkner and feminism said that her students feel emotionally "battered" when they read his texts and asked whether the audience thought it was "moral" to teach Faulkner. While we share her concern, we see this as an important and interesting pedagogical problem rather than a deterrent. One of us, teaching a recent seminar on the novels of Faulkner and Toni Morrison to women students, confronted repeatedly their anger at the way Faulkner's texts silence or marginalize white women and blacks and disclose a range of constrictions imposed by everything from politesse to rape, virtual imprisonment, and lynching. It was both an intellectual and emotional challenge to get the students even to consider that some comparable difficulties are faced by Faulkner's male characters, that the masculinist and racist discourse contains its own subversions, or that Faulkner's sociology might be regarded as descriptive rather than prescriptive, that his work must be considered in relationship to the cultural context in which it was produced. The classroom atmosphere was often charged with hostility, directed sometimes at the professor, whom they saw as consorting with the enemy, as well as at the author, whose work they blamed for being sexist and racist and compared unfavorably with Morrison's, despite their exposure to Morrison's own acknowledgment of her indebtedness to Faulkner. Still, it was evident throughout the semester that the intellectual energy produced in and by the class was exhilarating for all of us: the discussion of *Sanctuary* in particular had an emotional range and critical depth that distinguished it from any prior classroom experience, and one student's angry yet persuasively argued essay on racism in *Absalom, Absalom!* won an all-college prize. Thus, the initial negativity ultimately proved to have productive results for nearly everyone.

Along with such teaching challenges, certainly not confined to Faulkner or other male American authors—one must deal with Cather's, Stein's, and Wharton's racism, Wharton's and Cather's anti-Semitism, and the more subtle but ubiquitous issue of all of these writers' ambivalence toward the feminine—the feminist frequently confronts important conceptual difficulties when she undertakes criticism of a male writer. To be sure, in the Faulkner field, we have passed well beyond the taxonomic images-of-women stage and have moved toward a theory-based concern with topics such as voice and silence, toward efforts to "hear" his black and female characters, free of the usual patriarchal static that would ghettoize them as irretrievably Other, or toward relocating the authorial voice itself in diverse regions of the gender map, characterizing that voice as variously feminine, androgynous, bisexual, or even, provocatively, as lesbian. Feminist critiques have attempted to discern traces of the silenced female voices in *The Sound and the Fury,* to locate at the center of *As I Lay Dying* Addie Bundren's posthumous voice, speaking beyond and yet to the Symbolic order, to hear resistances in the non-sense of Temple Drake in *Sanctuary,* and to de-marginalize the hysterical speech of Rosa Coldfield in *Absalom, Absalom!* To date, the most attention has been directed to Faulkner's major fiction from the period 1929–1939 and has appeared primarily in article form; only one fully feminist book-length study has been published, Gwin's *The Feminine and Faulkner* (John Duvall's *Faulkner's Marginal Couple* is partially concerned with feminist issues). Clearly, there is more to be done, on lesser Faulkner texts, say, such as the intriguing *kunstlerroman, Mosquitoes;* but the publication data (only seven identifiably feminist articles in the 1989 *MLA Bibliography,* twelve in 1990) suggest that the erasure of the female in Faulkner's work is sufficiently pervasive that it has, in the past, limited the number of such archaeological projects as those listed above.[9]

A variety of inhibiting pressures affect other feminists at work in and on the male canon, in some cases aborting their efforts. In the most vivid example of pressures of this sort, a woman critic who has written extensively on both male and female writers told us that the extremely hostile and apparently *ad feminam* attacks elicited by many of her recent feminist critiques of male writers makes her wonder whether silence might not be the appropriate tactic, at least for the moment. Others report confronting more oblique but no less intimidating challenges. One who is midway through her second book on a nineteenth-century male writer says she occasionally resorts to odd self-interrogations. Like most feminists of our generation, she is a self-taught "resisting reader," but she still asks herself about the source and nature of her authority vis-á-vis male texts. Although she reminds herself that the process of training in gender criticism has taught her to "read like a woman," she can't help wondering as *whom,* in gender terms, she speaks. Another woman critic, completing a study of ways in which a group of twentieth-century women writers have inherited an earlier (male) tradition, is concerned that her strategy might seem hostile to feminist criticism and thus has taken care to demonstrate that it is not, all the while aware nevertheless of the "danger" that in studies such as hers the male tradition might once again swallow up the female. Yet another woman, who has done a good deal of work on canonical male writers, notes that her criticism is often labeled and sometimes assailed as feminist, even when its approach to the literature is not technically feminist, not grounded in the theory or exploring the issues commonly regarded as feminist; she sees equal hazards whether one operates in the mainstream or on the margins. Such pejorative labeling of criticism as feminist is also among the forms of intellectual harassment cited in the 1991 MLA report (*Concerns*).

These conceptual difficulties are further augmented by the fact that it is now seen by many as "conservative" or "old fashioned" to work on individual authors, even more so to be closely identified with one of them. As we all know, theory over the past decade or more has included frequent proclamations of the death of the author, and this seems to have been reified in the recent actions of our largest and most visible professional organization, the Modern Language Association. Since about 1988, the MLA has with increasing frequency rejected proposals for special sessions devoted to the work of a single author and has recently adopted guidelines for affiliated organizations that make it extremely difficult for author societies to gain allied status. Because of this, the American Literature Association, comprised of just such societies, was formed in 1989 and has begun holding annual conferences. While panel proposals on individual authors are much more easily accepted by the ALA than the MLA, the feminist critic presenting at ALA faces the paradox that in more readily gaining a public forum for her ideas, which may be at the theoretical cutting edge, she is functioning in an arena that is, in many ways, reactionary. A scholar relatively new to the profession implied something like this when she described her own work on nineteenth-century American literature; including both men and women in her study in an effort to break down the gender distinctions she sees as espoused by an "earlier generation" of feminists, she doesn't view herself as someone who "does" any particular author or authors, but rather as one who is interested in certain specific texts in their relationship to the larger cultural discourse.

As far as our own work is concerned, even if we put aside such issues as generational identification, location of authority, gendering of critical voice, or the mainstream-margin conflict, we confront still other questions whenever we turn back to Faulkner. The first of these has to do with the nature and origin of our powerful attraction (we use the term knowingly) to his fiction and poetry. The intellectual answers are relatively simple and easily understood by anyone who appreciates his rhetorical pyrotechnics and the multivalence of his texts, which endlessly reward frequent explorations and reconsiderations. Understanding the emotional mesmerization is somewhat more difficult. One of us remembers her first thrilling encounter with a Faulkner novel, which was soon followed by absolute certainty that he would be her literary "main man"; that the text was *The Sound and the Fury,* in which the female voices can barely be heard through the alterity of the masculine discourse in which they are embedded, mattered then not a whit. Although it does now, this awareness, even coupled with more intimate knowledge of an entire corpus in which female agency and subjectivity are minimal or absent, hardly mitigates the force and persistence of the attraction.

We also ask ourselves how legitimate, finally, is our enterprise. Because, as numerous critics have noted, Faulkner's texts give primary voice and agency to the male subject, we wonder whether it is appropriate—or correct, for that matter, though one hesitates to use this charged term—for us, as feminists, to continue to validate in any way this repressive textual strategy. About a decade ago, one of us suggested in an overview of critical approaches to Faulkner's female characters (Wittenberg 1982) that misogynistic assessments of the author constituted violations of Faulkner's fictional contexts, that any generalizations about Faulkner's presentation of gender-based issues are problematic, necessarily qualified by the multivalence of his texts; recently this essay was described as "overgenerous" to Faulkner's "sexism" (Crews 50). Such judgments, however typical of the ongoing critical dialogue, nonetheless, given the circumstances, lead us to wonder whether we have been complicitous in a rehabilitative enterprise of a questionable nature. We find it ironic, moreover, that in attempting to retrieve the feminine voices in Faulkner from silence and marginalization, we sometimes find ourselves stilled or viewed as off-center by the male critical community, the gynocritics, and our students.

Although these moments of discomfort occur, just as the doubts and questions persist and the facts of the external situation intermittently annoy, we continue our criticism and teaching of Faulkner and some other canonical males voluntarily and often with complete confidence. One of our colleagues attempted to explain why feminists should read Faulkner: "What he does so well is to show the *process* of women's silencing, the appropriative gesture of white male dominance—the naturalization of systems of oppression" (Gwin 1991). Another, now beginning her second book on the writer, asserts the importance of feminism to the Faulkner field: "We do it to redress the glaring absences in Faulkner criticism and to contradict mainstream critical positions." Moreover, despite a history of limited activity and inhibiting pressures, and despite the fact that one or two feminists may have recently "signed off" on Faulkner, there are now some indications that feminist voices are beginning to speak with increasing frequency. As of this writing, a double issue of the *Faulkner Journal* devoted to feminist critiques, all but one by women, has appeared, and there are reports of other such essays and full-length studies in press or in preparation; whatever the reasons for the earlier constraint, it shows signs of lessening.

Feminist critiques of Faulkner, like those of any "great" male writer, are part of the larger project of rethinking the canon and serve, as George Levine says, to "expand the canon by forcing new perspectives on now classic works" (1027). Furthermore, avers one female colleague, it is important for feminist critics to think about male writers, both because great literature may not be as sexist as some interpretations have suggested and because at least some male writers have as great a commitment to thinking through issues of gender as many women writers, even if their angles of vision inevitably differ. Since, as this colleague says, "gender is not simply a product of biology but is part and parcel of our socio-political, historical consciousness of ourselves, how can the male writers *not* tell us something about what it means to be a woman?" That we have much to learn about women, and about race, even from the often controversial texts of a writer like William Faulkner, is clear. As Thadious Davis, a woman and an African-American and one of the first critics to chart the intersections of gender, race, and class in Faulkner's fiction, argues, Faulkner's deeply conflicted and contradictory representation of race "is a central imaginative force" in his fiction which functions "both as concept and as character and becomes an integral component of the structural and thematic patterns in much of [his] art" (2). Certainly there is evidence of misogyny in Faulkner's work, and his fiction presents unresolvable ideological problems for feminists. Our job, as we see it, is to acknowledge these problems, to write about them, and, in the classroom, to help our students discover them for themselves so that they are able to make an informed choice about whether they can continue to study Faulkner and other modernists—male and female—whose poetry and fiction is, to a greater or lesser extent, similarly conflicted.

To those of us who live and work as feminists and are engaged by feminist theory, and who wish to speak from a position that coincides neither with the center nor the margins, it is necessary as well as enlivening to view the field of criticism as dialogic and carnivalesque, and the feminist critic as one who, in Cixous's words, "doesn't annul differences but stirs them up" (254). While the project of reexamining the traditional canon from a feminist vantage point may position the woman critic in an uncomfortable in-between space, it is a space, we believe, whose occupation is crucial both to critical theory and praxis and, ultimately, to the canon itself.

NOTES

1. In Faulkner studies it seems to be not so much the practice of feminist criticism that can create special challenges as it is the gender of the practitioner; the field now appears as hospitable to feminist criticism as it is to, say, deconstruction and new historicism, examples of all of which are found on current lists of critical works, though perhaps fewer than one might expect, given the amenability of Faulkner's rich texts to a variety of approaches. When we use the term "feminist(s)" in this essay, we mean women feminists unless otherwise indicated.

2. Judith L. Sensibar's work on Faulkner includes "Faulkner's Fictional Photographs: Beyond Patriarchy?" in *Out of Bounds: Male Writers and Feminist Inquiry,* eds. Laura Claridge and Elizabeth Langland (Amherst: University of Massachusetts Press, 1990), " 'Drowsing Maidenhead Symbol's Self': Faulkner and the Fictions of Love," in *Faulkner and the Craft of Fiction,* eds. Ann J. Abadie and Doreen Fowler (Jackson: University Press of Mississippi, 1989), *Faulkner's Poetry: A Bibliographical Guide to Texts and Criticism* (Ann Arbor: UMI-Research Press, 1988), *The Origins of Faulkner's Art* (Austin: University of Texas Press, 1984), an edition of Faulkner's *Vision in Spring* (Austin: University of Texas Press, 1984), and "Pierrot and the Marble Faun: Another Fragment," *Mississippi Quarterly* 32:3 (Summer 1979). She is completing a book about three women in Faulkner's life entitled *Faulkner and Love, A Family Narrative: Caroline Barr, Maud Butler Falkner, and Lida Estelle Oldham.*

Judith Wittenberg's work on Faulkner includes "Configurations of the Female and Textual Politics in *Mosquitoes,*" *Faulkner Studies* 1:1 (1991), "Gender and Linguistic

Strategies in *Absalom, Absalom!"* in *Faulkner's Discourse,* ed. Lothar Honnighausen (Berlin: Niemeyer Verlag, 1989), "Faulkner and Women Writers," in *Faulkner and Women,* eds. Doreen Fowler and Ann J. Abadie (Jackson: University Press of Mississippi, 1987), "Women in Light in August," in *New Essays on* Light in August, ed. Michael Millgate (Cambridge: Cambridge University Press, 1987), "The Art of Ending," in *New Directions in Faulkner Studies,* eds. Doreen Fowler and Ann J. Abadie (Jackson: University Press of Mississippi, 1984), "William Faulkner: A Feminist Consideration," in *American Novelists Revisited,* ed. Fritz Fleischmann (Boston: G. K. Hall, 1982), "Faulkner and Eugene O'Neill," *Mississippi Quaterly* 33 (Summer 1980), and *Faulkner: The Transfiguration of Biography* (Lincoln: University of Nebraska Press, 1979).

3. This drops to 60 percent in the 1990 and 1991 *MLA Bibliographies,* perhaps signaling a new trend.

4. For example, Joseph Blotner and Noel Polk have been preparing the Faulkner texts for Random House and Library of America; David Minter has published a Norton critical edition of *The Sound and the Fury;* Faulkner's letters have been published by Joseph Blotner, L. D. Brodsky, and James Watson; the manuscript facsimiles were prepared for Garland by Michael Millgate, Thomas McHaney, Joseph Blotner, and Noel Polk; and the concordances were overseen by Jack Capps and Noel Polk. Judith L. Sensibar's edition of *Vision in Spring* is one obvious exception to this all-male list.

5. It should be pointed out here that these incidents may not be typical; at least some women scholars working on other writers such as Dreiser, Twain, Whitman, and Hemingway report that they have had no difficulty gaining access to manuscript collections. At the same time, however, sometimes women scholars experience difficulty gaining access to the collections of women writers—collections to which their male colleagues have been readily admitted.

6. The proportions changed dramatically in the 1991 listing, in large part because of a special issue of the *Faulkner Journal,* "Faulkner and Feminisms," whose articles were mostly authored by women.

7. Showalter goes on to assert that "when male theorists borrow the language of feminist criticism without a willingness to explore the masculinist bias of their own reading system, we get a phallic 'feminist' criticism that competes with women instead of breaking out of partiarchal bounds" (143). We believe that, while her reading of the situation is both essentialist and more applicable to the early 1980s than the early 1990s, the issue raised remains relevant.

8. For an elaboration of the equality-difference issue, see Snitow, 18 and *passim.*

9. The number mushroomed to 21 in 1991, because of the situation explained in n. 6.

We are grateful to the female colleagues in American literature who shared their experiences and their insights with us. None of them is cited by name because they spoke to us "off the record" (which of course raises another issue of "silence"). They have enriched our own dialogue and our understanding of the conundrums faced by all of us.

WORKS CITED

Bauer, Dale M. *Feminist Dialogics: A Theory of Failed Community.* Albany: State University of New York P, 1988.

Cixous, Helene. "The Laugh of the Medusa." in *New French Feminisms*. Ed. Elaine Marks and Isabelle de Courtivron. New York: Schocken Books, 1981.

Crews, Frederick. "The Strange Fate of William Faulkner." *New York Review of Books*. March 7, 1991: 47–52.

Davis, Thadious M. *Faulkner's "Negro": Art and the Southern Context*. Baton Rouge: Louisiana State UP, 1983.

Donovan, Josephine. "Feminism and Aestheticism." *Critical Inquiry* 3 (1977): 605–608.

Duvall, John N. *Faulkner's Marginal Couple*. Austin: University of Texas P, 1990.

Fetterley, Judith. *The Resisting Reader*. Bloomington: Indiana UP, 1978.

Gwin, Minrose C. "Feminism and Faulkner: Second Thoughts: Or, What's a radical feminist doing with a canonical male text anyway?" *Faulkner Journal* 4: 1, 2 (1988–89) [published Fall 1991]: 55–65.

———. *The Feminine and Faulkner,* Knoxville: University of Tennessee P, 1990.

Levine, George. "Introduction: Victorian Cluster." *PMLA* 105:5 (October 1990).

Olsen, Tillie. *Silences*. New York: Delacorte, 1978.

Showalter, Elaine. "Critical Cross-Dressing: Male Feminists and the Woman of the Year." *Raritan* 3:2 (Fall 1983): 130–49.

Snitow, Ann. "A Gender Diary." In *Conflicts in Feminism*. Ed. Marianne Hirsch and Evelyn Fox Keller. New York: Routledge, Chapman and Hall, 1990.

Wittenberg, Judith Bryant. "William Faulkner: A Feminist Consideration." *American Novelists Revisited* Ed. Friz Fleischmann. Boston: G. K. Hall, 1982.

Women's Caucus of the Modern Language Association. *Concerns: Newsletter of the Women's Caucus* 21:2 (June 1991).

"The Great Unexamined": Silence,
Speech, and Class

Lillian S. Robinson

Tillie Olsen's San Francisco apartment is directly across the street from the Chinese consulate. In June of 1989, during the student occupation of Tienanmen Square, this location gave her a literal window on the local response to events in Beijing. "The Chinese students were alone out there today," she reported to me, after we learned that the troops had fired, "but tomorrow there's a much bigger demonstration. Do you have a marker I can borrow to make a poster?" She came to my apartment a block away and I gave her my red marker. The next day, as we gathered in the narrow street in front of the consulate, hers was the only sign I could read.

For us non-Chinese, it was the most silent of vigils. We were surrounded by loudspeaker announcements—the latest news of the massacre—foreign chanting, and angry ideographs; but the only statement we could make was with our bodily presence. From time to time, my ear would catch a Chinese word I recognized: *we . . . shame . . . people;* it made a found poem. And every so often, over the heads of the weeping, shouting crowd, I would glimpse Tillie's sign. DENG XIAO-PING, it cried out, red on white, DO NOT DESTROY CHINA'S BEAUTIFUL FUTURE. Inspired, I went back to my apartment for the other marker, the black one, and made a poster of my own. Where Tillie's was lyrical, in her style, mine was ironic, in mine: A PEOPLE'S ARMY DOESN'T SHOOT DOWN THE PEOPLE. And I returned to the demonstration. A group of Chinese students read my sign, bowed, and silently clapped their hands as they passed.

Like any good postmodern narrative, this anecdote authorizes speculation in a number of different and sometimes mutually contradictory directions. I am particularly interested in (not to say preoccupied or obsessed with) those that suggest the political dimensions of silence and speech in the overlapping universes of discourse and action. I have sometimes used it, an anecdote about two posters—actual *signs* at a moment when theory allows us to describe anything as a "sign"—to illustrate a lecture about the literary canon and multiculturalism. Perhaps, I mused, it is precisely this sort of literary influence, the "chain reaction of the empowered subject," that traditionalists are afraid of.[1] But, postmodern or no, I had to mutilate the story to make it fit my rhetorical rubric. That particular chain reaction matters because neither Tillie Olsen's writing nor mine is restricted to hand-made placards. Yet our writing does acquire some of its meaning from the interruptions, the necessary silences entailed in our activism. We are the kind of activists we are because we are writers, but we are also the kind of writers we are because we are activists.

More important, just as contemporary literary theory has enabled us to conceive discourse as action, it should make it possible for us to understand action as discourse and thereby to read political action as a form of articulation, rather than its absence, as speech rather than as silence. In other words, if this essay had an epigraph, it might be a testy, belligerent, "You lookin' at me? You lookin' at me? Who you callin' The Inarticulate, anyway?"

The word *circumstances* recurs throughout *Silences*. It is Tillie Olsen's way of characterizing the conditions that hamper creative life without resorting to value-laden jargon. "Circumstances" is a—well—*circumstantial* description, one that makes ready connections between external facts and the internal history they shape. It also conveys a certain flexibility. Not only do circumstances alter cases, but circumstances themselves alter and, with them, the meanings attached to social experience. If we are not equally free to create our own expressive destinies, neither are we necessarily the silent victims of history.

"Circumstances" is also—and I think usefully—imprecise, covering the joint and several actions of gender, class, and race with family, work, and political structures. There is no vagueness, however, about the hard material facts and their impact on the making, unmaking, and nonmaking of writers. In the years since Olsen first began speaking and writing on these issues, both feminist and multicultural studies have emerged as complex and powerful critical forces. They have developed in tandem with the changing creative situation of women and people of color and have simultaneously helped to chart the change and participated in the cultural process. *Silences* itself has become part of the rich and raucous history of breaking silence about the cultural realities of gender and race.

But what about class? Olsen's term *circumstances,* despite its apparent neutrality, was one of the critical tools that familiarized American readers with the cultural conjunction of sex, race, and class. *Silences* is usually characterized as a study of or meditation on women and writing, hence about gender. Olsen's observations on the situation of black writers—especially the quantitative exercise in which she examines how few blacks, as of the mid-1960s, had managed to publish a second book even if they'd brought out one—also strike the imagination and remain in the memory.[2] The sensitive reader of *Silences* will also be able to recall passages about the physical and spiritual weariness that impede the creative development of working people. In the brief passage called "Creativity: Potentiality. First Generation," in the section entitled "Deepenings, Roundings, Expansions," Olsen also considers the internal barriers that keep the working-class writer from coming to the written word.[3] And Olsen's own affinities as writer and critic are clearly proletarian as well as feminist.

Still, what *about* class? In contrast to race and gender, class is a critical and analytical category without a coherent voice of its own. Working-class experience not only silences those who live it, but silences the culture about class itself. Class is thus the Cinderella of cultural studies, left behind in the ashes (the literal dustbin of history?) while race and sex whirl off to the ball.[4] It is what Olsen herself, in the phrase I have borrowed for my title, calls "the great unexamined," thereby recognizing an interpretive silence about the phenomenon of mass silence, as if all we needed was this shamefaced metasilence.[5]

In *Silences,* Olsen describes the time- and spirit-consuming labor of housework and child-rearing, especially combined in the "double day" with jobs outside the home, and charts the toll exacted by working-class jobs in general, a toll very much at odds with the enabling conditions for the production of literature. But she tends, in so doing, to take an evolutionary view of the relation of class to literary production, one in which the children and grandchildren of the proletariat have access to some of the educational and creative opportunities that make it possible for them to write from within a working-class experience and community. It is this process that provides Olsen with her term "the first generation," which she frequently uses, in *Silences* and elsewhere, to describe the background of particular writers and also to identify promising literary trends or movements in the making. Thus, *Silences* is dedicated both to "our silenced people, century after century their beings consumed in the hard, everyday essential work of maintaining human life. . . . Their art . . . refused respect, recognition; lost" as well as to those of their descendants "by our achievement bearing witness to what was . . . silenced." It seems to me that it is time, as part of that process, to acknowledge and honor the widest possible range of expression as the speech—the articulate speech—of the oppressed.

In a provocative paper at the 1990 MLA convention, Michael Bennett hypothesizes a "poetics of divestment."[6] The divestment he refers to is not another negative state, a silencing, like disinheritance, disempowerment, or inarticulateness. Rather, he is using the term in the specific and localized meaning it acquired through the political activism of the 1980s: the movement to get foreign institutions to "deaccession" their shares in companies that do business in South Africa. Because American universities hold stock portfolios, much of the divestment activism in this country centered on campuses, with students and faculty applying pressure to the institutions' corporate decision makers to end their economic complicity in the policies of apartheid. Bennett's paper draws a parallel between the development of the divestment movement as he experienced it at the University of Virginia and the evolution of African-American critical theory. On both sides of the parallel, the issues of empowering an authentic voice of the oppressed and learning to hear it effectively were foregrounded.

But the divestment movement was manifested in a series of actions that may themselves be characterized as symbolic speech, and Bennett's discussion hints at, although it does not elaborate, a cultural theory that would understand the ways that form and content work together in such actions. In the Virginia scenario, I was particularly struck by Bennett's description of the concentric circles of protest and protection created by the supporters of divest-

ment. After listening to presentations at a student-sponsored divestment forum, the finance committee of the university's governing board

> refused to engage in a dialogue or make any commitments toward a policy
> review. This refusal triggered a sit-in which was amplified by the presence of
> several hundred protestors outside who had been attending a simultaneous
> public rally. . . . These protestors formed a human chain around the Ro-
> tunda, significantly slowing the process of the eventual arrest of those inside.
>
> Ironically, the arrest of the "Rotunda 31" was also slowed by the pres-
> ence of a group of suit-and-tied academics who were occupying the room
> until 5:00 to hear a distinguished historian deliver a paper touching on First
> Amendment rights. So the conference-goers sat in chairs placed around the
> students sitting on the floor and proceeded with their business.[7]

When he summarizes the history that culminated in this multifaceted
demonstration, Bennett notes as one important stage the construction of a
campus shantytown during a 1985 board meeting. He refers to this initial
shantytown, which the broad coalition of divestment forces was to repeat at
every subsequent board meeting for the next five years, as "our first foray
into *symbolic language.*" And, when he mentions the lawsuits over the movement's right to build shanties next to the Rotunda, a certified historic landmark, he calls the shanties "an effort to bring the *voice* of black South
Africans to Charlottesville."[8] Thus, for Bennett, the "symbolic language" of
the shanties expresses the "voice" of black South Africa. Although his analysis does not pause to acknowledge the metaphorical character of this "voice,"
I believe that it is precisely here that the poetics of political action has its most
profound application.

The construction, occupation, and meaning of the shanties that went up on
many American campuses in the 1980s were themselves a form of political
speech—speech, moreover, that was representative, rather than directly communicative. When black South African workers put up shantytowns, it is for
the purpose of utilitarian shelter in the urban areas to which they are restricted. The shacks are not a symbol of deprivation for them, they are part of
the actual deprivation, miserable housing. When privileged American students place replicas of these shanties in the shadow of ivied walls and ivory
towers, the shanties, whatever their scale and suitablity as residential accommodations, are translated into symbolic statements. Even on campuses
that cannot boast landscaping and architecture as splendid as Virginia's, there
was always an eloquent contrast between First World institutions and Third
World living conditions. But it is the immediate economic connection between
those institutions and the conditions elsewhere that support and enable them
that makes the eloquence effective. This is the case even in the bitterly ironic
situations where the elite campus is situated in the middle of an urban ghetto
or where local homeless people use the shanties for shelter against the elements. (In fact, the difference between a shantytown in South Africa and one
at Penn, Columbia, or Chicago is like the difference between homelessness
and street theater.) And the contrast persists on campuses where Olsen's "first

generation" is being educated and where it is a narrower version of academic privilege that is nonetheless supported by the labor of black South Africans.

This is not to say that South African blacks, any more than other oppressed people, lack the capacity and the means for symbolic speech. But, just as university students and faculty with all the resources of verbal rhetoric at their command still opt at times to create an architectural representation of oppression (or to occupy the administration building as the local *locus* of power), oppressed people select a medium appropriate to their condition, one that may or may not rely in the first instance on verbal discourse. It seems to me that the failure to recognize this full range of representation as political speech seriously falsifies the meaning of social and cultural resistance. The falsification has its own full range of dangerous consequences from, for instance, the tendency to equate dissidence with the activities of writers and intellectuals; to the imposition of narrow definitions of what constitutes a "prisoner of conscience"; to the assumption that the American blacklist victims of the 1950s were primarily or exclusively writers, directors, and performers in the entertainment industry. The literal danger inherent in each of these consequences should be obvious: by privileging one form of resistance over another, all of them tend to expose some of the most oppressed among us to further attack. Less directly, they can also have the effect of replicating the hierarchy of class within movements designed to resist it. Ultimately, they displace logocentrism from the universe of abstract theoretical polysyllables to that of potentially lethal weapons against those whose principal language is not necessarily language.

So far, however, in my own effort to avoid privileging the literary text over other forms of political speech, I have made a number of unwarranted assumptions. All working-class political texts may deserve to be read with the full range of interpretive attention, but it does not necessarily follow that all literary texts emanating from working-class experience can be read through the same political lens, particularly if that lens is one of self-conscious militancy. Tillie Olsen cautions the writer of the first generation against adopting the themes and tonalities of the dominant literature. But she does not reject the idea of "literariness" itself, which entails a vision of political speech that is often complex, covert, and subtle in its execution.

As a literature of the first generation—a "literary" literature, that is—emerges into being, not only can its politics not be read as if they were a poster painted in primary colors or written in "big character" ideographs, they often subsist at some remove from the discourse and even the possibility of activism. Far from being one means of political activism, contemporary American working-class writing often presents itself as a substitute for an activism that has been superseded, frustrated, or defeated.

Two recent anthologies, *Calling Home* and *Overtime,* embody different— and differently gendered—aspects of this phenomenon of surrogacy.[9] Janet Zandy's collection, *Calling Home,* brings together writings by American women of working-class origin from the whole of the twentieth century. It includes a generation of women who write (or are represented in the volume by oral histories or other forms of nonwritten witness) from the direct experience of the proletarian job, neighborhood, family, and culture, and a generation of women who are from working-class backgrounds, but whose development as writers coincides with if it does not directly reflect some distancing from that background. The difference, as I understand it, is between those of an earlier period for whom everything is problematic *except* their identity as women of the working class, and their descendants, for whom working-class identity is itself the (great, unexamined) problem. The very title, *Calling Home,* suggests that the subject, wherever she may be, is located somewhere other than at home and is attempting, through the act of making literature, to get back in touch with the place she is from. The tone is one of loss and the pain of remembering what has been lost, underlying a sense of not fully belonging anywhere. If long-distance telephoning means reaching out and touching someone, the someone most of Zandy's contributors are trying to reach is themselves. Zandy's introduction reflects her own awareness that the process she calls "circling back," even if possible and complete, is not sufficient, that the justice to be done to working people is material and historical, not only, or even primarily, textual. But she leaves unstated the possible connections between the narrative of working-class women's experience and the advent of that justice. The experience of estrangement at the center of so many of these narratives strongly suggests that, far from being a stage in the process of militancy, this writing could come into being only in the absence of collective struggle.

American resistance culture is informed by the politics of race, where the assertion of identity constitutes a challenge in itself, and the exploration of identity is a form of community action. The evocative power of *Calling Home* also resides in the search for identity, but raises troubling questions about whether, in the context of *class* identity, that search is the beginning of resistance or an acknowledgment of its end.

Overtime makes somewhat the same point, in a more overtly masculine register. Although its subtitle, "Punchin' Out with the *Mill Hunk Herald,*" implies a certain level of activity, if not of activism, that activity is chiefly one of valediction. *The Mill Hunk Herald,* published by Pittsburgh activists throughout most of the 1980s, served as an outlet for worker-writers around the country, chiefly male blue-collar workers from the "rust belt" cities of the industrial North. As a periodical, it was not only an outlet for personal narrative, but also a focus for action based on that narrative, specifically the rearguard action of fighting the plant-closings, sellouts, and give-backs that characterized the death agony of heavy industry in the United States. Selected from the periodical and collected into a book that won the Before Columbus Foundation's American Book Award, the pieces become something else: a statement of culmination.

In the mid-1980s, local director Tony Buba, with the cooperation of the *Mill Hunk* staff, made a film with and about the unemployed and soon to be unemployed steelworkers of Braddock, Pennsylvania. The footage ends with a pitch for the *Mill Hunk,* shot on the tracks leading to the defunct steel mill.

Gesturing at his Lech Walesa Solidarity T-shirt and mentioning the mutual support of the two movements, the editor says, "See this guy? He's crazy enough to organize in Poland. We're crazy enough to organize here in Pittsburgh!"[10] The big difference, of course, is that Solidarity won state power, while the American industrial workers lost even their oppressive base of action.

From the point of view of reading the discourse of working-class political action on the international level, Solidarity might have been a better case in point than the South African liberation struggle. I chose the latter because its discourse included a wider range of symbolic support activities on the part of Americans and others outside the country or the immediate frame of reference: symbolic activities that were nonetheless able, as with the shantytowns, to link the conditions in South Africa to a refusal on the part of First World activists, particularly within academic institutions, to benefit from those conditions. Americans also lent support to Solidarity but, except in the case of the *Mill Hunk* collective, they tended not to perceive and dramatize connections between their own situation and that of the Polish workers. (Indeed, few of the Americans who waxed enthusiastic about Solidarity experienced or identified such links as the commonality of alienated wage labor under state and "free market" forms of capitalism. And, of course, some of the most ardent wavers of the Polish flag were also ardently anti-labor, not to say anti-worker and anti-resistance, in their own country.)

The words and actions of Solidarity count as literature only in the expanded definition of political speech I attempted to outline earlier, whereas the contributors to *The Mill Hunk Herald* and its anthology were consciously making literature out of the stuff of their lives. It is tempting—if depressing—to relate this difference to the other difference, the one between success and failure. In a recent interview, the editor of the *Herald* and of *Overtime* confided that his then-wife had criticized his continued attachment to the project, which she saw as a lost cause within a lost way of life.[11] "What do you want?" She would ask, "to be the one who stays behind at the steel mills to turn out the light?" My own reply to this rhetorical question would be, "Why not? Somebody has to." Ultimately, *Overtime* is not only the chronicle of the decline of heavy industry in the industrial heartland, but the successful translation of that death into cultural expression.

So the female voices that are calling home in Zandy's volume are the voices of regret for the past. The male voices in Evans's collection (overheard while punching their timeclocks at the close of work, not *hitting* out at those responsible) are the voices of farewell. Jointly, both groups are the heirs to generations of ancestral silence, of attributed inarticulateness, and they find their own voice only in an essentially negative declaration. Despite their removal from the working-class experience, however, or *its* removal from them, the new first generation of writers of both sexes has not become something *other* than working class. Rather, they are moving, along with our entire social structure, into a new series of class relations that does not yet have a name, but where the same conditions of alienation and exploitation, the same denial of human creative potential, continue to prevail. In this sense, their empowerment through the word and the empowerment with which their writing endows their readers do not come too late, after all. It comes at the beginning. And it comes *as* the beginning.

NOTES

1. This version of my discussion of the canon has been presented at the University of Kentucky, the Hawaii Committee for the Humanities, the University of Oregon, Southern Oregon State College, Phi Beta Kappa Alpha of Hawaii, the University of Texas at Austin, Occidental College, Hastings College, the University of Nebraska, the University of Southern Maine, Bates College, New York University, the University of Alabama, the University of Arkansas, Virginia Tech, Wake Forest University, and East Carolina University. The lecture is excerpted, minus the Chinese consulate anecdote, in Lillian S. Robinson, "What Culture Should Mean," *The Nation*, 249, 9 (September 25, 1989), 319–21.

2. Tillie Olsen, *Silences*. New York: Delacorte-Seymour Lawrence, 1978, p. 9.

3. *Silences*, pp. 261–64.

4. This line comes from the discussion on the erasure of class as a category in my article, "Out of the Copper Mines, into the Canyon: Working-Class Feminism in the Fifties and the Nineties," in *Cinema and the Question of Class*, ed. David James and Rick Berg, U Minnesota P, forthcoming.

5. *Silences*, p. 264.

6. Michael Bennett, "The Poetics of Divestment/The Politics of Voice," presented at the Annual Meeting of the Modern Language Association, Chicago, December, 1990.

7. "The Poetics of Divestment," pp. 1–2. Michael Bennett generously gave me a photocopy of his typescript at the close of this conference session without knowing who I was or what use I planned to make of his work. Rather than repay this generosity by siccing a bunch of *sics* on a text for oral delivery, not for publication, I have taken the liberty of correcting obvious typos.

8. "The Poetics of Divestment," p. 9, emphasis added.

9. *Calling Home: Working-Class Women's Writing*, ed. Janet Zandy. New Brunswick, NJ: Rutgers U P, 1990. *Overtime: Punchin' Out with the Mill Hunk Herald*, ed. Larry Evans. Minneapolis: West End Press, 1990. See also my review of Zandy's collection and of the Cornell ILR press's reprint of Teresa Malkiel's 1910 *Diary of a Shirtwaist Striker*: Lillian S. Robinson, "Class Acts," *The Nation*, 251, 14 (November 12, 1990), 570–72.

10. Tony Buba, *Lightning Over Braddock*, 1988. When I interviewed Larry Evans, he showed me videotaped clips of several scenes, including this one, from Buba's film. I understand the scene does not appear in the final edited version.

11. Lillian S. Robinson, interview with Larry Evans, Baton Rouge, La., July 19–21, 1991.

Filling in the Silences:
Tillie Olsen's Reading Lists

ROBIN DIZARD

There is a little snapshot of Tillie Olsen beaming at the camera (and at Jack Olsen), seated at the feet of Marx and Engels, represented in larger-than-life-sized bronzes in a public square somewhere in the Soviet Union in 1984.[1] The photograph is more than suggestive of Olsen's background. Daughter of socialists who escaped czarist Russia, schooled by American rebels and friendly with America's West Coast Communist Party leaders, Olsen is a lifelong member of the old Left. Class consciousness is her second nature. (Whether she joined the CP-USA, or when she left is immaterial; she joined the Young Communist League in her teens. In her twenties she attended a party-sponsored school of labor organizers. In her thirties and forties, during the anti-communist crusades, when the FBI worked to make communists pariahs, she lived within the diminished but resilient red circles in San Francisco.) Her trip to the USSR was a return of the exile. The snapshot is a metonymy of her background.[2]

Her pose has the uncanny effect of splicing her into the sculptural composition. The sculptor set two massive bronze images of Victorian men in long-tailed coats, vests, and trousers, on a bench. Engels regards Marx, on his left, who seems to pause mid-sentence as he looks into the front corner of the oblong pink granite slab, straight at Olsen. Clad in blue slacks and jersey, one leg outstretched, the other flexed, hands clasped around her knee, she seems to be Marx's brain-child; pixie-like, she recenters the entire composition.

Statues don't speak, but the Olsens could have quoted the *Communist Manifesto:* "When people speak of ideas that revolutionize society, they do but express the fact that within the old society, the elements of a new one have been created, and that the dissolution of the old ideas keeps even pace with the dissolution of the old conditions of existence" (quoted in Solomon 50). Olsen's effort, in her fiction and in her advocacy for neglected women writers, can be read in the light of her enlightenment faith in the power of ideas and her conviction that the future is immanent now, in the downtrodden. Her imagination is fired by opposition, by vivifying indignation at the terrible conditions that "the apostles of harmony in the service of the ruling class" would veil, explain away, or aestheticize (Engels, *Anti-Duhring,* Solomon 73).

Olsen led the way into the current debate over the canon by compiling reading lists that insist the American experience begins not only at Plymouth but also at Ellis Island, Charlestown Bay, San Francisco, and on the great plains. As a thirties survivor, she discerned the flaw in pre-sixties American Literature curricula at once: in them labor's voice was stifled.

Olsen's bold achievement in challenging the canon may be judged by comparing her reading lists to the conservative reactions of Allan Bloom and E. D. Hirsch, Jr., in *The Closing of the American Mind: How Higher Education Has Failed America and Impoverished the Souls of Today's Students* (1987) and *Cultural Literacy: What Every American Needs to Know* (1987, 1988), respectively. Bloom and Hirsch hold that instilling a common culture is the paramount task for educators in a democracy, though they defend diametrically opposed positions regarding the best way to confront the problems of lower educational attainments conventionally blamed on newcomers in schools—immigrants and women—and on the emergent disciplines—Women's Studies and Ethnic Studies—which these newcomers have created on American campuses. Bloom would educate a cohesive elite. Hirsch would have every high school student understand a core of facts bounded by what literate Americans already know. Olsen, by contrast, holds a socialist-feminist position about a common literature, believing with Virginia Woolf that

> English literature will survive if commoners and outsiders like ourselves make that country our own country, if we teach ourselves how to read, how to write, how to preserve, how to create (quoted in *Silences,* 264).

This essay explains how Olsen's advocacy for outsiders led to her reading lists and how her ideas about the survival of literature play against the diagnoses of the crisis in liberal education proffered by cultural conservatives.

Bloom and Hirsch blame many forces, including timid administrators, for the demise of the liberal educational ideal, but they complain of intellectual influences from the sixties in particular.[3] It is my purpose to show that their diagnosis is mistaken, using Olsen's reading lists as my case in point. Her reading lists defend the ideals of liberal learning through an act of imaginative love. Where Bloom and Hirsch discern one endangered heritage and advocate its preservation, Olsen sees an eclipsed heritage and an acknowledged one, or, in other words, a struggle over legitimacy in intellectual terms. She would introduce "new classics" and thus preserve the common heritage by enlarging it. Olsen honors the canon by remedying its silences regarding women, men of color, and working people. Instead of repeating the past—lessons, errors, silences, majesty, and all—in curricula featuring those great books every university graduate has to know, Olsen wants scholars to come to know classics on subjects the old liberal curriculum never acknowledged, by writers the traditional canon never knew. By placing obscure and unknown authors on the shelf reserved for classics in 1972–1974, Olsen's lists challenged the teaching profession in its own academic home. This event was one of many small signals that heralded the paradigm shift in literary studies which is still underway, twenty years later.

Beginning about 1940, under the influence of the new criticism, college courses treated most literary works as originals within constellations of universal ideals. Matthew Arnold's theory that art is the touchstone "for the best that is thought and said" held sway. That the authors of touchstones were all Western European men was deemed irrelevant; literary critics abjured reductive biographical criticism. Study the work, forget the artist. Universals rather than biography filled in a generalized background. There was, for instance, a legend about the gradual dawn of individualism and democracy, ideas flowing westward from fifth-century Athens to Renaissance Italy to revolutionary France to the British empire and finally to the United States, evinced in Plato, Dante, Shakespeare, Molière, and the novels of the English "great tradition." This schema subsumed women into everyman's history. Likewise this legend subsumed the story of domination; hence those relationships based in unequal exchange sank from sight. "Class—problems of first generation—its relationship to works of literature [becomes thereby] the great unexamined" (*Silences*, 264).

Olsen's reading lists restore the material context, that complicated mingling of longstanding tradition and individual talent, seeing books as material results of human labor, written under particular conditions by particular writers. No figure is to her more salient than the immigrant, whose situation epitomizes twentieth-century humanity. The immigrant confronts intermeshed problems of nationalism, language, class, labor, and education. As the immigrant's dilemmas involve the broadest social problems, solutions suiting her would be the most useful for everyone excluded from ladders to upward mobility. When Olsen uses the term "first-generation" to describe immigrants *and* sons and daughters who are the first in their families to attend college, *and* first to write, she is using immigration as a trope for all kinds of arrivals. Immigration is where the questions of class and gender and the canon intersect. What is the common ground? How shall difference be regarded? Who is the learner?

Essentially the canon debate pits a Eurocentric account of culture, which puts Western European males at the universe's center, against a decentered system, which contemplates an immense plurality of influences. Bloom considers the decentered viewpoint immoral, irrational, and seditious. He locates a special evil in multicultural tolerance. "Cultural relativism succeeds in destroying the West's universal or intellectually imperialistic aims, leaving it to be just another culture" (*Closing*, 39). He locates his advocacy for classic authors within an intellectual nationalism: "The United States is one of the highest and most extreme achievements of the rational quest for the good life. What makes its political structure possible is the use of rational principles of natural right" (39). Hence dignifying traditions outside the previously established canon threatens to annihilate culture. As he stated in an interview, "I would hope I encouraged some people who still love Shakespeare, Plato, and Nietzsche to resist the powerful movement . . . to deprive younger people of books written by dead, white, Western males" (quoted in *Chronicle of Higher Education*). Bloom tries to establish an all-or-nothing choice: pledge allegiance to the European classics, or be damned.

Hirsch, on the other hand, argues that "the basic goal of education in a human community is acculturation, the transmission to children of the specific information shared by the adults of the group or polis" (*Cultural Literacy,* xvi). Hirsch focuses on the process and, like Olsen, pays attention to the problems of class, immigration, and social mobility. However, says Hirsch, "My colleagues and I decided that our list should aim to represent but not to alter current literate American culture" (*Cultural Literacy,* 136). The aim of schooling would be to teach all students, especially immigrants, the dominant consensus. Unlike Bloom, Hirsch admits that multicultural education has value: "it inculcates tolerance and provides a perspective on our own traditions and values" (*Cultural Literacy,* 18). But he sets multiculturalism aside from "our own" American literature culture, which reveals his educational nationalism's clay feet. His universal standard is actually white, Anglo-Saxon, male, mainstream culture. Although Hirsch countenances a broader interpretation of the term *culture* than Bloom (to Hirsch *culture* means the totality of the civilization rather than its aristocratic component alone), he preserves a distinction between more important items and less important items, which parallels class distinctions. Weighed in the balance against a (presumed) universal culture, justifications for Women's Studies or multiculturalism are, to him, frivolous.

Had not Olsen and the new awareness she helped stimulate succeeded in convincing American teachers and professors that their courses muted crucial voices in our national heritage, and consequently, that they should put *other* classics about the America of inequality and hard times and the color bar into courses and anthologies, cultural conservatives would not have deemed that the canon needed defense or repackaging.[4]

Olsen's work—the reading lists she began to produce in 1969 in response to requests from younger scholars, which were published in installments beginning in 1972 and handed around at the MLA in 1974—helped usher in the ethos that challenges unities and transcendencies however constructed or sponsored, from the viewpoints of feminism and ethnic studies. Olsen was one of the first to demonstrate how to recenter the prevalent system of literary taxonomy. She went to college campuses in the 1960s when she was in her fifties, fond of quoting Dickinson, Whitman, W. E. B. DuBois, Virginia Woolf. Her reaction, on finding what the curriculum contained, was to note erasures. Where were women writers, where was multiethnic America, what about the workers? Hers might resemble the position that flattens art with political corrections, judging books according to tendency and partnership, stipulating representatives from each district and faction. But she aimed deeper. If thirst for beauty and the impulse to create are our common birthright (which she, as a mother, Marxist, and humanist, believes), why are women only "one out of twelve" once curricula and anthologies are issued? If a pantheon of artists is all male and ruling class, a Marxist suspects the ruling standards are in fact, as Marx declared, the standards of the ruling class. One standard exists for mainstream works, while several other fluid, ad hoc, and inexplicit standards cull out "minor" stuff. Olsen demanded a single standard, a level playing field, applying the labor organizer's strategy.[5] She claimed intellectual authority for women and working-class men, thinkers conspicuously without credentials in the old arrangements or in Bloom's and Hirsch's newish ones.

As a class-conscious artist, Olsen wants to raise consciousness about an entire class of neglected writers. She would demonstrate that many women of genius existed, but that, due to "the blood-struggle for means: one's own development so often at the cost of others giving themselves up for us" (*Silences,* 262–63), many faltered. As with any producer, the artist's problem is access to the means of production: for writers, these include time, a publisher, and encouragement. Olsen argues that the absence of women from literature as it has been taught is one of the wounds of class, a shaming and a barrier to creativity. In a particular spirit, Olsen entered the life of the scholar, and produced her reading lists and her "Afterword" to "Life in the Iron Mills," to lift a hidden world to view and to help blaze the path for new courses and writers.

Olsen thinks about "the work of art" from the producer's position. She thinks art work means an occupation, a material reality, traces of which are in the finished article. To her, as to any Marxist, it is abberrant to divorce the worker, the work process, and the object. She insists that artistic achievement must be set within the context of production, that individual works are mere tips of icebergs, Over centuries, while countless art objects disappeared through neglect or decay, even more were and still are sacrificed because poverty, skimpy education, or censorship menace the artists themselves. Many an artist lacks good materials (like the hero of "Life in the Iron Mills," who sculpted in slag), or sacrifices the best for short-term survival (like Arnow's *The Dollmaker,* who cut up her artwork to make sellable toys). To Olsen, imagination is less an individual possession than an interactive power, for which the greatest use is to come to a sense of reality and be able to transmute it into art and into the stuff of daily living. She believes that life and art feed one another.

Tillie Olsen's reading lists came out of her encounter with American academia in 1969–1970, when she found that the women within, and many outside, were practically invisible. Her lists grew from her amazement at the depths of ignorance in ivory towers. In 1968 Professor Leo Marx of the American Studies program at Amherst College nominated Olsen for the college's Visiting Writer. She accepted, becoming the third person and first woman in the post.

Meeting her first classes at Amherst in the fall of 1969, she noted a profound innocence among her Amherst College students. For example, "They knew almost nothing about immigration except the Mayflower, and they had some idea about all these 'swarms' who came, but the real reasons why people came they did not know" (unpublished interview, December 11, 1988). Shocked, she added new items to her syllabus. The impetus to make reading lists came when she realized she could educate colleagues, too, as younger scholars sought her advice. The project began, Olsen says, in conversation with her friends Florence Howe and Paul Lauter, both then at SUNY-Old Westbury. Through them, she realized the power of the canon in higher education.

> Florence and Paul . . . were very eager to know what they could teach—
> because like the rest of the academics almost all of the reading I had done
> was absolutely beyond their ken— . . . I am not one of those confronta-
> tional people, you know; if I were I could have said, "How come you don't
> know about this? If you'd really been interested, you could have found it!"
> But when you are in academe, and it's still somewhat true, you only have
> time to learn that which is already in what they call the canon; and that was
> what they knew, that was what they knew (Interview, December 11, 1988).

Olsen sat down to make lists. She made hasty trips to sellers of used books in
New York City; she consulted librarians. Something suddenly crystalized: she
had for years known an answer; she had just found the question. Who were
the neglected women (she noted the secretaries, the faculty wives, the
"biddies" who tidied faculty offices) and who were the writers who knew the
silences of these women? She knew; professors did not. Olsen plotted an extra
course, titled: "The Literature of Poverty, War, and the Struggle for Freedom." She realized that Amherst, then a men-only college, like the academic
establishment generally, preserved a worldview congruent to that Elizabeth
Cady Stanton discerned in her speech to the International Council of Women
in 1888: "Thus far women have been the mere echoes of men. Our laws and
constitutions, our creeds and codes, and the customs of social life are all of
masculine origin," (Dubois 212).

Amherst's insularity was in these years extreme: its tenured professors
included one woman, and most of the faculty members were educated in the
big or little ivies. Olsen saw her duty (and she liked the looks of it). Amherst
College preserved the old customs of thought Stanton described, entirely
adjusted within white old-monied male dominance.[6] In such silence, the unspoken is, as Olsen reminds us, unspeakable:

> Unclean, taboo. The Devil's Gateway. The three steps behind; the girl ba-
> bies drowned in the river; baby strapped to the back. Buried alive with the
> lord, burned alive on the funeral pyre, burned as a witch at the stake. . . .
> Excluded from council, ritual, activity, language, when there was neither
> biological nor economic reason to be excluded. . . . The Jewish male morn-
> ing prayer: thank God I was not born a woman (*Silences*, 26).

Olsen set about correcting academe's evident indifference to sexism and the
injuries of class.[7] The cure she chose was the reading cure, stored up from
years when "public libraries were my college" (dust jacket, *Yonnondio*). Her
courses were the start; to publish reading lists was the logical next step.

Olsen's first list appeared in *Women's Studies Newsletter* in Volume I,
Numbers 2–4, (1972,1973) and Volume II, Number 1 (1974) under the title
"Excavations: Tillie Olsen's Reading List, A List Out of Which to Read,
Extend Range, Comprehension."[8] Reproduced on multilith for the MLA
Commission on the Status of Women by Elaine Reuben and Deborah
Rosenfelt, the list circulated from hand to hand at the Modern Language
Association meetings in 1974, bound between a "Minibibliography on Marx-
ism and Feminism" by Adrienne Rich and Marxist study guides from the

California State University at Long Beach.[9] *New America* reprinted Olsen's list in 1976 with minor changes and additions.[10]

The sweep of Olsen's list is broad and deep; it sparkles with imaginative variety: fiction, biography, autobiography, and poetry, old books and new, authors known and obscure. The list has four divisions: A Spectrum, Most Women's Lives, Mothering and Wifehood, and Forms and Formings: the Younger Years. In all, Olsen lists 216 titles. "A Spectrum," as its title announces, spans a range of experiences, from pioneer life, to coming of age, to revolutionary organizing. "Most Women's Lives" begins with a headnote about the importance of balance, for correcting the idea that women are cosseted, privileged, fragile creatures who "need to be helped into carriages and lifted over ditches," in Sojourner Truth's words. Olsen quotes Olive Schreiner's *Women and Labor* (out of print in 1972): "no work was too hard, no labor too strenuous to exclude us" to counter the double standard that deems ladies more feminine than laboring women, skewing the history of labor thereby. In a similar vein, the headnote to "Mothering and Wifehood" warns against the residual sexism Olsen found in some Women's Studies courses in the early 1970s, which bypassed institutions (like wifehood and motherhood) and experiences (like mothering and being a wife) that are still the defining realities for most women. "Women's courses do not know, or do not understand, the necessity of including the relatively few works that tell something of what mothering and wifehood mean and have meant in a world never, as yet, nuturing to—instead of harmful to—human life." Recently Olsen repeated the criticism that mothering warrants more attention in Women's Studies: even feminists, she says, perpetuate disdain for women if they sequester childrearing, so large a part of women's existence, away from their art, advocacy, and scholarship. She recalled the words of Virginia Woolf: the mothers "who could not be with us tonight because they are washing the dishes and putting the children to bed" deserve that their words be honored, their experience validated (Women and Nurturing Conference, Keene, November, 1991). "Forms and Formings: the Younger Years" repeats many of the other listings, but rearranges them: "These books are listed in their own kind of order . . . by the period of time they cover or in clusters for special reasons."

Olsen's categories are plural, decentered, dynamic. She favors clusters, thematic groups, constellations. She thus avoids spurious hierarchies. She also resists the dichotomy of the public world and the private home, which erases a major reality for women, housewifery, from descriptions of real life and labor. As Jessie Bernard would observe years later in *The Female World* (1981):

> As an occupation housewifery does not appear in any of the research on occupation as a dimension of socioeconomic status. . . . It is precisely the magnitude of this contribution that renders it almost invisible . . . almost too big to be seen (213).

By tracing literature in terms of life stages, Olsen renders household occupations (wifehood, mothering, domestic labor) visible. Thus she indicates an emerging genre where stock comic characters from earlier male-centered literature—the serving maid, the housewife, and the old maid—assume tragic stature. (This development occurred in books by women and men, but women writers are its vanguard.) The social fact that there is no adequate surrogate for households, that someone must see that children get sheltered, fed, and educated, becomes the tragic occasion for sacrifice in story after story ("Wagner Matinee," "Babushka Farnham," *Alberta Alone, This Chile's Gonna Live,* and *Daughter of Earth,* for example.)[11] Olsen's categories follow the divisions of biographers (girlhood, flowering and sexuality, one-hundred-year-old women), minimize the division between author and work, maximize attention to the author's circumstances, and consequently reaccentuate connections between art and life.

All things considered, contrasts between Olsen's reading lists and programs like Bloom's and Hirsch's demonstrate the difference between the academy's establishment and its outskirts. Bloom points out the endless fertility of the classics, their capacity to subvert and problematize themselves against new backgrounds. Hirsch pleads for "hazy familiarity" with the summarized ideas from some classics. But neither would alter the dominant position of Western Eurocentric masculine culture. Bloom pursues a Trojan horse tactic. He would return to the classics and make that the excuse to reinstall cold-war xenophobia and marginalization for all women and men of color. Hirsch's program, blander yet more pernicious, depends on teaching "facts," a diluted, highly mediated version of the dominant culture which he proposes that teachers shall deposit upon students.

Olsen managed to breach the academic consensus that Bloom and Hirsch in different ways seek to defend. Though to them Olsen might seem to be a destroyer, that is not her intent. Her language ("redress," "extend range and comprehension," "read as balancer, corrective of prevalent images of women as protected, passive, parasitic") signals her intent to augment, not replace the classics.[12] She wants to extend the roster of classics in the same way Sojourner Truth expanded the definition of woman: "And ain't I a woman?" She would not replace renowned works, but rather would recontextualize the classics by setting new ones around them. She would excavate the buried heritage of female and first-generation creativity. Revealing this heritage—even in a partial listing of literary achievements—is tantamount to questioning received wisdom about women and newcomers. Tillie Olsen's reading list is about lacunae in cultural memories and the serious partiality in misogynist literary traditions.

Bloom assumes culture is man-made, deserving honor as such. (Bloom and Stanton arrive at the same conclusion but differ on its significance.) Bloom appeals to resentment at the changes the sixties forced upon liberal universalism in order to argue a return to the order of the past. Bloom's ideal is the Greek "community of men seeking the truth" (*Closing,* 381). He does not include women in the term *men.* Bloom targets what he sees as intellectually vapid open-mindedness in college and university professors and their students, those slack and dilatory youth; he hates the influences of the sixties and seventies; he detests women who protest against rigid "feminine" stereotypes. Robert Hutchins's "Great Books" is the reading list Bloom calls "the royal road to learning" (*Closing,* 344). That summation of 3,000 years of Western culture quotes seventy-four white men. Even the essay on differences between men and women in the *Synopticon,* a book-length précis of the greatest ideas in the *Great Books,* quotes Aeschylus, Aristophanes, Bacon, the Bible, Boswell, Cervantes, Darwin, Euripides, Freud, Goethe, Hegel, William James, Tolstoi, Shakespeare, and twenty-five other male writers, but not one woman. Education on such a plan yokes great erudition with deep misperceptions. Like Bloom's *Closing,* it is self-congratulatory.

Hirsch believes an educated citizenry, the foundation for a sound nation, must possess a shared culture through knowing shared references, or facts. Hirsch's and his co-authors' special contribution is an alphabetical list of 5,000 references, publicized with the aid of large corporations, incarnate in a testing program and a new "Dictionary of Cultural Literacy." The core is a reading program, actually a sort of *Cliff's Notes,* keyed to American "facts" of the late twentieth century. But Hirsch's model of cultural literacy, apparently humane in intent, ignores the fact that all facts are polyvalent. Education designed to spur critical thinking, that part of literacy that makes for creativity, the encounter with full texts, education for imagination, is sacrificed for the expedient, communication.

In pursuing this goal, communication, Hirsch ignores the fundamental protean changeability built into language. He seems oblivious to ways in which core concepts can be understood differently from diverse positions. Should 1492 (Hirsch 152) mean the advent of exploration of the New World and escape from the Inquisition's persecution for Protestants and Jews, or the dawn of the destruction of the Toltec, the Carib, and the Maya? Does Custer's Last Stand (Hirsch 165) commemorate a cavalry hero or the tactical genius of Sitting Bull (Hirsch 204)? Might "The female of the species is more deadly than the male" (Hirsch 171) or "Hell hath no fury like a woman scorned" (Hirsch 176) or "What is good for General Motors is good for the country" (Hirsch 214) be taken ironically? Hirsch believes in a shared culture, but he sentimentalizes *sharing.* He has published a compendium of received ideas. He believes in a model of education similar to that which drives missionary schools. By eliding ways to contextualize and evaluate knowledge, Hirsch's plan conceals the mechanism deciding what shall be given behind the stupefying list of what shall be received.

Olsen makes the unacknowledged a major theme. Her reading lists tender evidence and supply a method that can detect the superficiality of the literary history Bloom and Hirsch rehearse. Compared to their books, her list is but a fragment, but the list, joined with *Silences,* forms a coherent program. Her list points to women shapers, makers, and triers, and so teaches where to search for flaws in received wisdom.

Olsen's method blends irony and passion, already evident in a 1938 note to herself:

> To write the history of that whole generation of exiles, revolutionaries, the
> kurelians & croatians, the bundists & the poles; the women, the foreign
> women, the mothers of 6 & 7, the housewives whose Zetkin and Curie &
> Brontë hearts went into kitchen and laundries and patching of old socks; and
> those who did not speak the language of their children, who had no
> bridge . . . to make . . . themselves understood . . . (Rosenfelt 401).

Olsen's dilemma is how to translate the truths of mother-revolutionaries,
unnameable in the terms and schema standard literary history supplies, into
literature. Sentimental clichés and brutal taboos shunt so many to dusty obliv-
ion. Even Clara Zetkin, cofounder of the German Communist Party, Lenin's
and Rosa Luxembourg's friend, has disappeared from literate people's common knowledge. Olsen writes to render justice to these great originals.

When received wisdom designates creation an all-male affair, women are
creativity's exiles. Olsen's metaphor, her bridge, has the revolutionary heroes
Zetkin, Curie, and the Brontës stand for American immigrant women; she
likens crossing gender barriers in politics, science, and literature to crossing
national frontiers. Cooking, cleaning, patching—primitive, ill-paid drudgery
to tend others—are at once the mother-artist's duties to her family, and the
work that threatens her existence as an artist. They are a succinct symbol for
her struggle against self-doubt, distraction, poverty, and despair.[13] Olsen
means to make the immigrants metonymic figures for all kinds of artists who
are first generation, whether first-generation in the United States, in college,
in the middle class, or in formerly all-male pursuits.

Olsen's metonymy yoking the immigration ordeal to an artist's struggle
with materials is apt for a writer's struggle with language. Masculine culture
tests women revolutionaries and path-breakers much as language tests mothers whose children speak another tongue from theirs; immigrants' children
become their mothers' translators. Olsen makes the figure explicit in dedicating *Silences:*

> For our silenced people, century after century their beings consumed in the
> hard, everyday essential work of maintaining human life. Their art, which
> still they made—as their other contributions—anonymous, refused respect,
> recognition, lost.
>   For those of us (few yet in number, for the way is punishing), their kin
> and descendants who begin to emerge into more flowered and rewarded use
> of ourselves in ways denied to them—and by achievement bearing witness to
> what was (and still is) being lost, silenced.

Descendants of exiles, foreigner's children, live between cultures. As Werner
Sollors observes, immigrants to the United States tend to misread American
cultural icons whether they celebrate their new culture or take it ironically.[14]
Either way, the immigrants in effect move into the temple of culture and dare
rearrange the altar. Indeed, writers whose gender, family origin, or class make
them outsiders in their new (American) culture need the classics because their
mothers' tongues are other tongues ("I'm nobody, who are you?"). Mainstream
culture is their passport out of dispossessed status, but it dangerously tempts
immigrants to "pass" or alter themselves to fit in completely and risk alienation.

First-generation artists' first creations are themselves; to become self-made, they compose original systems. (Olsen in such a spirit started as a girl to read everything in the Omaha public library, but quit part way through the M's.) Olsen's list is as all-American as she, a self-taught scholar from nowhere.[15] She proceeded, I think, from the writer's insight that fired her 1938 ambition into her plan for her reading list. Her first list foregrounds texts that are bridges for children of mothers "who had no bridge to make themselves understood." The novels of the list's first section, "A Spectrum," are *Story of an African Farm, Middlemarch, The Mill on the Floss, The Awakening, To the Lighthouse, Cement, Daughter of Earth, The Man Who Loved Children, The Dollmaker, The Time of Man,* and *The Gadfly.* (Later Olsen would add Cora Sandel's *Alberta* trilogy, Margaret Walker's *Jubilee,* and Edith Summers Kelley's *The Devil's Hand.*) Each of the novels has a major figure who breaches gender barriers. In each are themes of the stranger arriving in an alien land. First-generation writers are well represented (Schreiner, Eliot, Smedley, Chopin), likewise expatriates (Stead, Richardson, Sandel). Every one explores a variant of the wife's tragedy. As in any immigrant neighborhood, disparate traditions jostle. Olsen's list rubs realism against modernism; a soviet tractor novel, *Cement,* lodges between Virginia Woolf and a *bildungsroman* from the American plains. Stops, disjunctions, and wild jazzy improvisations abound.

Hirsch and Bloom ignore the location of literature within the larger setting of human life. They overlook the links between received wisdom (social myths) and the class system. Hirsch treats facts as unidimensional and flattens the social use of language into simple communication; Bloom would use literature as a social shibboleth. Taken together, their proposals would reinscribe the class-division myth that teaches why the powerless deserve poverty and the powerful deserve property: the powerless do not know enough. Because Olsen's reading lists pay attention to class and gender, they show how many more Great Books there are than Bloom imagines and how to become more fully literate than Hirsch proposes.[16]

Among the most important things a teacher can do is to point to ways to transcend the course. In this respect, Olsen outdoes both of the professors to whom I compare her, as a glance at one of the most famous tropes in education will demonstrate. Plato illustrated the problem of trying to learn the truth in a fable about people chained in a cavern underground, who would, if they ever got out to the surface, squint and doubt their own senses when they saw sunlight instead of flickering torchlight. Philosophers use the allegory to show the difference between partial enlightenment and "universal" truths.[17] If, instead, one recalls that in fifth-century Athens, slaves chained inside mineshafts dug silver ore, the fable reveals its material basis. Read in the light of Olsen's advice to "[b]egin counting the numberless and nameless 'little maids' and slaves or slaveys who populate fiction of the past," Plato's cave becomes interesting in a whole new way. Bloom says the fable is the most powerful image about social life and the most important inspiration for his life and work (*Closing,* 381). "[A] culture is a cave" (and we are prisoners in it). In his thinking, though, the cave's prisoners and chains are abstractions. If you follow Olsen's instruction to count the slaves and slaveys, you have more than an abstraction, you have Plato's allegory of teaching and its barbaric context, a reminder that ignorance does not just happen, it is imposed.

To learn, we match something new to what we already know. We begin with some arbitrary form—a design, an image, some pattern, a schema—then lay out and stitch together experiences in terms of that beginning "word."[18] Teachers of literature guess what basic schemata their students are already using, then link those to the texts they teach; this pedagogy recalls Socrates's doctrine of reminiscence. In the dialogue with Meno, he says teachers lead students not to discover but to recollect truths their souls knew from previous existences. The difference between the ancient theory of instruction and post-modern thought lies in the prevailing assumption today that cultural patterns, especially language, supply both preconscious memories and the schemata of conscious learning. Cultural patterns, it is thought, also supply ways to oc-clude or simply bury inconvenient memories. Olsen's project shows there are other ways to see women and other ways to read if one remembers to read like a novelist, listening for the multiplicity of voices from myriad directions. Not surprisingly, Olsen, an outsider, whose sensibilities were trained in other ways and other settings, was one who could supply what she saw higher education needed.

Reading lists always concern pedagogy, that is, theories about memory and transmission. Decisions about what ought to be remembered mold every reading list. Recent cruxes in pedagogy have concerned the decisions about the shadow side of memory, the forgotten, fogged-over, and repressed scenes that seemed not to fit into the schema scholarship provided for educating Americans in mid-century, from 1945 to about 1968. Fittingly, it was a woman from another field, the country of the socialist organizers of the thirties, who excavated American national literature to bring back its missing women.

NOTES

1. "Chronology" *Tillie Olsen*. Mickey Pearlman and Abby H.P. Werlock. Twayne United States Authors Series. Boston: 1991, xviii.

2. The Olsens were not uncritical apologists. During the same trip, they also visited and photographed a memorial obelisk in Minsk commemorating the destruc-tion of thousands in the old Jewish ghetto.

3. Hirsch says, "cafeteria-style education" causes cultural fragmentation. This education is rationalized by "educational formalism" which explains "the indiscrimi-nate variety of school offerings as a positive virtue. . . . Formalism has also conve-niently allowed administrators to meet objections to the traditional literate materials that used to be taught in the schools. Objectors have said that traditional materials are class-bound, white, Anglo-Saxon, and Protestant, not to mention racist, sexist, and excessively Western" (*Literacy*) 21. Hirsch's anonymous "objectors" have to be the feminists, Marxists, and proponents of Ethnic Studies whose presence affected education, starting about 1965. Bloom's account of this period is apocalyptic and

elitist: "Neither aristocrats nor priests, the natural bearers of a high intellectual tradition, exist in any meaningful sense in America. The greatest of thoughts were in our political principles but were never embodied . . . in a class of men. Their home in America was the university, and the violation of that home was the crime of the sixties" (*Closing*, 321).

4. The MLA Survey of the readings and teaching goals in upper division courses in a random sample of English departments shows that among recent additions in nineteenth-century American Literature courses, *Life in the Iron Mills* has earned a place in six percent of such courses. Here is a solid indication of Olsen's effect on scholarship and advocacy. Cf. *MLA Newsletter* (Winter 1991)23:4, 12.

5. According to this strategy, it matters less which standard applies than that it applies to all players. In an academic tenure case, for example, one would believe a double standard is operating if the tenure committee argues that a man who publishes in various fields is "multifaceted" while a woman who does the same is "unfocused." I never have heard or read Olsen's definition of a literary standard, but would guess she agrees with Emily Dickinson that one recognizes great poetry by the way it blows the top of one's head off.

6. Olsen's discomfort was increased because her husband, Jack Olsen, was forced to accept employment at the *Wall Street Journal,* then printed in Chicopee, Mass. An organizer, labor educator, and typesetter by trade, Olsen could claim priority placement by the terms of his standing in the typesetters' union. Ironically the only place with work available was the *Journal,* what he called a ruling-class mouthpiece, where he had to keep quiet about the rights of labor. He kept teaching, though, by posting evidence of "Crimes in The Street" as published in *WSJ,* to counteract his workmates' indignation at crime in the streets.

7. Olsen was by 1969–70 aware of more than just Amherst, but I have focused my attention there because she lived in Amherst when she assembled her lists. She had of course been at Stanford in 1956–57, and at the Bunting Institute at Radcliffe in 1962–64. She was in correspondence and visiting with professors from University of Massachusetts-Amherst, Smith, Mt. Holyoke, Hampshire, SUNY-Old Westbury, and MIT during her year at Amherst College.

8. The Feminist Press, Old Westbury: New York, 1972–1974.

9. *Affirmative Interactions in Literature and Criticism: Some Suggestions for Reading and Research* December, 1974. The other lists in this compilation were Judith Dansker's "Selected Bibliography and Diagrammatic Analysis of Feminist Scholarship and Aesthetics" and David Peck's "The New Marxist Criticism: A Bibliography."

10. *New America* is a small-circulation socialist newspaper. The text I have is a photocopy without a date; efforts to locate a microfilm copy for verification were unsuccessful. Additions to the lists published in 1972–1974 made by the editor, Gail Baker, at Olsen's request, were Edith Summers Kelley's *Weeds* and *The Devil's Hand,* both in the "Spectrum" section. The section titled "Most Women's Lives" adds two short stories: Susan Glaspell's "A Jury of Her Peers" and Willa Cather's "Wagner Matinee." A handwritten direction places Margaret Walker's *Jubilee* in the Spectrum section. Another entry in Olsen's handwriting in the copy she supplied to me is Cora Sandel's *Alberta,* a trilogy. The section on mothering and wifehood adds *Weeds,* Elizabeth Madox Roberts' *Time of Man,* and Ann Petry's *The Street.*

11. I mention "surrogates" for households rather than the division of work within households for two reasons. First, in many of the works listed, the heroes are women who head their households all or most of the time, so there is no other adult present to

share thier burden. Such heroes, like their real counterparts, are at risk precisely because their necessary household work is unpaid, so they must produce wages by some extra, different effort. Their dilemma is cruel: work or starve; meanwhile, leave your children to fend for themselves. (Cf. Davis, Richardson, Wright, Sandel, Smedley, Gladkov, Chekov, Hurst.) Second, the current crisis of the homeless demonstrates the negative: no institution is quite so reliable, flexible, and responsive as a household for dispensing food, encouragement, and some supports for mental and physical health.

12. "Just as, to the bourgeois, the disappearance of class property is the disappearance of production itself, so the disappearance of class culture is to him identical with the disappearance of all culture. That culture, the loss of which he laments, is for the enormous majority a mere training to act as a machine (*The Communist Manifesto*, Solomon, 49).

13. Virginia Woolf's "angel in the house" and her essay about "Shakespeare's sister" enter Olsen's musings about the immigrant women, too. Olsen states that there are "necessary angels" who must be kept, because without them life cannot continue. Mothers are sometimes children's sole shelter from harsh conditions. In a similar vein, Olsen insists that there are really Shakespeare's sisters among us now, perhaps living as mothers in large families. I do not know when Olsen read Woolf's essays, yet I believe that her dialogue with Woolf sets the realities of immigrant existence beside Woolf's inspired abstractions.

14. Introduction. *The Life Stories of Undistinguished Americans as Told by Themselves*. Ed. Hamilton Holt. New York: Routledge, 1990, xxi.

15. According to "Biographical Sketch," Olsen was born either in Omaha, Mead, or Wahoo, Nebraska, in either 1912 or 1913. I take a playful delight in this indication of a self-made start, to resistance to being pinned down (Pearlman and Werlock 9).

16. A document Tillie Olsen urges as essential reading (which she distributed as assigned reading at Amherst College when she was preparing the reading list) is "The Universal Declaration of Human Rights" adopted by the General Assembly of the United Nations December 10, 1948. Article XX in her copy is marked and underlined: "Everyone, as a member of society, has a right to social security and is entitled to realization, through national effort and international cooperation and in accordance with the organization and resources of each state, of the economic, social and cultural rights indispensable for their dignity and the free development of their personality." Olsen changed the pronouns in the original from "his" to "their." Interestingly, this document is one text in the Stanford course "Europe and the Americas" which Bloom, among others, considers a scandal.

17. Bloom, for instance, in an interpretive essay, comments on one "fatal temptation of the mind" illustrated in the account of the cave. There are "men who insist on the significance of the images in the cave and constitute themselves as their defenders and hence the accusers of the philosophers. They are often men of very high intelligence who are forced to hate reason by their unwillingness to renounce the charm and significance of their particular experiences and those of their people. They are enemies of whatever lies in the direction of universality" (*The Republic of Plato*, trans. Allan Bloom 405).

18. Piaget introduced the term *schema*, now widely used by cognitive psychologists and educators. According to Hirsch, "A person learns something new by building on a schema already known, and in practical knowledge the already known term is a productive 'schema' for performing a task" (*The Philosophy of Composition*, Chicago: University of Chicago 1977, p. 159).

Works Consulted

Bernard, Jessie. *The Female World.* New York: Free Press, 1981.

Blair, Hugh. *Lectures on Rhetoric and Belles Lettres.* Philadelphia: Troutman and Hayes, 1853.

Bloom, Allan. "Books by Dead, White, Western Males." Quoted in *The Chronicle of Higher Education* 24 Jan. (1990): B-34.

———. *The Closing of the American Mind: How Higher Education Has Failed America and Impoverished the Souls of Today's Students.* New York: Simon and Shuster, 1987.

Bloom, Allan, ed. *The Republic of Plato.* Translated by Allan Bloom. New York: Basic Books, 1968.

DuBois, Ellen Carol, ed. *Elizabeth Cady Stanton–Susan B. Anthony: Correspondence, Writings, Speeches.* New York: Schocken, 1981.

Hirsch, E. D., Jr. *Cultural Literacy: What Every American Needs to Know.* New York: Vintage, 1988.

———. *The Philosophy of Composition.* Chicago: U of Chicago P, 1977.

———. *Validity in Interpretation.* New Haven: Yale UP, 1967.

Hirsch, E. D., Jr., Gayatri Spivak, Roger Shattuck, Jon Pareles, and John Kaliski. "Who Needs the Great Works: A Debate on the Canon, Core Curricula and Culture." *Harper's Magazine* 279:1672 (1989): 43–53.

Hutchins, Robert. *The Great Conversation: The Substance of a Liberal Education.* Chicago: Encyclopedia Britannica, 1952.

———. *The Higher Education in America.* New Haven: Yale UP, 1936.

The Life Stories of Undistinguished Americans as Told by Themselves. Ed. Hamilton Holt. Introduction by Werner Sollors. New York: Routledge (1906) 1990.

Martin, Jane Roland. *Reclaiming a Conversation: The Ideal of the Educated Woman.* New Haven: Yale UP, 1985.

"MLA Survey Casts Light on Canon Debate." *Modern Language Association Newsletter* 23:4 (Winter 1991): 12–14.

Moi, Toril. *Sexual/Textual Politics: Feminist Literary Theory.* New York: Routledge, 1988.

Nussbaum, Martha. "Undemocratic Vistas." *The New York Review of Books* 34:20 (1987): 25–26.

Olsen, Tillie. "Excavations; A List Out of Which to Read, Extend Range, Comprehension." *Women's Studies Newsletter* 1:2 (Winter, 1972); 1:3 (Spring 1973); 1:4 (Summer 1973); 2:1 (Winter 1974).

———. *Mother to Daughter, Daughter to Mother.* Old Westbury: The Feminist Press, 1984.

———. *Silences.* New York: Delacorte/Seymour Lawrence, 1978.

Pearlman, Mickey, and Abby Werlock. *Tillie Olsen.* Boston: Twayne Publishers, 1991.

Reuben, Elaine, and Deborah Rosenfelt, eds. "Affirmative Actions in Literature and Criticism." MLA Commission on the Status of Women. December, 1974.

Rosenfelt, Deborah. "From the Thirties: Tillie Olsen and the Radical Tradition." *Feminist Studies.* 7 (Fall 1981): 371–406.

Scholes, Robert. "Three Views of Education: Nostalgia, History and Voodoo." *College English* 50, 1988: 323–24.

Solomon, Maynard, ed. *Marxism and Art: Essays Classic and Contemporary.* New York: Vintage, 1974.

United Nations. "Text of the Universal Declaration of Human Rights." *These Rights and Freedoms.* United Nations Department of Public Information, 1950, 170–76.

Contributors

Kate Adams is a doctoral candidate in American Civilization at the University of Texas. She is completing a dissertation entitled "Paper Lesbians: Feminism, Publishing, and the Politics of Lesbian Literary Identity in the United States, 1950–1990," the first chapter of which has been published in *Lesbian Texts and Contexts,* eds. Karla Jay and Joanne Glasgow (New York University Press, 1990).

Norma Alarcón is an Associate Professor of Ethnic/Chicano/Women's Studies at the University of California, Berkeley. She is the author of a book on the Mexican writer, Rosario Castellanos, *Ninfomania: El Discurso de la Diferencia en la Obra Poetica de Rosario Castellanos,* numerous essays on Chicana writers, and editor and publisher of Third Woman Press. She has also published *Esta Puente Mi Espalda,* a Spanish translation of the influential anthology, *This Bridge Called My Back.*

Joanne M. Braxton is Frances and Edwin L. Cummings Professor of American Studies and English at the College of William and Mary. She is the author of *Sometimes I Think of Maryland* (1977), a collection of poetry, and of *Black Women Writing Autobiography: A Tradition Within a Tradition* (1989). With Andree N. McLaughlin, she is co-editor of *Wild Women in the Whirlwind: Afra-American Culture and the Contemporary Literary Renaissance* (Rutgers, 1989).

King-Kok Cheung is Associate Professor of English and Associate Director of the Asian American Studies Center at the University of California, Los Angeles. She is the author of *Articulate Silences: Hisaye Yamamoto, Maxine Hong Kingston, Joy Kogawa* (Cornell University Press, 1993), in which the present essay also appears, and co-editor of *Asian American Literature: An Annotated Bibliography* (Modern Language Association, 1988).

Constance Coiner is Assistant Professor of English at the State University of New York at Binghamton and a member of the editorial board of *Radical Teacher.* She is the author of *Better Red: The Writing and Resistance of Tillie Olsen and Meridel LeSueur* (Oxford University Press, 1995). Among other publications, she contributed an essay on Olsen and Le Sueur to *Left Politics and the Literary Profession,* edited by Lennard J. Davis and M. Bella Mirabella (Columbia University Press, 1990). Coiner is currently working on a book about poet Carolyn Forché, and, with Diana Hume George, editing a collection of personal narratives addressing the difficulties and benefits of combining a full academic life with caring for children, aging parents, and significant others. Coiner serves on the Modern Language Association Com-

311

mission on the Status of Women in the Profession's Subcommittee on Family-Care Issues.

Robin Dizard lives and works in western Massachusetts. She teaches composition at Greenfield Community College. She is the author of *Changing the Subject: The Early Novels of Christina Stead* (1984) and also writes about ethnic writers of the United States.

Shelley Fisher Fishkin is Professor of American Studies at the University of Austin, Texas. She is the author of *Was Huck Black? Mark Twain and African-American Voices* (Oxford University Press, 1993), and of *From Fact to Fiction: Journalism and Imaginative Writing in America* (Johns Hopkins University Press, 1985; Oxford, 1988). She has published essays on writers including W. E. B. DuBois, James Agee, Tillie Olsen, Gloria Anzaldúa, Frederick Douglass, Charlotte Perkins Gilman, and Maxine Hong Kingston. She is co-editor of the Oxford book series, "Race and American Culture," and is Executive Director and Co-Founder (with Elaine Hedges) of the Charlotte Perkins Gilman Society.

Diana Hume George is Professor of English and Women's Studies at Pennsylvania State University in Erie, Pennsylvania. Her critical studies include *Blake and Freud, Oedipus Anne: The Poetry of Anne Sexton,* and *Epitaph and Icon* (with M. A. Nelson). She is the editor of *Sexton: Critical Essays* and co-editor, with Diane Middlebrook, of *Selected Poems of Anne Sexton*. She writes essays and poems for a number of journals and freelances for *Ms.* magazine. Her most recent book of poems is *The Resurrection of the Body*. She is writing a study of Maxine Kumin and a book of feminist travel essays.

Elaine Hedges is Professor of English and Coordinator of Women's Studies at Towson State University. She is the author or editor of numerous books and articles, including the "Afterword" to The Feminist Press edition of Charlotte Perkins Gilman's "The Yellow Wallpaper" (1973); *In Her Own Image: Women Working in the Arts* (1980); *Land and Imagination: The American Rural Dream* (1980); *Ripening: Selected Writings of Meridel LeSueur* (1982); and *Hearts and Hands. The Influence of Women and Quilts on American Society* (1987). She is also an editor of *The Heath Anthology of American Literature* (1990,1994). She is President and Co-Founder (with Shelley Fisher Fishkin) of the Charlotte Perkins Gilman Society.

Carla Kaplan is Assistant Professor of English at Yale University, where she teaches courses in American Literature and feminist theory. In 1992–1993 she was a Visiting Scholar at the Center for the Humanities, Oregon State University. She is completing a book entitled *The Erotics of Talk: Women's Writing and Feminist Paradigms*. A study of black and white women's writings of the American 1920s is in progress.

Patricia Laurence is Associate Professor of English at the City College of New York and author of *The Reading of Silence: Virginia Woolf in the English Tradition* (Stanford University Press, 1991). She has also published on women and war, the history of the English novel, and feminism and ethnography. She is currently at work on a book on the influence of China on Bloomsbury writers.

Rebecca Mark is an Associate Professor of American Literature at Tulane University, where she teaches Southern literature. She is the author of *The Dragon's Blood: Feminist Intertextuality in Eudora Welty's "The Golden Apples"* (University of Mississippi Press, 1994). She has published articles on gay pedagogy and an edition of Gertrude Stein's *Lifting Belly* (Naiad Press, 1989). She is currently working on a new book, *The Killing of Sister Femme,* which explores mass media images of butch-femme sexuality.

Diane Middlebrook is Howard H. and Jessie T. Watkins University Professor of English at Stanford University. She is the author of *Worlds into Words. Understanding Modern Poems* (W. W. Norton, 1978) and of *Anne Sexton: A Biography* (Houghton Mifflin Company, 1991; Virago, 1991; Vintage Books, 1992). With Marilyn Yalom she co-edited *Coming to Light: American Women Poets in the Twentieth Century.*

Carla L. Peterson is a Professor of English at the University of Maryland, College Park. She is the author of *The Determined Reader: Gender and Culture in the Novel from Napoleon to Victoria* (Rutgers, 1986) and *Doers of the Word: African-American Women Writers in the Antebellum North, 1830–1880* (Oxford University Press, 1994).

Lillian S. Robinson currently holds the C. C. Garvin Endowed Professorship of English at Virginia Polytechnic Institute and State University. She is the author of *Sex, Class, and Culture* and *Monstrous Regiment: The Lady Knight in Sixteenth-Century Epic,* and co-author of *Feminist Scholarship: Kindling in the Groves of Academe.* She has been Citizens' Professor of English at the University of Hawaii, Distinguished Professor of Women's Studies at San Diego State University, Hartley Burr Alexander Professor of Humanities at Scripps College, National Endowment of the Humanities Professor at Albright College, and Visiting Scholar at the Harry Ransom Humanities Research Center, University of Texas. She is currently working on a study of the politics and esthetics of the literary canon.

Deborah Silverton Rosenfelt is Professor of Women's Studies and Director of the Curriculum Transformation Project at the University of Maryland, College Park. Previously, she was Director of Women's Studies at San Francisco State University. She has published books and essays on women's literature, feminist criticism, and Women's Studies in higher education, including the co-edited anthology, *Feminist Criticism and Social Change* (1985), which contains a previous essay on Tillie Olsen. She is also the mother of Miranda, seven, who during the long evolution of the essay in this book matured from consistently demanding preschooler to frequent partner in parallel work.

Judith L. Sensibar is Associate Professor of English at Arizona State University. She is the author of three books—*Faulkner's Poetry: A Bibliographical*

Guide, The Origins of Faulkner's Art, and an edition of *Vision in Spring.* She is also the author of numerous articles on Faulkner and of essays on Edith Wharton and Henry James. She is currently completing a biography of the women in Faulkner's family.

Judith Bryant Wittenberg is Professor of English at Simmons College. She has published a book and several articles on William Faulkner and was co-editor of "Faulkner and Feminisms," a special issue of the *Faulkner Journal* (1991). Her scholarly publications also include essays on Faulkner's prótegée, the novelist Joan Williams, and on Thomas Hardy, Ellen Glasgow, and Sarah Orne Jewett.

Sharon L. Zuber is a graduate student in American Studies at the College of William and Mary, where she also teaches composition in the English department.

Index

Stowe, Harriet Beecher, 27, 99, 104
Street, The (Petry), 307
Sula (Morrison), 83
Swan, Barbara, 17, 19
Swirnoff, Lois, 17
Swoboda, Frank, 207
Synopticon, 303

Tannen, Deborah, 157
Tarule, Jill, 157
Tate, Claudia, 97, 98, 102
Taylor, Jill McLean, 226
Teasdale, Sara, 19
Tell Me A Riddle (Olsen), 6, 7, 31, 33,
49–69, 71–92, 197
"Tell Me A Riddle" (Olsen), 17, 50,
51–57, 67, 76–78, 87–90
This Bridge Called My Back (Anzaldúa
and Moraga), 30, 143
This Chile's Gonna Live (Wright), 302
Thoreau, Sophie, 14
Thoreau Society, 276
Thorman, George, 214
Three Guineas (Woolf), 156
Tiano, Susan, 271
Tillman, Katherine Davis Chapman, 28
Time Magazine, 35, 39
Time of Man, The (Roberts), 305, 307
To Bedlam and Part Way Back
(Sexton), 17–18
To The Lighthouse (Woolf), 161–62,
305
Todorov, Tzvetan, 158
Tolstoy, Leo, 17, 303
"Toward a Woman-Centered
University" (Rich), 252, 255
"Transformation of Silence into
Language and Action, The"
(Lorde), 4
Treichler, Paula A., 13, 172, 189
Trials and Triumphs (Harper), 98, 104,
108
Trueblood, Valerie, 38
Truth, Sojourner, 28, 301
Tunberg, Jacqueline, 200, 201
Twain, Mark, 30–31, 285

Updike, John, 55
Universal Declaration of Human
Rights, 308

University of Illinois Press, 27
"Unlearning to not Speak" (Piercy), 4
Urrutia, Elena, 271

Vance, Carol S., 189
Virago Press, 27
Viramontes, Helena María, 31, 34
Voyage Out, The (Woolf), 161, 165–66

"Wagner Matinee, The" (Cather), 302,
307
Walker, Alice, 31, 34, 97, 128, 171,
173, 174, 176, 216, 218
Walker, Margaret, 305, 307
Ward, Victoria, 226
Warner, Michael, 187, 190
Warner, Susan, 27
Washington, Booker T., 110
Washington, Mary Helen, 28
Watson, James, 285
Waves, The (Woolf), 161, 165–66
Wayne, Joyce, 113, 120
Weddington, Sarah, 37, 40
Weeds (Kelley), 307
Wells-Barnett, Ida B., 28
Werlock, Abby, 33
West, Cornel, 269, 271
West, Dorothy, 27
West, Robin, 31
Wharton, Edith, 28, 279
Wheatley, Phillis, 28
"When We Dead Awaken" (Rich),
4
White, Martha, 18, 20
White Negro, The (Mailer), 68
Whitman, Walt, 18, 28, 277, 285, 295
Whittmore, Reed, 143
*Wider Giving, A: Women Writing after
Long Silence* (Zeidenstein), 32, 38
Wildmon, Donald, 34
Williams, Joan, 279
Williams, Raymond, 51, 55, 68, 91
Wilson, Edmund, 199
Wilson, Elena, 199
Winkler, John Jay, 247
Wittenberg, Judith Bryant, 11, 12, 283,
284–85
Wittig, Monique, 189
Woman Warrior, The (Kingston), 128
Women and Labor (Schreiner), 301